'Brilliant'
Simon Carr, *Independent*

'Boris ... ation's
buffoo... n. The

*Also by Andrew Gimson*

THE DESIRED EFFECT

GIMSON'S KINGS AND QUEENS: BRIEF LIVES OF
THE FORTY MONARCHS SINCE 1066

# BORIS

## *The Adventures of Boris Johnson*

ANDREW GIMSON

**SIMON &
SCHUSTER**

London · New York · Sydney · Toronto · New Delhi

A CBS COMPANY

First published in Great Britain by Simon & Schuster UK Ltd, 2006
This edition published by Simon & Schuster UK Ltd, 2016
A CBS COMPANY

1 3 5 7 9 10 8 6 4 2

Simon & Schuster UK Ltd
1st Floor
222 Gray's Inn Road
London WC1X 8HB

www.simonandschuster.co.uk
www.simonandschuster.com.au
www.simonandschuster.co.in

Simon & Schuster Australia, Sydney
Simon & Schuster India, New Delhi

A CIP catalogue record for this book is available
from the British Library.

ISBN: 978-1-4711-6234-3
eBook ISBN: 978-0-8572-0739-5

Typeset and designed in the UK by M Rules
Printed and bound by CPI Group (UK) Ltd, Croydon, CR0 4YY

# Contents

# *Preface*

In the summer of 2016, the most passionate, unpredictable and momentous political drama for many years unfolded in the United Kingdom. Boris Johnson played a starring role in all three acts, and was at once identified by some as the villain of the piece, while others hailed him as the hero.

In Act One, Boris led the Leave campaign to victory in the EU referendum, held on Thursday 23 June, by 17,410,742 votes to 16,141,241: a triumph which astonished and dismayed the establishment. Here was a rebellion by the people, or 52 per cent of them, against the experts, who had warned in the most emphatic terms that leaving the EU would be disastrous. The losing side, which included most of the intelligentsia, accused Boris not just of populism, but of opportunism: telling lies, stirring up racism and wrecking the economy in order to seize power for himself. For the first time in his life, Boris was not just scorned by his enemies, but hated.

At the start of Act Two, David Cameron resigned as Prime Minister, and Boris became the frontrunner to succeed him. But the Tory leadership race unleashed dark passions and unspeakable vanities. Civilised individuals revealed their unexpected capacity for treachery. Within six days, Boris was destroyed by the very people with whom he had just spent six months in close alliance. He saved the day only to the extent that he contrived, in one of the great pieces of political theatre of modern times, to announce to his astounded followers his own downfall.

People groped for Shakespearean analogies to describe this assassination. Boris himself referred to Brutus, who killed Julius Caesar. Others nicknamed his chief assailant's wife Lady Macbeth. I was reminded of a line spoken by Hamlet about his father's murderer: 'That one may smile, and smile, and be a villain.' But there is no Shakespeare play which quite prefigures the plot of this Tory drama.

In Act Three, although it looked as if Boris had been buried, it turned out he was not dead, but sleeping. From the first weekend after the referendum, he had maintained quiet but friendly contact with Theresa May, the inscrutable woman, eight years older than himself, who on 13 July became Prime Minister – and installed Boris as Foreign Secretary! People were so astonished they compared this to the raising of Lazarus, but that occurred after only four days, while Boris had lain for 13 days in the political tomb. Once again, the analogy did not quite fit, especially as Boris himself is a thorough-going pagan.

I wanted to set down my account of these convulsions as soon as I could, while the excitement of them was still fresh in my mind, and working against the clock to get the story finished. Other historians, including the admirable Tim Shipman of the *Sunday Times*, will offer more detailed accounts of what has occurred. But here, I hope, is a sense of the sheer unexpectedness of what happened, by one who lived through those almost sleepless days and nights.

It is followed by the account of Boris's early life on which I began work as long ago as 2004, and which I have been updating ever since. In this edition, two short new chapters at the end of the book touch on his performance at the 2012 London Olympics, when he first sprang to worldwide attention, and on his return in 2015 to the House of Commons, the narrow chamber in which he has never yet shone. Without some knowledge of his background, his style of politics, including his compulsion to combine seriousness with frivolity, becomes incomprehensible. Can such a bizarre character ever become Prime Minister? The question has still not been fully answered.

A difficulty arose over the book's original subtitle, *The Rise of Boris Johnson*. Once he was knocked out of the leadership race, we changed this to *The Rise and Fall of Boris Johnson*. His elevation to the foreign secretaryship led my older daughter, Eliza, to propose that this in turn should be modified to *The Rise ~~and Fall~~ of Boris Johnson*. On the day after his promotion, the BBC published a profile under the title *Boris Johnson: His rise, fall, rise, fall and rise*, which shows what a zigzag path he has taken. But we have settled for *The Adventures of Boris Johnson*, as being less likely to become almost immediately out of date.

Andrew Gimson, Cagnes-sur-Mer, August 2016

# Act One: Triumph

Before the EU referendum campaign began, Boris admitted he was 'veering all over the place like a supermarket trolley' on the subject. But at teatime on Sunday 21 February 2016, he emerged from his family's handsome, end-of-terrace Georgian house in Islington to announce to the milling crowd of journalists and photographers which side he was going to back. The media were out in such force not just because Boris can be relied on to provide good copy, but because on his decision the whole story could turn. In a close-run fight, his powers as a campaigner might well make the difference between victory and defeat.

Two days earlier, David Cameron had returned from Brussels bearing the meagre fruits of his renegotiation of the terms of British membership, on the basis of which he would be urging people to vote to stay in the EU. Five Cabinet ministers, of whom the most eloquent and influential was Michael Gove, the Justice Secretary, had already announced they would be campaigning on the opposite side to the PM. Now the nation waited to see which way Boris would jump.

All who saw or spoke to him during that weekend agree he agonised over the decision. He went down to the family farmhouse near Thame, in Oxfordshire, to think things over. Ben Wallace, his leading supporter in Parliament, warned that siding with Leave would mean losing thirty votes in any future leadership campaign. The decision had to be made by Sunday evening, when Boris must file his column for Monday's *Daily Telegraph*.

He composed two columns, one for and one against. According to someone who read both, the case for staying in the EU was stronger than that for leaving.

Some have pilloried Boris for his indecision, which they take as proof of his disgraceful insincerity. But this variable state of mind was shared by millions of voters, and by many politicians too. As no less a figure than Hugo Young, writing in *This Blessed Plot: Britain and Europe from Churchill to Blair*, has pointed out:

> On no question of this period did more people in British public life change their minds than on Europe. There were conversions from one side to the other, and sometimes back again, each position often being held with a passion summoned from the realm of faith more than reason, where there are secret uncertainties that only the loudest voice can mask. Many, who first opposed British entry, later decided they had been wrong. Many others, who helped take Britain in, became virulent critics of their own handiwork.

On Sunday morning, Cameron went on the *Andrew Marr Show*, where he issued a final plea to Boris: 'I think the prospect of linking arms with Nigel Farage and George Galloway and taking a leap into the dark is the wrong step for our country. And if Boris and others really care about being able to get things done in our world, then the EU is one of the ways in which we get them done.'

Farage, then the leader of UKIP, and Galloway, the ex-Labour MP who leads Respect, are eloquent mavericks, whose company Boris would find slightly less off-putting than Cameron does. Nor would Boris sympathise with the suggestion that it is necessary to belong to the EU in order to get things done. In Boris's view, you get things done by wanting to get them done. He thought Cameron's new deal was so pathetic because the PM lacked the guts to threaten to walk away if the UK did not get what it wanted.

For almost thirty years, ever since he went to Brussels as a correspondent, Boris knew he could make a good thing out of ridiculing the EU. Nor had these attacks diminished in recent years. In his disrespect for supranational European institutions, and his sense that these could impinge on national freedoms, he has been entirely consistent – a word not often applied to him. He has always been willing to say things which sensible, sober, temperate people like Cameron would consider it reckless to say, but which were music to the ears of Eurosceptics, including many Conservatives.

A single example suffices as a reminder of how outspoken Boris liked to be. In 2012, during the agonisingly protracted crisis over Greece's unsustainable debts, the British Government took the polite view that the solution to the Eurozone's problems was fiscal union. Boris thought differently: 'It is frankly unbelievable that we should now be urging our neighbours to go for fiscal union. It is like seeing a driver heading full-tilt for a brick wall, and then telling them to hit the accelerator rather than the brake.'

In the manner of a surgeon proposing a radical operation, Boris urged 'a north/south bisection' of the Eurozone.

But it would be wrong to assume, as many people do, that he simply needed to see which side Cameron was on before joining the opposite and more dangerous one. The Prime Minister had already indicated that in the 'unity reshuffle', which he intended to make after persuading the British public to stay in the EU, Boris would be rewarded with the foreign secretaryship. Unity matters to Boris: he is a natural unifier, and knows the Conservative Party has to maintain some kind of unity or it is finished. There was a strong case for being loyal to the PM, building a record of reliability, and being ready to seize the crown when Cameron chose to step down. Several ministers with records of Euroscepticism were indeed induced to back Cameron.

If Boris took the opposite course, he would open himself to the accusation of bad faith. For on the great question of parliamentary sovereignty – the principle Enoch Powell and his descendants within the Conservative Party have long regarded as sacred – Boris has always been regarded by his fellow MPs as 'incorrigibly wet', as he himself put it when I interviewed him for the Christmas 2012 edition of *Weltwoche*, a magazine published in Zurich. The truth is that his views are inconveniently close to Cameron's, except that Boris thinks the British renegotiation should have been conducted by someone really bold and brilliant, namely himself.

In the end, Boris decided he could not bear to become a subordinate cog in the Cameron machine. So after some preliminary remarks, he told the waiting press, 'I will be advocating Vote Leave, or whatever the team is called – I understand there are many of them': a jokey reference to the divisions on the Leave side of the argument.

Boris added that 'what I won't do is take part in loads of TV debates against other members of my party'; already he was worried about being written off as a divisive figure. He began his Monday morning column for the *Telegraph*, in which he sought to justify what he had done, by insisting: 'I am a European ... It is ... vital to stress that there is nothing necessarily anti-European or xenophobic in wanting to vote Leave.'

A few hours later, when Cameron reported to the Commons on his European deal, he took a swipe at these windy assurances by Boris, and at the argument that by defying the EU one could end up with a more harmonious relationship: 'Sadly, Mr Speaker, I have known a number of couples who've begun divorce proceedings, but I do not know of any who've begun divorce proceedings in order to renew their marriage vows.'

This was pointed, for everyone knew that Boris had gone

through occasional moments of marital discord. When it came to more precise arguments, Boris had in fact clearly borrowed from his wife, Marina, a liberal-minded lawyer who had protested in print against 'judicial activism' by the European Court of Justice. There's 'too much judicial activism' by the ECJ, he loyally declared.

But Sir Nicholas Soames, a Tory grandee whom I interviewed for ConservativeHome, hastened to accuse Boris of bad faith:

> I know for a fact he's not an Outer, because he told me, and I think that he went through agony to come to this decision, and that's his look-out, but I spoke to him, actually from the car park at Ascot Racecourse, where I was about to go and enjoy a nice day's steeplechasing, and it was on the day before he announced, he announced on the Sunday, and he was under great personal pressure, and he said, 'You don't know how awful this is.'

However awful, it was also enjoyable. Here he was at the very centre of national attention, by far the most newsworthy figure in the Leave campaign, with Michael Gove, his fellow Conservative, lending intellectual credibility to the enterprise.

Boris did not have to worry too much about intellectual credibility. His task was to be an insurgent: the champion of the forgotten, unfashionable people of the provinces, and also of the outer boroughs of London, who felt spurned by Cameron. There was a widespread expectation at this time, and indeed right up to the night of 23/24 June, that the Prime Minister's gamble in holding the referendum was going to pay off. Boris was the underdog: a role he embraced with gusto, for it made him look plucky and deserving of support. As he declared up and down the country, and also to Michael Cockerell, who at the end of the campaign made a short film for *Newsnight* about the rivalry between Boris and Cameron: 'This

is a David and Goliath fight. This is a struggle of the little pla-
toons against the big battalions, and they have the CBI, and
Goldman Sachs, and Peter Mandelson.'

Who the hell wants the CBI, and Goldman Sachs, and Peter
Mandelson? Not Boris. He preferred to commit a series of indiscretions which would win him even greater attention. One of
these was his attack, in the *Sun*, on President Barack Obama,
who in April arrived in London intent on promoting the official
Washington line that Britain is worth far more to the United
States as a member of the EU than as an independent power.

Boris issued a pre-emptive strike by dragging up the hoary old
story of how, on entering the White House, Obama removed the
bust of Winston Churchill from the Oval Office. In Boris's words,
'some people' said this was 'a snub to Britain' and 'a symbol of
the part-Kenyan President's ancestral dislike of the British
Empire – of which Churchill had been such a fervent defender'.

The term 'part-Kenyan' was at once translated into a racial
slur at Obama's expense. At his press conference, the President
struck back with overwhelming force, exploding Boris's accusations. As I observed at the time in a piece for the *Mail on Sunday*,
Obama got very much the better of him.

Yet who emerged as the victor of this exchange? Almost certainly Boris, for daring to take on the most powerful man on the
planet. And the key point advanced by Boris – namely that it was
nauseatingly hypocritical of the President to tell us we must go on
giving up sovereignty to the European Union, when the United
States would never dream of sacrificing its national prerogatives to
some pan-American body – still stood. Many voters felt it was a
bit off for Obama to come over here and tell us what to do.

On 11 May, Boris launched his Vote Leave battlebus campaign
by brandishing a Cornish pasty, and later some asparagus and an
ice cream, while touring Cornwall. These pictures raised
people's spirits, and conveyed the idea that calling for Brexit was
an enjoyable thing to do, which could even be accompanied by

the consumption of one's favourite foods. His companions in Vote Leave, including those whose primary loyalty was to Gove, spoke very highly of him. As one of them put it to me: 'I was impressed by several things about the way that Boris handled the campaign. The first is that he had a genuinely team-spirited approach. He mucked in. He threw himself into campaigning with brio. He performed very well in both of the major TV debates. So my opinion of Boris rose.'

This praise was returned. Boris appeared often with Gove, could be seen relishing his company, and when Gove appeared for Vote Leave in a Sky News debate, fired off a volley of encouraging tweets:

Brilliant stuff by the Gover
Exactly right Michael Gove
Dead right Gover
Spot on Gover and great appeal at the end!
Gove hit it out of the park tonight at Sky News debate.

Gove was at this time admired by people in every part of the Conservative Party, for he was so courteous, lucid, good humoured and intelligent. He had declared, with attractive modesty, that he lacked the qualities needed to be Prime Minister, but Paul Goodman, editor of the ConservativeHome website and a man with a profound knowledge of the party, urged that once the contest was over, Gove be made Deputy Prime Minister in order to help bring the two sides back together. I was myself very well disposed towards Gove, because when I managed to fall out, in a most ridiculous fashion, with the *Daily Telegraph*, he was kind enough to invite me to lunch, at a point when he was at the height of his fame as a reforming Education Secretary. It was true that the teachers could not abide Gove, but most people at Westminster were charmed by him.

Meanwhile, Boris attracted, from the Remain side, some very

bad reviews. Here, they thought, was a man so consumed by
ambition that he would stop at nothing. Matthew Parris did a
ferocious hatchet job on him in *The Times*:

> Somebody has to call a halt to the gathering pretence that
> if only you're sufficiently comical in politics you can laugh
> everything off. Somebody has to remind us that it's not
> enough for those who seek to govern us simply to be: they
> have to do. Incompetence is not funny. Policy vacuum is
> not funny. Administrative sloth is not funny. Breaking
> promises is not funny. A careless disregard for the truth is
> not funny. Advising old mates planning to beat somebody
> up is not funny. Abortions and gagging orders are not
> funny. Creeping ambition in a jester's cap is not funny.
> Vacuity posing as merriment, cynicism posing as savviness,
> a wink and smile covering for betrayal . . . these things are
> not funny . . . When the media turn nasty, as it will, his
> powers of laughing everything off will falter.

Parris, himself a former Conservative MP, warned that 'we on
the centre-right should end our affair with this dangerous
charmer'. His piece was remarkably nasty, for it insinuated that
Boris's private life was so disreputable it would not bear scrutiny.
But the article could also be seen as a compliment to Boris, for
it was predicated on the appalled realisation that his chances of
becoming Prime Minister were getting better and better.

Space precludes listing, let alone quoting from, all the hatchet
jobs on Boris which appeared during the campaign. Perhaps the
most elegant and enjoyable was by Ferdinand Mount, a cousin as
it happens of Cameron, in the *London Review of Books*. Mount
observed that 'Johnson . . . changes his ideas once a fortnight',
and cited Boris's by now abandoned proposal for a second referendum, in order to endorse the improved membership terms we
would obtain by voting No in the first one. Since that time,

Mount remarked, Johnson and other Leavers had suggested, in rapid succession, that our future trading arrangements should be based on those of Norway, Iceland, Switzerland, Canada and Albania.

This was not, in fact, a question the Leavers were capable of answering, for they were split down the middle about what kind of country they wanted Britain to be. Some of them (though certainly not Boris) were motivated primarily by hatred of immigration and a longing to get back to the 1950s. Others regarded immigration as a good thing, and looked forward to a future as a global trading nation open to the world.

So Vote Leave soon refused to talk about trade policy, let alone offer any plan for how we would leave the EU. This struck people like Parris and Mount as a contemptible dereliction of duty. But the Leavers retorted that they were not a government in waiting, and it was for the actual Government to do the planning – something Cameron was not willing to set in train, for he did not wish to suggest leaving the EU would be anything less than a total disaster.

Relations between the two sides became appallingly bad. The campaign degenerated into a barren and repetitive exchange of insults, with each side accusing the other of lying. This was an inglorious way to settle things, but the protagonists had too much at stake to help themselves. Cameron's side kept saying we faced total economic collapse if we left the EU: an argument dismissed by their opponents as 'Project Fear'. Boris's lot kept playing to the xenophobic gallery, while pretending not to do so.

The Prime Minister declined to face Boris in any television debates. During the 2010 general election, Cameron had made the mistake of giving Nick Clegg, the Liberal Democrat leader, the chance to shine against him on TV, and it was even more likely that Boris would do so. After all, he had already outshone Cameron in 2012, during the London Olympics.

But Boris was performing, in the months leading up to the

referendum, a trickier balancing act than his enemies were prepared to allow. As Cameron had warned, he found himself in awkward company, and obliged to defend awkward propositions. Short of denouncing his own side's campaign, which would have been an act of unpardonable sabotage, there was not much Boris could do to correct the claim, painted on the side of Vote Leave's bus, that if we left the EU, we would have £350 million more a week to spend on the National Health Service – an assertion which omitted the very considerable funds flowing back to Britain from Brussels.

The more threatened the Remain side felt by Boris, the more it yearned to cut him down to size. Amber Rudd was deployed in the ITV television debate held on 9 June and came armed with two carefully devised lines which were supposed to turn him into a laughing stock. Rudd was Secretary of State for Energy and Climate Change, and also the brother of Roland Rudd, a successful PR man who was one of the prime movers behind the Remain campaign, and who also makes a fleeting appearance on page 65 of this book. Perhaps the theory was that Boris would find it harder to cope with an attack not just from a woman, but from the sister of an old friend. Nowadays they often try to pep up a movie by giving the job of hitman to a hitwoman.

Agent Rudd fired off one of her missiles in an exchange about immigration, during which she worked round – with a momentary stumble on the word 'interested' – to this jibe: 'But you need to look at the numbers, although I fear the only number that Boris is interested in is the one that says Number Ten.'

Her other attack was more personal, and contained a touch of old-fashioned sexism: 'He's the life and soul of the party, but he's not the man you want driving you home at the end of the evening.'

These lines were funny, even faintly outrageous, so were widely reported. But whether they did Boris any harm may be doubted. By refusing to answer back, he demonstrated a self-restraint which not everyone knew he possessed. Like other attacks on him, this one had the paradoxical effect of building him up, by showing his enemies regarded him as a serious enough player to wish to destroy him. And it confirmed that whatever game Rudd was playing, Boris could not be written off as an establishment stooge.

Two days afterwards, I received a message from Boris which said: 'See Daily Telegraph page 35.' I went out, bought the paper, turned to that page, which carried the obituaries, and read all three without being able to detect what relevance they might have. In a further message, he said: 'The man is holding something very helpful in elucidating our future.' And there was a picture of Gordie Howe, a famous Canadian ice hockey player, holding an ice hockey stick.

I remembered then that about a week before, Boris had changed his prediction of what would happen to the economy after Brexit from a Nike tick, which goes down before it goes up, to a hockey stick, and had insisted: 'If you study a hockey stick closely, it just goes up.'

This, I wrote, was simply wrong: 'I happen to have a hockey stick, recently purchased by one of the sportier members of my family, standing beside my desk. In the vertical position, the end with which you hit (or try to hit) the ball undoubtedly goes down before it goes up.'

But Boris now pointed out that 'if you rest the bottom' of an ice hockey stick, which is straight, 'flat on the ice as they do in order to perform a slap shot or a wrist shot the shape is first horizontal and then turns 45 degrees upwards'.

Your view of Boris may depend on whether you are amused that he found time, in the midst of a campaign on which the future of Britain depended, to discuss this question, or are, on the contrary, contemptuous of him for allowing his attention to be diverted.

A week before polling day, Jo Cox, the Labour MP for Batley and Spen, was murdered while carrying out an engagement in

her constituency. This crime, the first killing of an MP since the
IRA blew up Ian Gow in 1990, appalled the nation and led to a
temporary halt in the campaign. A suspect was arrested at the
scene, but at the time of writing has not yet been tried.

Cox's husband, Brendan, said: 'She would have wanted two
things above all else to happen now, one that our precious children are bathed in love and two that we all unite to fight against
the hatred that killed her.' He later added that he believed she had
been killed because of her political views. Cox had worked for
Oxfam, campaigned in Parliament to alleviate the terrible suffering of Syrian civilians, and wanted Britain to remain in the EU.

On Sunday morning, when campaigning resumed, Boris
made his most heartfelt statement yet about immigration: 'I am
pro-immigration, my friends, I'm the proud descendant of
Turkish immigrants and let me stun you perhaps by saying I will
go further, I'm not only pro-immigration, I am pro-immigrants
and I am in favour of an amnesty for illegal immigrants who
have been here for more than twelve years.'

A couple of days before the referendum, InFacts – an organisation 'making the fact-based case for Britain to remain in the
European Union', with Boris's old schoolfriend Hugo Dixon
(last encountered on page 51 of this book) serving as editor-in-
chief – published a list of Boris's 'top ten errors' about Brexit.
The first of these read:

> Boris Blunder: 'Our gross contributions to the EU budget
> are now running at about £20 billion a year... the net
> contribution is £10 billion.'

> InFact: Our gross contribution is £12.9 billion and our net
> contribution is £6.3 billion.

The third item on the list exemplified the slightly humourless
pedantry of the InFact approach:

Boris Blunder: The EU has rules on 'how old a child has to be before he or she can blow up a balloon'.

InFact: The EU has merely recommended adult supervision.

More telling is the absence of any evidence that Boris had himself fomented racism or xenophobia.

On Tuesday 21 June, Boris delivered the closing speech for his side at the final television debate, held at the Wembley Arena. He received a loud ovation after declaring: 'And if we stand up for democracy we will be standing up for hundreds of millions of people around Europe who agree with us but who currently have no voice. If we vote Leave, and take back control, I believe that this Thursday can be our country's Independence Day.'

But there was still no general expectation that Boris's side was going to win. At Downing Street, Cameron's pollster, Andrew Cooper, assured the PM that Remain was heading for victory by a margin of ten or even twenty percentage points, and texted Vote Leave to boast that this would be so. The City likewise expected a Remain win. The polls could not be relied on – we had seen that at the 2015 general election, when Cameron won an overall majority which the pollsters failed to foresee – but old hands pointed out that in referendums, there is almost always a last-minute swing back towards the status quo, as voters react against the risk of tearing up familiar arrangements in favour of some untried proposal. That, after all, was what appeared to have happened in the Scottish referendum in September 2014, when voters opted by 55 per cent to 45 to remain in the UK rather than go for independence. On the evening of 23 June, I went to bed early, convinced that when I woke in the morning, Britain would have voted to stay in the EU.

# Act Two: Treachery

By five in the morning on 24 June 2016, it was clear that Britain had voted to leave the EU. From the declaration of the first results, soon after midnight in Newcastle and Sunderland, the tide had been flowing strongly in that direction, and it never altered course.

Boris watched the results at home in Islington, along with his closest advisers and his wife, who was reclining under a duvet on a chaise longue. Gove had gone to bed in his house in Notting Hill, and had to be woken at 4.45 by a call from one of his special advisers, who told him the news.

Neither of the leading figures in Vote Leave displayed the slightest euphoria. Nor did any other key personality in the campaign. Everyone was too drained to rejoice. The country had surprised itself by voting to leave the EU, and no one yet knew the meaning of this revolution. The old regime had been overthrown, and there was a power vacuum.

The Remainers were plunged into mourning. Many of them believed, as they said during the campaign, that leaving the EU would precipitate national disaster. But their defeat had been so close – 51.9 to 48.1 per cent – that they could not help wondering if it could be reversed, perhaps by means of a second referendum. Meanwhile, they looked round for someone to blame.

The Leavers were just as disconcerted but in a different way. They were like people who have been pushing with all their strength at a door which seems as if it is going to remain firmly shut, but at the last moment springs open, precipitating them forward. They were caught completely off balance.

At about 8.15 in the morning, David Cameron emerged into Downing Street, accompanied by his wife, Samantha, who stood a few yards to the side of him as he spoke. He announced his resignation, to take effect as soon as a new leader could be chosen. As he reached the end of his statement, his voice began to crack.

Neither Boris nor Gove had known Cameron was going to resign so quickly. The buck now quite clearly stopped with them. They faced the daunting prospect of sorting out the situation they had themselves helped to create. The world was waiting for them to say how they proposed to achieve this, but they had no plan. Meanwhile, Norman Smith, reporting for the BBC from Downing Street, said Boris was 'likely to be taking up residence' there, and was 'absolutely in pole position'.

It was a beautiful, clear morning in London, the sun shining from a cloudless sky. On College Green, the triangular patch of grass across the road from the Houses of Parliament, a strange kind of garden party was in progress, with several hundred politicians and media people milling about in front of the tents being used by various broadcasters. Here Lord Mandelson, the eurocrats' eurocrat (for he had been a European Commissioner as well as right-hand man to various Labour leaders), wore a stricken air as he took questions on the debacle. Here too could be found some of the leading Brexiteers such as Iain Duncan Smith, looking goggle-eyed with exhaustion.

In Islington, the mood was uglier. As Boris left his house, a band of protesters jostled him, hurled obscenities at him and shouted that they would like to kill him. For a man who prides himself on being able to defuse hostility by exerting irresistible personal charm, this was something of a shock. He was driven to the headquarters of Vote Leave. Here he appeared before the cameras with Gove and with Gisela Stuart, the leading Labour campaigner for Brexit.

She spoke first, and reminded people that Vote Leave was a cross-party organisation. Boris came next. Some people thought he looked frightened, but that was not my impression. To me, he looked not just very tired, but almost as if he was bereaved: as sombre and untriumphalist as in 2008, when he defeated Ken Livingstone. He began by paying tribute to Cameron: 'I know I speak for Michael [Gove] when I say how sad I am that that he's stepped down.'

Boris then took it upon himself, in this first public statement after the referendum, to speak not just for Gove but on behalf of the whole political class: 'Today I think all of us politicians should thank the British people, because in a way they have been doing our job for us.' He added that 'there is now no need for haste', and he insisted 'this does not mean the United Kingdom will be any less united, nor indeed that it will be any less European'.

But actually, there was a crying need for haste. A new Prime Minister had to be chosen, or confidence in the British economy, already shaken by the referendum result, might collapse. Boris drew Gove aside into a room at Vote Leave. Here Boris said he hoped to run for the leadership of the Conservatives, and asked what Gove thought. Gove replied that he was disposed not just to give Boris a clear run, but to support him. Some of Gove's admirers, including two Cabinet ministers, urged him to run instead, but he told them he was probably backing Boris, and on the Saturday morning he confirmed to Boris that this was so.

Boris chose this moment to go off and play cricket against his old friend Charles Spencer at Althorp, the latter's estate in Northamptonshire. To some, this seemed a quintessentially English way to relax after the rigours of the campaign. But to others, including some of Gove's supporters, it demonstrated an almost criminal lack of seriousness. The German Foreign Minister, Frank-Walter Steinmeier, said later that 'instead of taking responsibility', Boris 'went to play cricket'.

The problem was compounded on the Sunday, when Boris held a barbecue at his house near Thame. Team Gove were invited to this festivity, and were appalled by what they saw as the lack of professionalism in the Boris camp. As one Gove supporter put it, 'Boris was surrounded by jolly good sorts, but they weren't sharpening their machine.'

The truth was that Boris did not have a machine. He had a small group of supporters in the Commons, including Ben Wallace, Nigel Adams, Jake Berry and Amanda Milling, who before the referendum had held a series of parties at which their man could meet members of the 2010 and 2015 Commons intakes. For Boris did not know most of these still quite new Tory MPs. He had left the House in 2008, immediately after his election as Mayor of London.

Nor in his earlier period as an MP, for the seven years from 2001, had he made a uniformly good impression on his fellow parliamentarians. For Boris combined a number of irritating characteristics. He was far more famous than most of them, and far less assiduous. While they were full-time MPs, working every hour that God gave to serve their constituents and make their way at Westminster, he was also editing a magazine: a dual role which ended in the embarrassments of 2004, chronicled in chapters 21 to 23 of this book.

The question for his fellow MPs was whether Boris could be trusted. He had done little enough to reassure them, and on Sunday night, when the electronic version of his column for Monday's *Daily Telegraph* appeared, he unsettled them further. For Boris asserted:

It is said that those who voted Leave were mainly driven by anxieties about immigration. I do not believe that is so.

After meeting thousands of people in the course of the campaign, I can tell you that the number one issue was control – a sense that British democracy was being undermined by the EU system, and that we should return to the people that vital power: to kick out their rulers at elections and to choose new ones.

It strained credulity to downplay, only three days after the referendum, the importance of immigration. When voters said they wanted 'control', they meant in particular the control of our borders. Immigration was the Leave campaign's trump card: the one to which Cameron and his allies never found an answer. Yet here was Boris declaring he did not 'believe' it to be important. Lewis Carroll's heroine put the objection to this kind of thing very well:

Alice laughed: 'There's no use trying,' she said; 'one can't believe impossible things.' 'I daresay you haven't had much practice,' said the Queen. 'When I was younger, I always did it for half an hour a day. Why, sometimes I've believed as many as six impossible things before breakfast.'

One might say, in Boris's defence, that he was asking his readers to believe only one impossible thing before Brexit, namely that immigration didn't really matter. But for stern, unbending Tory Eurosceptics, this looked like clear evidence that he was getting ready to betray them. As a leading Conservative in the Leave campaign put it to me, he was 'fudging the free movement issue'; was in fact 'going weak' on it.

Boris's motive for doing this was clear: in order to 'build bridges' with the Remainers, he thought he needed to downplay the importance of ending the free movement of people from the EU to Britain. For the Remainers had just spent months telling anyone who would listen that it would be impossible to preserve satisfactory trading arrangements with the EU, while at the same time inducing Brussels to abandon the principle of free movement.

For the purposes of this argument, it does not matter whether the Remainers or the Leavers are right. We cannot yet know for certain who is right, for the terms of our withdrawal from the EU have still to be negotiated. But what we do already know for certain is that there is an irreconcilable difference between the two sides.

Whoever ended up leading the Conservative Party would have to show that he or she was capable of uniting it. This was a very difficult problem, for the unfortunate fact was that the party was split between two factions. Hence Cameron's stratagem of promising, in his Bloomberg speech in January 2013, to hold a referendum on British membership of the EU, provided he won the 2015 general election, and after he had obtained thorough-going reforms from Brussels.

The first part of this programme worked out surprisingly well: in 2015, he won an overall majority. But the second part blew up in his face: as we have seen, he did not obtain sufficient reforms from the EU, so lost the referendum.

It was time for someone else to have a go, and Boris sought, with his *Telegraph* article, to show he should be that person. He had taken the precaution of showing what he had written to Gove, who was by now his campaign manager. They were both of them successful and prolific journalists by trade, so when it came to making sure an article struck the right note, they reckoned they knew what they were doing, and were unlikely to be too fussy. After all, if one article came out wrong, one could always write another. And on this occasion, the whole thing had to be dealt with in a tearing hurry: this was the day of the barbecue, and both men were still so short of sleep their judgement was scarcely likely to be reliable.

Whatever emendations Gove had proposed were quite

insufficient to persuade his followers that Boris could be relied on. For the two teams had failed, when they met on the Sunday, to meld with each other. The problem was not, as some have supposed, that Boris and Gove were too different from each other. The trouble was that they were too similar, and had for a long time been conducting a subterranean rivalry. They were gifted columnists who were useless at running things: brilliant figureheads for the Leave campaign, which was a protest against the way Cameron was running things; quick-witted mavericks who placed an alarming degree of faith in their own bold judgement. They attracted the support of other quick-witted mavericks, while the prudent, weighty types who are the ballast of a successful party generally regarded them with suspicion.

Of the two men, Boris was the more aware of what he lacked. While Mayor of London, he realised he simply had to recruit capable and well-informed individuals to cope with the administrative side of things: first Sir Simon Milton and then Sir Eddie Lister.

But unlike Boris, Gove did at least have a detailed knowledge of the parliamentary party. For Gove had been an MP since 2005 and had served, briefly, as Chief Whip. He was, however, said by his critics to have been the worst Chief Whip in living memory. During his time there, the whips' office leaked like a sieve, as often as not because Gove himself enjoyed gossiping about what was going on, instead of remaining as close and confidential as a good whip should.

Gove's outstanding achievement, as Education Secretary from 2010 to 2014, was to rough up the educational establishment in order to drive up standards of education. In this endeavour, he was ably assisted by his special adviser, Dominic Cummings, a man of such fiery convictions that not content with assailing the teaching profession, he also assailed Cameron, and Cameron's quietly professional, self-effacing chief of staff, Ed Llewellyn. As one observer remarked, 'Cummings has zero interest in pleasing anyone, even the Prime Minister.'

At length, Cameron wearied of this. At the urging of Lynton Crosby, the rough Australian brought in to run the Conservatives' 2015 election campaign, Gove was sacked. Cummings had already been forced to step down as a special adviser, but continued to help Gove in an informal capacity.

This history mattered, for Boris had a tremendously high opinion of Crosby, who had run his successful mayoral campaigns in 2008 and 2012, and whom he had now called in to help run his Tory leadership bid: another instance of Boris well understanding the need for professional assistance. Meanwhile Cummings was advising Gove, after playing a crucial role in the Vote Leave campaign, where he had as usual made bitter enemies, but had helped mastermind the insurrection which swept Cameron out of Number Ten.

Cummings was anxious that Gove should insist on the role of Chancellor of the Exchequer, in order to provide the 'buttressing' that Boris would require as Prime Minister. Gove's three special advisers – Henry Cook, Henry Newman and Beth Armstrong – meanwhile formed a low opinion of Boris's team.

And Boris himself was regarded with very widespread suspicion. On the Saturday after the referendum, a shire Tory told me, 'I can't bear the thought of him being our Prime Minister.' Another old friend rang to say that for the first time since moving to London over thirty years ago, she had been insulted as a foreigner. She was so angry not only with Boris, but with me for saying a few words in defence of Boris on the *Today* programme, that she said she would never talk to me again.

Anecdotal evidence, soon backed up by statistics, multiplied of people feeling emboldened by the referendum result to insult and threaten those whom they regarded as foreign, either by word of mouth or by the yet more despicable method of anonymous letter. I naturally deprecated these disgusting attacks. But although I had myself voted, after a long period of indecision, for Remain, it seemed to me unfair to blame Boris for the horrible things being said or done by the various creeps who claimed him as their champion.

Not all the news was bad for Boris. On the morning of Monday 27 June, a reassuringly strong case for supporting him was made on ConservativeHome by Nick Boles MP, who was one of Gove's closest friends and allies:

> We need to elect someone who is a natural unifier, and consensus builder, a fully paid-up member of the human race, who doesn't just spout the rhetoric of One Nation, but lives and breathes an approach to politics that is warm, generous, open and inclusive . . . I am going to spend the next three months doing my best to explain to them, as the spirit of my late father explained to me, why the national interest must come first and why, in the national interest, we must elect Johnson.

In the words of one of Boris's supporters, Boles had 'dipped his hand in the blood'. And an increasing number of MPs were declaring for Boris. But behind the scenes, all was not well. The Gove camp claimed Boris was 'curiously unenergised', and disastrously unprofessional, about becoming Prime Minister. It also said it was obtaining promises of support from a much larger number of MPs than Boris's people were managing to recruit.

But Boris's people complained in a fury that they were not even allowed, by the Gove team, to see which MPs had pledged their support to the Boris/Gove 'dream team'. Nor, they lamented, was it possible for them to feed in valuable intelligence which would then be acted upon.

One of Boris's backbench supporters canvassed Amber Rudd, the Energy and Climate Change Secretary, on his behalf. As a

Remainer who had gone out of her way to attack Boris during the final stages of the referendum campaign, and was widely seen as a rising star, she would have been a real catch, confirmation that he was indeed building bridges to the other side.

Rudd did not ask to be promised a job in some future Boris/Gove administration. All she wanted was a commitment on climate change: something Boris was ready to give. But after her request was fed in to the campaign, nothing happened. It is hard to know whether this was simple inefficiency, or an act of sabotage. Gove's people said Boris was 'addicted to doing things on the fly'. But instead of pulling together, the two sides were at loggerheads, and there was not much time to get things right: nominations were due to close at noon on Thursday 30 June, only a week after the referendum. Conservative MPs would then whittle the candidates down to only two by means of a series of ballots, after which the two finalists would compete for support from the Tory membership.

On Tuesday, an extraordinarily disturbing email was published by Sky News after Gove's wife, Sarah Vine, had apparently sent it by mistake to the wrong person. It was addressed by her to Gove himself and two of his special advisers, Henry Cook and Beth Armstrong, and in it she said:

Very important that we focus on the individual obstacles and thoroughly overcome them before moving to the next.

I really think Michael needs to have a Henry or a Beth with him for this morning's crucial meetings.

One simple message: you MUST have SPECIFIC assurances from Boris OTHERWISE you cannot guarantee your support.

The details can be worked out later on, but without that you have no leverage.

Crucially, the membership will not have the necessary reassurance to back Boris, neither will Dacre/Murdoch,

who instinctively dislike Boris but trust your ability enough
to support a Boris/Gove ticket.

Do not concede any ground. Be your stubborn best.
GOOD LUCK.


Vine's email is not just uncollegiate: it breathes suspicion that
Boris is going to betray her husband. She urges Gove not to
yield an inch, and assures him Boris needs him more than he
needs Boris. For without Gove, the Tory membership will not
have the 'necessary reassurance' to back Boris. Nor will Boris
win the support of Paul Dacre, the editor of the *Daily Mail*, who
had made Vine one of his star columnists, or of Rupert
Murdoch, the proprietor of (among other papers) *The Times*,
where Gove was a rising star, and was seen as a likely future
editor, until he opted to go into politics instead.

Her reference to Murdoch reminded people of a curious
dinner thrown by that magnate in 2014, at which Gove had
denounced Boris as unfit to be Prime Minister: 'Boris is incapable of focusing on serious issues and has no gravitas. He isn't
a team player and plays to the gallery the whole time.'

And Vine, too, could be staggeringly indiscreet in her column
for the *Mail*, a newspaper with about four million readers. On
Wednesday 29 June, so the day before nominations closed, she
announced to them: 'Given Michael's high-profile role in the
Leave campaign, that means he − we − are now charged with
implementing the instructions of 17 million people. And that is
an awesome responsibility.'

Awesome indeed, but few spouses would assume joint responsibility in this grandiose manner for fulfilling the voters' wishes.
There is something about Tory leadership races which brings out
the worst in people. Passions are released which have been sup-
pressed for years. For a few days, every MP matters, or thinks
that he or she matters, which amounts to the same thing. The
Commons is full of disappointed people. Walk around the Palace

of Westminster, and you will see hundreds of men and women who, with a few happy exceptions, cannot reconcile themselves to the discrepancy between their ambitions and their achievements.

They have taken great trouble to get elected to this place, only to find on arrival that they do not matter at all, and are treated as so much lobby fodder. They have to defer like so many new boys and new girls to their seniors, unless they rebel, and neither way do they get anywhere near the top.

But in a leadership contest, everything suddenly seems, and perhaps even is, possible. The most implausible candidates come forward, and sometimes they win. In the Labour Party, one has only to look at the ascent in 2015 of Jeremy Corbyn, from the backbenches to the leadership in a single leap. But the three great leadership contests of the post-war era – great in the sense of being amazing spectacles – have all been in the Conservative Party.

Here the front-runner has not won a contest since Sir Anthony Eden succeeded Sir Winston Churchill in 1955. In 1963, the 14th Earl of Home came through and won, despite not being, at the start of the race, a contender. A law permitting the renunciation of hereditary peerages had just been introduced, and after he had won he converted himself into Sir Alec Douglas-Home. He was in many ways a worthy winner: a shrewd man of unimpeachable integrity, who helped restore the party's scandal-shaken reputation, and almost led it to victory in 1964.

But the manner in which he was chosen was regarded as unacceptable. Humphrey Berkeley, a Conservative backbencher, said it was 'More appropriate for the enstoolment of an African chief'. The accusation in 1963 was that Home had been chosen by a 'magic circle' all but one of whom had been, like him, to Eton. He reluctantly decided it was necessary to adopt a system of election 'where from start to finish everything was seen to be open and above board'.

The next really memorable contest (though the intervening races were by no means uninteresting) was in 1990. The fall of Margaret Thatcher was one of the great stories of modern times. She was replaced by the relatively unknown John Major, who had the decisive merit, in the eyes of Conservative MPs, of not being Michael Heseltine, who had brought Thatcher down. That contest, and the history of Tory leadership contests, are related with wit and learning by Alan Watkins in *A Conservative Coup*. He points out that although everything was meant to be 'open and above board', many Conservative MPs did not understand the rules, and were 'frivolous' in their attitudes, more concerned to administer a shock to whichever candidate they disliked than to choose the best person. Although the rules had been modernised, many disgraceful things occurred.

The contest of 2016 is the third great one of modern times. As it unfolded, I kept reminding myself that the frontrunner has not won a Tory leadership race for over sixty years. Yet on Tuesday 28 June, Boris still seemed to be on course for victory. That afternoon, Sir Nicholas Soames, who had been so cross with him for siding with Leave, posted an encouraging tweet:

Gave @BorisJohnson proper stick during Campaign but only one way ahead now. Boris will be great PM. The Gover makes it a top team.

On the morning of Wednesday 29 June, the *Sun* – one of Murdoch's titles – carried the headline IT'S BORIS DAY and assured its readers that 'BoJo storms ahead', with '100 MPs backing him for PM'.

Yet behind the scenes, things were going from bad to worse. Gove and his advisers were increasingly worried by Boris's failure to write the speech to be delivered at the launch on Thursday morning. They refused to accept that his method of composition on such occasions was to rise at 5.45 in the morning and knock it off at high speed. He was not a committee man, who wanted a lot of drafts by other people. Yet that is what Gove and his team set out to provide. After all, this was a very important speech, which was meant to tell people what a Boris premiership would be about: what its theme would be. Yet Boris just was not getting on with it.

On Wednesday afternoon, Gove, Boles and a couple of advisers set aside a couple of hours 'to sort of bash ideas around'. Boris was supposed to have written something overnight, 'but there wasn't really much there . . . And then Michael stood up and recited what he thought the speech should be, and it was brilliant, it was fantastic, and he was giving this for Boris.'

Gove, as we have noted, possesses many of the same strengths as Boris. Like him, he is a gifted speaker, who was elected President of the Oxford Union. Indeed, on page 70 of this book he cheerfully admits that while at Oxford, 'I was Boris's stooge. I became a votary of the Boris cult.'

Perhaps it was time, thirty years later, to stop being Boris's stooge? The writer Logan Pearsall Smith once remarked, 'Every author, however modest, keeps a most outrageous vanity chained like a madman in the padded cell of his breast.' Something similar could be said of politicians. And part of the point about Gove is that he really is very gifted, and very good at taking on vested interests. The way he set about reforming the prison system, on becoming Justice Secretary after the 2015 general election, was a case in point. It won him golden opinions.

Meanwhile Boris, who had not yet served in the Cabinet, was making a hash of landing Andrea Leadsom, a major new recruit to his campaign. She was a hitherto almost completely unknown Leaver who had won good reviews during the referendum campaign and was now picking up a lot of support from the kind of ideological Eurosceptic who regarded Boris as flaky.

Gove was almost certainly not aware that Lord Tebbit, a stern upholder of Thatcherite verities who as Norman Tebbit had served as a minister under Margaret Thatcher, had rung Leadsom on Tuesday evening and urged her to run. She may have had an incentive to present Boris with a series of demands which he would feel unable to meet, whereupon she could go ahead on her own account. She considered there would be two top jobs in a future Johnson government, either Chancellor of the Exchequer or Deputy Prime Minister in charge of the Brexit negotiations, and on Wednesday evening she wished to receive both a letter and a tweet guaranteeing she would get one or other of those posts.

My guess is that Boris did not want to be bounced into accepting such an extravagant demand, so prevaricated. Nor was it sensible to treat him as a kind of postmaster, responsible for the safe delivery of letters. But the Gove camp presented his failure to land Leadsom as yet more evidence of his unfitness for high office.

On Wednesday night, Boris returned home with Boles from the Conservatives' summer party at the Hurlingham Club. The idea was that they were going to do yet more work on the speech. During this journey, a text from Leadsom arrived on Johnson's phone, of which Boles had taken charge, announcing that she would be standing herself. This news burst like a thunderbolt on the Gove camp. Boles was summoned by Gove to a late-night conclave at his house, attended by Sarah Vine, Simone Finn (once Gove's girlfriend) and Gove's three special advisers.

At about one o'clock in the morning, Gove told them that over the last few days he had lost faith in Boris's ability to be Prime Minister, which meant he could no longer urge people to vote for him. He nevertheless thought a Brexiteer should run for the leadership, and since Leadsom was too inexperienced, he proposed to run himself.

No one spoke against this idea, for he was surrounded by his little court. None of these people would shrink from telling Gove how brilliant he is. Boles had always wanted his old friend to run rather than Boris. The three special advisers were in various states of despair at the hopelessness of the Boris campaign.

Vine had already shown she thought Boris was going to betray her husband. Some of Gove's friends blame the blunder he was about to make on his wife. They say her father is a wealthy, self-made man, who does not recognise other people's good qualities unless they too have made money. They believe she wanted to lift her husband in her father's eyes, and making Michael Prime Minister would not be a bad way of doing that.

It amused a wider circle of people to call her Lady Macbeth. This strikes me as wrong. Gove needed less persuading than Macbeth did. Sarah Vine is a high-spirited, warm-hearted woman, who is good company and has bolstered the family finances by spilling quite a lot of beans in the *Daily Mail*. Ben Wallace, a staunch Boris supporter, was later to say this was one reason why Gove could not become Prime Minister: 'UK citizens deserve to know that when they go to sleep at night their secrets and their nation's secrets aren't shared in the newspaper column of the Prime Minister's wife the next day, or traded away with newspaper proprietors over fine wine.'

Vine became good friends with Cameron's wife, Samantha, though the two of them fell out once Gove decided to back Vote Leave. Vine, at this meeting of dead-tired amateurs in the early hours of the morning, lacked the austere temperament to say what a spouse should have said: 'Don't be such a damn fool, darling.'

So the crucial point was not made that to abandon Boris now, only hours before the campaign was launched and having promised only a few days before to support him, would be an act of the most monstrous and conspicuous treachery, which was sure to rebound on its perpetrator. The feeling in Gove's circle was that he was at long last doing the right thing. He nevertheless said he would sleep on it, which he did for about five hours. That took him yet nearer to the hour of Boris's launch, which was to take place at 11.30am at St Ermin's Hotel in Westminster.

At 9.02 on Thursday morning, so just after the *Today* programme came off the air, Gove launched his surprise attack on

Boris with an email to journalists which said: 'I have come reluctantly to the conclusion that Boris cannot provide the leadership or build the team for the task ahead. I have, therefore, decided to put my name forward for the leadership.'

Dominic Raab, who would always have preferred Gove to run, had been assigned to go on the *Today* programme to make the case for Boris, but was told of the change of plan and pulled out. It was, however, too late to pull his article in that morning's *Sun*:

> I am backing Boris Johnson to be our next leader because he has the vision, the optimism and the raw fire to take Britain forward . . . The Conservatives must be the party of the aspirational underdog. Boris and Michael Gove will make a formidable partnership . . . Boris is a natural-born winner. He's got the Heineken effect that refreshes the parts that more conventional politicians cannot reach.

A ringing endorsement, one might have thought. But Raab now took to the airwaves to complain that Boris had behaved in a 'cavalier' manner, and to claim that Gove 'is the right leader' and 'can speak out to the aspirational underdog in our society'.

An hour and a half earlier, so soon after 7.30 on Thursday morning, Boles sent out a mysterious text to some of the MPs who were supporting Boris, which is printed here for the first time:

> We are calling a top priority meeting for a small number of colleagues to discuss the campaign at 9am sharp in Room 26, on the Upper Ministerial Corridor of the House of Commons. Michael wants you to drop anything you can to be there. Please be aware that this message has been sent to a small group and Michael trusts you not to mention this meeting to anyone else. Thanks Nick.

At nine o'clock Gove entered Room 26, a handsome office next to Big Ben which had been allocated to him because he was Justice Secretary. He informed the hastily assembled MPs, who included Boles, Raab, Ed Vaizey and Nick Gibb, he had just sent out a press release in which he announced he was himself going to stand for the leadership. He was sorry this was so late, but had decided Boris was just not up to it. He went round the room asking for support. Vaizey, who had been best man at Gove's wedding, said he had always thought Gove was brilliant, and joined up, as did the others named here.

A few minutes before this, Gove had rung Lynton Crosby: 'Hi Lynton, it's Michael Gove here. I'm running.'

'Running what?' the rugged Australian enquired.

'I'm running for the leadership myself.'

Crosby asked if Gove had told Boris. Gove said he hadn't, but intended to. This, however, was a call that was never made. Time was short, and it would have been an awkward conversation, but that was because what Gove was doing was such a betrayal. Only five days before, he had promised Boris his support. For Gove to claim that in those five days, he had discovered Boris's unfitness to be Prime Minister is an insult to our intelligence. He had known for many years of Boris's strengths and weaknesses. Gove spoke of the need to build a team, yet here he was smashing the team to smithereens. One should, in fairness, repeat that he and almost everyone else were very short of sleep. But what really warped his judgement was his vanity: the irresistible belief that he would be better than Boris at being Prime Minister. Gove's numerous denials of his fitness for the prime ministership were so many attempts to keep that raging vanity chained, as Pearsall Smith put it, 'like a madman in the padded cell of his breast'. Now the madman was out, and Gove struggled to sound sane.

Ben Wallace, Boris's principal parliamentary supporter, has described how he learned what was afoot:

When on Thursday morning, just before 9am, I got a call from a journalist asking me if it was true Michael Gove was deserting Boris, I denied it. It couldn't have been true. Only the night before we had confirmed 97 names of supporters, and I knew of three more coming over that day. Michael hadn't said anything or hinted at any frustrations over the previous four days so I presumed it was just another story from the 'rumour mill' that accompanies leadership campaigns.

I walked round the corner to see Lynton Crosby, ashen white, taking a call from someone who turned out to be Michael Gove. 'He has done the dirty on us, mate,' were the words I remember most afterwards. Boris was at his home rehearsing for his speech unaware that the press knew before him.

Crosby was furious. 'On a scale of one to 100, I'd say 928,' as one observer put it. An emergency meeting took place at Boris's campaign headquarters in Greycoat Place, off Victoria Street. A ring round of his parliamentary supporters swiftly established he had lost about half of them, including all the ministers. Some of his admirers thought he should fight on, and continued to say so in the coming days. Forty supporters was not such a bad start. Support for Liam Fox, a veteran Eurosceptic who was also standing, was in single figures. But Crosby and others gave the grown-up view, namely that Boris could not now do it.

At about this time on Thursday morning, Theresa May launched her leadership campaign. The whole affair went off very well. She had been Home Secretary since 2010, and she sounded calm, confident, decisive and professional. Here were no convulsions, of the kind which were even now shattering Boris's campaign. She even had one quite good joke at his expense: 'Boris negotiated in Europe. I seem to remember last time he did a deal with the Germans he came back with three nearly new water cannon.'

Those were the water cannon which he as Mayor of London bought from the Germans, and the use of which she as Home Secretary banned.

Over at St Ermin's Hotel, a late-Victorian edifice just round the corner from St James's Park Underground Station, the excitement was intense. No one seemed to know what Boris was going to say. One guessed he would arrive by the main entrance, at the end of the long, narrow forecourt between two high, red-brick wings of the building. Here taxis drove in and out, cameras had been set up, and I waited at the top of the steps, along with Alexander von Schönburg, special correspondent for the *Bild Zeitung* from Berlin. We saw the two dozen MPs who had remained loyal to Boris, and scores of journalists, pouring in for the show. Among the MPs I spotted were Andrew Mitchell, Zac Goldsmith, Mark Field, Edward Garnier, Jesse Norman, Nadine Dorries, Kwasi Kwarteng and Jo Johnson, Boris's younger brother. One of them said 'the most serious crisis since 1940' was no time to play games. Another said: 'I shook his hand. I pledged myself. It is too soon to write him off.' A French tourist asked who all the cameras were for, and fled with the words, 'I'm not staying for him.'

Word suddenly ran round the throng that Boris had entered the hotel by another entrance. We hurried to the Caxton Suite, a meeting room with a high ceiling of sugary plasterwork painted dead white. Here Boris had already been greeted with whoops and cheers by supporters who assumed he was going to make a stand. He told them this was 'a time not to fight against the tide of history but to take that tide at the flood and sail on to fortune': a reference to a line by Brutus in *Julius Caesar*, but what did it mean? Boris had not yet revealed whether he was going to fight. He said more about his record in London, including his favourite transport joke – 'bus crime down by 50 per cent, obviously crime committed on buses rather than crime by buses' – than one would have expected in a speech launching a national campaign. At last, after a passage about foreign policy, he said:

This is our chance to think globally, to lift our eyes to the horizon, to bring our unique British voice and values, powerful, humane, progressive, to the great global forums without being elbowed aside by a supranational body... That is the agenda for the next Prime Minister of this country. But I must tell you, my friends, you who have waited faithfully for the punch line of this speech, that having consulted colleagues and in view of the circumstances in Parliament, I have concluded that person cannot be me.

People gasped. This was not what they had been expecting. The room went quiet. An MP who had been sitting in the front row told me Boris 'looked crushed' and had 'water in his eyes'. Nadine Dorries, one of his most devoted supporters, began weeping. But from the back of the hall, where I was standing, his voice still sounded resolute, and his demeanour, though not joyful, was robust. Moments later he left the room by a side door. He was photographed leaving the hotel in a taxi with his wife, Marina.

People milled about in a daze. Ann Sindall, who had worked for many years for Boris at the *Spectator* and City Hall, said to me, 'Has that taken the wind out of your sails?' Or did she mean, out of my sales? Some of Boris's supporters were so emotional they could not speak. 'I'm off to join Theresa,' one MP who had supported Boris said in a fury. Another MP, Jake Berry, tweeted about Gove: 'There is a very deep pit in Hell for such as he.' This remark echoed, with an important modification, what had been said by one of the Cameroons just after Cameron lost the referendum and was forced to resign: 'There is a special place in Hell reserved for Boris.' Gove had replaced Boris as the villain of the piece. Berry later deleted his tweet, but replaced it with this no less definitive formula: 'I do not for one moment resile from my opinion that as a traitor Gove leaves Judas Iscariot standing.'

# Act Three: Comeback

Boris kept silent. He did not recriminate, or write lachrymose articles. I cannot recall any occasion when he has responded to a setback or a personal attack, however hurtful, by answering back. In politics, this is a valuable trait, for one is bound at times to have to work with people who have behaved badly.

During the 2005 Tory leadership contest, which was won by Cameron and in which (as related on page 236) Boris was in no condition to stand, he was interviewed by a Dutch journalist, Patrick van IJzendoorn. Their conversation ended with Boris asking, 'Do you know that number by Chumbawamba?' and singing: 'I get knocked down, but I get up again. Tedumtedum. I get knocked down, but I get up again. Tedumtedumtedum. I get knocked down, but I get up again. Tedumtedum. You're never going to keep me down.'

After Gove's knock-out blow, the spirit of Chumbawamba had once more to be channelled. But behind the scenes, perhaps things were not quite as grim as they seemed. Theresa May sent him a text of condolence. She had tried to ring him, but he missed the call. As early as the weekend after the referendum, there had been contact between the two of them. Justine Greening, the International Development Secretary, wrote a piece published on Sunday 26 June on ConservativeHome in which she urged: 'A leadership contest is not in the interests of our country... Boris and Theresa should agree to forge a deal which means they are a united leadership, under one or the other.'

*Boris*

Everything the two candidates did was designed to leave open the way to an eventual deal. Even while trying to defeat each other, they were developing a relationship. For both of them, and indeed for the party, this made sense. Whoever won the leadership would have to reunite the Conservatives, which would mean bringing senior figures from both Leave and Remain into the Cabinet. The harder the battle, the greater the need for a workable peace. As soon as Boris had conceded he was not going to be Prime Minister, there was a community of interest between himself and May.

Not that this was apparent to most people at the time. May was regarded with suspicion by the Leavers. They had hoped she would join their side, but instead she sat out the referendum campaign as a largely silent Remainer. She was an unknown and probably unknowable woman, who might very well try to betray the vote for Brexit and stitch up some compromise which left the UK for most practical purposes still inside the EU.

So May knew she would need some important and visible Brexiteers in the Cabinet. Who could these be? After what Gove had just done, no one would trust him. She did not trust him, for she had suffered at his hands in Cabinet. In 2014 he took it upon himself to interrogate her, in his clever-clever way, and with prime ministerial cover, about her proposed immigration cap, which he tore apart, and about Islamic extremism, on which he thought he knew better; and in 2013 he did likewise when she gave a speech to ConservativeHome which was interpreted as her attempt to profile herself as a future leader. As James Forsyth, of the *Spectator*, had remarked: 'It is hard to imagine relations between these two ever recovering.'

May had certainly had various disagreements with Boris about the London riots, water cannon and other matters. But how good he was at mending fences once the latest row was over, and how tactful he was about not demanding some particular post if she won. And unlike Gove, he did not suck up to

Cameron in order to pull rank on her. And he was popular with the Tory rank and file. And he would stop her Cabinet looking too dull. Already, one can be sure, she was thinking carefully about her ministerial team, for she would need to form it quickly once she had won, to show she was really in charge. And the only person who stood between her and Number Ten was the inexperienced Leadsom. May knew the Conservative Party backwards, and had been in the Commons since 1997, and a frontbencher since 1999. Leadsom had been in the Commons since 2010, and a junior minister since 2014. She didn't stand a hope.

The Duke of Wellington said the test of a great general was to know when to retreat, and to dare to do it. Boris had dared to retreat. Michael Heseltine, who overthrew Margaret Thatcher and served as Deputy Prime Minister, denounced Boris for having 'ripped the party apart... he's like a general that led his army to the sound of guns, and at the sight of the battlefield abandoned the field'. Max Hastings, who had hired Boris at the *Daily Telegraph*, danced in the *Daily Mail* on the grave of 'this dangerous charlatan'.

But Boris had avoided the opprobrium, and the bloodshed, which would have accompanied a fight to the death. He lived to fight another day, and discomfited his betrayer, Gove, who had assumed that Boris would fight on, and was now left to take the entire blame for what had happened. Compared to Gove, Boris looked trustworthy. Gove was accused by Boris supporters of being a 'Machiavellian psychopath' who was always plotting to stab their man, and chose the most damaging possible moment to wield the dagger.

It soon became clear that Gove's position was hopeless. He held his launch and gave the speech he had wanted Boris to give, but did not win a single convert. At the first hustings, held in Committee Room 14 at the Palace of Westminster, where the leadership candidates addressed and took questions from their

fellow Tory MPs, one of Boris's supporters, Nigel Adams, contrived to sit facing Gove, and very close to him. 'His eyes bored
into Gove the whole time,' a witness related. 'It was an unfor-
gettable sight.'

In the two rounds of voting by the 330 Tory MPs which
were needed to whittle down the candidates to the final two,
Gove's vote fell back from 48 to 46, while May's rose from 165
to 199. The effect of his treachery had been to destroy himself.

Boles too was in a desperate state. As Gove's courtier, he had
urged his prince to commit an act of betrayal which was not
merely immoral but suicidal. If Gove could not get into the final
two – and after the first round of voting, held on Tuesday 5 July,
it was clear the Eurosceptics were flocking to Andrea Leadsom
rather than to him – the whole exercise would have been a disaster. So on Wednesday 6 July, Boles sent a number of potential
supporters a text which even by his own standards was foolish
and disreputable:

> You are my friend. I respect the fact that you want Theresa
> May to be PM. It is overwhelmingly likely that she will be.
> And if she does I will sleep easily at night. But I
> am seriously frightened about the risk of allowing Andrea
> Leadsom onto the membership ballot. What if Theresa
> stumbles? Are we really confident that the membership
> won't vote for a fresh face who shares their attitudes about
> much of modern life? Like they did with IDS. I am not
> asking you to respond unless you positively want to have a
> chat. But I hope that you will reflect on this carefully.
> Michael doesn't mind spending 2 months taking a good
> thrashing from Theresa if that's what it takes but in the
> party's interest and the national interest surely we must
> work together to stop AL?

This message was leaked. If anyone had doubted before whether the Gove camp was treacherous, now proof was to hand. The text also indicated an insulting distrust for the membership, which was suspected of being opposed to modern life, including reforms such as gay marriage which had distressed many older Conservatives. In vain Boles apologised for what he had done, and said Gove did not know about it. When asked about this message at a meeting of Conservative MPs, all Gove could do was giggle. As one of Boris's supporters said to me, the Boles text showed how 'inept and poisonous' the Gove operation actually was.

Gove himself attempted, in a preposterous interview with the *Spectator*, to bring out the heroism which lay behind his abandonment of Boris: 'I compare it to a group of people standing outside a collapsing building, wondering who is going to rescue a child inside. I thought: well, I don't think I've got either the strength or the speed for this, but as I looked around, I thought, God, I'm at least as strong and at least as fast as the others. I've got to try to save the child.'

Boris backed Leadsom, his fellow Eurosceptic, but in an unemphatic way. He was good at being friendly without being irretrievably committed. On the evening of Thursday 7 July, Team May again reached out, very quietly, to Boris, who was uncritical of her in interviews, and remarked that either woman would make a great leader. He said Leadsom's qualities included zap, kindness and trustworthiness, and he even went to a fundraiser for her in Northampton, also held on 7 July, the day of the second ballot, in which she gained the support of 84 Tory MPs. That was 115 fewer than May but 38 more than Gove, so Leadsom went through to the final. The 125,000 Tory members now had the task of choosing between May and Leadsom, with the winner due to be announced on 9 September.

So there was unprecedented interest in Leadsom's character and opinions, and she agreed to give an interview to Rachel

Sylvester of *The Times*, for the paper dated Saturday 9 July. Here is a transcript of the passage in that interview which was to destroy her leadership bid:

> SYLVESTER: Does your family inform your politics?
> LEADSOM: Oh, totally.
> SYLVESTER: During the euro debates, you said several times 'as a mum'. Do you feel like a mum in politics?
> LEADSOM: Yes.
> SYLVESTER: Why and how?
> LEADSOM: So, really carefully, because I am sure, I don't really know Theresa very well but I am sure she will be really sad she doesn't have children so I don't want this to be 'Andrea has children, Theresa hasn't', because I think that would be really horrible but, genuinely, I feel being a mum means you have a very real stake in the future of our country, a tangible stake. She possibly has nieces, nephews, lots of people. But I have children who are going to have children who will directly be a part of what happens next. So it really keeps you focussed on what are you really saying, because what it means is you don't want a downturn but never mind, ten years hence it will all be fine, my childen will be starting their lives in that next ten years so I have a real stake in the next year, the next two.

Leadsom appeared to think that if you have children you care about the country's future, while if, like May, you are childless, you don't care. This was offensive not only to May, but to anyone without children who cared deeply about what became of the UK. Whether or not this was what Leadsom believed, it was plain she was too naïve to become Prime Minister.

Boris acted over that weekend as a channel of communication

between May and Leadsom. He conveyed reassuring messages from May to her: 'We want a fair fight, we can see you're being hard done by, this isn't coming from us.' The British press in full pursuit of some suddenly newsworthy victim must prompt a twinge of sympathy from all but the most stony-hearted. Leadsom denied, protested, clarified and wriggled, but could not escape. On Monday 11 July, she withdrew from the race, and May was declared the winner.

Boris at once published a series of three loyal tweets, which are given here with his original numbering:

1/3 Theresa May has the authority & the leadership necessary to unite the Conservative Party & the country.

2/3 Andrea Leadsom's decision is both brave and principled & allows that process to begin immediately.

3/3 I've no doubt Theresa will make an excellent Prime Minister and I'm encouraged that she's made it clear that Brexit means Brexit.

Two days later, after Cameron had taken his last Prime Minister's Questions, May went to Buckingham Palace and was asked by the Queen to form a government. That night the new Prime Minister made her first ministerial appointments.

As Boris said, May had already declared, repeatedly, that 'Brexit means Brexit': a reassuring formula, but no one could tell what, in practice, it would mean. She now went a step further, and in a stroke of genius – which like many such mental leaps looks like common sense once it has been made – she put three Brexiteers in charge of Brexit. And the greatest of the three was Boris. It was a staggering comeback. The conventional wisdom at Westminster was that he would be lucky if he scraped into the Cabinet as Culture Secretary, yet here he was as Foreign

Secretary, one of the great offices of state. On the BBC's *News At Ten* this was described, with perfect accuracy, as 'a jaw-dropping shock'; I had the pleasure of seeing the jaw drop of the first person to whom I told the news. The *Daily Mail* headline was 'BORIS BOUNCES BACK!' Sue Cameron, a journalist with a deep knowledge of Whitehall, happened to be in the Foreign Office at 7.45 in the evening, when news of the appointment broke, and next day told listeners to Radio Four:

> It was quite amazing. There was a lecture in the Foreign Office and we were in one of their very grand rooms at the top of the very impressive staircase and the place was thick with former Cabinet secretaries and top civil servants and academics, and suddenly everybody started looking at their phones and the word went round that it's Boris, and you can't leave the room just now because Boris is coming up the stairs. And they were gobsmacked, absolutely gobsmacked.

On that Wednesday evening, Gove went to a club dinner, attended by MPs and journalists. As the Cabinet posts were announced, everyone looked down at their phones to see who had been appointed. The first collective buzz revealed 'Hammond, Chancellor' – the widely predicted news that Philip Hammond was moving from the Foreign Office to the Treasury. The next buzz revealed 'Boris, Foreign Secretary'. Gove went white as a sheet. He was out, banished along with most of Cameron's other friends, or former friends, to the back benches, while Boris, whose hopes Gove had blighted only thirteen days before, attained new heights.

Paddy Ashdown, a former leader of the Liberal Democrats, said it was 'the silliest appointment since Caligula made his horse a consul'. In Germany, a spokesman for the Social Democrats asked, 'What next, Dracula as Health Minister?' The French

Foreign Minister, Jean-Marc Ayrault, claimed that during the referendum campaign Boris 'lied a lot to the British people'. In Washington, the State Department spokesman was unable to keep a straight face when asked about Boris.

Quite a lot of people wanted to believe this was an absurd appointment, though some of them just thought that was how they ought to react. The media trawled through Boris's articles for rude things he had said about foreign leaders, and came up with a rich haul. He had likened the American presidential candidate Hillary Clinton to 'a sadistic nurse in a mental hospital', while of the Russian leader, Vladimir Putin, he wrote: 'Despite looking a bit like Dobby the House Elf, he is a ruthless and manipulative tyrant.'

American journalists were especially scandalised that Boris had not always been strictly truthful. They take a puritanically unforgiving view of such behaviour. A correspondent from the *New York Times* who rang me up in July 2016 to ask a few questions for a profile she was writing of Boris was still appalled, rather than amused, by his attempt in 2002 to play a joke on that paper, by getting it to print a picture of me under the impression that it was him (a prank related on page 157 of this book). On Tuesday 19 July, when Boris did his first joint press conference with the American Secretary of State, John Kerry, another correspondent from that newspaper, Gardiner Harris, expressed the deep disapproval felt by him and his colleagues: 'I understand that you don't want to revisit the past but you have an unusually long history of wild exaggerations and frankly outright lies which few Foreign Secretaries have prior to this job and I am just wondering how John Kerry and others can believe what you say.'

In a reply to a similar enquiry at this press conference from James Landale of the BBC (who on page 116 of this book can be found declaiming that 'Boris told such dreadful lies'), the new Foreign Secretary had declared, in a reply which would have to do for the Americans too: 'I'm afraid that there is such a rich thesaurus now of things that I have said that have been one way or another, through what alchemy I do not know, somehow misconstrued that it would really take me too long to engage in any full global itinerary of apology.'

Letting bygones be bygones was the only sensible line to take. The lapses of the past could be overlaid by his record in office. He seemed to be getting on well with Kerry, and on the previous day he had got on well with his opposite numbers in Brussels, where he made a favourable impression by being the first British Foreign Secretary for a long time who actually enjoys speaking French. His predecessor but one, William Hague, addressed some advice to him: 'Make the most of your unusual advantage of being both very well-known and underestimated at the same time. You can ignore the ribaldry that has greeted your appointment in some quarters – wherever you travel, people will want to hear the words of one of the most recognisable Foreign Secretaries in history.'

Pippa Crerar of the *Evening Standard*, who had followed him for eight years on his travels as Mayor of London, said that 'for every rugby-tackled Japanese schoolboy' – a reference to a celebrated occasion in 2015 when Boris flattened a ten-year-old boy in Tokyo – there were 'thousands of pictures promoting what would otherwise have been a dry trade mission'. She went on: 'Boris is a world-class salesman. He has become a globally recognised figurehead and if anyone can persuade our international partners that a Brexit vote was one of a self-confident nation keen to secure existing relationships and strike new alliances, he can.'

One of the first tasks of a journalist is to make things interesting. Boris acknowledges an absolute obligation to do this, and is not especially scrupulous about how he achieves it. Whatever he may have to say, he sets out to make it as vivid, paradoxical and arresting as he can. He coins new words, mixes common terms with learned ones and is rude about self-important people. He is not one of the best writers at work today, but he is one of the most energetic and inventive. Journalism becomes, for him, an imaginative art, not a precise one: an approach his critics can neither understand nor forgive.

As a politician too, he feels compelled to make things interesting. He is a master of the theatre of politics. He lives in the moment. After the show, it may seem that not much remains. He has not yet shown he can deliver much except a series of brilliant performances. What he cares most about is the greatness of Boris, to be obtained without any diminution in the personality of Boris. For him to be bored is a kind of offence against his idea of himself. He has a genius for making things amusing. He makes whatever he is doing – municipal government, foreign relations – a better spectacle than it usually is. He has an instinct for freedom, and an almost complete lack of interest in administrative detail, but that does not mean he is merely slapdash: the way he found his way through the summer of 2016, and emerged in a high position, was no mere fluke, but the fruit of deeper thought and greater self-discipline than he would care to admit.

His greatest weakness is that people do not trust him. It is possible, though by no means a foregone conclusion, that in his first Cabinet post, he can do something to reassure them. On 20 July 2016, Theresa May took her first Prime Minister's Questions: a commanding performance. And there was Boris sitting on the front bench, looking happy, as well he might. For although he had not obtained the office which for a few days at the end of June 2016 seemed within his grasp, only Amber Rudd, the new Home Secretary, and Philip Hammond, the new Chancellor, now sat between him and the Prime Minister.

# Introduction

'It was at Rome, on the 15th of October 1764, as I sat musing amidst the ruins of the Capitol, while the barefooted friars were singing vespers in the Temple of Jupiter, that the idea of writing the decline and fall of the city first started to my mind.'

—Edward Gibbon, *Autobiography*

It was at London, on the 4th of June 2004, as I sat musing amidst the ruins of breakfast, while my wife said she supposed she would not really mind if we all went barefoot, that the idea of writing the life of Boris Johnson first started to my mind.

Like Gibbon, Boris is a historian of Rome, but that was not why his name occurred to me. In the summer of 2004, Boris's star shone with amazing brightness. Reputable judges predicted he would be the next Conservative Prime Minister, and that June morning he was all over the newspapers, which were enthralled by a scoop he had gathered while waiting on his bike at a traffic light.

An hour or two later I rang Boris and left a message on his mobile, telling him that I'd had an idea. I have known Boris since 1987, and in January 2000 he gave me the unpaid post of Foreign Editor of the *Spectator*, but it was almost unprecedented for me to ring him with an idea.

Two minutes later he rang back. Almost his first words were:

'Hang on, Andrew. A very beautiful girl has got to get off the train.'

Boris was at this time much bothered by girls who did not appreciate that he had editorial duties.

As soon as she had gone, Boris said, 'I met this rather beautiful singer. She just directed a coy, backward glance at me.'

I asked Boris if I could write his biography. He laughed for a long time before saying, 'Such is my colossal vanity that I have no intention of trying to forbid you.'

He said he would introduce me to the people I wanted to talk to, and provide photographs of himself as a child. He also declared, in the manner of a Victorian statesman, 'I will of course give you full access to my papers.'

Boris himself pointed out that the book could be 'the most fantastic piss-take'. Nobody is quicker than Boris to spot his own life's comic possibilities.

But then he asked: 'What about poor Allegra?' Allegra was Boris's first wife, and although for some years he omitted her from his entry in *Who's Who*, she is not omitted from this book. I wondered if he was worried what Allegra would say about him. I was already more worried about Marina, his present wife. It is one thing to write about a marriage that is over, quite another to intrude on a marriage which is still going.

Boris reminisced about our past: 'You introduced me to journalism. You gave me pork chops in your flat. We both got very drunk. Basically you introduced me to T. E. Utley, who introduced me to *The Times*, who gave me the traineeship.'

Boris has a remarkable memory and is one of the great flatterers of our times. It was delightful of him to say that I had introduced him to journalism, but the truth was that a number of people, all of them far more powerful than myself, helped Boris into journalism, and he has left each of them with the heart-warming impression that he or she was solely responsible for launching him. It is also true that Boris was more than capable of launching himself. His energy, ambition and talents were so remarkable that he could have pushed into almost any profession that attracted him, though it is true that he has failed to become a concert pianist.

For a time Boris continued kind. He loves reciting poetry, and when next we spoke he burst out into a great chunk of 'Lycidas', by John Milton:

> Alas! What boots it with uncessant care
> To tend the homely, slighted, shepherd's trade
> And strictly meditate the thankless Muse?
> Were it not better done, as others use,
> To sport with Amaryllis in the shade,
> Or with the tangles of Neaera's hair?
> Fame is the spur that the clear spirit doth raise
> (That last infirmity of noble mind)
> To scorn delights, and live laborious days:
> But the fair guerdon when we hope to find,
> And think to burst out into sudden blaze,
> Comes the blind Fury with the abhorred shears
> And slits the thin-spun life.

I put it to Boris that sporting with Amaryllis might be preferable to fame, but he made no reply. He was at this time doing so well that it seemed he could have everything he wanted. There was a risk, from my point of view, that others would hit on the idea of writing his life, but he said he would 'actively dissuade' anyone else who tried to do so before I had finished.

Boris also enquired, in the words of Sir Arthur Conan Doyle, whether his life was like 'the giant rat of Sumatra, a story for which the world is not yet prepared'. I took this as false modesty, but in retrospect it can be seen as his first note of caution.

During our third talk about the book Boris very sportingly gave me his father, mother and sister's telephone numbers. He also invited me to his fortieth birthday party, which was soon to take place, and to the cricket match between a *Spectator* side, captained by himself, and the team of his friend Lord Spencer, brother of the late Princess of Wales. The game was to take place on the ground at Althorp, the Spencer estate near Northampton.

Boris again mentioned Allegra, his first wife. I said I was having lunch with her that very day.

'Oh no!' he said. There was a pause, after which he went on: 'My life is literally in your hands.'

A few days later I had lunch with a friend of Boris's mistress, Petronella Wyatt, who told me that in 2003 she had got pregnant by Boris, and had aborted the child, but that Boris had told her he would look after any child she had by him.

No word of any such pregnancy had yet appeared in the newspapers, but on 16 June 2004 I found, not altogether surprisingly, that Boris was getting cold feet about the book. I met him that evening outside the House of Commons, in New Palace Yard, having rung him on his mobile while he was voting at 7 p.m. As we walked out into Parliament Square and across the road into Whitehall, Boris pushing his bike, he said in a worried tone: 'If it's a piss-take that's OK.' But he also said, 'Anything that purported to tell the truth really would be intolerable.'

I contended that politicians almost always get into trouble not for telling the truth but for trying to conceal it. Painful episodes in Boris's past would lose their power to hurt him once they were known, and it would be much less dangerous to deal with this stuff now than when he became Prime Minister.

In George Otto Trevelyan's classic book about another brilliant Old Etonian politician, *The Early History of Charles James Fox*, we are reminded that 'the senatorial habit of regarding the daily press as a criminal organisation' was already fully developed in the eighteenth century. Trevelyan described why in 1770 the Prime Minister tried to suppress the reporting of Parliament:

'Conscious of belonging to the class with regard to whom truth is the worst of libels, Lord North and his followers esteemed the reporter an equally dangerous enemy with the pamphleteer.'

Boris is not a member of 'the class with regard to whom truth is the worst of libels'. He is a man of immense energy, who was no more brought up to be faithful to a single woman than Charles James Fox was brought up to abstain from gambling.

As we sauntered into Whitehall, Boris gave his reluctant consent to the book, but it was becoming clear that his family were worried. His mother, Charlotte, sounded wonderfully sympathetic on the telephone, but deferred by a month a meeting I was to have with her.

His sister, Rachel, was the only one of his three siblings and two half-siblings with whom I was already acquainted. A week or two after I rang her, she sent me an e-mail, in which she referred to Boris as 'Al', the name by which the Johnsons call him, and said: 'There is little appetite among the siblings for sharing, much as we love Al, which we really do, but these are complicated issues and until Al has talked to us all about the "*grand projet*" I don't think I can have our meeting. In fact, it's because we love the bugger and regard our shared childhood as so precious that there is reluctance to turn it, like so much else, into public knowledge.'

Worst of all, I heard from a friend of mine that Marina, Boris's wife, and her parents Charles and Dip Wheeler were very worried about the book and had tried to enlist this friend's help to stop it. Marina is loved by all who know her, while her father, who died in 2008, was one of the most respected correspondents the BBC has ever had.

Perhaps at this point I should have renounced the project. This book may inflict some pain, especially since, in an attempt to convey some flavour of Boris, I have quoted with impudent freedom from private conversations I have had with him.

I might claim I owed it to history to leave my impressions of this great man. But that would be the most unutterable balls. Like Boris himself, I have been selfish. I found him too enjoyable to give up. There was too much laughter in him, and almost everyone to whom I mentioned the idea of the book responded by laughing, or at least by smiling. Boris is filled with a vitality which bursts the bounds of good taste. He is a figure from the eighteenth century, a magnanimous Merry England Conservative who has the gift, very unusual in a politician, of cheering people up. Nobody could be less sanctimonious, or more anxious to win our love by telling jokes. He reaches far beyond the ranks of those who are interested in politics, and attracts support even among those who hate politicians.

I was attracted by the idea of writing about a politician before he had achieved Cabinet office. It is such a relief not to have to go into the details of Boris's sixth budget, or the third administration which he will form at the age of eighty-one. If you want that sort of thing, there are plenty of great works where you can find it. But where else can you find a sketch of a shadow Conservative spokesman on higher education (as he was when this book first came out), or of a brand-new Foreign Secretary?

Boris is a celebrity, which is a bizarre thing for a man with his classical education at Eton and Balliol College, Oxford, to have become, or to want to become, and I wanted to see how he had done it. The celebrity living a life above the rules is the epitome of our tabloid culture, and to write about him in a completely sanitised way would be to misunderstand him. He or she appeals to our fantasies of effortless success, a sort of modern version of the effortless superiority once attributed to Balliol men.

The celebrity has sex without responsibility and is attractive enough never to be without a lover. As Boris himself once boasted to a woman: 'I haven't had to have a wank for twenty years.'

Some months after starting my research, I decided the time had come to speak to Boris himself about his childhood. I went one morning to the *Spectator* and waited for him in his office.

Boris looked shocked to see me when he arrived. In what now strikes me as a rather gauche way, I said I wanted to talk to him about his childhood. Boris said, 'Oh my God,' and held his head in his hands. He went on to say, 'What I'm worried about is that stuff will come out, no matter how delicate and tactful you are . . . Other people will use the appearance of the book to fan old coals and heat up long-dead issues.'

When I remarked that I was writing the book anyhow, and urged him to have his say, he responded: 'As the *News of the World* would say' – and here he switched into a brutish accent – 'your name's going to be in this anyway. We'd just like you to put your side of the story.'

I reminded Boris that he had agreed to the book. He replied: 'I wasn't thinking straight then.'

Boris asked how large an advance Simon & Schuster were paying me for the book, which I refused to tell him. He offered to buy me out, and as the book progressed, his bids increased in size. I am inclined to think that all this must have been a protracted joke. At one of our last encounters before the book went to press, when I bumped into him in Trafalgar Square, he raised the amount in large jumps, as if bidding in an auction, and for a fleeting moment offered me £100,000 not to write the book. In a subsequent communication, he thought better of this approach and offered instead to give my children free Greek lessons.

Boris had moved from complete agreement with the book to total disagreement. He began by sounding utterly confident, and ended by sounding strangely vulnerable. It was a curious transformation, but also, as I was to discover, a rather characteristic one.

So this is not an authorised biography, nor can I pretend that it is exhaustive. I have tried to be fair to Boris and to those near to him, and if I have failed the fault is mine alone, but I have not attempted to monopolise this colossus of our times. In years to come, there will be any amount of work for younger, fitter Johnson scholars.

I sought the advice of other writers. Tony Blair's biographer, John Rentoul, warned: 'The sex is difficult.' Charles Moore, who is at work on Margaret Thatcher's authorised biography, said of Boris: 'You'll need 200 pages for his foreign policy' – a remark which until July 2016 sounded satirical rather than prophetic.

But time has given out, and those 200 pages remain unwritten. All I can offer is a sketch drawn from life, by one who was lucky enough to know Boris.

# Acknowledgements

My greatest debt is to Boris, for providing such good subject matter, and for remaining generally good-tempered. I would like to thank his mother, Charlotte, and father, Stanley, for outlining the family background, and his sister, Rachel, for supplying a couple of anecdotes. Their cousin Sinan Kuneralp provided valuable information about the Johnsons' Turkish ancestry, as did Geoffrey Lewis, Andrew Mango and David Barchard.

Boris's first wife, Allegra Mostyn-Owen, was immensely helpful, and Marina Wheeler, his present wife, kindly broke her rule of not talking to journalists (apart from members of her own family) and corrected some inaccuracies. Max Benitz undertook some last-minute research. Among the many other people I must thank are Darius Guppy, Shusha Guppy, Conrad Black, Charles Moore, Frank Johnson, Ann Sindall, Nick Garland, Nigel Howard, Alan Davidson, Clive and Rowena Williams, Eric Anderson, John Lewis, Martin Hammond, Michael Meredith, Penny Hatfield, Chris Bayston, Andrew Gilmour, Jesse Norman, Giles Stibbe, James Hughes-Onslow, Johnnie Boden, Joshua Neicho, Jasper Griffin, Jonathan Barnes, Anthony Kenny, Lloyd Evans, Justin Rushbrooke, Radek Sikorski, Frank Luntz, Patrick Hennessy, Gary Gibbon, Toby Young, Michael Gove, Jessica Pulay, David Ekserdjian, John and Sarah Biffen, Miriam Gross, Susanna Gross, Peter Stothard, Charles Wilson, George Brock, John Bryant, Simon Heffer, Paul Hill, Rory Watson, David Usborne, Michael Binyon, Sarah Helm, Charles Grant, John

Kerr, Douglas Hurd, Philippe Sands, James Landale, Max Hastings, Dominic Lawson, Trevor Grove, Marcus Scriven, Sue Lawley, Ian Hislop, Richard Ehrman, Stuart Reid, Mary Wakefield, Peter Oborne, Peter McKay, Olivia Walmsley, Henrietta Malcolm-Smith, Stephen Glover, Sarah Sands, Anne Jenkin, Tom Henry, Matthew Pencharz, Guto Harri, Ken Livingstone, Melissa Crawshay-Williams, Lynton Crosby, Susan Clarke, Robert Davis, Ray Lewis, Nick Boles, Quentin Letts, Robin Harris, David Cameron, Alistair Cooke, Oliver Letwin, Henry McCrory, Paul Goodman, Francis Elliott, Sam Coates, Andrew Grice, James Forsyth and Michael Cockerell. Many other people helped but asked not to be quoted by name. I am acutely aware that there are yet others to whom it would have been desirable to talk, and would urge anyone with memories of Boris which he or she is willing to share with a wider audience to get in touch. I am grateful to those writers from whose articles I have quoted.

My agents, Rivers Scott and Andrew Gordon, and Angela Herlihy, Mike Jones, Rory Scarfe, Ian Marshall and Jo Whitford at Simon & Schuster all gave indispensable help. My wife Sally encouraged me in a way that nobody else could have done. This book is dedicated to her with my love.

Andrew Gimson
Gospel Oak
July 2006 and December 2011;
Cagnes-sur-Mer August 2016

# – 1 –

## The Birth of Boris

BORIS WAS BORN TO BRITISH PARENTS IN NEW YORK City on 19 June 1964. His mother, Charlotte, who was only twenty-two years old, relates that even at birth he had the thick yellow hair for which he was later to become so celebrated: 'We didn't cut it, so it turned into ringlets.'

His father, Stanley, who was twenty-three, wrote a radio talk about the birth which was broadcast later that summer in Britain on the Light Programme. In it he recalled that Charlotte 'received a constant stream of letters and cables from England entreating her to go back and have the child there'. Their friends said it would be appallingly expensive to have the baby in America, and they also pointed out that the child would be a US citizen, 'eligible to be drafted and like as not dispatched into the jungles of Vietnam'. They must also have doubted whether Stanley would be able to look after Charlotte and the baby properly.

By Stanley's account, the most powerful argument 'was, of course, the financial one'. Doctors in New York were not cheap: when Charlotte broke her toe, her treatment cost $70. But then they heard of 'the Clinic', a place where you paid only what you could afford. Respectable New Yorkers did not go to the Clinic:

'Socialized, or as it is more sinisterly called, communistic medicine is in America evil almost by definition.' But as Stanley said in the radio talk, 'we were neither respectable nor New Yorkers'.

For five weeks, Stanley attended ante-natal classes, before asking himself: 'Did real men bother themselves with all this?'

One detail which he omitted from the talk, but mentioned in conversation to me, was that he had been 'doing my stuff', rubbing Charlotte's back and uttering words of encouragement during her labour, but had 'popped out for a pizza at the crucial moment'.

On his return, Stanley was surprised to see that the soles of their new-born baby were black. This was because his footprints had been taken, to ensure that no baby-swapping took place.

The boy's full name was Alexander Boris de Pfeffel Johnson. The name Boris was in honour of Boris Litwin, a White Russian in Mexico City. On leaving Oxford in 1963, Stanley had won a Harkness Fellowship to study in the United States. In the same year, he married Charlotte, who was herself an undergraduate at Lady Margaret Hall, Oxford. They met when he won the Newdigate Prize for poetry, which led to his being invited to dine at All Souls', where she too was dining, because her father, James Fawcett, was a fellow of that college. She deferred the final year of her degree, and they went together to America, where Stanley started by attending the State University of Iowa in Iowa City for one term.

From Iowa, where Boris was probably conceived, they moved to New York, where they lived in a loft on West 23rd Street, opposite the Chelsea Hotel and above a café called the Star Bar, where Stanley first heard the Beatles.

A condition of the Harkness award was that he must do at least three months' travel each summer, for which purpose he was given a brand new Chevrolet Bel Air.

At the end of May 1964, when Charlotte was eight months pregnant, they drove from New York to Laredo in Texas, a distance of 1,700 miles as the crow flies, which as Stanley says was 'quite a long haul'.

Stanley, it has been said by one who knew him over a long period, does not believe in comfort or sickness. He neither admitted to sickness himself, nor noticed it in others. The same is true of Boris, of whom this observer said: 'I'd never put him in charge of hospitals.'

The young couple were not allowed to take the car out of the country, so left it on the border and took the Greyhound bus to Mexico City, about 600 miles farther on, where they met Boris Litwin, whose daughter was a friend of a friend of Stanley's at Oxford.

When Litwin saw Charlotte's condition and heard that Stanley proposed to take her all the way back to Laredo on the bus, he was appalled, and the following exchange took place:

LITWIN: 'I want to give you a first-class ticket to New York.'
CHARLOTTE: 'Oh Mr Litwin . . .'
LITWIN: 'Call me Boris.'
CHARLOTTE: 'Oh Boris, whatever the baby is, I shall call it
        Boris.'

In the event, Charlotte and Stanley accepted two tickets from Litwin to get them back to the United States and then drove back to New York. Soon afterwards, Boris was born, and the next day Stanley typed a letter to Litwin:

I write at once to tell you that Alexander BORIS de Pfeffel Johnson was born at 2.00 p.m. yesterday and that both he and his mother, Charlotte, are very well and happy.

    It is a source of immense satisfaction to me, sir, that we have thus been able to redeem the promise which we made to you in Mexico, so long ago, that, should it be possible, the child would be named after you in some small recognition of the kindnesses which you showed to us then.

Alexander BORIS weighed 9 pounds 1 ounce at birth and is a remarkably lusty child.

Litwin had unfortunately died, so never received this news. As for the lusty child, he is still known to the Johnsons as Al, and his first articles for *The Times* appeared under the byline Alexander Johnson, but we shall call him Boris, the name under which he was to become famous. As someone fated to devote so many of his prodigious energies to public performance, he was lucky to have been given such a simple and memorable stage name.

# 2

# The Death of Ali Kemal

BORIS'S FOREBEARS WERE CLEVER AND COSMOPOLITAN. HIS father's family was notable for its recklessness, while his mother's family are distinguished for their learning. In the direct male line, Boris is descended from a Turkish polemicist who went into politics and was murdered after backing the wrong side. His great grandfather, Ali Kemal, was a handsome, brilliant and provocative Turkish journalist before and just after the First World War, during the last years of the Ottoman Empire. Ali Kemal's own father came from Kalfat, a village in north-west Anatolia where there were many children with blond hair, perhaps descended from the Goths. This is thought to be the origin of the remarkably fair hair, more white than gold, which is found to this day in the Johnson family and is one of Boris's most distinctive characteristics.

Ali Kemal's mother was a Circassian, reputedly of slave origin. The Circassians were an unruly, good-looking race of mountaineers from the western Caucasus. Their fighting spirit and willingness to risk life and limb are seen in Boris, but appeared with even greater force in Ali Kemal. He was first arrested in 1888, for setting up a students' society, and spent many years before the First World War in exile from Ottoman Turkey.

Ali Kemal was an educated man, a poet and novelist who

enjoyed living abroad. But even before he was murdered it was said of him that 'the life of a predatory bird tends to be short', and according to Andrew Mango, the foremost British authority on the period, 'his pen ran away with him. He was clearly a difficult man with an angry temperament. In Britain today he would be a vituperative journalist.'

At the end of the First World War, Ali Kemal became one of the most prominent advocates of co-operation with the victorious Allies, including the British, and the sworn enemy of the Turkish Nationalist movement which was emerging under the leadership of Kemal Atatürk.

Atatürk, who at this point was still known as Mustafa Kemal, was a senior army officer who had distinguished himself at Gallipoli. He was about to achieve worldwide renown as the founder of modern Turkey, but not before Ali Kemal tried to stop him.

In May 1919 Ali Kemal was made interior minister. On 16 June he instructed post offices to refuse the flood of protest telegrams being sent by Anti-Annexation Societies all over Aegean Turkey to the government in Istanbul and to the Allies. These telegrams contained demands for protection against Greek troops, who had landed with Allied help in Izmir and were driving out the Muslim population with heavy loss of life and wholesale destruction of Muslim property.

Ali Kemal immediately understood how vital the telegraph system was to the Nationalists. Boris shows a similar ability, both as a journalist and as a politician, to see how power works.

Atatürk, who was later to say that he won the War of Independence by using the telegraph wires, hit back on 20 June 1919 with a circular to post offices in which he threatened to court martial any official who obeyed Ali Kemal's ban on telegrams. Three days later, the government backed down and allowed the transmission of telegrams, on condition that these were approved by the local authorities.

On the same day, 23 June, Ali Kemal sent a circular to the provincial authorities ordering them to have nothing to do with Atatürk. But Ali Kemal was dangerously isolated. He was the only minister who was determined to get rid of Atatürk, and he became embroiled in a furious argument with the war minister, with the result that on 26 June they both resigned.

While Atatürk led the Nationalists to victory, attained in August 1922, Ali Kemal returned to journalism. He edited a newspaper called *Peyam-i Sabah*, or 'Morning Message', and attacked the Nationalists very violently in print, telling them that by opposing the British they would get a worse deal. In the view of the Nationalists, he was a traitor who wanted to turn Turkey into a British colony.

On 10 September 1922 Ali Kemal published an editorial in which he attempted to make his peace with the Nationalists, expressing his joy at their victory. This last editorial did not save him. On 4 November 1922, he was kidnapped by Nationalist agents outside the Cercle d'Orient club in Istanbul, bundled into a boat and taken across the Bosphorus to Izmit, where he was handed over to Nurettin Pasha, a brutal general who dealt with enemies by handing them over to a mob which could be relied upon to lynch them.

Nurettin had already disposed of Chrysostom, a Greek Archbishop, in this way, and he applied the same bloodthirsty method to Ali Kemal. The mob finished him off with sticks, stones and knives, before hanging him up in a tree in the square of Izmit. Atatürk was furious, declaring, 'We're not bandits operating in the mountains,' and sacked Nurettin.

Boris is a passionate defender of Turkish entry into the European Union: a position which in 2016 contrasted oddly with lurid warnings by Leave campaigners including himself that the EU intends to allow 77 million Turks to come to the UK.

It is usual on these occasions for the presenter to be filmed in the places from which the artefacts are drawn, but Boris had travelled no further than the RA in Piccadilly, where he repeatedly described the exhibits as 'magnificent'.

Boris has also related how, when accused at a meeting during the 2001 General Election of stoking up base feelings against asylum-seekers, he responded by announcing, 'I am the grandson of an asylum-seeker.'

This too is incorrect. Ali Kemal's first wife, who was half-English and half-Swiss, gave birth in Bournemouth in September 1909 to a son, Osman Ali. It had been thought she would be safer in England than in Turkey, but she died in childbirth. Her son was brought up by her mother, Margaret Johnson, and was renamed Wilfred Johnson.

On 27 June 1919, Margaret Johnson wrote a formal letter from 15 Foxholes Road, Southbourne-on-Sea, just east of Bournemouth, to the British Delegation to the Versailles Peace Conference:

Sir,

I beg leave to inquire if you can inform me whether I should be able to have an interview with one of the Turkish Delegates at present in Paris, under the following circumstances:

(1) The Delegate referred to is ALI KEMAL BEY, who I am informed is at present staying at the Château de Monteclin, Jouy-en-Josas, near Paris.

(2) He was married to my daughter, who died in the year 1909, leaving two children, a girl now aged 12, and a boy now 10 years of age. By arrangement with their father, the above mentioned Delegate, these children were, on the death of their mother (my daughter), left in my care, and were both baptised into the Church of England. Both are now being educated here.

(3) Since the outbreak of war with Turkey the father has not contributed anything towards their maintenance.

(4) As I am, unfortunately, left without means, the support of these dear children has been a very great strain on my efforts.

(5) Knowing that their father is now in Paris in connection with the preparation of the Treaty of Peace with Turkey, I am very anxious to see him, if possible, in order to get money from him towards the support of his two children. That is my sole and only reason for seeking an interview with him, and I am most anxious not to take any steps that would not meet with the approval, and be in strict accordance with the permission, of the British Delegation.

This enquiry brought no joy: the British Delegation informed Mrs Johnson that Ali Kemal had already left Paris. But several things emerge from the letter. One is that Mrs Johnson was bringing her grandson up as an Englishman, and indeed as a member of the Church of England. Another is that Ali Kemal had made no attempt since the end of the war to see his English children, or to send them money, although money was certainly needed.

Ali Kemal contracted a brilliant second marriage in 1913, to Sabiha, daughter of Zeki Pasha, a distinguished soldier who was head of the Ottoman artillery. They had one son, Zeki Kuneralp, whom Sabiha brought up in exile in Switzerland after Ali Kemal's murder. Sabiha sold Ali Kemal's collection of oriental manuscripts to the British Library after his death and gave the proceeds to Mrs Johnson. Zeki, her son, was a man of great ability and charm. He entered the Turkish diplomatic service, in which he rose to become ambassador in London and then in Madrid, where in 1977 his wife and her brother, the Turkish ambassador in Oslo, were murdered by Armenian terrorists.

The Turkish and English sides of the family were by this time in friendly contact. But the panache with which Boris plays the part of stage Englishman can be traced to the determination of the Johnsons to be seen as English. It is a role they have perfected over three generations.

Wilfred Johnson, known as Johnny, did not care to be reminded of the Turkish father who had abandoned him. Boris's grandfather grew up in England, farmed in Canada and then went to Egypt, where he worked on the farms of various Swiss cousins. It was here that he met Boris's grandmother, Irène Williams, known as 'Buster' because of her kick-boxing prowess. Johnny saw her do a camel kick to get rid of a cheeky soldier who had molested her in a bar. They were married in 1936.

Buster was half-French and half-English. On the English side, she was descended from Sir George Williams, who in 1844 founded the YMCA, or Young Men's Christian Association. His grandson, Stanley Williams, married Marie-Louise de Pfeffel, daughter of the Baron de Pfeffel, who lived in a fine house in Versailles which is now the Chamber of Commerce. In August 2008 the BBC investigated Boris's ancestors in an edition of *Who Do You Think You Are?* The programme, which is well worth watching, made the startling discovery that the Pfeffel line leads back, via an illegitimate liaison, to King George II. Boris is a Hanoverian! He received the news of his royal ancestry with a fitting mixture of satisfaction and humility.

During the Second World War, Johnny served in Coastal Command in the RAF, and on one occasion, when Buster was watching from the ground, he tipped the wing of his plane to her and crashed, injuring himself quite severely. This was later spoken of by the family as a great joke. A mangled fragment of this wrecked plane – it looks like the joystick – is preserved at Nethercote, the 500-acre sheep farm on Exmoor which Johnny and Buster bought with her money after the war.

# 3

## Small Blond Heads

SOON AFTER BORIS WAS BORN, HIS PARENTS CAME BACK WITH him to England so that Charlotte could return to Oxford and finish her English degree. She was the first married undergraduate her college, Lady Margaret Hall, had ever had, and during her final year she became pregnant for a second time: 'The Principal never spoke to me again when she learned that Miss Fawcett, as I continued to be known, was pregnant again.' In the autumn of 1964, the Johnsons took a modern flat in Summertown, Oxford. Here Charlotte looked after Boris with the aid of a woman next door, and studied for her exams. She remembers Boris as an 'incredibly good baby' who never cried. She would be writing an essay and he would sit on the floor at her feet, with a box or saucepan to amuse him. On looking down, she would sometimes find he had fallen asleep on his back. Once, when he was being looked after by her old nanny at her parents' large house in Cavendish Avenue in St John's Wood, London, Charlotte's mother and the nanny, Miss Reid, were having coffee downstairs and heard a crash. Boris's cot had broken and they found him lying fast asleep on the mattress on the floor.

Until the age of eight or nine he was very deaf, and had to undergo several operations to have grommets put in his ear.

According to his mother, 'I think that not hearing very well made him quite quiet.' Although he always had the gift of amusing people, he was not the rumbustious figure he later became.

Boris's aversion to eggs dates from early childhood, when he claims to have been fed too many of them. His rough and ready attitude to food reflects an upbringing where he was expected to eat pretty much anything. He has recalled with pride how he was able to eat the disgusting food which was served in one of his early primary schools.

Charlotte took her finals in June 1965, when Boris was a year old and she was about six months' pregnant with Rachel. At the end of her exams, when she was wearing subfusc – formal academic dress – made out of black-out curtains to accommodate her bump, Stanley and Miss Reid, the Fawcett family nanny, brought the one-year-old Boris to celebrate with her. The photograph of this occasion shows Boris with a magnificent head of fair, curly hair, attempting to drink some his mother's champagne, with Miss Reid looking on.

Charlotte's ancestors included Henry Fawcett, the Radical MP for Brighton, who was blinded by his own father in a shooting accident and became known as 'the blind Postmaster General', a position he was given by Gladstone in 1880. His wife, Millicent Garrett Fawcett, was one of the most famous campaigners for votes for women. Charlotte is herself one of the five children of Sir James Fawcett, an international lawyer who was described in his *Times* obituary as 'an intellectual colossus'. He was educated at Rugby and at New College, Oxford, where he obtained a double first in Mods and Greats before becoming a fellow of All Souls.

From his mother's family, Boris has inherited a tradition of humane and erudite liberalism. For twenty-two years, from 1962 to 1984, Sir James Fawcett was a member of the European Commission of Human Rights at Strasbourg. As a politician, Boris displays similar instincts to his grandfather. In an obituary piece for the *Independent* published on 1 July 1991, Lord Lester summarised some of the principles upheld by Sir James during his long period at the Commission, including the right to respect for family life of unmarried mothers and their children, the degrading nature of judicial corporal punishment, the right to free speech in a democratic society, the right to equal citizenship without racial discrimination, and the need for adequate safeguards against the misuse of necessary powers of clandestine surveillance.

In retirement Sir James pursued his interest in astronomy: 'Behind his house in Combe in the Berkshire hills was a telescope through which friends would share his love of the Heavens.' Lord Lester said of him: 'James was a gentle, considerate and private man, of extraordinary charm and dignity, and strikingly handsome. What mattered most to him were his marriage to his beloved Bice, and their delightful children and grandchildren. Bice was his constant and adored companion.'

The Fawcetts were great friends of the Pakenhams – Lord and Lady Longford – one of whose daughters, the novelist Rachel Billington, is Charlotte's best friend, and Boris's godmother. If Boris had taken his party allegiance from his mother's family, he would have joined Labour, and the Fawcetts were somewhat shocked when Charlotte married, in Stanley, a Tory.

Charlotte's mother, Beatrice Lowe, or Bice, was a Catholic convert of partly Jewish extraction. She was the daughter of Elias Lowe, né Loew, an immensely learned Lithuanian-born palaeographer of Latin manuscripts who worked at Oxford before becoming a professor at Princeton. His wife, Helen Lowe-Porter, was American, and for fifty years enjoyed the exclusive right to translate Thomas Mann's works into English. Mann had the highest opinion of her, but some rival scholars considered her translations to be stunningly inaccurate.

When I spoke to Charlotte, she was plainly thinking far more about the need to protect and help others, including her children, daughter-in-law and grandchildren, than about herself.

Stanley took a second degree, in agricultural economics, and in the spring of 1965 he also joined the Foreign Office, from which he resigned in the autumn of the same year, because 'by then the World Bank had come through with an offer for me to go to Washington'.

Charlotte, Stanley, Boris and Rachel spent the winter of 1965–66 on Exmoor, in a house they rented between Nethercote and Dulverton. Charlotte looked after the children while Stanley wrote his first novel, *Gold Dust*. On 22 February 1966 they flew to Washington. A year later, their third child, Leo, was born – a birth for which Charlotte returned to London. In 1968, when Stanley was already leaving the World Bank, he played a successful April Fool on its senior staff by putting forward a proposal to finance the building of three new pyramids in Egypt.

Charlotte was not keen to stay in America. According to Stanley, she was 'badly shaken by the riots in spring 1968' involving Martin Luther King. The Johnsons remained in Washington until the middle of 1968, when they moved to New York, where Stanley had got a job funded by John D. Rockefeller to look into the question of overpopulation. He had become convinced that the world was going to perish from this cause, and travelled 35,000 miles to research a book called *Life Without Birth*.

Stanley admitted in his first chapter that he had not himself practised the birth control which he had come to regard as an urgent necessity. It is one of the first references to Boris (still known as Alexander) in print, and also indicates one of the origins of Boris's style. Stanley is urging the need to do something now to save the world from overpopulation:

Act now. Act now. Oh God! I look at my guilty face in the shaving mirror as my children clatter down to breakfast –

it's too late to act. By all means bolt the stable door but the horses have gone. Where were you, *New York Times*, with your full-page advertisements [warning against over-population], when we added Rachel to Alexander? Where were you, conservationists of the world, at the getting of Leo? How can I face that row of small blond heads bobbing over the cornflakes knowing that I am statistically accountable for the burdens they will add to society?

We can be confident that Stanley could face the small blond heads with no trouble at all. He is immensely proud to have six children, four by Charlotte and two more by his present wife, Jenny.

Stanley had soaked up the progressive opinions of the day. He remarks that he has married a Catholic, but this does not stop him condemning the Pope (as did many Catholics too) for in July 1968 issuing *Humanae Vitae*, the encyclical forbidding birth control:

> If any single human being is to be brought to the bar of history for crimes against humanity in this last third of the twentieth century, it must be Pope Paul VI – for he has consigned countless millions to misery and anguish, mental and material. I believe that *Humanae Vitae* may come to be ranked as one of the most massive errors of judgment ever made . . . Paul VI, on the black day in July 1968, sacrificed the whole world to save the Church's soul.

This does not sound like Boris, who never denounces anyone in such harsh terms. But Stanley was only about twenty-seven when he wrote this, and his impetuousness, and urge to talk up the story he is telling, could be said to characterise some of the reports from Brussels which Boris was to write at the same age. In May 1969 the Johnsons returned to London, where they

lived in Blomfield Road, Maida Vale. Stanley says he was 'actually quite rich – the Ford Foundation had given us rather a
valuable scholarship to be in London studying demography'. He
also had 'a variety of jobs', including one as the first environment
desk officer in the Conservative Party's Research Department,
where he shared an office with Chris Patten. Lord Patten, as he
later became, remembers Stanley as 'absurd but harmless'.

There is a precarious feeling to all this. Nothing is solid or
permanent. As Charlotte recalled: 'We moved thirty-two times
when I was married to Stanley.' He was quick-witted and energetic, and had an eye to the main chance, but he had not hit the
jackpot, and was not by birth a man of substance. The farm on
Exmoor lost money and was subsidised out of Stanley's scholarships. Boris had a privileged upbringing, but also a rather rackety
and hand-to-mouth one. As I worked on this book, I came to
believe that he suffers to this day from a sense of insecurity, and
a worry that he is about to be rumbled, which outsiders seldom
detect. Along with his boundless optimism goes the fear that he
and his family are only a couple of meals away from the poor
house.

# 4

# Learning to Be a Johnson

FROM HIS EARLIEST YEARS, BORIS DEVELOPED A PASSION FOR coming top. His sister Rachel recalls that when asked as a small boy what he wanted to be, he would say 'the world king'. Nor has he ever grown out of this ambition. He has simply learned to conceal it. His manner is so shambolic and laid-back that, as with the insecurity mentioned at the end of the last chapter, this side of him can easily be overlooked. You will never find a more ferocious competitor than Boris, driven on by that sense of insecurity, but also by what he himself has called, with the intention that we should presume he is merely joking, his megalomania. He was not born to ease and comfort, but to wage a ceaseless struggle for supremacy. No Prussian militarist with a bankrupt estate in the barren depths of Brandenburg could be more single-minded than Boris in pursuit of knock-out victory.

In Boris's case, the estate which could never be made to pay, and which made it necessary for him to go out and win a place in the sun, was his grandparents' farm on Exmoor. Boris was almost five years old when the family left London and bought Nethercote Cottage, smallest of the three houses on the farm. It might be thought that in this remote spot, playing with his siblings rather than with other children, he would be sheltered from competitive pressure, but the Johnsons knew how to make their own competition. His grandmother would ask Rachel, a precocious four-year-old, to sit at the kitchen table and read the *Times* leader, and would tell her how well she had read it. This praise for his sister, who was just over a year younger than him, drove Boris mad with rage.

Another favourite family story has Boris playing table tennis with Rachel, losing a point to her during the knock-up, and kicking the wall so hard that he broke his toe. He is also supposed, when playing snooker with her, to have got so angry that he ripped the cloth and broke the cue, after she got a fluky shot in.

Julia Johnson, one of Stanley's two children by his second wife, Jenny, has described a Johnson upbringing:

> My father has six children, of which I am the last but one, and as long as I can remember there have been cut-throat mealtime quizzes, fearsome ping-pong matches, height, weight and blondness contests, and, of course, academic rivalry of mind-numbing magnitude. When my brother Jo gained a First from Oxford, Rachel rang Boris to tell him the 'terrible news'. If I came second in Latin, my father would instantly demand: 'Who came first?' It became a standard catchphrase in our household and a vigorous deterrent against being anything except top.

According to Julia, 'If anyone is coming top in the Johnson league table, it would be the one my father refers to as: "Boris, that great prodigious tree in the rainforest, in the shade of which the smaller trees must either perish or struggle to find their own place in the sun."' The comparison is comic, but also slightly chilling. We find ourselves watching a struggle for the survival of the fittest, though one should add that they all proved fit, with five of them going to Oxford while Julia herself went to Cambridge.

For a year after they came back from America, when they were living in her parents' house in Cavendish Avenue, Charlotte taught all three children – Boris, Rachel and their younger brother Leo – herself: 'Stanley was going round the world as usual – he used to leave me for periods of six months – so I got very close to the children.' She remembers this as 'one of the happiest times'. Each child had an exercise book, even Leo, who was too young to write, and each morning she would teach them many different subjects. They made lots of things and Boris was very artistic. Charlotte is a painter by profession, and Boris continues to paint with great enthusiasm, and with more ability than many amateurs.

Here was a gentler world, which still exists in Boris, but was overlaid by rivalries. Boris's sister Rachel told Julia: 'There was always tremendous competition to climb trees higher, or learn to read first. I think the last time I beat Boris at anything was when I won the Scottish dancing prize at the age of twelve. It's been a rapid ascent for him ever since. He planted his flag first on the summit of so many Mount Olympuses that we younger siblings have to content ourselves in tooling quietly around the foothills of our own careers.' The expression 'tooling quietly around' is a ridiculous way for Rachel to refer to her own immensely energetic attempts to become a top author.

Boris himself told Julia: 'As the oldest, I've always known that my position was basically unchallengeable. It is the fixed point about which my cosmos is organised. I smile indulgently on everybody else's attempts to compete with me. Bring it on, I say.'

Julia ended her account by commenting: 'I must e-mail this to my father, so he can check that there's more about him than anyone else.'

The Johnsons are very loyal to each other, but also compete like mad against each other. This is perhaps true, to some extent, of all families, but they present an extreme case. What can sometimes amount to deep hurt and bitter rivalries are covered up by jokes, and by laughing at the jokes we become complicit in the cover-up. But one reason why Boris attracts people is that this cover-up, though maintained with such heroic fortitude that it has become second nature to him, is never sufficient to hide his humanity. People love him because he makes them laugh, but also because they glimpse the hurt young kid behind the laughter. The English pretence that all is well is accompanied by an un-English depth of feeling, which survives even when he performs on television. Boris's vulnerability is akin to someone like Marilyn Monroe's: it is part of his attraction, and like her he can use it to seduce audiences pretty much at will.

Boris has described how he felt when a man was unexpectedly nasty to him on a plane: 'I quivered, like a puppy unexpectedly kicked.' Not everybody is prepared to tolerate a grown man who behaves like a puppy, but the English are exceptionally fond of animals and a lot of people find Boris refreshing, especially when they compare him to more mature and stilted politicians.

In August 2005 I visited Stanley at Nethercote. He arranged for Mr Whitley, the local taxi driver, to pick me up from Taunton station. For almost an hour Mr Whitley drove westwards past Combe Florey, where the journalist Auberon Waugh lived, into the Exmoor National Park and over the Brendon Hills, before descending into the deep valley of the River Exe, which rises on Exmoor and runs through the Johnsons' farm, between Exford and Winsford, before turning south on its way to Exeter and the sea.

In Winsford, where about 300 people live, we drove through a small ford and up to the old village school. This was where Boris went to school, a white building next to the church, with the headmistress living in a house next door. The school closed some time ago.

We drove out of Winsford, past the Old Vicarage, and turned up Stanley's drive. It was a perfect summer's day and as we came into the valley we seemed to be entering heaven upon earth. Two girls on bicycles, a young man and a labrador noted our arrival and raced off up the track ahead of us. The drive runs for a mile and three quarters under trees beside the River Exe. When Boris was young, this track was very rough, so that visitors would sometimes lose heart before they got to the farm buildings and turn back, but a new and smoother surface has recently been applied. The valley still has a shaggy, unimproved feeling, its sides a mixture of rough pasture, bracken and woodland.

There are three houses grouped together at the end of the drive, after a final bridge over the river. The welcome party had gone into the second house, which belongs to Rachel, Boris's sister. Stanley's is the last house you come to, beyond an empty farmyard. The patriarch was sitting outside drinking a glass of white wine, with a volume of Cavafy's poems in Greek and English. His farmhouse, where his parents used to live, is long, low, stone, an old and scruffy building, though also very clean, whereas visitors who went there when Boris was a lad remember it being very dirty. It has a huge open fireplace and smells of woodsmoke. It has not been tarted up, and none of the outbuildings has been turned into a house. There is nothing prissy about the set-up, or about Boris himself, which is yet another reason why people like him.

Stanley said Boris had rung the previous day, before taking Marina and the children on holiday in Uzbekistan, and was highly suspicious of my visit. I felt I had penetrated an Arcadian sanctuary, but one which – as Stanley's own mother found – could also be a prison.

Stanley walked me round to Nethercote Cottage, where he installed Charlotte with their three small children some time after their return from America. As we walked up to the cottage he said: 'Charlotte maintains I left her here for a year while I wrote a book called *The Green Revolution*. I've looked at my diaries. I did three longish trips but it doesn't add up to a year.' Charlotte remembers living at Nethercote without a car, washing machine or television, but having 'actually a wonderful time'.

A small wooden building to the left of the cottage served as the children's playroom, though now it is fitted up as a work-shop. Here Stanley showed me 'Alexander's first known literary effort'. At the age of about five, Boris painted a message on the wall in clear blue letters: 'Boo to grown ups!'

Birdie, Stanley's sister, who lives here, had made herself scarce, but he led me inside and up the stairs. Near the top on the left, a small door, only a few feet high, opened into a kind of box room – a long, narrow space, with a sloping roof, and a small window at the far end.

A grown-up could not stand in here, but one could imagine that a small boy would love it, though he would need to climb on to the stairs with some care or he would tumble down. It is the room where Boris slept. Some childish pictures were still attached to the wall at the far end. We could make out a rain-bow, a frog (or possibly a flying saucer) and some birds, and these two words in capitals:

MAMA
ANDER

The second of these words is short for Alexander, or it could also be that the first four letters of the name by which Boris was then known have been obscured.

It seemed extraordinary that these pictures should still be here. Stanley said later, when we were on our way back to Taunton: 'I had no idea they were still there. Like cave art.'

Hanging on the stairs is a framed poem by Buster, Stanley's mother, which starts:

We have come to the end of the track
And must part

For our journey together is ended
For the last time I pause and look back
Sick at heart
While my hand in farewell is extended.

The poem continues for about another twenty lines in the same vein. At the bottom of the stairs is a framed photograph of a man in RAF uniform – Stanley's father.

Stanley said: 'When my father came here he had no other thoughts but to farm it. It has turned out to be a wonderful place to have. I consider myself to be the son of a farmer. My mother was different. She read modern languages – French and Russian, I think – at Oxford, and had been at Cheltenham Ladies' College. She thought she might have married a diplomat. I think my mother did see Nethercote as a gilded prison. The high point of her life was often driving down to the bottom of the drive to see if someone had left a letter for her.'

Buster took great trouble with Stanley's education. Her money was sufficient to send him and his brother Peter to school at Sherborne. Stanley was head boy, played rugby for the school and won a scholarship in classics to Exeter College, Oxford.

Stanley did not seem to wish to linger any longer in his sister's cottage. This could be impatience on his part. He likes to get on with things, and had already waited while I transcribed the start of the poem.

On the way back we looked inside Rachel's house. Four children were there, two of them Rachel's and two friends who were visiting. A young man – an Australian – seemed to have the job of looking after them. Rachel was said to have gone for a very long walk.

Stanley asked the children if they wanted to come up to the top of the farm with us in the back of the Land Rover. This suggestion was met with wild enthusiasm. We got into an incredibly old, battered Land Rover, four children and two dogs in the back, and set off up the hill. Stanley has two of these vehicles, neither of which is licensed for use on the public road.

The children took it in turns to open gates, and to clamber back in as the Land Rover moved on.

'Look out for the brambles!' Stanley cried as we ground our way up a steep track between high banks. He could remember horse-drawn hay wagons coming down this way in the 1950s. In 1951, when he was ten and moved here with his parents, the farm had no electricity, and they used Tilley lamps and Aladdin stoves. They got a generator in the 1960s, and mains electricity in the early 1990s.

The farm is 960 feet above sea level, rising to about 1,200 feet. We emerged into a field of thistles. Stanley said: 'I'll have to tell my chap to cut some of these thistles.' There were screams of delight from the children, and marvellous views in all directions. To the north we could see Dunkery Beacon, which at 1,703 feet is the highest point on Exmoor.

When Stanley's father gave up active farming in the autumn of 1969, Stanley got the train down from London with Boris. They drove to the farm and saw all the stock penned in for auction. This, Stanley says, was the worst day of his father's life. The ashes of his parents were scattered on these fields above the farm.

When we returned to the cottage, Stanley left me in the garden with some wine and a pile of old photograph albums while he went inside to cook some pork chops.

The first pictures I saw were small, colour photographs taken when the Johnsons were living on an island in Norwalk, Connecticut, when Boris would have been about four years old and Stanley was working in New York. My host came by and said: 'An absolutely fabulous house – it really was.' He is a man with a great enthusiasm for houses and remembers many of the places he has lived with affectionate relish.

Charlotte, I thought to myself, looked lovely in the pictures – very attractive. I then realised that this young woman, perhaps only nineteen or twenty, who was kneeling with the children and smiling so happily, is not Charlotte, but the au pair girl. Stanley, who is himself only about twenty-seven, is stripped to the waist.

We come to Charlotte: she too is very young, and looks sweet and beautiful, but also vulnerable and unhappy. We see Charlotte breast-feeding – Leo perhaps – and Boris naked. Boris looking out of a train window. Boris in a beige sun hat. Boris up to the age of five or six does not look particularly happy.

There are also some pictures of a safari in East Africa. Boris stands on an ant hill, striking a pose.

We lunched in the garden and Stanley drove me at high speed in his little Subaru back to Taunton. As we descended into Taunton Vale, he remembered the very hot summer of 1976, when 'our au pairs wore nothing – I do remember them certainly parading down by the river – Oliver Walston says they wore nothing in the house too – he sent a card afterwards saying "Thanks for the mammaries".'

They usually had a pair of au pair girls, in the hope that they would not both leave at once, though on a couple of occasions they did. Stanley mentioned that Vreni, a Swiss girl who came to live with them in America, had looked after Boris. She must be the girl in the photographs.

Once the au pairs refused to cook lunch because it coincided with the arrival of the stag's heart, borne by Stanley and Charlotte's fourth child, Jo. Boris has written a fine description of this scene, at the start of an article in which he defends hunting, reprinted in his book *Lend Me Your Ears*:

All the warning we had was a crackling of the alder branches that bend over the Exe, and then the stag was upon us. I can see it now, stepping high in the water, eyes rolling, tongue protruding, foaming, antlers streaming bracken and leaves like the hat of some demented old woman, and behind it the sexual, high-pitched yipping of the dogs. You never saw such a piteous or terrible sight.

In that instant we would have done anything to help the stag get away. I think we vaguely shouted and flapped our arms, but too late. In a trice, the stag had been brought to bay by the hounds, almost at our feet in the meadow. And then a man with an ancient-looking pistol, a bit like a starting gun, blammed it in the head and they cut it open in a kind of laparotomy.

I can remember the guts steaming, and stag turds spilling out on to the grass from within the ventral cavity. Then they cut out the heart and gave it to my six-year-old brother, still beating, he claimed ever afterwards, or still twitching, and he went dancing home singing: 'We've got the heart! We've got the heart!' So we cooked it up with a bit of flour, and the German au pair girl left the next day.

In the winter of 1970 the family moved to London, first back to Blomfield Road, then to Princess Road in Primrose Hill, and in about November 1972 round the corner to Regent's Park Road, where they occupied a house they later sold to the journalist Simon Jenkins. Boris went to Primrose Hill primary school until April 1973, when Stanley took the family to Brussels, where he had secured a job as one of the first Britons to join the European Commission. Stanley became the first head of the Prevention of Pollution and Nuisance Division. It might not be a glamorous title, but he was and is an ardent environmentalist, and had secured a post at the most wide-ranging and least accountable bureaucracy in Europe.

Boris went to the European School in Uccle in Brussels, where he met a girl of exactly his own age called Marina Wheeler. She arrived in Brussels from Washington wearing an 'Impeach Nixon' badge and taught Boris the meaning of the word 'impeach' – a process he tried, many years later, to apply to

Tony Blair. Boris took a great liking to Marina, and would try to amuse her by rolling out of the car on to the ground when he was dropped off at school each day.

Marina would just think 'Oh God' when she saw this trick, which became a bit of a joke in her family. Nor was she any more impressed when, for her benefit, he rolled into a boat during a school trip to some caves. She was much less impressed by Boris than he was by her, and decided he was 'generally to be avoided'. But because their parents already knew each other from Washington, the two families continued to see a certain amount of each other.

To Marina and her sister, the Johnsons seemed 'incredibly rough – they were all so wild and out of control'. If you were playing a ball game with them, the ball would hit you hard on the nose, you would burst into tears and would feel you were being feeble. Marina's mother, Dip, one day relayed the exciting news that Boris had actually been shot with an air pistol by his brother Leo. To visit the Johnsons on Exmoor was also for Marina a shocking experience, 'so much harsher than I was used to'. It was freezing cold and everyone had holes in their socks. She thinks Stanley has 'mellowed' since.

Boris's intelligence was already apparent. He was an ardent reader: when his siblings wanted him to play with them, they would sometimes receive the unsatisfactory reply, 'Let's play reading.' At the European School, his mother was one day taken aside to be informed that he was '*un enfant doué*' – a gifted child.

In 1974, a year after moving to Brussels, when her and Stanley's youngest child, Jo, was still very small, Charlotte had a nervous breakdown. She was in the Maudsley Hospital, in London, for nine months, suffering from depression. As she herself says, 'It was terrible because I'd had before this all that time when I was so, so close to the children, and then I disappeared.'

It is painful even to think how harrowing this period must have been for Charlotte and her children: 'They used to come and see me. It was so mad. I would suddenly see my children running down the passage. And when they had gone I would feel completely destroyed.' Until she and Stanley were divorced, Charlotte was 'in and out of hospital quite often'.

Brussels was to become, in the early 1990s, the scene of Boris's first journalistic triumphs, and also of the collapse of his first marriage. In the 1970s, it was the place where Stanley and Charlotte's marriage fell apart. But before they parted, Boris had already been sent away to school in England.

# 5

# Greek before Breakfast

IN 1975 BORIS ARRIVED AT ASHDOWN HOUSE PREP-
aratory school in East Sussex. Here the process started, as he later
put it, of filling him 'up to the gills with the finest education
England can provide'.

This period is so recent, yet in many ways it already seems
impossibly remote. Boris caught the last years when Latin and
Greek were at the heart of the curriculum. Ashdown's tradition
of brilliant classical teaching had been set by Billy Williamson,
headmaster from 1949, whose pupils won many awards to Eton
and Winchester. Among them was Clive Williams, who got a
scholarship to Eton and returned as a young man to Ashdown
first as an assistant master and from 1974 as headmaster.

Some readers may assume from this account that the school,
accommodated since 1886 in a fine country house at Forest
Row in East Sussex, was simply a machine for getting scholarships, but this would be unfair. As Williams says of his
predecessor: 'Billy was a past master at getting Eton awards – that
was what he liked to do and he was very good at it – but he also
took a great deal of trouble with those less able.'

Boris had a meteoric career at Ashdown. He went there as a
boarder in the autumn term of 1975 when he was eleven years

old, so the school had only two years to prepare him for Eton. It is normal for a boy destined for public school to spend five years, from the age of eight, at a preparatory school, so Boris had a vast amount of catching up to do, especially as he had never studied Latin or Greek.

We see Boris moving with almost unbelievable rapidity up the school. Williams showed me a notebook containing a record of all his pupils, including their form lists, aggregated marks, what prizes they won and which schools they went to. At the end of his first term Boris was placed fifteenth out of the fifteen pupils in Form II B, so he must have been struggling. At the end of his second term, the Lent term of 1976, he had already moved up to sixth place: as Williams remarks, 'he was getting the hang of things'. At the end of the summer term, he came top of II B and was awarded the form prize.

Half-way through that summer term someone brought Williams a piece of Boris's work: 'For the first time I thought there was something rather special about this boy. We had a discussion about this fantastically able boy in the common room.'

For his last year Boris was placed in Form I. Williams now taught him himself. Form I was divided into Division I and Division II, with Boris placed at first in the lower of these. Williams remembers: 'I don't think I've ever taught anyone who learned quicker. He was very good, very good, but I think it was the speed at which he learned which was so impressive. He just lapped it up, and the great thing was that he found it fun. Not all children enjoy Latin and Greek, but he did. He thought the paradigms of *luo* was rather fun – we used to do those before breakfast.'

*Luo*, the basic Greek verb, has an extraordinary number of different forms, and at Ashdown some of the pupils studied these at early school from 7.30 in the morning, while the rest did PT outside. As Williams remarked in a modest tone: 'We

1. Boris's great-grandfather, Ali Kemal, journalist and politician – a caricature drawn shortly before his death at the hands of a lynch mob in 1922.

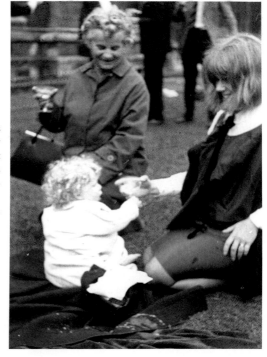

2. Boris, aged one, comes to celebrate with his heavily pregnant mother Charlotte at the end of her Oxford exams in 1965, and is determined to have some of her champagne. Charlotte's family nanny, Miss Reid, looks on.

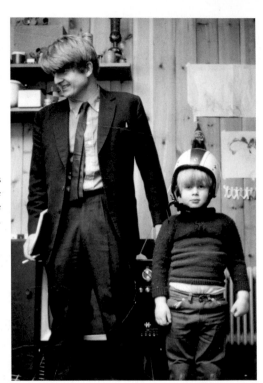

3. Boris with his father Stanley, whose motorcycle helmet he is wearing.

4. Boris at the age of about seven, sketched by his mother, Charlotte.

5. Boris with his mother, Charlotte, and sister Rachel.

6. Sibling rivalry in Brussels: Boris runs faster than Rachel, Leo and Jo.

7. The Johnson family (from left): Charlotte, Jo, Stanley, Rachel, Leo and a not very happy Boris.

8. Father's Day at Ashdown House: Boris takes tea with his father, who has longer hair.

9. Ashdown House: the three successful scholarship candidates (from left): Meyrick Cox (Eton), Boris (Eton) and Tim Moon (Winchester).

10. A commanding figure: Boris, wearing his Pop waistcoat, dominates this photograph of College at Eton in 1982. His housemaster, Martin Hammond, composer of penetrating reports of Boris's progress, sits in the middle of the front row.

11. Balliol rugby XV: Boris standing at the extreme left.

12. Boris (in odd socks) as a member of the Oxford dining club, the Bullingdon, in 1986. Darius Guppy is standing fourth from right; to the left of Guppy is Andrew Gilmour.

13. Boris as President of the Oxford Union, flanked by the Greek actress Melina Mercouri and by Gavin Stamp, with Jonathan Barnes next to Stamp and Allegra Mostyn-Owen behind them.

14. Allegra as cover girl, just after David Bailey has told her to 'fuck the camera'.

15. Boris and Allegra celebrate in 1987 after his final Oxford exams: but he perhaps already suspects that he has not done quite enough to get a first.

16. Boris and Allegra on their wedding day, 5 September 1987.

did seem to be a street ahead in basic grammar which in something like Greek makes quite a bit of difference.' The boys in Form I did fourteen periods of Classics a week, which in Williams's opinion 'you can't possibly justify'. Like all successful upholders of tradition, he saw the need for change: 'I think in those days we were rather too keen on our Latin and Greek.'

Ashdown was not one of those dangerous schools where all the pupils are unusually bright and tend to drive each other mad, but Boris was stretched by two other boys in Form I. As Williams said: 'Having two pretty competitive characters in Meyrick Cox and Tim Moon brought out the best in him. The rivalry in the top three was fairly intense, though never less than friendly. Meyrick Cox was much more a mathematician, so they were nicely balanced. Tim Moon was good at them all.'

Williams nevertheless doubted whether Boris would be ready for the Eton scholarship exam: 'The papers were quite difficult in those days.' But after only five terms of preparation – for the exams took place early in the summer term – Boris duly won a scholarship to Eton. Stanley still remembers how moved Williams was on ringing him in Brussels to give the good news. Meyrick Cox also won a scholarship to Eton, while Tim Moon was fourth on the scholarship roll at Winchester.

Boris's education was not confined to the Classics. Children at Ashdown were expected to take part in a wide variety of activities, whether they showed much aptitude or not. For example, as Williams says, 'Everybody was always in teams. He was certainly in the rugby side because of his size, and was quicker on his feet than you'd think. He enjoyed participating in all his games. He was not a great expert but he was by no means hopeless at any of them. But the things he did well he was astonishingly good at. He was a wonderful King Rhesus in the Greek play [performed in Greek]. He was particularly good as counsel for the prosecution in the mock trials we used to have. He was a good debater and he won the poem prize. He had a marvellously optimistic outlook – he would always go for anything – and he was also genuinely entertaining – he always was funny as a boy.'

Williams found Stanley an ideal parent: 'He was marvellous at encouraging us all to get on with it. He took lots of interest, but never interfered. He was always very jolly and extremely supportive. Running a school in those days was less complicated.' In the age before the mobile phone, anxious parents had much less scope to interfere in the running of boarding schools, which meant children enjoyed greater independence than is the case today.

Stanley had only one unusual demand, concerning Boris's sister: 'He told us we'd got to take Rachel. It was marvellous for us – we had already decided in 1974 to take girls. My predecessor was fairly old-fashioned, he ran the school on military lines. We wanted to be different, and the great different thing we wanted to do was have girls. Stanley's support was crucial. Stanley said, "I'll provide you with your first pupil," and sent us Rachel. She was not as brilliant as Boris, but she won a scholarship to Bryanston. Rachel was very good as a pioneer girl. She was tremendous.'

Boris and Rachel's younger brothers followed them to Ashdown: 'Leo and Jo – they were terrific too. Leo was a terrific chap. He only just missed a scholarship to Eton. Leo was a commanding figure in the school – an excellent games player and head boy too.'

This distinction eluded Boris. As Williams put it: 'He's always rather cross with me – in joking asides – not to have been made a dorm captain or a prefect.' But as Williams explained, it would have been 'rather unusual' to confer such posts on a boy who had only been in the school for one year.

Williams's wife, Rowena, who was involved in every aspect of the school, said: 'He wouldn't have been nearly such a good head boy as Leo.'

'He'd have given a very good speech,' Williams countered.

The Williamses remember Boris's mother with great affection: 'She gave us a lovely present – she gave us a portrait of us – a jolly nice thing to do.'

Stanley, Boris and Rachel have all been down to Ashdown to give away the prizes. As so often with Boris, he had a problem with his clothes. The zip on his trousers was broken. Rowena Williams said: 'I had to safety-pin his flies. If I was around a bit more often I might have saved him a lot of trouble.'

She added in a maternal tone: 'I always get nervous watching him on anything. Our feelings are nothing but affectionate towards him and his family.' When the news broke in November 2004 of Boris's affair with Petronella Wyatt, Rowena found herself having to explain it to her father 'as if Boris was one of my own children'.

Ashdown, like many independent schools at this time, was immersed in a headlong process of liberalisation, in which the admission of girls played a key part. Williams one night came upon a number of children, including Rachel, having a midnight feast of Coke and crisps. He offered Rachel the choice of losing two half-holidays or being beaten. She confounded him by opting to be beaten. Williams realised he could not beat a girl, nor could he have half the school eligible for a beating and half not, so corporal punishment ended at Ashdown.

Conrad Black, who was later to make Boris editor of the *Spectator*, said: 'His schooldays were one of the few subjects where he became quite serious and even quite believable – he is a passionate opponent of corporal punishment. He told me how when he was at school he would hear the younger boys crying, in terrible pain, and just how awful it was.'

Boris told me it made him deeply angry when he was chastised at Ashdown, not that he harbours any personal grudge.

Here was another English tradition of which he caught the final years, but not one which, like the study of Latin and Greek, he would spend the rest of his life celebrating. For while the Classics uplifted him, he was degraded by being beaten, and Boris is too proud to accept that.

# 6

# An Etonian Performance

WHEN BORIS WAS FOURTEEN YEARS OLD HIS PARENTS got divorced. Stanley broke the news to the children, against Charlotte's wishes, when they were all at Nethercote. Boris lined himself and his three siblings up in the yard, stepped forward and said: 'Why did you have us?'

Charlotte and Stanley made it their policy to get on with each other. She says Stanley has been 'a very good father', while he is loud in her praises. But however well people behave – and the Johnsons behaved much better than many couples – divorce is still deeply miserable.

Charlotte returned to London and moved in to a maisonette at the top of a high, stuccoed building in Notting Hill with her four children. She was still a very attractive woman, only thirty-six years old, by vocation an artist and by birth a Fawcett, with grand Catholic friends, not one of those rackety Johnsons. For a time the roof leaked, but she loved filling the rooms with a rich profusion of things, and all the time she painted and drew. Her friends gathered that Stanley had been 'one amazing womaniser', and she was fed up with it. According to Charlotte, 'I couldn't stay with him. He was so inaccessible, not to say completely unfaithful. I couldn't live with him never allowing anything to be serious. That's the essential difference between Boris and his father. I can talk to Boris about anything.'

When Boris and his siblings were with their mother, he felt he was the man in the family, who must protect her. Charlotte's friends remember that he had a kind of seriousness about him, and a gentle reticence, and was conscientious and careful when given a responsible task, such as looking after a smaller child. He was tall for his age, and shy, and blushed when he spoke, gazing out through his hair like Lady Diana.

This is not the Boris the public have come to know and love. A friend of the family said: 'He had a dignity about him. You could see he was a very nice person. He understood what had happened to his mother, he knew it was dreadful and humiliating, and he was enduring it.'

Boris has continued to care for his mother. She lived in Notting Hill for ten years, supporting herself by selling portraits. In 1988 she married an American academic, Nick Wahl, with whom she went to live in an apartment in Washington Square, New York. He had no children of his own and was very fond of hers, but died in 1996, after which she moved back to Notting Hill.

As early as 1982, Charlotte noticed something wrong with her foot, which felt like a flipper when she went swimming, but it was not until 1989 that she was diagnosed with Parkinson's disease. It has progressed very slowly, but makes her hand tremble and is exhausting, and if she did not take her pills she could not swallow. She said Boris is very, very protective of her, often comes with her when she goes to see her consultant, and minds people talking about her illnesses.

The atrocious pain of the divorce encouraged Boris to create a mask which hid how he felt from the outside world. Many years later he confided to a woman with whom he was in love that after his parents split up, he decided to make himself invulnerable.

Any sensitive adolescent might hope to do this, but few have been able to model their escape bid on quite such a father. Stanley claims that apart from sending his children to good schools, 'My parental impact has been strictly zero. I'm quite ready to concede that a good school is probably going to do a better job of bringing up your kids than you're likely to do. In my view it took the pain out of parenting. It was a safer bet, particularly in the circumstances of Charlotte and me splitting up. Probably kids would prefer their parents to stay together. In many ways it was more difficult for Jo [the youngest of the four children]. Boris was already at Eton.'

The pretence that he has had no parental influence is Stanley at his most preposterous. Anyone who has met both father and son is struck by the extraordinary resemblance between them. They talk in an amazingly similar way, and Boris has learned a great part of his comic art from his father. They behave like stage Englishmen, often pretending to be impossibly baffled and stupid, while behind this screen they calculate what would be to their own advantage. This manner makes it hard for them to do seriousness, nor do they detect any great public demand for it.

Stanley said as he recounted his own political career, 'Nothing is more gloomy than making a speech that has no jokes in it. I don't think that on the whole people can take too much seriousness.'

In the late 1970s, as the first European elections in Britain approached, Stanley looked around for a seat where he could stand as a Conservative. He was interviewed in Leicester, where the Duke of Rutland, chairman of the selectors, asked if he had ever been there before. Stanley says he replied: 'Your Grace, I have never been to Leicester before but I have been to Leicester Square.' This joke went down badly.

After failing at three selection contests for European seats, Stanley put in for the Isle of Wight and East Hampshire. The other contenders were Bill Cash 'and his very scenic wife

Biddy', and Sir John Peel. Stanley said: 'I was in the process of separating very amicably from Charlotte. I was the only person of the three of us who didn't visibly have a wife there.'

The selection committee asked Stanley, 'Will Mrs Johnson be coming to live with you in the constituency?'

Stanley replied: 'Mrs Johnson will possibly be coming to live in the constituency, but certainly not with me.'

This joke went down well, and Stanley got the seat, which he held from 1979 to 1984.

But while Stanley joked about his divorce, it would be wrong to suggest he is completely incapable of seriousness. The stage Englishman usually has a hobby which he invests with the sanctity of a religion: his golf clubs mean everything to him.

Stanley cares deeply about the environment. As the lawyer Philippe Sands recalls: 'He used to instruct me a lot fifteen years ago in a lot of environmental cases. Stanley's terribly principled, even if it's totally unfashionable.'

Not that Stanley is unable to leaven even his environmentalism with humour. At the World Trade Organization meeting in Seattle, he dressed up as a turtle. Sands said: 'There are some great photographs of Stanley dressed up as a turtle haranguing Al Gore.'

When I put it to Stanley that Boris has followed him in many things, but not as an environmentalist, the father leapt to the son's defence: 'He's been jolly good on the Brazilian Macau question; but that was I think partly under my influence. And he has been particularly sound on the hunting question.'

Boris has entered the same competitions as his father. Like Stanley, he is a passionate rugby player who won a classical scholarship to Oxford, married young, had lots of children, and pursued careers as a writer and a Tory politician. But Stanley grew self-deprecating when I mentioned some of the similarities between him and his eldest son: 'Boris does almost all of those things better than I did. He gets very large advances [for his books] and I over the years have not had those. I think the talent comes from Charlotte – she's a wonderful lady.'

When an interviewer asked Boris about his parents' divorce, he replied: 'Yes, I was upset when they broke up.' But a minute later he added: 'Oh good Lord, they will read this,' after which he tried to retract it, before saying: 'No, it had some effect. They handled it brilliantly.'

Boris had to handle the divorce soon after he started at Eton, the most famous school in the world. It stands on the low ground on the other side of the Thames from Windsor Castle, whose towers can be seen in the distance. Eighteen British Prime Ministers have been educated there.

Eton is synonymous for many with idle privilege, but what people often overlook is how hard the school has worked to avoid becoming an irrelevant survival, and to stay at the top on its merits. Patrick Hennessy, who went to Eton slightly ahead of Boris, recalled, 'I disapprove of it fantastically and in many ways it's a disadvantage to have been there. But the education, and the way you were treated as an adult, and taught to become extremely independent, and have a very, very questing mind – there was nothing you couldn't do. McCrum [the headmaster] was very keen on the pursuit of excellence.'

As often happens, Boris spent his first half (as the school term is called at Eton), the autumn of 1977, in another house, D. J. S. Guilford's, before there was room for him in College, the house where the scholars live.

Boris's hair made him immediately recognisable, but there were about 1,200 boys in the school, and one should bear in mind that Boris would have been unknown, except by appearance, to many Etonians. Hennessy said: 'We didn't have much to do with Collegers. I do remember him though, very well, because he looked exactly as he does today. He was incredibly scruffy and had that sort of straw-coloured hair. Collegers had to wear gowns, which made him look all the more extraordinary.'

Boris's first housemaster, John Lewis, who in 1980 left to become headmaster of Geelong Grammar in Australia before returning to Eton as headmaster, remembers very little about Boris in his first three years at the school: 'He had a touch of the self-deprecating air which has become part of his political persona now, but he certainly wasn't a clown.' This period when Boris's parents were divorcing was no time for clowning. Boris, by Lewis's account, was a model schoolboy: 'He was a very good member of College: humorous, loyal and (in the politest possible way) irreverent.'

It is during his last two and a bit years at Eton that the familiar Boris emerges into the limelight. We see him develop into a public performer who is one of the great Eton characters of his generation, but who does this at the expense of the steady, unglamorous work needed to make the most of his intellectual gifts. Boris adores the Classics, but he cannot give them his exclusive devotion.

Boris has often said that for him 'the really inspirational teacher was Martin Hammond'. Hammond became Master in College in September 1980. A distinguished classical scholar, in 2006 he published a new translation of the *Meditations* of Marcus Aurelius, which was followed by a translation of Thucydides for Oxford University Press. By great good fortune, or perhaps by sheer efficiency, Hammond has kept copies of the seven school reports he wrote on Boris. These take the form of a letter to Boris's father at the end of each term, and Hammond wrote to me: 'I would gladly release these reports to you, but that of course must depend on the agreement not only of Boris but also of Stanley Johnson, to whom they were addressed.'

When I rang Stanley to ask for his agreement, he laughed and said yes. When I rang Boris he said: 'Um, er, um, um, I don't see why not.'

These reports almost constitute a biography in miniature of

Boris, unclouded by hindsight and throwing brilliant shafts of illumination into the future. Nobody has ever been in a better position than Hammond to try to get the best out of Boris, and a fascinating duel develops between the master, who knows how things ought to be done, and his apprentice, who is intent on following a more risky but amusing path to success.

The first letter, which would have accompanied a sheaf of other reports by Boris's teachers, was written on 30 December 1980:

Dear Mr Johnson,

I had of course met Boris before this half, and had come to know something of his considerable intellectual ability . . . Closer acquaintance this half has enabled me to get to know him much better . . . I've found Boris a quite delightful person, a real life-enhancer. I like his open friendliness of manner, and his ready wit . . . I remember in particular a magnificent performance in Prayers, when he read with spectacular effect the hell-fire preacher's sermon from *Cold Comfort Farm*.

In his next report, dated 3 April 1981, Hammond says Boris has 'a finger in a wide variety of pies', is 'asserting his intellectual ascendancy powerfully but modestly' and presents 'the *disiecta membra* of a very considerable scholar'. But '*disiecta membra*' is the Latin for 'scattered limbs', and Hammond is growing worried that amid a diversity of other activities, Boris will fail to do justice to himself as a scholar.

This worry becomes even more pressing in Hammond's third report, written on 22 July 1981:

Boris' favoured pace is the amble (with the odd last-minute sprint), which has been good enough so far, and I suppose enables him to smell the flowers along the way. It's time, though, that with a greater commitment to the real business of scholarship (reading widely and deeply, unbidden; approaching each task with a craftsman's eye and a craftsman's deliberation; constantly probing for something deeper, or truer, or more accurate) Boris could turn himself into a classicist of real distinction, one of the best that we've had for years. To do that he must become a professional: and the first step, on which I think we must insist next year, is the production or preparation of work on time.

Similar criticisms – gross unpunctuality, failure to organise himself, refusal to submit to the discipline needed to become a professional – were to be levelled time and again against Boris in the decades to come. In his fourth report, written on 29 December 1981, Hammond is relatively content with Boris: 'His success in the Newcastle Classical Prize was deserved, narrow though the margin was.'

But the report after that contains one of the fiercest attacks on Boris which can ever have been written, the effect heightened by the friendly and fair-minded praise which is heaped on him at the start and finish.

Each boy at Eton has his own room, and every evening after house prayers, Hammond would walk the corridors of College from 8.45 until about 11.15, dropping in on one boy or another. There was, he says, 'virtually never any disciplinary aspect to these visits', though one can guess that the housemaster's presence helped to keep the peace.

'The Bill' which is mentioned refers not to the police, but to the form of punishment at Eton which entails being fetched from one's classroom before lunch by a praepostor, or prefect, and hauled before the headmaster. Boris's offence was to have done no work. The post of Captain of the School means the head boy of College. The letter was written on 10 April 1982 and is given in full:

Dear Stanley,

I was delighted that Boris achieved some success in the Newcastle [Divinity Scholarship], and he deserved it. He did in fact work quite hard towards the examination (which is not to say that he could not have worked harder): I was pleased to find him one evening reading St John's Gospel in Greek, and exclaiming, 'This is really exciting!' – as indeed it is.

Of course Boris did take on several large extra commitments this half, and one does not want to discourage diversity: but there is no doubt, as these reports make very plain, that his regular academic responsibilities were sadly neglected as a result. The tone of Andrew Hobson's letter is pretty damning, but its contents can hardly be gainsaid, and a very similar picture is painted by Ian McAuslan. Boris really has adopted a disgracefully cavalier attitude to his classical studies, and the scandal of the Bill would be followed by an even greater scandal if he did drop a grade at A level through sheer fecklessness. It is a question of priorities, which most of his colleagues have no difficulty in sorting out. Boris sometimes seems affronted when criticised for what amounts to a gross failure of responsibility (and surprised at the same time that he was not appointed Captain of the School for next half): I think he honestly believes that it is churlish of us not to regard him as an exception, one who should be free of the network of obligation which binds everyone else. I'm enormously fond of Boris, and saddened that he should have brought upon himself this sort of report. All is not lost, by any means: he can easily effect a full return to grace by showing obvious commitment next half.

I thought very well indeed of his contribution to the success of the College Play. He worked hard at it, and made Sir Politique Would-be a memorably comic figure (who

reappeared, with suitable adjustments, in the French Play):
he handled the dropped-stick episode superbly, and
throughout kept a marvellous rapport with the audience,
communicating his enjoyment to them.

Will the decision on Harvard have to be made at the
very beginning of the half?

Yours ever,

Martin

There was at this time some question of Boris going to Harvard,
the most famous university in the United States. According to
Stanley, 'Harvard came through with a terrifically generous
financial offer – who can tell what would have happened if he'd
made his life in America?'

Mr Hammond's next report, written on 25 July 1982,
brought little respite:

Although there has been no repetition of the disgrace of last
half's academic torpor, it's clear that Boris has still not been
working at anything like the limit of his capacity in any of
his three subjects – in fact, in comparison with what might
have been, this has been a pretty disappointing year. Boris
is pretty impressive when success can be achieved by pure
intelligence unaccompanied by hard work (he shines in
unseens, which are of course unprepared): but he doesn't
have the instincts of a real scholar, and tends to 'sell himself
short' when an exercise requires intellectual preparation.
He is, in fact, pretty idle about it all ... Boris has
something of a tendency to assume that success and
honours will drop into his lap: not so, he must work for
them.

Efficiency and organisation have been constant problems
(there was trouble this half with his running of the Political
Society, and an unprecedented rebuke from the Provost).

The Provost of Eton, Lord Charteris of Amisfield, had spent most of his life in royal service, latterly as Private Secretary to the Queen, and although he was a genial man, he liked things done properly. When the Queen Mother felt like visiting Eton, which she did at fairly regular intervals, Lord Charteris would make the arrangements. He also acted as host for the eminent speakers who came to address the Political Society, which Boris was then running.

Lord Charteris died in 1999, so it seemed unlikely that anyone but Boris would be able to say what the 'unprecedented rebuke' was for. Even Boris appeared, when I put the question to him, to have difficulty remembering what had gone wrong: 'Oh yes. I got into terrible trouble – he got terribly cross with me because I wanted to invite Ronald Reagan – I think that might have been it.'

It is amusing to find that even then, Boris had no hesitation in pursuing the famous. One of his strengths as a journalist is that he has always pushed for an interview with the most powerful person.

But Boris then corrected himself about his trouble with the Provost: 'No. I'm afraid I just turned up late to see him one day. I mean I wasn't very late. About forty-five minutes.'

Most schoolboys would not have dared to turn up late to see Lord Charteris, and even most of those with the self-confidence to do such a thing would have tried to avoid it, assuming they liked the Provost, because they would know it to be so rude. One suspects that Boris aggravated his offence by appearing not to understand how rude he had been.

Boris liked the Provost very much indeed: 'He was such a nice man. A wonderful man, Martin Charteris. I used to have to pour the wine [at Political Society events].' Boris did not mention to me that the Provost was also a friend of his mother's parents.

The next sentence of Martin Hammond's report, immediately after the reference to the 'unprecedented rebuke', marks an astonishing change of tack:

It was perhaps a bit of a risk to make Boris Captain of the School: but he clearly has the personality and the respect necessary for the job, and it's my hope that the imposition of a public responsibility will energise all else. It's a particularly important job in the Michaelmas, and involves a number of administrative tasks which simply must be done well. Certainly I look forward to working with him – he's excellent company, and has a mature understanding of people and things.

Boris has triumphed. Even though 'efficiency and organisation have been constant problems', he has been given a post which 'involves a number of administrative tasks which simply must be done well'. Hammond has been forced to recognise that Boris's claims to the top job are too strong to deny. The Captain of the School is the top boy in College, and not in the entire school, where the other two grandees were the Captain of the Oppidans, appointed from the rest of the boys by the headmaster, and the President of Pop, appointed by the boys.

Looking back on Boris, Hammond said: 'He was passionately loyal to his House, his school. In an odd way, he likes an ordered world, not a random world. Boris was not a rebel at all. He was a fully signed up member of the tribe. He was jolly nearly the custodian of the ark. Everything that went into the traditions of being at College Boris embraced whole-heartedly – Latin prayers, bellowed hymns.'

Another Eton tradition into which Boris threw himself wholeheartedly, and which still means a lot to him, is the Wall Game. The main match of the year takes place on or near St Andrew's Day, 30 November, between a team drawn from the 70 Collegers and one from the more than 1,100 Oppidans, and Boris played three years running in the College team.

Part of the charm of this game is that it is almost incomprehensible. But an article in the *Eton College Chronicle* – the fortnightly school newspaper – of St Andrew's Day 1982 by Oliver Van Oss, who taught at Eton and was Headmaster of Charterhouse, allows one to get some flavour of the contest. The Wall Game turns out to be the perfect preparation for life. Substantial quotation is needed even to begin to convey its strangeness:

The ground is about 100 yards long, bounded on one side by a high brick wall and on the other by a furrow. At no point is it more than 15 yards wide. The object is to drive an under-sized football over a line, beyond which the aggressors may attempt to score. One end is called Good Calx, because the ball cannot go over the dead ball line; the other Bad Calx, because it can, which offers some slight advantage to a hard-pressed defence.

Each team has 10 players . . . The centre of the battle is the Bully (scrum) and the leaders of it are the three Walls, men chosen for their huge size, physical strength and that exceptional length of arm which so seldom correlates with intellectual power . . . At first nothing happens . . . The lull seems permanently established when suddenly the Bully erupts . . . This pattern of alternating trance and frenzy continues until one side has forced its way into Calx and is in a position to score . . .

It sounds bizarre, almost Boeotian [stupid, dull], yet all who have played it rate it one of the great games. It is enormous fun and utterly exhausting. It demands secret skills and an equable temperament. Though Rule XII forbids 'tripping, kicking, stamping, striking' and now alas 'knuckling' and goes on to disallow 'any methods of play whose sole purpose is to cause pain', it can be excruciatingly uncomfortable.

The Wall Game is the supreme non-spectacle, the last sport totally to disregard the spectator . . . As a preparation

for life, the Wall Game has two special merits. It teaches
one to push oneself to the limit of endurance and
discomfort without losing one's temper. It provides the
perfect training for later work on boards, committees, royal
commissions and governing bodies. The unmovable and
the irresistible are poised in perfect balance. Nothing is
happening and it seems unlikely that anything ever will.
Then, for two seconds or so, the situation becomes fluid. If
one can take one's chance – and there may not be another –
the day is won. If one miskicks or mistimes or is timid or
was not attending, all may be irretrievably lost.

The *Chronicle* was in the custom of publishing short descriptions of the players. Boris first appears on St Andrew's Day 1980,
when he is described as 'Completely non-directional, has to be
pointed the right way or he may push the Wall over.' A year later
we find: 'He plays the Wall Game like an echidna on heat,
according to his homespun philosophy, "If it moves, grunt at it.
If it moves again, kill it, then grunt at it." The only Colleger able
to take on the Oppidans at their own level.' For his last St
Andrew's Day we read: 'Hey, hey, A.B.J. How many Oppidans
did you kill today? Watch the Blond Behemoth crud relentlessly
through the steaming pile of purple-and-orange heavyweights,
until he's knocking on the Lower Master's door.'

Johnnie Boden, who played the Wall Game against Boris,
said: 'I was bitten by someone and it could well have been him.'
Boden in later life launched a mail-order clothing company, of
which Boris is a strong supporter, sometimes referring to
Boden as his tailor. When I asked Boris if he had ever bitten
Boden, he replied: 'I might have done. No, no, I wasn't a biter.
My tactics in the Wall Game are sudden spasms of uncontrolled
aggression.'

Boris adopted a similar style of play on the rugby field, where
he played for the First XV. In Hammond's words, 'On the rugby

field Boris was an absolute berserker. There was a lot of yelling and hurling of himself reckless of life and limb, both his own and other people's. He took it very seriously.'

I suggested to Hammond that Boris was not a typical Etonian, having in mind Boris's willingness to have a go at things he does not know how to do, and to risk making a fool of himself. But Hammond had detected another quality which distinguishes Boris: 'He's much more generous-hearted than most Etonians are. I didn't know him at school be unkind to anyone.'

Andrew Gilmour became friends with Boris at Eton. He remembers Boris performing at Speeches, an Eton tradition where Sixth Form Select – the top ten scholars and the top ten Oppidans – recite pieces of poetry or prose.

Boris recited the first page of *Decline and Fall* by Evelyn Waugh, which begins: 'Mr Sniggs, the Junior Dean, and Mr Postlethwaite, the Domestic Bursar . . .'

Gilmour recalls: 'The way he said "Sniggs" made people laugh, and then he turned to the prompter and said, "What's his name again?" That brought the house down. Even the Provost I remember roaring with laughter. I think from that time Boris realised that if you forget your lines and carry it off with aplomb, then you're made. He performed in a Molière play in French, *L'Ecole des Femmes*, with a very strong English accent and had to be prompted throughout.'

Unpreparedness had become one of Boris's hallmarks. Sir Eric Anderson, who was Tony Blair's housemaster at Fettes and Boris's headmaster at Eton, says: 'Boris had some similarity with Blair as a boy – both of them opted to live on their wits rather than preparation. They both enjoyed performing. In both cases people found them life-enhancing and fun to have around, but also maddening.'

But while the young Blair rebelled against the system at Fettes, 'Boris wasn't a rebel at all – a satirist and a humorist rather than a rebel,' in Anderson's words. He paid tribute to another of

Boris's qualities: 'Boris has terrific intellectual energy and terrific physical energy as well. The great Dr Arnold said there is more difference in the amount of energy of boys than in the amount of intellect, and that it was more important. Energy matters.'

Boris agrees with this and may well have heard it first from Anderson. As Boris put it in an interview in 2003: 'Intelligence is really all about energy. I mean you can have the brightest people in the world who simply can't be arsed. No good to man or beast.'

Eric Anderson taught Sixth Form Select once a week: 'I tossed them an intellectual bone and let them chew it. I wrote "Business, Industry, Commerce" up on the board and asked them to spend ten minutes writing down what these words suggested to them. Boris wrote: "These three words suggest to me that the headmaster dined in London last night."'

'Correct,' Anderson responded with a smile.

Boris went on: 'Some ignorant people attacked him for not sending enough Etonians into industry or commerce. What they do not realise is that industry is making things, commerce is selling them, while business is making all that happen, which being much more interesting is what Etonians head for.'

Sir Eric admired this answer for its intelligence and wit, but it also betrays the arrogant, or confident, or perhaps just the realistic belief that Etonians will end up running the show.

'I do remember,' Anderson said, 'that he was a member of the Headmaster's Essay Society – twenty-four bright boys on a Sunday evening three times a term – one of them read a paper and the others tore it to pieces. I do remember meeting him at Sunday lunchtime and he said he hadn't started working. But we still got a very stimulating paper.'

The word 'stimulating' is possibly a charitable way of concealing the annoyance Anderson felt at the time. As Boris himself was later to remark, Anderson 'was frightfully anti-me at school'.

Anderson offered his last anecdote of Boris: 'My third story is not particularly to his credit. At that time – it's now ceased, partly no doubt because of his performance – there used to be something called Shakespeare in the Cloisters, where members of College acted some scenes from Shakespeare out of doors. This had become less interesting as school drama became more developed. They were doing some scenes from *Richard III*, with Boris as the King. He hadn't had time to learn the lines, so had pasted them up behind various pillars. The whole performance consisted of him running from one side of the stage to the other and failing to read it properly.'

Boris wrote some of his first journalism at Eton. In the *Chronicle* of 10 October 1980, when Boris was sixteen, we find a short and unexciting report of a visit by Edward Heath to the Political Society. Boris ended with the words, 'Good sense like this must continue to provoke' – a sentence which could be ironical. One cannot pretend, in his articles for the *Chronicle*, that Boris stands out from his contemporaries. Nothing comes off all that well. In one piece, published on 4 June 1982, he is 'filled with a name-less horror' at the idea of becoming an Old Etonian banker.

But as a performer, Boris is already in a class of his own. On 2 November 1980 the Debating Society held a debate on the proposition 'This House would rather be tight than loose', pro-posed by Boris and by Hugo Dixon, a fellow scholar who had also been at Ashdown and became a lifelong friend. We are told that Boris 'spoke in such an authoritative manner that the audi-ence almost believed him'.

In the autumn of 1981, Boris was elected to Pop, the self-perpetuating group of the grandest Etonians. We also find Dixon and Boris, 'whose speeches are always full of sound and fury, even if signifying nothing,' in the final of the House Debating Competition, which they lost. A quarter of a century later, Dixon recalled what happened. He was still cross about it, for a competitive Etonian is as competitive as anyone in the whole wide world: 'This was the high point of my debating career. Boris stood up and he hadn't prepared a speech. The judge said basically I'm afraid Dixon and Johnson have lost, although Dixon made the best speech of all four.'

One of the effects of glancing through these *Chronicle*s is to start to get a sense of a whole generation.

On 15 May 1982 Hugh Fearnley-Whittingstall published a poem entitled 'Whither Apathy?' which was so bad that I did not bother, during an enjoyable day spent reading back numbers of the *Chronicle* in the library at Eton, to copy it. I did not then realise that many years later Boris would still be raging, as we shall see, against Fearnley-Whittingstall.

Near the end of Boris's time at Eton, a few articles by a boy called David Cameron appeared in the *Chronicle*. But it seemed clear to me – I carried out this research in July 2005 – that Cameron was unlikely to become so prominent as to make it worth asking the Eton archivist, Penny Hatfield, to go to the trouble of photocopying his juvenilia. Within six months, Cameron had become leader of the Conservative Party. In May 2006, when he went on *Desert Island Discs*, he attracted a certain amount of adverse criticism by choosing a cookery book by Fearnley-Whittingstall.

In the *Chronicle* for 5 June 1982, we read of a visit by a group of Etonians to debate with the girls at Wycombe Abbey. Boris received by far the most mentions in this short account: 'Boris Johnson was still asking if anyone wanted to speak instead of him, as we got into the minibus . . . Boris . . . unlikeliest cult-hero, won the debate on gestures . . . Boris was nearly left behind a tree.'

Almost everyone who remembers Boris at school remarks at some point on his acting. Jesse Norman remembers the College production of *Othello*. Boris played Brabantio, the father of Desdemona, and Norman said: 'I very much remember Boris looking out through a window and Iago telling him, "An old black ram / Is tupping your white ewe."'

Andrew Gilmour said: 'He had a great rivalry with Kabir Nath. There were two genius musicians in my year. Paul Richardson won the piano competition every year, except one year when Kabir Nath got it. Boris found this insufferable. He took up the piano, thinking he'd win it next year. He had no idea how difficult the piano was. He had such confidence in his own ability he just thought he'd come sailing in.'

Chris Bayston, who was a singer by profession, taught Boris the piano: 'He came to me for piano lessons as a beginner. It very soon became evident that he was incredibly bright, but he found the business of reading notes on two staves simultaneously, and also co-ordinating his hands, really remarkably difficult.'

Many people would either have decided the piano was not for them, or would have continued with the lessons but done virtually no practice. Eton has over 1,000 music lessons a week, given by 64 teachers, and as Bayston said, 'the tail of the dragon is very, very long – a large number of boys did very little practice'.

But Boris reacted quite differently: 'Whether it was the novelty of finding something he couldn't do easily, or a fascination with music, I've never taught a senior boy who struggled so manfully.'

Boris's housemaster, Hammond, could hear Boris struggling, and wrote in his report of 30 December 1980: 'As to his piano work, I can testify both to his determination and to the glacial progress: Boris plies his art on the instrument in Lower School, just across the passage from my study.'

A year later, on 29 December 1981, Hammond wrote: 'I could not fail to be aware of his flurry of preparation for the piano exam, sitting as I was just a few yards from the instrument that shared his agony.'

But Bayston has no bad memories of Boris: 'It was a joy to

teach him. He loved doing something very, very difficult. He never lost his temper – our lessons were such fun. What made the experience of teaching him the more memorable was that I plied him with very old-fashioned pieces by Walter Carroll, whom I learned from in my own childhood. Walter Carroll's first book was called *Scenes at a Farm* and had desperately outmoded pictures of peasants in smocks. I think he eventually graduated to a second book called *Sea Idylls* which had little poems. I taught him as if he was a young child, but he lapped it up, he derived enormous pleasure from it. I can't remember whether he took Grade One in his last year, but I do know he went on to the end, even when he was in Pop, and reached the standard of Grade One. I just felt that I actually achieved something heroic in getting him that far.'

Grade One is the lowest of the eight grades which pianists can sit. As Bayston observed, Boris understands what it is like not to be successful.

One of Boris's closest friends at school and university said: 'Boris read the Classics and was very influenced by the Classics. He likes the heroism. And I think that secretly – but unfortunately you can't say this in politics – he likes the aristocratic value system of the ancients, meaning rule of the best – the heroic values. I would imagine he's always found it slightly frustrating to have to say what the newspapers want. I secretly think he would have preferred it in ancient times.'

Hammond's last report on Boris, written on 2 January 1983, contains forebodings about the future:

Of course I was delighted by the news of Boris' Scholarship at Balliol, a real achievement in a year of extremely tough competition. His performance was described as 'very powerful' by Jasper Griffin: oddly, though, they could not get very much out of him at interview. The Scholarship is a happy ending to an academic career here which in its latter stages was not always quite so happy: and this last half, as these reports show, was no significant improvement on those that went before. My fear is that Boris may take his easy-going ways with him to Balliol, and add to the damaging statistics of Etonians who do little work at Oxbridge. I very much hope that this does not happen, and that Boris sets himself with proper determination at the First which should be within his capability. I think it true to say that Boris has no real academic bent, and he'll be an easier prey than some to the temptations of Oxford life: but he has a penetrating mind and a very sharp intelligence (not to speak of a big helping of personal charm), which should ensure a response to the intellectual stimulus of Balliol.

Boris remains intensely proud of his achievements at school, and loved being a leader there. But his page in the College Leaving Book, which every member of College fills in, referred to a different form of competition. It contained a large photograph of himself, with two scarves and a machine gun, together with an inscription about his determination to achieve 'more notches on my phallocratic phallus'.

# 7

## *Genuine Bogusness*

WHEN BORIS ARRIVED AT BALLIOL COLLEGE, OXFORD, IN THE autumn of 1983, he had several ambitions, not all of them quite normal for a nineteen-year-old. A close friend recalls: 'He came to Oxford wanting to find a wife.' Boris believed Oxford was the place where one would find the pick of the potential wives.

His Eton friend Charles Spencer (then known as Viscount, or Charlie, Althorp) pointed out to him: 'Your parents did that.'

Boris refused to be put off: 'Well, they did pretty well. Twelve years.'

There is a kind of ambitious man who wants to get married just in order to have his private life settled, so he can get on with the serious business of his career. Boris's urge to marry so young seems more likely to be a sign of his desire to emulate his father's achievements. He may also have wanted to create a new and intact family.

Boris was optimistic, and willing to throw himself into enterprises which others would have regarded as too danger-ous. He was certainly precocious. Toby Young, who went up to Brasenose College, Oxford, in the same year, noticed that Boris was more grown-up, or more focused, than other undergraduates: 'Boris had a real head-start on the rest of us. He seemed so fully formed, even in those days.'

At a time when many of us are still in a state of utter confusion, Boris knew where he wanted to go. A close friend said of him: 'At the age of eighteen he set himself the target that he was going to be in the Cabinet by the age of thirty-five.'

Toby Young was not nearly as close as that friend to Boris, but offered a grander, though less reliable, version of our man's ambitions. Darius Guppy, an Etonian who was later to go to prison for fraud and drag Boris into his misfortunes, told Young that while at school, Boris had confided in Charles Spencer that his secret ambition was to be President of the United States. Boris had an American passport, so this was not beyond the bounds of legal possibility, but as a leap of imagination it is worthy of Ian Fleming, the Old Etonian author of the James Bond stories.

As a more immediately practical step, Boris set out to become President of the Oxford Union. He also yearned, with a passion barely conceivable to some of us, to take a first-class degree.

Boris aimed higher than most of his contemporaries, but was not alone in being ambitious. Born at the height of the post-war baby boom, this generation of students was alarmingly competitive. Some of them must have led quiet and meritorious lives, but the ones who chased the glittering prizes could be rude, nasty, spiteful, petty and arrogant. Boris was not like that, except for a hidden well of arrogance, but he noticed the obnoxious behaviour of many of his contemporaries, and when he returned to Oxford in 1999 to give a speech, he reported that the students seemed 'nicer' than they were in his day.

David Ekserdjian, who came to Balliol as a junior research fellow in October 1983, was struck by the careerist atmosphere: 'They were terribly keen on working out what they were going to do and how they were going to get there. In my recollection, the thing people in Cambridge in about 1976 thought was incredibly cool was to get into the BBC. Boris's generation I don't think gave a stuff for the BBC. They thought the *Spectator* was frightfully gripping.'

Balliol has long been a nursery of statesmen. The last great crop consisted of Edward Heath, Roy Jenkins and Denis Healey, who all held high office. Before them came Asquith, Curzon, Macmillan and a host of others. This history mattered to Boris. Like other men who have aspired to greatness, he scorned to measure himself merely against his contemporaries. When an interviewer tried to console him, at the age of thirty-nine, by telling him, 'You've come a long way very young,' Boris replied in a gloomy tone: 'Not by historical standards.'

Balliol was founded in about 1263, but rose to pre-eminence in the nineteenth century under Benjamin Jowett, who encouraged public service as well as intellectual brilliance. According to Jowett, 'One man is as good as another until he has written a book.' Jowett's pupils and their successors took so many leading positions that Cyril Asquith, a son of Asquith the Prime Minister, observed: 'At the "top of the tree" in every profession we find a sort of congested arboreal slum of Balliol men.'

When Boris went up to Oxford, *Brideshead Revisited* had been shown only two years before on television, and undergraduates could be found who were attempting to imitate Evelyn Waugh's version of undergraduate life in the 1920s. But Balliol was not that kind of place. It was a friendly and informal college, architecturally one of the less distinguished parts of the university. In the main quadrangle, Garden Quad, students were at liberty to lounge about on the grass in the summer, dons and students drank in the same bar, and like most of Oxford it was allergic to the then Prime Minister, Margaret Thatcher, and clung to the faded dogmas of the 1960s.

Jonathan Barnes, who was one of Boris's college tutors and later became Professor of Ancient Philosophy at the Sorbonne, says it was no advantage at this time to have been to Eton if you wanted to go to Balliol: 'On the contrary, there was a pretty strong prejudice against public schools. I should say that it was the college's policy – powerfully urged by some tutors and implicitly accepted by most – that, other things being equal, a candidate from an "unfavoured background" should be preferred to one from a favoured background (anglice: prefer the rotten schools to the good).'

Boris had entered a college where Tory politics were virtually unknown. As the Master of Balliol in Boris's time, Anthony Kenny – now Sir Anthony – recalls: 'The Balliol JCR [Junior Common Room, representing the undergraduates] was in those days very, very left-wing. The Communist Party was the right wing of it. Boris avoided it. An SDP MP approached me, to ask if I could recommend a young man to work for him. I asked Boris if he would be interested. Boris burst out laughing and said: "No, I'm a true-blue Tory."'

Boris, it will be seen, did not wear his Conservative colours on his sleeve, and even such an astute and friendly observer as Kenny supposed he would support the SDP, the new party launched by Labour rebels in 1981 with the intention of breaking the mould in British politics.

Lloyd Evans, who went up to Balliol from a left-wing household and a state school in 1982, said of the JCR: 'They were all these stupid public-school idiots who were showboating – it was a lifestyle choice for them – pretending to have a bond of affection for the working man.' According to Lloyd, these lefties had 'posh accents, donkey jackets, working men's boots and Mummy and Daddy paying the battels [college bills]'.

Boris, like Lloyd, was repelled by this kind of politics. He has since said, in the kind of language some might use to describe how they discovered they were homosexual, that he was 'conscious of right-wing feelings' and 'realised I had Tory tendencies' when he saw students at Oxford collecting money during the miners' strike, which lasted from March 1984 to early 1985. As Boris told *GQ* in May 2003: 'I was appalled by the way middle-class kids were going around supporting Arthur Scargill when it was quite obvious he was leading the poor miners to utter perdition and doing them no bloody good at all.'

Lloyd had heard Boris's name before meeting him: 'The first time I saw him he was standing in the quad. There were a group of people standing round him and he said: "I think I might pop up to my room and have a peek at Plato."

'So I said: "Why, have you got him in the cupboard?" I got this enormous laugh. The thing about him is how personally warm and charismatic he is. You always get this gale of laughter. He leaves you with a terribly good feeling about yourself.'

Jasper Griffin, who has spent most of his life at Balliol, was one of Boris's teachers and remembers him with much affection: 'He was a very entertaining figure about the place. He was generally liked. He was a conspicuous figure.' Griffin added that Boris 'doesn't have the stuffy and tiresome habits' which might be thought to go with his manner.

Barnes, brother of the novelist Julian, remembered Boris's charm, and described the impression Boris made:

The charm was part of the Old Buffer persona which he already had at Balliol. Not a Young Fogey – he wasn't in the least fogeyish. Rather, a young Old Buffer. It showed up in his clothes (suits, not jeans and T-shirt; occasionally a tie; shoes, not trainers; etc), and in his speech (the drawl; 'a tome' for 'at home', 'orften' etc; and especially the Gollys and the Goshes), and also in what for want of a better word I call his manners (he was polite, courteous, witty). He wasn't the only Buffer in the world; but at the time bufferdom was not at all widespread, and it certainly marked Boris out. It was, I think, generally supposed that the bufferdom was sedulously cultivated. I can't judge – but, cultivated or natural or a mixture of the two, he wore it very well.

As Hammond had feared, for most of the time Boris did virtually no academic work. Barnes said: 'My exiguous tutorial notes read "feeble", "hasn't read the text", "no essay", and so on. He wasn't lazy, and he wasn't uninterested in Plato (at least, I don't think he was). Rather, there were other things which engaged most of his interest.'

Ekserdjian claims that Barnes one week reproached Boris for copying a piece of work word for word out of Loeb, which gives a straight English translation next to the original Greek or Latin text.

Barnes said: 'Oh Boris, I'm incredibly offended that you should underestimate my intelligence to such a degree that you thought I wouldn't realise you'd just nicked this out of Loeb.'

Boris gave the amusing reply: 'I'm terribly, terribly sorry, I've been so busy I just didn't have time to put in the mistakes.'

Barnes does not remember this, but says of his attempts to teach Boris philosophy: 'If you're intelligent enough, you can rub along in philosophy on a couple of hours a week. Boris rubbed along on no hours a week, and it wasn't quite good enough.'

At the end of each term Balliol has a ceremony called 'hand-shaking', when each undergraduate appears before the Master and tutors in his subject. The tutors report on how well or badly the student has done, and Barnes recalls telling Kenny: 'This term, Master, Mr Johnson has been a pain in the arse.'

Yet all Boris's teachers remember him with affection. Barnes said:

On the whole, I find politicians perfectly odious (and I haven't the slightest interest in what they do). Balliol has produced more than its fair share of MPs: while I was a Fellow I met many of them, and taught three or four. Most of them strike me as frightful people – vainglorious and yet very stupid, moralistic and yet deeply dishonest. Boris

strikes me as one of the few exceptions. I might even be
tempted to vote for him . . . I confess that I have forgotten
the irritations, and am left with the conviction that, at
bottom, Boris is really a Good Egg.

Justin Rushbrooke, a Harrovian who was also reading Classics
at Balliol, became a lasting friend of Boris when they had rooms
next to each other, and defends him against the charge of idleness: 'Considering how thinly he spread himself, he was
disciplined, and he did *love* certain parts of the subject. He was
by no means a slacker. I was a complete slacker. Boris viewed me
with a degree of horror. We had different lifestyles: I would still
be in bed at eleven o'clock in the morning. We both had scholarships but I lost mine in my third year and took a gentleman's
third.'

Boris played rugby for Balliol for four years running, as a prop
forward, but his social life extended far beyond the college. In
Oxford terms, though not by any more demanding standard,
Boris was a toff, having been to Eton; but he tended to be seen
more as an exotic flower, or an English eccentric, than as a toff.
What Boris carefully hid from view, or at least took care not to
emphasise, was that many of his friends were toffish – a fact not
readily apparent among the workers, peasants and intellectuals of
the Balliol JCR.

Yet Boris was also one of the most conspicuous undergradu-
ates in Oxford, and had other conspicuous friends. Patrick
Hennessy, who had gone from Eton to Oxford ahead of Boris,
recalls: 'When he was at Oxford he associated with Darius
Guppy. Guppy was an obviously dodgy character. It was a flaw in
Boris in my view. I found Guppy very unpleasant.'

In a later chapter, we shall describe Guppy's downfall, and
how Boris became ensnared in it. But at this time Guppy was
enjoying social success and a relatively innocent notoriety. He
was at Magdalen College, as was his great friend Charles

Spencer. Boris was very fond of Guppy, and also on close terms with Spencer.

A large number of undergraduates were ready to take offence at the ostentatious behaviour of some members of this circle. A body calling itself the Magdalen Women's Group passed the following motion by an overwhelming majority: 'Henceforth, Magdalen women will not pander to the whim of Darius Guppy.'

Guppy revelled in such attention, which only made him more provocative. To insult the spirit of the age was part of the point. It was around this time that Peregrine Worsthorne, the then editor of the *Sunday Telegraph*, coined the expression 'bourgeois triumphalism' to describe the vulgar behaviour of some beneficiaries of Thatcherism, and such triumphalism could certainly be found among Oxford undergraduates.

Boris was elected to the Bullingdon, the most famously riotous dining-club in Oxford, which had only twenty-four members. The dress for the Bullingdon, including a navy-blue tailcoat with white silk facings and gold buttons, cost nearly £1,000 at 1984 prices, and the dinners, at which vast amounts of drink were consumed in the most expensive restaurants, about £400 a time. But according to Guppy the less wealthy members were subsidised at this period, and allowed to pay only £200 a dinner, by a rich benefactor who some believed had been elected to the club for this purpose.

Champagne breakfasts were held once a term at hotels such as The Bear in Woodstock and were attended, Guppy has recalled, by 'two or three top-class strippers from London' who 'would be heralded into the dining-room when the champagne had been flowing for some time' and 'would always be well-paid for their services and would never become annoyed, even when the more drunken undergraduates went too far'.

Elections to the Bullingdon took place in one or another member's rooms late at night at the end of each term, and

were often hotly contested. Boris had great difficulty persuading the other members to agree to admit Guppy, who in turn
faced a titanic battle to get Radek Sikorski in, at an election
held in the rooms of Toby Mansell-Pleydell in University
College.

By Guppy's account, some of the members did not want
Sikorski because he was a foreigner and, as they put it, 'not suitable material'. Sikorski was a fiercely anti-Communist Pole who
had managed to get out of Poland and into Oxford, where he
was elected President of the Union. In 2007 he became Poland's
Foreign Minister.

Sikorski told me: 'I vividly remember the night of my election
to the Bullingdon, which happened as I was asleep in my room
in Walton Street. In the middle of the night a dozen screaming
figures burst in to my room and demolished it completely with
my hi-fi and books piled up in the middle of the floor and my
heavy desk chair put through the wall. I vividly remember Boris,
a very solid and friendly man, saying, "Congratulations, man.
You've been elected."

'The secretary or mistress of the landlord came down the stairs
and screamed: "What do you think you're doing?"

'And Darius Guppy ran up the stairs, put his face very close to
her and said: "Don't worry, baby, it's his birthday."'

The tradition was to smash up a new member's room, but
when Andrew Gilmour was elected, Boris warned the other
members not to break up his room, telling them that if this were
to happen, Gilmour would refuse to join.

Gilmour went to the first dinner after he was elected, at Le
Manoir aux Quat' Saisons, Raymond Blanc's restaurant outside
Oxford. In Gilmour's words, it was 'a pretty awful occasion –
someone vomited'.

After dinner the members asked each other, 'Who shall we go
and trash?' This prompted a protest from Gilmour: 'I got rather
pompous and said as the only member who was the son of an

old member, that didn't used to be done. I had the coat and all that – it was my father's.'

Gilmour's father is Sir Ian Gilmour, one of the patrician Tory wets who were appalled by Margaret Thatcher. He was ennobled as Lord Gilmour of Craigmillar. While still a young man he bought and for a time edited the *Spectator*.

Charles Spencer, who shared a house with Gilmour, was also elected to the Bullingdon, but declined to join. As with so many institutions which are popularly regarded as smart, it seems it may have been smarter not to belong to the Bullingdon.

Patrick Hennessy, himself an Old Etonian, said: 'It's often thought the Bullingdon was crammed full of Old Etonians. Quite a lot of Old Etonians wouldn't have gone within a mile of the Bullingdon and thought it was a load of tossers.'

The club still invited Gilmour to its farewell dinner, held at Cliveden, reached by boat down the Thames: 'I had an argument with Boris about Israel – Boris had read Conor Cruise O'Brien's book – don't give an inch of Gaza ground – Boris and I were arguing about it even as we went down to this ludicrous event in our Buller tails. I remember Guppy being anti-Semitic and Boris getting really very, very angry about that.'

In the photograph of the Bullingdon that can be found in the plate section, Boris is sitting on the steps, and although he appears to have the correct kit, he manages to subvert the effect by wearing odd socks. Most of the Buller men look very young and vulnerable, but determined to seem manly and self-assured. The pressure at that age to enjoy oneself, and to do supposedly glamorous things, can be pretty much intolerable.

Toby Young recalls that Roland Rudd, a Social Democrat ally of Boris who was President of the Union and later built up a financial PR company worth many millions of pounds, was debagged by the Bullingdon 'and took it very badly'.

According to Gilmour, Boris backed out when the Bullingdon went after Rudd. Boris seems to have kept a more level head than some Buller men. But if one moved in these circles, one was bound to find oneself witnessing the odd debagging. When Charles Spencer celebrated his twentieth birthday with a group of Oxford friends including Boris at the Notting Hill restaurant La Paesana, they tried to debag the disc jockey Tony Blackburn, who told the press: 'I got the message that Althorp and co. wanted to get my trousers off. I thought it was all very odd, but the waiters stepped in and asked them to return to their tables. There was a lot of shouting and suddenly a rubber plant hurtled across the room and landed in somebody's meal.'

In March 2003, by which time Boris was editor of the *Spectator*, he got Peter Oborne to include this incident in a cover piece for the magazine about the decline and fall of the Hooray Henry. But Boris exercised his editorial prerogative of removing all reference to himself from the piece.

Toby Young, who has himself achieved a degree of fame as a journalist in later life, is not sure where he first met Boris, but thinks 'it may have been at a Cheese and Wine Appreciation Society' meeting. Chapsoc, as it was usually known, just as the Lesbian and Gay Society was known as Gaysoc, was 'an opportunity for male undergraduates to meet secretaries'. Guppy and Spencer were both members.

According to Rachel Johnson, Boris's sister, who went to New College, Oxford, Chapsoc was 'easily the raunchiest society in Oxford, far surpassing the tame transvestitism of the Piers Gaveston . . . The bacchanalian quality of its meetings derives not so much from the amount of wine drunk as from the sexual excitement generated by the proximity of so many secretaries. Rendered incapable of small talk, difficult at the best of times in noisy rooms, the boys throw French sticks and packets of supermarket cheese at the girls they fancy.'

This account appeared in Rachel's essay on sex in *The Oxford Myth*, a collection she edited of ten pieces about the university, published by Weidenfeld in 1988. The book was denounced by reviewers, partly because of Toby Young's unpleasant and inaccurate account of the people he found in Brasenose: 'Small, vaguely deformed undergraduates would scuttle across the quad as if carrying mobile homes on their backs . . . In America, these people would be called "nerds". In Brasenose we referred to them as "stains".'

Rachel and her collaborators were recognised, as Young later conceded, as 'a bunch of insufferable jumped-up prats who deserved criticism'.

But even as Boris pursued earthly glory, he could see with perverse amusement how bogus it all was, and how the words of a poet might long outlive the power of a ruler.

One of the debates Boris had many times with his friends in his room at Balliol was whether 'bogusness' or 'bogusity' is the noun that goes with the word 'bogus'. Twenty years later, when telling *Esquire* magazine why the Rolling Stones are one of his favourites, he plumped for 'bogusness': 'What I like is the bogusness of them. I love the idea of these four middle-class white kids pretending to be rough around the edges.'

Oxford offered an inexhaustible supply of bogusness, and for Boris that was part of its attraction. He himself has a kind of genuine bogusness: a ludicrous manner which has nevertheless become part of him. And at Oxford he was about to demonstrate that he could conquer a far wider public than at school.

# 8

# The Oxford Politician

BORIS THE WOULD-BE POLITICIAN REFINED HIS ORATORY, and the no less necessary crafts of intrigue and deceit, at the Oxford Union, where so many statesmen have taken their first steps. In the Union's Victorian debating chamber are found the images of Gladstone, Salisbury, Asquith, F. E. Smith, Curzon, Macmillan, Roy Jenkins and Michael Heseltine. But none of these great men has left so penetrating an account as Boris of how to get on in Oxford politics. His analysis of how to become President of the Union is worthy of Machiavelli.

Boris's twenty-page treatise, simply entitled 'Politics', appeared in *The Oxford Myth*, the collection edited by his sister Rachel. The triviality of the subject matter in no way invalidates the fascination of the work.

Boris understands the bogusness of democracy. He has an infallible eye for the distinction between the high-flown theory of how the Union is supposed to work, and the sordid reality. Rule 33 of its constitution expressly forbids the soliciting of votes, yet this is the 'distinctive activity' during the elections in which the President and other officers are chosen.

To succeed at Union elections, Boris explains, what you really need is 'a disciplined and deluded collection of stooges' who will get the vote out for you in their respective colleges. The key word here is 'deluded', for you attract stooges by implying that you are going to do as much for them, in their attempt to gain election to a junior committee, as they will do for you in your campaign to become supreme leader, or President.

Yet as Boris says, the 'brutal fact' of the candidate–stooge relationship is that the candidate can never do as much for his stooges as they can do for him. No candidate can give effective support to more than one stooge, while he must have support from several stooges if he is to become President. In short, 'The relationship . . . is founded on duplicity.'

Why then, he asks, do people consent to become stooges? There are several reasons: they can be flattered into doing so, they are vain enough to think that they themselves could have a shot at the top job, and their empty lives are given meaning by their humdrum activities within the organisation, or machine, which they have joined.

The essence of the stooge's role is a kind of wilful self-deception. In Boris's words, 'The tragedy of the stooge is that even if he thinks this through, he wants so much to believe that his relationship with the candidate is special that he shuts out the truth. The terrible art of the candidate is to coddle the self-deception of the stooge.'

One cannot pretend that Boris does justice to every motive which might inspire a man or woman to a political career. It does not seem to occur to him that some people might enter politics with disinterested motives, and he appears to think that everyone down to the humblest party worker secretly believes he can get to the top. On the other hand, the way in which many Tory MPs who were totally unknown to the outside world either entered the contest in 2005 to succeed Michael Howard as Tory leader, or seriously considered doing so, more than confirms Boris's view that politicians are amazingly vain.

So much for the theory. What of Boris's practice at the

Union? Michael Gove, who became a successful journalist at *The Times* and in 2005 followed Boris into the Commons as a Tory MP, cheerfully admitted: 'I was Boris's stooge. I became a votary of the Boris cult.'

Gove recalled how Boris hooked him: 'The first time I saw him was in the Union bar. He was a striking figure with sheep-dog hair and penny loafers, standing in a distinctive pose with his hands in his trouser pockets and his head bent forward. He seemed like a kindly, Oxford character, but he was really there like a great basking shark waiting for freshers to swim towards him.'

This vision of Boris as a shark does not, of course, do full justice to him. Gove, who had himself become an accomplished debater while still a schoolboy in Scotland and who appeared at the Union in a kilt, said of Boris: 'He was quite the most brilliant *extempore* speaker of his generation. I can still remember him mentioning "the Bell curve distribution", after which he went on: "I'm sure we all know what a Bell curve is. It is a curve which is shaped like a bell."'

As Gove said, 'Boris has the capacity apparently to lose his way in a sentence, like a child in a nativity play. You want him to succeed, and when he does you share in his triumph.' Gove also recalled that Boris was much more interesting to talk to than most of the Union hacks, and did not just take a 'close-the-deal' approach.

But a deal was closed: 'The real reason why I became a stooge in the Boris machine was that Oxford politics was essentially a matter of the college that you found yourself in. I was in Lady Margaret Hall [LMH], which was a small satrap of Balliol, like a colony in Sicily aping the manners of our betters. Slates need balance, and an LMH debater fitted into the balance.'

The recruitment of a team of stooges such as Gove was not the only means by which Boris became President. He also practised a series of bold deceptions about his own political opinions, in order to appeal to several different constituencies at the same time.

This behaviour was witnessed by Frank Luntz, an American at Oxford, whose outrage at Boris's conduct can be heard even down a transatlantic telephone line twenty years later. Luntz says: 'He renounced his Conservative affiliation and fully embraced the SDP and the principles and people who supported the SDP to help him get elected. At that time being a member of the Social Democrats was the best thing to be at Oxford. I said to him, "You don't do this, this is a very small country and it's not right and it will come back to haunt you." He abandoned them to get elected and after he was elected he said he was a Tory again.'

Radek Sikorski confirmed this: 'Boris made these SDP speeches at the Union which was how he got elected.'

But Luntz also remembered that Boris was capable of saying unpopular things: 'He was probably the most popular debater – when he spoke he was entertaining and emotional and effective. But he also stood up for Israel, which was not a popular thing to do. He stood up and said this thing about the bully in the school yard. The Jewish students at that moment just wanted to make him king.'

Luntz has since become a successful pollster in the United States, where he prides himself on having helped 'move the language' so that, for example, 'school vouchers' become 'opportunity scholarships'. His name cropped up in British politics in October 2005 when the Cameron campaign team distributed footage of a focus group organised by Luntz which showed that Cameron was 'exactly what swing voters are looking for in a Conservative leader' and represented 'the future of Britain and a new generation'. Some people thought this footage, which was shown on *Newsnight*, was unduly favourable to Cameron.

Whether or not that was so, Luntz still has close links with

Boris: 'I see him, I like him, I think he's a great guy.' At the Republican convention in 2004, Boris arrived without the right pass, but Luntz got him in and he ended up sitting in the seats reserved for the family of Vice-President Dick Cheney.

To pass himself off as a Social Democrat was not Boris's only deception. At Balliol, according to Lloyd Evans: 'He never stood in the Conservative interest. When he stood for the Union he told us he was an environmentalist.'

Jessica Pulay, of Christ Church, who was herself to become President of the Union, and is a great admirer of Boris, admits that he was 'extremely clever at not really revealing his political cards at any point'.

How did he veil his real opinions? Pulay said: 'His humour. And the fact that he's not an ideologue – or if he is, he keeps it very well-concealed. He's a life-enhancer. He had a lot of acolytes who maybe he didn't regard as friends. I was sure that he was going to be a success, absolutely. He just had an aura about him that made him instantly recognisable. Boris was a great showman – without doubt the best showman of his generation. He just made people laugh when he opened his mouth.'

Pulay recalled that Boris only succeeded in becoming President of the Union at the second attempt: 'The second time he was running against someone from Christ Church [her own college]. It was not the done thing not to support your own college, but I was a college renegade. The Balliol machine was very much the SDP machine. The Christ Church machine was the Tory Reform Group machine – the slightly wet Tory machine.'

Boris has since sought to diminish his great essay about how to succeed at the Union. In 2003 he said: 'I think my essay remains the *locus classicus* of the English genre of bogus self-deprecation.'

One can see what Boris means. In his essay, he undervalues his own talents as a debater, which were plainly a major factor in his success. He stood as a debater, the alternative being to commend himself as an administrator who would save the Union by means of tight financial control. For the administrative side of things, he relied on Brenda Goodall, who is now dead, one of the first in a line of strong-minded women, devoted to his interests, who have helped Boris.

But Boris's essay on politics is not bogus. His Union career was over when he wrote it, so he could afford to be amazingly, though not completely, candid about a political process in which he himself had played a leading role. Although we find no mention in his account of his SDP period, we still see a sophisticated and instinctive grasp of the role played by deceit in the electoral process, and a joyful, one might even say an honest, willingness to play this game.

And although the Union is easily mocked or despised, it is one way in which Oxford keeps in touch with the wider world of politics, and it is a very good way to meet people from London. Charles Moore, who was at that time editor of the *Spectator*, said: 'I first met Boris at the Oxford Union. It's the only time I've met a President of the Union who I thought was really, really interesting. We had a conversation about creationism.'

At Boris's final debate, the speakers included Melina Mercouri, the Greek actress and politician who was determined to retrieve the Elgin Marbles from the British Museum. Jonathan Barnes said: 'He was a splendid President of the Union – he looked and acted the part, and generally managed to juggle the thing along thanks to a mixture of authority and bonhomie. He asked me to speak once or twice – always at the shortest of notices, because one of the speakers he had booked jacked at the last minute. I only did funny speeches (and not very funny at that).'

If the Union politics of this period seem tawdry, Oxford journalism was truly atrocious. For callow nastiness, it is hard to beat some of these publications. As Alexander Connock observed in *The Oxford Myth*, 'Writing such magazines requires a ruthless willingness to sell one's friends down the river.'

Many of these student journalists made it to Fleet Street in one capacity or another. Toby Young passed on the editorship of *Tributary*, an Oxford imitation of *Private Eye*, to Boris, Guppy and Charles Spencer. According to Toby, 'When I did it, it was like the first half of *Private Eye*, with stories about real people. Boris didn't want to make any enemies, so he made it more like the second half of *Private Eye*. I think he's got an absolute anathema to being disliked. He clearly thrives on popularity and adores winning popularity contests of any description.'

Boris's most amusing cover, published in May 1985, had a picture of a nude woman on the cover who was saying, 'Why am I so lonely at Oxford . . .? But wait!' A small phial of liquid was sellotaped to her hand, and on page two it was explained that this was a 'LOVE-PHILTRE' which would make you 'positively sexy'.

Lloyd Evans and Aidan Hartley were the next editors of *Trib*, as it was usually known, and Evans recalled a decisive intervention by Boris:

He could get really angry. There's a real toughness to him. When we were editing the magazine, and he was going for the presidency of the Union, he became fixated about what we were writing about him, and he came down to Aidan Hartley's house in the middle of the night – Aidan was living somewhere in Jericho and it was three o'clock in the morning – and picked up the thing we'd written and it contained a whole stream of abuse of Boris. We called him an exiled Armenian chicken farmer. The other thing we called him was the Aryan bull pig, victim of a hideous Nazi war experiment in Munich in 1936. We'd also called him incompetent. That was the thing he picked up on. He said,

'You can call me an Armenian chicken farmer or an Aryan bull pig, but don't call me incompetent.' He was absolutely incandescent. He really went mad. He grabbed the typewriter and said, 'Damn it, I'm a journalist,' and started writing his own version of the whole thing. We ended up not publishing any of it. I was surprised by how angry he was. He's a war leader. He is one of the two or three most extraordinary people I've ever met. You just feel he's going somewhere. People just love him. They go along with him and they enjoy being led.

To make people enjoy being led by him was an aspect of leadership which Boris mastered at a very young age. He made people helpless with laughter, and so great was their enjoyment that they scarcely cared what he did with their support, as long as he kept on amusing them. Only in retrospect did people start to ask whether this comedian could ever be serious. In Oxford, he looked to many of his contemporaries like a future Prime Minister.

# 9

# Boris in Love

BORIS FELL IN LOVE WITH THE MOST BEAUTIFUL GIRL IN Oxford. He met Allegra Mostyn-Owen in early 1984, half-way through their first year. She was a radiant beauty, of such sweetness that it was virtually impossible not to fall in love with her. If you managed to amuse her, you were rewarded with an eager, loving smirk. If you annoyed her, she could get frosty.

Boris had many drawbacks – he was poor, scruffy, unreliable about practical matters and obsessed by student politics – but he amused her very much indeed. With unflagging single-mindedness he set out to win her. He decided to make her, first his girlfriend, then the wife whom he had always intended to find at Oxford.

They met because of an error on his part. He was invited to a party in her rooms at Trinity College, next to Balliol, which she had thrown jointly with another girl, and arrived on the wrong night with a bottle of wine.

Allegra was reading a book: 'The problem was I was reading this economics textbook. Quite a big textbook. I think it's by R. J. Lipsey. The fifth edition. Or the seventh edition. In fact I was falling asleep. I was lying on the carpet, reading it on the carpet in my lovely double set in Garden Quad. A lovely living-room with two huge windows looking on to the garden.

'There's this stranger at the door who goes, "Oh, oh, oh, oh, oh." I'd never met him but he said he'd seen me at a Union debate, and he was known to the girl I'd co-hosted the party with.

'So we drank the bottle and talked. I don't know what we talked about. I think we got on very well and he became my best friend, a much better friend than any of the girls I knew at the time. Because anyway he made me laugh. He introduced me to poetry, which I didn't know at all, and there were lots of good jokes, and lots of bad jokes. And in my own way I didn't really think he was making a play for me, despite the fact that there was lots of curry *à deux* at the Kismet Tandoori.'

Unlike many of the bolder male students, Boris did not spend his time at Oxford chasing women in general. He pursued Allegra in a manner that made him faithful, and continent, compared to some of his disreputable friends. His girlfriend before Oxford was called Alexa de Ferranti, who went to school at Bryanston with his sister Rachel.

Allegra was struck by her new friend's early intellectual development: 'When I got to know him I was very impressed that he'd started to read *Economist* editorials at the age of ten.' Some of Boris's uncles on his mother's side worked for *The Economist*. Boris used to ask Allegra: 'If I added up the IQ of my father and my mother don't you think they'd be more than the IQ of your father and mother?'

Allegra was too young to dismiss this ghastly question: 'I thought he must know what he was talking about, but of course he didn't. He was just talking from his own insecurity.'

Boris's scholarship-boy question, filled with cringing awe for the conventional measures of intelligence, does not begin to do justice to Allegra's parents. Her father, Willy, traces his ancestry to Owen Glendower. Woodhouse, the family seat in Shropshire, was remodelled in 1798, and he also had a castle at Aberuchill in Perthshire. While Willy was still at Eton, his father and both his brothers died, leaving him a man of independent means, free to go touring in his Rolls-Royce and to pursue his love of the arts.

Willy married Gaia Servadio, a high-spirited young Italian whom he met after returning to London from Florence, where he worked for five years for the great art critic Bernhard Berenson. Gaia as a tiny girl spent the Second World War on the run in Italy with her sister, their father, who was Jewish, and their mother, who was not. The father's mother and grand-mother were murdered at Auschwitz, after spending a dreadful time in an internment camp in Italy from which they were able to send only one message: 'I need money and a comb.' Allegra is a Jewish name.

Gaia's first book, *Melinda*, was a spectacular success, and was translated into many languages. Willy became Director of Old Masters at Christie's. They had three children, but their marriage did not survive Gaia's stardom.

When Allegra disapproves of something, she can be quite severe. Boris once told her: 'What I like about you is that you've got principles.'

They saw more and more of each other, and at Easter they went on holiday together in Turkey, visited some of Boris's rela-tions in Istanbul and saw Troy and Ephesus: 'In Seljuk, close to Ephesus, we rented a motorbike. We spent at least half a day in this place. I liked sketching – every child seemed to be called either Attila or Genghis – and a small number had yellow hair, just like Boris did.

'We had a lovely time, and at some point quite late in the summer term we were just saying goodbye at the gate of Trinity and he said, "I don't know if I'm coming or going. If you don't go out with me I'm not going to devote so much time to being your friend. I'm actually going to devote most of my time to the Oxford Union." Which he did anyway. No, it was fine.'

Boris had pushed Allegra into a commitment. His ultimatum, and the priority he went on giving to his own career, indicated a ruthless determination to run their relationship on his own terms. Whether he had found, in Allegra, a woman strong enough to tolerate his egotism, is not the kind of question Boris has ever allowed to hold him back. He had won the most desirable woman in Oxford, whom any number of undergraduates would have been happy to call their own, and together they made a glamorous sight. Boris and Allegra became the Posh and Becks, or Mick and Jerry, or Bogart and Bacall, of their generation.

Toby Young said: 'Allegra was by common consent the most attractive undergraduate of her year. Boris very quickly became a legendary figure, scaling the wall between Trinity and Balliol to bed Allegra.'

That was not how Boris got into Trinity, but Young expresses a common feeling of admiration. Radek Sikorski said: 'He and Allegra were the perfect couple. She was the girl from the cover of *Tatler* and he was the future Prime Minister.'

Allegra was photographed by Terence Donovan for *Vogue* and by David Bailey for *Tatler*. Bailey began by saying to her: 'You're a bit posh, aren't you?'

His next words were: 'Go on then, just fuck the camera.'

Allegra says of the resulting cover: 'That's my look of horror and shock when he's telling me to fuck the camera.'

The bad aspects of this picture did not end there: 'Having done the cover shot for *Tatler*, people decided I must be beautiful because *Tatler* says so. Then I got these declarations of love every day. I didn't want anything to do with them. Boris felt like a safe place, but not for very long. Like most human beings, he'll exploit weakness.'

One of her innumerable admirers was Hugh Fearnley-Whittingstall, who had been at school with Boris and has since achieved fame as a food writer. He sent her a note which said: 'Why have steak and chips when you can have *foie gras*?'

Allegra was amused by this: 'It really made me laugh. Of

course I responded to Hugh with a note saying I found *foie gras*
ethically repugnant.'

Boris was less amused. In November 2005, in a brief contribution to the *Observer Food Monthly*, Boris said: 'As for Hugh
Fearnley-bloody-Whittingstall, he's got a lot to answer for. That
man has persuaded thousands of innocent people to pick nettles
and boil them up in the delusion that they are making something
fit for consumption.'

Many undergraduates were inhibited by a proper sense of shy-
ness from approaching Allegra. Michael Gove remembered:
'Allegra, an Oxford goddess, and editor of *Isis*, seemed unimag-
inably distant.'

Not everyone liked Allegra: to some people she seemed cold.
In the pages of *Cherwell* she became Ms Allergic Mostyn-Owen.

Boris and Allegra showed from the first some irreconcilable
differences of taste. She could never understand what he could
see in Darius Guppy, of whom she said: 'I got on with him OK.
It seemed to me he didn't have much respect for women in general. We had arguments about that. I think he's the only person
I've ever thrown a glass of beer over.'

Guppy would say to Allegra: 'Do you love me?'

Allegra would reply: 'Come on, Darry, you're too sweaty and
feverish.'

But because Allegra was with his friend Boris, Guppy 'didn't
step over the line with me'.

Boris and Allegra were in adjacent colleges, but wrote to each
other continually: 'We really enjoyed the pigeon post. I respond
very strongly to the written word and so does he. We would
leave each other notes at least twice a day.'

Many of Boris's notes are jokes. He would tell her that she had
been selected to play on board one for Atletico di Roma chess
club against the USSR, against Boris Spassky, and should bring
a packed lunch. Or he would ask her what is Plato's Theory of
Recollection, to which the answer is 'I forget'.

In another note, Boris said Allegra reminded him more and more of his mother. He perhaps found some of the same moral seriousness, and sensitivity, and sweetness, in Allegra as in his mother.

But as if to make up for this confession, the note ran immediately into a joke about whether her bed was made, to which the answer was that it was made in Birmingham. He added that he had been making this joke since about the age of eight.

Trinity, Allegra's college, made Boris welcome, despite the fact that he was from Balliol: 'He would regularly borrow books from our library – Trinity was remarkably tolerant. The Trinity porters were always very courteous to him.'

Work occasionally intruded. Boris usually wanted to see her that very evening, and would suggest an amusing range of possible diversions, but once, when Jasper Griffin had told him he would get a delta in Greek lyric poetry, he asked if she could face not seeing him for a whole week.

During his first long vacation, or summer holiday from Oxford, Boris went with his sister Rachel to stay in Israel on a Kibbutz. Through their stepmother, Jenny, who was the stepdaughter of Teddy Sieff, the chairman of Marks & Spencer, they were connected to one of the most prominent Jewish families in Britain. Rachel recalled with pleasure that on the Kibbutz, Boris was forced for six weeks to do the washing-up. According to Allegra, 'He was in a subterranean room being punished for his blondness.'

In his second long vacation, he went with Rachel and her boyfriend Sebastian Shakespeare to Spain and Portugal to investigate animal cruelty. During this expedition he wrote on 8 August 1985 from the Pension Amazonas in Lisbon to Allegra, asking her if she had broached the subject of marriage yet with her parents. Boris wondered on paper if she could bear the idea of getting married to him – a characteristic piece of self-deprecation – but also asked if she might emasculate him.

Allegra's parents were appalled by Boris. Her father, Willy, described him as 'rapacious', and would get into competitive conversations about Eton with him, in which it would invariably emerge that of the two of them, Boris had had the more glittering schoolboy career. Boris dressed in a wilfully scruffy manner, which might have been calculated to upset the Mostyn-Owens, who valued elegance and beauty. When he went on a skiing holiday with Allegra, her brothers and her mother, Gaia, he left his passport behind, which meant he had to catch a later flight, and when he opened his suitcase it turned out to contain only his dirty sheets from Balliol. Such behaviour added to Gaia's general sense of horror. Boris went skiing in his normal clothes, a tweed jacket and moleskin trousers, and liked going very fast straight downhill.

One way Boris saved time was by simply not doing some of the chores which fall to most students. Allegra said: 'He never had the time to wash laundry or buy shampoo and somehow he was terribly good at getting other people to do things. I ended up doing all his laundry at Trinity.' Boris pretends to be old-fashioned partly in order to hide the fact that he really is old-fashioned. He most likely believes laundry is for women, but would never be foolish enough to say it. Instead he has brought the art of masculine incompetence to such a pitch of perfection that women take pity on him. But it was still quite an achievement, albeit ungallant and not very good for his character, to get the most desirable girl at Oxford to wash his clothes.

Allegra liked the fact that Boris had to dress formally for the Union and the Bullingdon, as then he 'looked quite handsome'.

In the summer of 1986, Boris and Allegra engaged in a journalistic collaboration which caused her deep embarrassment. An article which Boris had helped to write appeared under Allegra's name in the *Sunday Telegraph*. It described the descent on Oxford of Tina Brown, a famous British journalist working in New York. Brown wanted to find out all about Olivia Channon, daughter of the Trade and Industry Secretary, Paul Channon, who had been discovered dead, choked on her vomit, in the rooms at Christ Church of Gottfried von Bismarck.

A delightfully hostile portrait was drawn of Brown on her hunt for 'tasteless details', but Allegra had made a disastrous error. She pretended she had been at a lunch which Brown threw for a group of fashionable undergraduates, when in fact only Boris had been there. It was the kind of mistake which would have counted for less than nothing in Oxford journalism, but it would not do in a national paper, for it enabled Brown to get one of her sidekicks to dismiss the whole article as 'untrue'. One of the distinctive products of Boris's journalism had already emerged: the powerful and amusing article, utterly convincing in its general drift, but weakened by cavalier treatment of mere facts.

Because Boris was reading Mods and Greats, as the undergraduate course in Greek and Roman literature, history and philosophy is known, he spent four years at Oxford, while Allegra left after the more normal three. After she had finished finals, they went on holiday in Perthshire, in Scotland. On the way back down, Boris insisted they have a picnic at Windscale, as the Sellafield nuclear reprocessing plant used to be known.

Allegra started work in London for the *Evening Standard*. She was on the paper's gossip column, 'Londoner's Diary', but did not enjoy it, and resigned the following April.

The separation during this year was difficult. Boris wrote many letters in which he tried to mend things after unsatisfactory telephone conversations. It is clear that he loves her deeply, and is determined to keep their relationship going. His passion and his fighting spirit are fully engaged. Where a faint heart might have decided things were not working out, Boris presses forward. He is worried whether he will get a first in his final exams, and the prospect of taking a job in the then fashionable field of management consultancy fills him with dread, but they are engaged to be married and that at least he regards as certain. But in a postscript to one letter he warns her to watch out for men and adds that they are all the same.

In March 1987 the great world came to Oxford, when two former Balliol men, Edward Heath and Roy Jenkins, contended for the chancellorship of the university, for which Lord Blake was also a candidate. Boris was entranced by the contest, and by the sight of Heath and Jenkins canvassing in Balliol with the quad full of bodyguards, and correctly predicted that Jenkins would win.

At the end of his Oxford days, Boris knocked on Anthony Kenny's door and asked for extra tuition in Aristotle's ethics before being viva-ed – interviewed – to see whether, despite written papers which were not on their own quite good enough, he could be given a first. 'But alas,' Kenny said, 'my efforts were in vain.'

Allegra remembered: 'He did really want a first. He had nightmares after it. He had one about his viva. The stumbling block in the viva was lyric poetry.'

Jasper Griffin said: 'He just cut it a bit too fine.' Griffin asked the don who had marked Boris's finals papers how he had done. The don replied: 'He got the top 2:1 in his year.' Griffin said of this don: 'I could have spat in his eyes, you can imagine.'

Boris in years to come was to make a speciality of cutting things too fine. A more humble – or humdrum – character would have said to himself, 'I really want a first and I'm quite clever enough to get one as long as I prepare carefully for the exam.' Boris instead said to himself, 'I really want a first and I'm so clever I can wing it.' It was with this enterprising attitude that he entered the world of work.

# 10

# Troubled Times

ON 5 SEPTEMBER 1987 BORIS AND ALLEGRA WERE MARRIED AT St Michael and All Angels, West Felton. It was a grand and elegant occasion. Anna Steiger, the daughter of Rod Steiger and Claire Bloom, sang from *The Marriage of Figaro*. The congregation also heard the world premiere of a piece by Hans Werner Henze called 'Allegra e Boris – Duetto Concertante per Violino e Viola all'Occasione delle loro Faustissime Nozze il 5 Settembre, 1987'.

The reception was held on a perfect summer's day in the garden at Woodhouse. The guests were cosmopolitan, drawn from London, Italy and Oxford. A string quartet played in the drawing-room and the confetti were proper sweetmeats – sugared almonds – as in Italy, instead of the pieces of coloured paper which are flung about at weddings in England. To a guest like myself who was barely involved with the two families, it looked like a stylish and light-hearted Italian film shot on location in the green depths of Shropshire. The bride and groom were both only twenty-three years old.

Boris misquoted P. G. Wodehouse in his speech and was corrected by a man who had arrived in a helicopter, whereupon Boris recovered by saying: 'Good chap. Give the man a coconut.'

During the wedding, Boris did something which Allegra described as 'hilarious and totally exasperating', though many other brides would have used stronger language. As she described it, Boris was not taken by the idea of wearing a ring (after all, Stanley never did). 'Strangely, it fell to Darius to bring the rings up to Shropshire; I think Boris may have forgotten to fetch them from Hatton Garden. Rings were exchanged, but by the time we had lunch he no longer had his. He always insisted he knew where it was, i.e. somewhere in the garden, but he had somehow dropped it and lost it within an hour of receiving it.'

This is not the behaviour of a man who is going to be very solicitous of his wife's feelings. The normal course for an Englishman who disliked wearing a wedding ring would have been to accept it and gradually get used to it, while a few die-hard conservatives might have indicated before the wedding that they were not going to go along with the modern custom of men wearing rings. But Boris accepted his ring only to get rid of it immediately afterwards.

Nor did his bounderish behaviour end there. He also arrived for his own wedding without the right clothes. As Allegra said, after relating the story of the ring: 'What's more, he was wearing John Biffen's trousers at the time [Biffen then being MP for Oswestry] . . . Some weeks later I had to send the mortgagees our wedding certificate, but it was nowhere to be found. Naturally Bozzer showed not the slightest interest. Months later the Biffens were much amused to find the missing document in the pocket of the famous trousers.'

When Lady Biffen was reminded that Boris got married in her husband's trousers, she replied with indignation: 'And in his cufflinks, and the reason he didn't get married in my husband's shoes is that his feet were larger – he would have limped to the altar, which would have been worse than the holes in the soles of his own shoes.'

One reason why Boris delights audiences so much is his

willingness to burst the bounds of good behaviour. He offers a joyful liberation from all the petty inhibitions which weigh so heavily on respectable and conscientious people. As he crashes about like a bull in a china shop, the result is general hilarity. But the joke is often lost on whoever happens to be running the china shop.

All the Johnsons stayed with the Biffens for the wedding, where they made a very poor impression on Lady Biffen. According to her, Boris and his brothers had hired 'a job lot' of morning coats and other wedding clothes in Taunton without trying anything on, and found they had shirts which needed cufflinks to fasten, 'and things that didn't fit'. They therefore had to borrow clothes off their host, John Biffen.

Lord Biffen, who seems to have been less affronted than his wife by the chaotic behaviour of his guests, said in a mild tone: 'Something borrowed, something blue.'

Lady Biffen added that there had been a dinner at the Gowries' house the night before the wedding – Lord Gowrie had served as arts minister from 1983 to 1985 – at which Stanley Johnson 'behaved disgracefully, sticking a sort of cine camera up everyone's nose'. Charlotte Johnson, Boris's mother, was staying with the Gowries.

At the wedding itself, Stanley suddenly stood up and started making a speech, but Lady Biffen stopped him by saying, 'Shut up, Stanley.'

Looking back on her wedding, Allegra said, 'When we got married, that was actually the end of the relationship instead of the beginning.' Boris's hunt for her had been crowned with success, but he was already embarking on another hunt, for success in his career, which would prove almost impossible to combine with any kind of settled married life.

They went on honeymoon in Egypt with no money, bought a flat in Sinclair Road in west London, and Boris started work as a management consultant, at the then very high salary of

£18,000 a year. But he knew immediately that he had made a mistake: 'Try as I might, I could not look at an overhead projection of a growth-profit matrix, and stay conscious.'

Many of us would have struggled on, in a dispirited way, for months or years before conceding defeat, but Boris was decisive enough to cut his losses. In his *Who's Who* entry we read: 'LEK Partnership, one week, 1987.'

According to Stanley, Boris stayed at LEK 'long enough to get the joining fee'.

It was time for Boris to activate the contacts he had made in journalism. At the end of 1986 a select party had driven from London to Shropshire to see in the New Year at Woodhouse: the literary journalist Miriam Gross, her then boyfriend Frank Johnson, and the novelist Edna O'Brien.

O'Brien said they should take a present of some champagne: 'I don't think a bottle, darling. I think half a dozen at least.'

Frank had won a reputation while writing the *Times* sketch as one of the wittiest writers and talkers in England. He was grateful for Boris's company: 'He kept me laughing and engaged the whole weekend. He was a throwback to minor, marginal figures in history I'd read about before the First World War. He had a knowledge of all sorts of things young people by then didn't have to pay attention to. I thought he was too original and had too little command of detail to become a politician. I said to him: "If you want to try journalism, give me a ring after your finals." He did, and I got him in to see Charlie Douglas-Home [then the editor of *The Times*]. That was why he got the job. I then went abroad for *The Times*, first to Paris and then to Bonn, so I wasn't working with Boris.'

Miriam Gross recalled meeting Boris with Allegra when he was at Oxford: 'And I was completely bowled over by Boris. I thought he was exceptionally charming, sophisticated, witty, erudite at that age, and he didn't at all have that slightly bumbling thing which he has now, which is a defence mechanism.'

Perhaps Miriam put Boris at his ease, and made him feel appreciated, which was why with her he did not need his defence mechanism. Miriam immediately became a fan of his work, and thought she could detect traces of it even in pieces by Allegra: 'I was fond of Gaia Mostyn-Owen, so I read Allegra in the *Evening Standard* – it was absolutely brilliant – I just knew having met Boris he must have had a hand in it. I immediately started telling every editor I knew they should employ Boris, and was slightly influential in getting him appointed to *The Times* and the *Daily Telegraph*, where I was at that time Arts Editor. When I was at the *Sunday Telegraph* I used to say how attractive he was – all my male colleagues thought I was mad – but I've been proved right. Everyone I know including Barbara and Conrad Black is completely charmed by Boris.'

That winter *The Times* sent Boris to train for three months on the *Wolverhampton Express & Star*. He lodged with a woman called Brenda. She lived near Bilston and had two other lodgers: a man on the run from his wife and children, and a probation officer who introduced Boris to some of the grittier realities of Wolverhampton, and who reappeared many years later in Boris's novel, *Seventy-Two Virgins*.

Brenda loved doing a cooked breakfast, and quite heavy cooked dishes in the evening. According to Allegra, 'She was particularly delighted that Boris liked her special oven dish of meat, potatoes, cheese and butter. It was quite tasty. Boris could finish it off – Brenda was radiant with pride.'

Allegra and Brenda got on well: 'She liked this combination of ginger wine and whisky – I would drink it with her quite merrily. In the bathroom you would find her discarded mules and wig.'

It was quite a difficult time in the marriage and when Allegra was there, Brenda once turned to Boris and said to him: 'Boris, you've got to treat her like porcelain.' But that was not Boris's way. He was in too much of a hurry, and too full of energy and ambition, to treat his fine and delicate wife with the tenderness she needed.

In a letter to Allegra written from the *Wolverhampton Express & Star* in February 1988, Boris reported that his task for the day was to write the caption for a picture of a man drinking a pint of beer while having his hair cut. But the opening paragraph on his neighbour's screen was: 'When Mrs Jean Perry thought she'd clean out her budgie's cage, she did not reckon with the suction power of her new Hoover.' This, Boris thought, was bound to make the front page.

He also reported that he had been out for a drink the night before with a belligerent social worker called Bruce who drank seven pints of beer incredibly fast and at one point grabbed Boris's lapel and told him not to patronise the Black Country.

Boris added that without Allegra, life was a cold cup of urine. It was an unromantic image, and indicated that he was not enjoying himself. Some of the toughest jobs in journalism are at the very bottom, where you are given the feeble stories nobody else wants to do, and have no scope to write them in the way that might suit your talents.

After Wolverhampton came the task of proving himself on *The Times*. George Brock, who was then Foreign Editor, remembered Boris as 'an immediately striking figure with red braces and albino hair. Inevitably, he was found a bit woolly and shambolic: news editors expect you to be sharp. But he wasn't in the slightest bit difficult, just a bit messy. I think he always thought people at *The Times* took life a bit seriously.'

Boris has written, in the introduction to his volume of collected journalism, *Lend Me Your Ears*, that Brock 'had the misfortune to be my trainer'. Brock was not appreciative of Boris's efforts, many of which resulted from the inglorious activity of rewriting stories supplied by news agencies. According to

Boris: 'It seemed to be one of the rules that you could rewrite agency copy, and claim it as your own, if you made at least one phone call to show that you had "added value" to the story.'

Peter Stothard, who later became editor of *The Times* and was already an influential figure, said: 'I was responsible for the Graduate Trainee Programme. It was quite radical. The idea was to try to attract clever people into journalism instead of merchant banking, by making sure that they didn't have to start on the local paper in Hemel Hempstead.

'Boris was one of the early ones. He was a classicist, which obviously appealed to me, and he came with the strong backing of Peter Utley, whom I had rescued from the *Telegraph*.' T. E. Utley, known as Peter, was blind from childhood, a distinguished Tory thinker, and also very good company. For a long period he was an adornment of the *Daily Telegraph*, and of the King & Keys, the low pub next door to it in Fleet Street, where he drank whisky and held court amid clouds of tobacco smoke in the most democratic manner. That was one of Utley's paradoxes: he had a deep understanding of the need for authority and hierarchy, yet he himself was the least hierarchical of men. He was encouraged to leave the *Telegraph* by Max Hastings, and spent his last years at *The Times*. Utley would try to help any stuttering young man or woman who sought his advice about getting into journalism, and his recommendation of Boris would certainly have carried weight.

The story that led to Boris's sacking from *The Times* came, Allegra says, from their neighbour in Sinclair Road. Stothard remembers things slightly differently: 'The trainees worked in different bits. Boris was in the newsroom and had been given a "new discovery" story. These stories almost always turn out to be wrong, for the discovery is seldom, in fact, new. Boris was given the story because he was the person who might have the best idea of who Edward II was. The news desk could be quite rough and Boris felt under the gun to add to the agency copy. So he concocted a quote to add to the Press Association story, to boost it up a bit.'

The quote was by Colin Lucas, a history don at Balliol who also happened to be his godfather. Lucas would not have been most people's first choice to comment on London in the reign of Edward II, or even their second choice, since his speciality was the French Revolution, which took place in Paris nearly 500 years later. But Boris has never allowed himself to be discouraged by a technicality of that kind, and duly concocted a racy comment for Lucas to make. Boris was unfortunately unable to contact Lucas, to check he was happy for his name to be used in this way.

The story 'by Boris Johnson' duly appeared in *The Times* on 20 May 1988, under the headline 'Edward II's "Rosary" Palace found in London'. One can see the kind of not particularly inspiring material Boris had to work with, as well as the manner in which he used Lucas to perk it up:

Archaeologists working on an urban development site on the South Bank of the Thames have discovered the long-lost palace of King Edward II. They have also found the remains of the large house of Sir John Fastog, thought to be the model for the Shakespearean character Sir John Falstaff.

A large stone corner of the royal palace, built in about 1325, first came to light at the Hay's Wharf site last week, but excavators have tried to keep the discovery quiet because of the danger of attracting treasure hunters . . . The palace was a large moated building, about 80 yards square. Known to historians as the 'Rosary', it was a retreat on the far side of the river where the king could escape the cares of office.

According to Dr Colin Lucas, of Balliol College, Oxford, this is where the king enjoyed a reign of dissolution with his catamite, Piers Gaveston, before he was gruesomely murdered at Berkeley Castle by barons who felt he was too prone to foreign influence.

The story continued for several more paragraphs, ending with a dubious speculation about the 'new light' cast on Sir John Fastog: 'The discovery near the house of riverfront installations suggests that Sir John was quite unlike the rumbustious devil-may-care Shakespearean character.'

The note of parody struck by Boris in this last sentence is worthy of Kingsley Amis. But that was not what caught the eye of readers. At high tables the length and breadth of the kingdom, a roar of laughter went up at Colin Lucas's expense.

Boris had scored a hit, but it was not the hit he had intended. He had managed to sex the story up – a catamite, after all, is a boy kept for homosexual purposes – but had also committed a grotesque historical error. Gaveston was beheaded in 1312, so could hardly have cavorted with Edward II in a palace built in 1325.

As Andrew Gilmour, who had been at Eton and Balliol with Boris, put it: 'Lucas was a laughing stock. Every sub-lecturer from Sheffield wrote in to point out his error.'

Lucas himself failed to see the joke, and wrote a letter of bitter complaint to *The Times*. He naturally took his own reputation and career prospects more seriously than anyone else did. For although he was at this point a relatively obscure history don, who had risen from an assistant lectureship at Sheffield to a fellowship at Balliol and lectureship at Oxford, he soon afterwards became a professor at Chicago University. From there he returned to become Master of Balliol and Vice-Chancellor of Oxford, and a knight as well as a member of the Légion d'Honneur.

Boris said that Lucas's behaviour 'lent a new meaning to the word godfather'. Lucas has declined to talk about this painful episode, but the estimable Brock has not failed us, and it has proved possible to reconstruct a rough outline of what took place. Boris was sunk not by the original story, but by his foolish attempts to deny or make light of it.

According to Brock: 'Colin Lucas complained and someone wrote back to him saying that our reporter stands by the story. Lucas then wrote back to *The Times* and said there was no way on earth Boris could have spoken to him. What got Boris into most trouble was lying about it. He had got the first *Times* person who wrote to Lucas to lie to Lucas.'

Brock's recollection that Lucas was at first rebuffed is supported by the following bizarre story which appeared in *The Times* of 24 May 1988, four days after the first piece, under Boris's name and bearing the sober headline, 'Timber may show date of Edward II's palace':

The discovery of timber supports near the 'Rosary' palace of King Edward II may help to determine the exact date of the building, archaeologists said yesterday. Two walls of a stone building, which is believed to have been the royal residence, were found on an urban development site at Hay's Wharf, south London.

The timber includes stakes and planks, which served as wharfing at two inlets, as well as wooden revetments supporting the palace moat.

The find shows how the Thames has shifted since the Middle Ages. Trading and wharf facilities at the time were much greater than had been suspected. The age of the timbers will be accurately determined using the dating technique of dendrochronology.

The only documentary evidence of the Rosary dates it to 1325, two years before Edward II was killed at Berkeley Castle. He would have had little time to use it as a retreat, as has been described.

Dr Colin Lucas, of Balliol College, Oxford, said:

'Edward II is reputed to have led a life of wine and song with his catamite Piers Gaveston. But if 1325 is correct, that could hardly have taken place in this building since Gaveston was executed in 1312.'

One can well see why Lucas might have regarded this contorted quote as inadequate recompense for making him a laughing stock.

Boris was summoned to appear before Charlie Wilson, the editor of *The Times*. Even at this late stage, he could almost certainly have saved himself if he had shown a fitting sense of how badly he had behaved. But according to Frank Johnson the following dialogue took place:

Wilson: 'All the quotes are made up.'

Boris: 'But so are most of the quotes in your paper.'

As Frank later remarked, 'This was perfectly true, but it was the wrong reply.'

John Bryant, who was then number three on *The Times*, remembers an 'inquest' on Boris in which Wilson said, 'You can't make up quotes on *The Times*,' to which Bryant replied, 'You can't make up quotes on any paper.'

Wilson himself cannot remember exactly what was said to him – Boris was, after all, an insignificant figure at this time. But Wilson does remember the general drift of his errant trainee's remarks: 'At the time Boris didn't seem to take making up quotes as a very serious matter. I thought it was a heinous crime. However, during my time as editor we had to dispose of only two trainee graduates and the other one was Toby Young, so you could argue that being fired by Charles Wilson was a guarantee of career success.'

The plain fact was that these Oxford men had no idea how to behave. This could have been the end of Boris as a journalist. The editor of *The Times* had found him wanting. Part of the trouble was that Boris also found the editor of *The Times* wanting: he was later to describe Wilson as 'a man straight from a Britflick gangster movie'. But Wilson was not the first or the last person who decided that Boris simply would not do. The general verdict of journalists at *The Times* on Boris was summed up by Brock: 'It was not clear he was going to be a success.'

# 11

## Our Man in Brussels

BORIS THREW HIMSELF INTO THE SEARCH FOR A NEW job. Frank Johnson remembered: 'Boris phoned me up one day and said he was in a bit of a spot – it could be a P45 job. I said don't be so ridiculous, Boris.' But when Frank realised how grave the situation was, he promised to see if there was an opening for Boris at the *Daily Telegraph*.

Frank summed up his contribution: 'I have both given this man his start in life, and saved him, but history will not remember it.'

The greatest credit for giving Boris his second chance in journalism should actually go to Max Hastings, the then editor of the *Daily Telegraph*. Hastings was unimpressed by Boris's brilliant career at Eton and Oxford, which he knew was 'often the precursor of a lifetime of obscurity', but agreed to take him on as a leader-writer. There was a cavalier dash to Hastings, seen when he scooped every other correspondent in the Falklands war by being the first man into Port Stanley. He saw the point of Boris, a man as energetic and competitive as himself, and less than a year later he made him the *Telegraph*'s man in Brussels.

Allegra had meanwhile abandoned journalism and enrolled at law college. In the spring of 1989 Boris started the job where he was to make his name. His stories about the idiocies of the European Union were received with rapture by an ever-growing circle of fans, and he became the only Brussels correspondent of whom ordinary mortals have heard. His work was so marvellously enjoyable because he debunked an institution which almost everyone else reporting from Brussels was still treating with reverence.

Boris infuriated many of his colleagues. According to Rory Watson, an experienced and scrupulous correspondent who was at that time working for the *European*: 'He made stories up. The classic one was the Berlaymont. It was when the Commission decided to leave the Berlaymont building because it was leaking asbestos. Boris's story was that the Berlaymont was going to be blown up.'

Charles Garside, the editor of the *European*, was so excited by this news that he rang Watson and told him: 'It's a pity you missed that great story about the Berlaymont. Find out which company is going to get the contract to blow it up.'

The *European* wanted to arrange for one of its readers to push the plunger on the detonator. The problem for Watson was that there was actually no plan to blow up the Berlaymont. An explosion seems to have appealed to Boris as being the cheapest, quickest and most dramatic way to get rid of a building, or at least to get his story into the *Daily Telegraph*. But dynamite is not an approved method for dealing with asbestos and the structure of the Berlaymont is standing to this day, with the asbestos-ridden cladding replaced by what looks like a completely new building.

David Usborne, the *Independent*'s Brussels correspondent, said of Boris: 'He was fundamentally intellectually dishonest, in my view. He was serving his masters in a very skilful way but I never felt he believed a word.'

Sarah Helm, who observed Boris while working as the *Independent*'s diplomatic correspondent, agreed with this: 'I

remember developing an instinctive feel that Boris was a complete charlatan. He was a highly intelligent man, much cleverer
than I was, he could see all these nuances and subtleties, but he
wasn't conveying them in his writing. It was a cheap thrill – a
stunt, and quite a dangerous stunt really.'

But Usborne, who had been in Brussels since 1984, recognised that the press corps was ripe for shaking: 'Boris came in to
a Brussels that was populated by correspondents who had either
been there a very long time – probably too long – or by people –
I would include myself in this – who were probably a little bit
guilty of becoming part of the institution they were reporting
on, and were inclined to defend it.'

Boris and Usborne became 'intense and friendly competitors'
for stories: 'Boris was always very flattering, telling me I was
number one, and like an idiot I probably believed him. To begin
with we were playing the same game, to see who could get the
best scoops and the best secret documents. But I began to realise
over time he was ploughing his own furrow, and a very different
furrow from me. Boris understood immediately what the
*Telegraph* wanted to hear and he delivered in spades. Once he got
his confidence up he started firing every torpedo he could at the
Commission. He was writing things without really believing in
his heart what he was writing. He would take something that
might make a few paragraphs and turn it into an atomic bomb.
He really began to eclipse all of us. He was having fun. He didn't
have to worry about all that serious stuff. He could just cherry
pick. I don't really think he was pursuing a political agenda about
Europe – I think he was pursuing his own future. I don't think
he was half as antagonistic to Delors as you would think.'

Jacques Delors, the President of the European Commission,
was driving forward the process of European integration and tri-
umphing over the British. A bitter power struggle was in
progress and Boris admired the ruthlessness with which Delors
and his henchman, Pascal Lamy, were waging it: 'With his

virtually shaven head and parade-ground manner, Lamy runs the upper echelons of the Commission like a Saharan camp of the French Foreign Legion.' British officials were, Boris lamented, 'limp-wristed' and 'impotent' by comparison: 'With their shy grins and corrugated-soled shoes, they are no match for the intellectual brutality of Lamy and his stooges.'

Like a brilliant caricaturist, who knows exactly what parts of his subject to exaggerate, Boris knew how to ridicule the European Union because he saw so clearly what was going on. He may have been a wrecker, but he was a highly intelligent wrecker. He revelled in the chaos he caused.

When asked if Boris often 'went the extra mile' in pursuit of a good story, Usborne replied: 'He often went the extra five hundred miles I think just for the pleasure of watching the rest of his colleagues scurry the next morning to catch up.'

Boris has confirmed that this could be a pleasure. He has related, in the introduction to his book of collected journalism, how 'the great George Brock', who had been so unimpressed by Boris's work at *The Times*, arrived in Brussels as the correspondent for that paper: 'One of my keenest pleasures was to hunt for scoops, exclusive stories that might cause *The Times* to ring Brock up, long after he was tucked up in bed. "Stand by your phone, George," I would say, tapping my nose. I like to think that Mr and Mrs Brock had several interrupted nights on my account; and at least once, annoyingly, I was rung by the *Telegraph* and asked to chase up one of his.' The playful tone and the concession in the last line save this from being nasty, but Boris has never been averse to getting even with those who disparage him.

Michael Binyon, Brock's predecessor as the *Times* man in Brussels, said: 'What he realised was that there was a cartel of Brussels correspondents, and if you broke the cartel you would stand out. He wrote some grotesquely exaggerated stories. He would get a story and then he would speculate on it. This drove everyone berserk, because they all had to follow it and it all turned out to be a load of tosh, but it didn't matter. He was never malicious. There was one about how Brussels was going to build the highest tower on earth.'

Boris had a highly personal style, symbolic of his determination to plough his own furrow. Binyon remembered Boris always arriving late for the daily press conference at noon, a fixed point around which the journalists' day revolved. Boris would shamble in at about 12.10 looking as if he had been pulled though a haystack, and a French journalist once asked Binyon: '*Qui est ce monstre?*'

Some of Boris's competitors were crippled by an excessive scrupulousness, which prevented them from cutting through the monstrous quantities of mostly very dull material with which they were confronted. Meanwhile Boris fell with joy on stories about changes in the rules governing crisps and sausages, which could so easily symbolise the threat posed by Brussels to the British way of life. Allegra said, 'He knew he could get a front page with a sausage.'

Boris could not have shone in Brussels without a big story to cover, and this he got. Charles Grant, *The Economist*'s correspondent, arrived in Brussels at the same time as Boris, in April 1989, 'just when the subject was getting interesting'. Jacques Delors, the President of the Commission, that month published his report on economic and monetary union, and in June, at the Madrid summit, Margaret Thatcher tried and failed to stop progress towards the single currency. The fight had begun which would lead to Thatcher's downfall. Brussels had become a British news story.

For a man with an anarchist streak, it was a marvellous opportunity to do some vandalism in a good cause. Boris has often fallen back on a favoured image, of throwing rocks over a garden wall, to describe his activities in Brussels. As he put it on *Desert Island Discs* in October 2005:

I saw the whole thing change. It was a wonderful time to
be there. The Berlin Wall fell and the French and Germans
had to decide how they were going to respond to this
event, and what was Europe going to become, and there
was this fantastic pressure to create a single polity, to create
an answer to the historic German problem, and this
produced the most fantastic strains in the Conservative
Party, so everything I wrote from Brussels, I found was sort
of chucking these rocks over the garden wall and I listened
to this amazing crash from the greenhouse next door over
in England as everything I wrote from Brussels was having
this amazing, explosive effect on the Tory party, and it really
gave me this I suppose rather weird sense of power.

Thatcher fell as a direct result of the Rome summit in
October 1990, at which she was ambushed by the Italians, who
sprang the date of 1999 on her for the launch of the euro.

Her message on 30 October 1990, when she reported to the
House of Commons on the Rome summit, was: 'No, no, no.'
On 1 November, Sir Geoffrey Howe resigned the post of
Deputy Prime Minister, in protest at Thatcher's European policy,
and on 22 November she herself was forced to resign. Like many
Tories, Boris felt this as a deep personal blow. He has written
that his future wife, Marina Wheeler, says 'she came upon me,
stumbling down a street in Brussels, tears in my eyes, and claiming that it was as if someone had shot Nanny'.

Boris did not invent euroscepticism, but he became one of its
most famous exponents. According to Grant, who was strongly
pro-European, 'For his first year or two, Boris wasn't very sceptical at all – he was a reporter. He does work incredibly hard. He
hasn't got a swottish image, but the truth is that he's always put
his career first. It's probably true that very successful journalists
have to do that. His supreme point is to entertain so he doesn't
worry too much if his facts are wrong. He'd always put a good

joke above the facts. I do remember as Boris became more sceptical, thinking it was an act, because he did it to make his name in the *Telegraph*. He wasn't particularly happy when I said that.'

But Boris remained on friendly terms with many people who found his growing euroscepticism abhorrent. This puzzles Grant: 'The interesting thing is why pro-Europeans like Boris. Why? I don't know, except he doesn't take himself seriously. I suppose he's not an extreme eurosceptic. Some of the more visceral eurosceptics are quitters.'

There is something about euroscepticism which can turn sensible men into cranks. They decide, quite reasonably, that the European Union is a mortal threat to our ancient liberties, including our form of government, and adopt a tone of intense hostility towards Brussels which starts to make them seem narrow and paranoid. On finding themselves ignored or dismissed by the pro-Europeans, the anti-Europeans become ever more vehement and ever more suspicious, until in the end they can only preach to the converted.

Boris never started on that downward path. He delighted in showing up the absurdities of Brussels, but he did it in a humorous rather than a bitter tone. And he began to make a European reputation. When European Foreign Ministers held an informal meeting at Guimaraes, in Portugal, on the first Saturday in May 1992, the Maastricht Treaty had recently been signed, but had yet to be ratified. Grant said: 'I remember Boris running around very excited at Guimaraes.'

Boris has written: 'I remember going to a payphone at teatime that Saturday, standing in the dusty square and watching the dogs lying in the sun, and ringing Frank Taylor, the Foreign Editor of the *Sunday Telegraph*, to find out what had happened to my story . . . "We've made it the splash," he said with his beardy chuckle, "and I've called it 'Delors Plan to Rule Europe'."'

And as Grant has written in his biography of Delors: 'The next day Britain's *Sunday Telegraph* carried an article which may

have changed the course of European history ... Boris
Johnson ... reported that Delors wanted to scrap the rotation of
the EU presidency and to centralise power in Brussels. The
member states would lose their remaining veto rights ...
Meanwhile Denmark was in the thick of a keenly fought referendum campaign on the Maastricht treaty. The *Sunday Telegraph*
article, widely reprinted in Denmark's newspapers, had a huge
impact. The "Nej" campaign, which had argued that the new
treaty would centralise power in Brussels and deprive small states
of their rights, claimed vindication. Before the article opinion
polls had suggested a narrow vote in favour of the Maastricht
treaty on 2 June; afterward they pointed to a narrow vote
against.'

Boris is naturally happy to accept Grant's verdict that his article helped sway the Danes: 'My boast, and I make it in the
confidence that no one gives a monkey's, is that I probably did
contribute to the Danish rejection of Maastricht.' Twenty-four
years later, Boris was to contribute rather more decisively to the
British rejection of the EU.

Thatcher formed a very high opinion of Boris, telling his old
headmaster, Sir Eric Anderson: 'He's my favourite journalist.'
But Douglas Hurd was greatly irritated as Foreign Secretary by
Boris's coverage. According to Charles Moore, who was then the
Deputy Editor of the *Telegraph*, 'Douglas Hurd made a serious
attempt to get Boris sacked while in Brussels. Max was very def-
erential to Hurd, who kept on at Max about how awful Boris
was. Max was in the end OK, but he did listen to Hurd a bit.
Boris was always a bit vulnerable because his stories weren't
always wholly accurate. I went to see Boris in Brussels when I
was Max's deputy. I told him about the Douglas Hurd risk, and
that I was completely on his, Boris's, side, but I noticed how
exceptionally worried Boris was at that point.'

Hurd denied to me that he ever tried to get Boris sacked: 'I
wouldn't have dreamed of it.' Nor does it sound quite like Hurd's

style. He said he and Boris 'were on cosy terms given the basically mischievous nature of his activities'.

John Kerr, then the UK Permanent Representative in Brussels
and, later, as Lord Kerr, the head of the Foreign Office, respected
Boris: 'I found him challenging in briefings. Disconcertingly, he
made few notes. Even my usual ploy, when on thin ice, of
attempting to distract with a battery of facts and numbers, some
of doubtful relevance, rarely worked with Boris. He had the
knack of spotting what I wasn't saying, and his subsequent product often drew heavily on intuition. Some of his flyers were way
off-beam, sometimes irritatingly so, but some were spot-on,
even more annoyingly.'

Boris's competitive instinct was not sated, as some people's
might have been, by the ceaseless struggle to get stories into
the *Telegraph*, and better stories than his rivals were getting into
their papers. He was also becoming increasingly determined to
go into politics himself: he and Charles Grant would discuss
their ambition to become MEPs, Boris as a Tory and Grant for
Labour. Meanwhile Boris took on a challenge of a quite different sort against Binyon of *The Times*. As Binyon recalled:
'We used to enjoy going down to Strasbourg – a weekend
away from Brussels – we all had cubby-hole desks next to each
other, and would be trying to hear what the other fellow was
saying.'

Boris asked where 'the true, the blushful Hippocrene' comes
from, to which Binyon replied: 'That's Keats. "Ode to a
Nightingale".'

Boris said: 'No, it's not. It's "Ode on a Grecian Urn".' He
went away, looked it up and having discovered that Binyon was
right, came back and said: 'OK, but I bet you can't recite it.'

A general challenge then arose between Binyon and Boris to
see who could recite all the great poems ever written in English.
Binyon made an alarming discovery about his opponent: 'Boris
to my horror had a considerable knowledge of long poems. He

could recite reams of Milton. I said: "That's absolutely impossible. We have to have short poems."' So they drew up a list of about 130 poems which they would learn. The challenge was to be held at the Dublin summit. A week before the summit, Binyon said to Boris: 'I say, Boris old chap, how are you getting on?'

It emerged that neither of them was prepared, so they postponed the contest until the Rome summit. They decided that a public challenge would be humiliating if it went wrong, so they started with a private challenge, held in a restaurant with vaulted ceilings and marble floors.

Binyon said: 'All right, Boris. Sonnet 18.'

Boris responded: 'Shall I compare thee to a summer's day?'

When the sweet trolley came, Binyon waved it away with the words: 'Not now, he's in the middle of Gray's "Elegy".'

Binyon remembers that Boris did not care for many of the modern poems and would say, 'Awful tosh, that stuff.' But the private challenge had gone well enough for them to decide to hold a public challenge once they were back in Brussels.

And so one night they went to Kitty O'Shea's, the Irish pub near the Commission, with eight or nine other correspondents, and began the challenge. Binyon was getting 'awfully tied up' in the middle of 'The Love Song of J. Alfred Prufrock' when another correspondent burst in and announced: 'Shevardnadze's resigned and we've all got to go and write reaction stories.'

And that, for some reason, was the end of the great poetry challenge. But when Boris met Binyon he would greet him in verse: 'Ah, Binyon. They told me, Heraclitus, they told me you were dead / They brought me bitter news to hear and bitter tears to shed.'

# Twelve Days a Bachelor

AS BORIS'S CAREER TOOK OFF, HIS MARRIAGE COLLAPSED. Allegra joined Boris in Brussels in the summer of 1989, after her law exams. She disliked the district in which he had found a place for them to live: 'I never understood what had drawn him to the flat in Woluwe St Pierre except that the ground floor was taken by a dentist called Goris. It was quite a Flemish suburb, and on the whole it wasn't very friendly. The newspaper shop was unfriendly after two years, and if you left the rubbish out on the wrong day you got anonymous notes.'

Nor could she detect any enthusiasm in her husband for the glories of Flemish culture, including the paintings and the food: 'It didn't work with him. His favourite food was sausages. It's true! I'm sure he'd still say so now.'

Boris recently declared, in a short interview about food: 'My favourite thing is bangers, mash and mustard, with red wine.'

When they went on a skiing holiday, and Allegra was feeling low, Boris said to her: 'What you need is a bit of buckismus.' She found that comment 'absurd and funny and totally alienating'. Things were past the stage when a bit of bucking-up would mend them.

Allegra witnessed the beginnings of Boris's fame: 'He was

included in some more obscure version of *Who's Who*, and under hobbies he put scuba diving, which was my hobby, which he was rather bad at – I did laugh. He uses up his oxygen too fast. I don't think he ever repeated it [scuba diving], so it was just a bit of a fib, but kind of vaguely revealing.' On another occasion, Boris returned from an EU summit and said with satisfaction: 'I was recognised by John Major.'

She remembers feeling 'a bit alienated' from the British journalists in Brussels: 'They were an interesting lot, the British press corps, but all they could do was this competitive stuff.' Boris himself specialised in the competitive stuff, which was not how Allegra, with her gift of sympathetic appreciation, could bear to live.

To Charles Grant, Boris and Allegra at first seemed fine: 'I used to go to their rather nice flat by a church. They gave nice parties and I rather liked Allegra. She was gorgeous to look at.'

In a letter written from the Holiday Inn, Strasbourg, Boris told Allegra that he had spent all day in the bowels of the Parliament building, waiting for any one of the MEPs to say or do something remotely unexpected. He said the place felt like a huge new airport, built by a third world government in the middle of a jungle, and totally pointless.

Boris went on to say how vital it was to him that Allegra had come and joined him in Brussels, though he feared she did not really respond to that sort of rhetoric, which was why he had not used it much.

She might have responded better if she had not come second to his work. Boris is a humane man, in the sense that he feels things deeply, and this emotional warmth has always drawn people to him, and has saved his jokes from ringing hollow. People sense that there is a suffering man behind the comic act.

But he could also be quite staggeringly inconsiderate. Intent on doing exactly what he wanted to do, or what he must do to maximise his chances of getting a piece in the next day's *Telegraph*, he accepted no obligation even to tell his wife where he had gone. One of his many gifts as a journalist is a willingness to board an aeroplane at the drop of a hat: he is excellent at rushing towards the sound of the gunfire, which in those days came with increasing frequency from the Balkans. As Yugoslavia disintegrated, Boris would fly in with whichever Brussels panjandrum was trying in vain to sort things out. Allegra often didn't know where he was: 'The really bad times were when he didn't tell me he was going to be away. There were two times when I had to ring the foreign desk to find out where he was. He got ribbed really badly. Then he was cross with me for having put him in that position. I used to get the paper – yesterday's news – and there's his by-line in fucking Zagreb. You get past caring and you start drinking malt whisky. But you know, I think he rather regrets all that stuff now. Though he finds it very difficult to play the part of a sensitive husband – it just doesn't come easily. He hasn't got a blueprint for that one.'

Allegra also said: 'I used to get a short haircut at the Flemish barber's because I wasn't very happy. I was very apprehensive that the Johnson family history would repeat itself. I adored his mother Charlotte but I was anxious to avoid the kind of experiences she had when she was married to Stanley.' When life in Brussels with Stanley had got too much, Charlotte checked herself into a clinic. Allegra felt she too was heading for a breakdown if she stayed with Boris. No note of recrimination entered her voice: that was just how things were. She could not take this kind of life: 'Boris didn't do much for my peace of mind. Bearing in mind that my own family was completely disintegrating at the time, and I was cut off in Brussels, I think I must have been vulnerable. But what the hell – it's all in the past.'

In February 1990 she left. This was a disaster which Boris could not conceal. As Charles Grant said: 'When Allegra left Boris, Boris was distraught. I do remember having a heart-to-heart with him at the Dublin summit in April 1990. Edmund Fawcett [one of his mother's brothers who worked at *The Economist*] and I and Boris had dinner together and Boris let it all hang out. He desperately wanted Allegra. That was probably the only time when the comic mask dropped. He was very, very unhappy.'

Allegra was very, very unhappy too. A male acquaintance got a lift back to London with her at about this time: 'She was driving and she poured out her heart to me. She was obviously fantastically affected by the break-up. She was in a terrible state. She said she'd been shocked by some of his behaviour. You thought you knew someone so well and then you found out things about them.'

Boris wanted to make Allegra happy, and to this day he says he feels 'guilty' about her, but he could not make the sacrifices of his own inclinations which would have been required. Allegra complained to people at the time that he never did the shopping or the washing-up, but really he did not attend enough to her at all. There was a kind of selfish impatience about him. He was twenty-five years old and it was natural for him to please himself.

Some people in Brussels thought Allegra was histrionic and over the top, but she found most of them pretty frightful too. She would not enter into the rivalries of his career, nor was she careerist when it came to her own work, nor could she sit quietly at home waiting for him to return at some unknown hour from his latest triumphs. At the end, he asked her something about politics, and she said, 'I can't believe it. I'm not going to talk about that. I'm leaving you.'

Boris and Allegra started divorce proceedings which reached the *decree nisi* stage, but then they had a reconciliation. In September 1990, Allegra began her Law Society finals course in London and commuted to Brussels every weekend. In September 1991, she enrolled at the Université Libre de Bruxelles for a Masters in EU law, as recommended to her by Boris's old childhood friend Marina Wheeler, who had taken the same course the previous year. According to Allegra, 'Marina lived in crappy digs and I'd have her round to dinner.'

Boris had never entirely lost touch with Marina, and on one occasion he invited her to some festivities at Eton. There was a bit of tittering from his friends, who asked him if she was his girl-friend: a question that made Marina indignant.

Marina is insistent that although Boris had been keen on her between the ages of nine and eleven when they were at school together in Brussels, she was not keen on him and did not become romantically involved with him until it was all over between him and Allegra. According to Marina, Boris was a bit frightened of not having anyone around and would quickly get lonely. Allegra had taken the furniture with her and Marina was there as a friend, helping him to pick up the pieces. They would go and do things together, and slowly their friendship became more romantic.

By the time Allegra made her last attempt to save the marriage, Boris was having none of it. He had reverted to the style of life, the chase, which came most easily to him. Marina resisted, but that only intensified his pursuit. She remembers crying with frustration that he would not go away. One of her friends said: 'Boris chased her mercilessly in Brussels. I do remember seeing her in Brussels and her saying this guy had absolutely targeted her and was going for her.'

Marina is the daughter of Charles Wheeler and his wife, Dip Singh, who is of Sikh descent. Boris's Tory politics were abhor-rent to Marina, a left-wing lawyer. She went to Bedales, a rather bohemian private school, read law at Cambridge, and had already been called to the Bar in London. She was tough, intelligent, level-headed and nice, and whatever else she did she was going to pursue her own career in the law.

But she fell madly in love with Boris. Friends who went to see her in Brussels found she cancelled meetings with them so she could see Boris.

When she introduced Boris to her friends in London, they were appalled. The first meeting took place at the birthday party of a lawyer who had known her since Cambridge, Philippe Sands, who has since become a Professor of International Law and a well-known critic of the legality of the Iraq war.

Sands said: 'The first time we met Boris was at my thirtieth birthday party in London. Marina turned up with Boris – the first time in front of her friends – and at the moment he made his grand entry there was no one who wished she was Marina. We were all totally appalled a) by the physical appearance – large and white. He was fucking ugly. I think he's become more attractive since – and b) when he actually opened his mouth. In October 1990, a month before Thatcher went, in comes our dearest, darlingest, teeniest Marina with a Tory – it was a ghastly moment. The idea of Marina turning up with a Tory was painful, hilarious and devastating all at the same time. This guy turned up and defended Margaret Thatcher. We were revelling in her misery. But I have to say that 98 per cent of people were won over.' Boris has always been brilliant at winning the support of lefties, including the lefty who became his second wife.

Yet Boris and Allegra continued to attend the odd event together. I happened to see them on the weekend of 9/10 November 1991, for the wedding of their Oxford friends, Andrew Gilmour and Emma Williams, at Lichfield Cathedral. Before the wedding, Boris had to go from Brussels to Rome for the *Telegraph*. The idea was that Allegra would go too, as her grandmother was dying in Rome, and she went with her suit-case to meet Boris at his office. Boris – who was finishing an article before he set off – told her it would cost £1,000 for her to fly to Rome and then to England for the Gilmour wedding, and then back to Brussels. Allegra took her suitcase home, went to watch a football match on the television with some British students and decided, as she put it, 'to change friends'. The end was now near, but she still appeared with her husband at the Gilmour party, which included a dance on the Saturday night.

A group of us, including Boris and Allegra, stayed the weekend with Nick and Madeleine Budgen on their farm at Rugeley. On the Sunday, Nick Budgen, who had succeeded Enoch Powell as the MP for Wolverhampton South-West, took Boris and myself to the Remembrance Day parade in Wolverhampton. A huge variety of people joined in the parade, including a Sikh mayor and a contingent of firemen in silver helmets: middle England did not seem to be disintegrating. Afterwards we went to a reception where Boris asked Budgen what he thought of John Major, who was at that time Prime Minister and the leader of Budgen's party. Budgen said Major would make a highly competent head of the social security office in Wolverhampton.

In about January 1992, however, Boris and Allegra's marriage finally collapsed. In October that year, I spent a couple of weeks in Brussels with Sally Malcolm-Smith, my future wife, who was working for the *European*. We stayed in the flat above the *European* offices, and one night had dinner with Boris and Marina. They picked us up in a car which had something badly wrong with the door on the passenger side – a chronic problem, it seemed, which Boris had not got round to fixing – and we went to a restaurant in one of the arcades in the middle of Brussels, where we ate Belgian delicacies with names such as Waterzooi.

There was a certain symmetry about the evening, for while Boris and I are Tories of some description, Marina and Sally are natural Labour Party supporters. Marina asked Sally how she could possibly marry such a right-wing man as myself. Sally explained that I wasn't homophobic or racist, so the gap was not as huge as it might seem. Marina was worried that the political gap between her and Boris *was* huge, but she was also crazy about him.

It was at about this time, October 1992, that Marina got pregnant by Boris. Allegra agreed to an accelerated divorce, but time was short. Paul Hill, foreign desk manager at the *Daily Telegraph*, said Boris 'got in a bit of a tizz' when getting married to Marina as he 'hadn't quite divorced his old wife yet'. Boris needed a copy of his birth certificate and Hill 'had to run over and get one'. Almost at the last moment a DHL delivery van came up a drive in Umbria to deliver a document for Allegra to sign. The divorce was straightforward and Allegra was a litigant-in-person. One of the questions she had to answer was: 'On what date do you think the adultery began?' Allegra answered: '1 April.' As she afterwards said, 'It was a grim business with one feeble joke.'

Boris and Allegra still get on well, on the rare occasions when their paths cross, but it is clear that they were not cut out to be man and wife. For him, the role of husband was fulfilled by going out and working immensely hard at getting on in the world, which happened to be what he wanted to do anyhow. But for her, his self-preoccupation was disappointing. She finished her legal studies but did not pursue a career in law. She instead became an artist, and taught a weekly art class at the Minhaj-ul-Quran mosque in Forest Gate, east London. After becoming Mayor of London, Boris held a question and answer session at the mosque during which he said he looked forward to the day when being a Muslim was no more remarkable than being a red-head. His audience was more impressed that his great-grandfather, Ali Kemal, was a hafiz, someone who knows the Koran by heart, than by Boris being mayor. In 2009 Allegra married a 23-year-old Pakistani Muslim, without herself converting to Islam.

Boris was a bachelor for twelve days. His divorce came through on 26 April 1993 and on 8 May he married Marina at Horsham town hall in Sussex, near her parents' home. Marina was by now extremely pregnant and there was some doubt whether the Belgians would allow her to travel, but she told her gynaecologist: 'There's a wedding I want to go to in England.' The wedding was small, consisting of close family, including Marina's aunt from

India, and five or six friends each. Marina had never envisaged her father walking her down the aisle. They had a splendid honeymoon in East Grinstead, where they stayed for one night at an absurdly over-decorated hotel.

Their first child, Lara Lettice, was born a month later, on 12 June, and at the end of that month Boris wrote a piece in the *Spectator* headed 'Congratulations! It's a Belgian'. The difficulty was that although Marina and Boris were both British citizens, they were also both born abroad, and this meant, under the terms of Willie Whitelaw's 1981 British Nationality Act, that they could not transmit their nationality to any of their own children who were also born abroad.

The purpose of the Act was to prevent British citizens living in the Caribbean or the Indian sub-continent from transmitting their nationality to their descendants, who might then arrive in 'tidal waves' in the United Kingdom.

Boris addressed a humorous yet heartfelt plea to the then Home Secretary, Michael Howard, not to let Lara become a Belgian by default: 'Do you wish to see her claimed by a nation which refused to sell us ammunition in the Gulf war? Shall she scamper, her face gleaming with chips and mayonnaise, as thousands of Bruxellois did the other day, to watch the National Day firework display, her heart beating at the sight of the black-red-yellow flags?' Five years later they managed to have Lara registered as a British citizen.

Sally and I met Boris and Marina quite soon after at a dinner in London and a memorable argument broke out, during which it emerged that Boris thought North Korea was South Korea, and vice versa.

When Boris left Brussels in 1994, James Landale, who was working for *The Times* but has since joined BBC television, composed some verses in his honour. They were closely modelled on 'Matilda', by Hilaire Belloc, with the *Telegraph*'s foreign desk taking the place of Matilda's aunt, and they began:

Boris told such dreadful lies
It made one gasp and stretch one's eyes.
His desk, which from its earliest youth
Had kept a strict regard for truth,
Attempted to believe each scoop
Until they landed in the soup.

In Belloc's story, Matilda tells a lie – that her house is burning down – with the result that nobody believes her when her house really is on fire, and she is burned to death. In Landale's version, Boris tells a lie – that Britain is to leave the European Community – and all the other correspondents have to follow it without any time to check the facts, and are forced to retract when John Major and Douglas Hurd deny the story. Boris then tells a second, even more implausible story, which the correspondents refuse to believe:

For every time he said 'Delors' the Messiah',
We only answered: 'Nah, it's a flyer.'

In journalism, a 'flyer' is an eye-catching story based on guesswork rather than fact. To round off his verses, Landale wrote:

The moral is, it is indeed,
It might be wrong but it's a damn fine read.

The details of what Boris wrote might often be wrong, but his general understanding of what was happening was right. He saw that Brussels was intent on gaining much greater power over the member states, and he dramatised this process more entertainingly than any of his rivals. Boris had begun to show his extraordinary ability to reach the widest possible audience.

# 13

# The Fall of Darius Guppy

WHILE BORIS'S CAREER WAS STILL IN ITS INFANCY, IT was nearly ruined by the sympathy he showed for one of his friends. No scandal, or alleged scandal, has pursued Boris for longer than the bizarre case of his tape-recorded conversation with his Eton and Oxford chum Darius Guppy. After leaving university and spending a brief period as a bond dealer, Guppy had embarked on a criminal career. In March 1990 he arranged to have himself and his business partner tied up in a hotel room in New York, and to make it look as if they had been robbed of precious stones worth £1.8 million, a sum they successfully claimed from Lloyd's of London.

In the summer of 1990 Guppy became annoyed by the inquiries of Stuart Collier, a journalist on the *News of the World*, and decided to arrange for him to be beaten up and frightened off. Guppy rang Boris in Brussels and asked him to supply Collier's private address and telephone number. This twenty-one-minute conversation was bugged by Peter Risdon, who had been paid £10,000 to tie Guppy up in New York, but had now decided to betray him.

As on a number of other occasions, Boris would have got into fewer difficulties if he had managed to give a straight answer. If he had kept his wits about him, he would have said something like: 'For heaven's sake, Darry, you know I can't do that. Just forget about this wretched journalist.'

But which of us can claim never to have had a telephone conversation which would look bad in print? Boris allowed his friend to talk, and can be heard prevaricating. He is plainly reluctant to provide the number, but also to say that he will not provide the number. Guppy has rung him before, and Boris has undertaken to get Collier's details from one or another of his contacts at News International, publishers of *The Times* as well as the *News of the World*. But Boris has not yet done so and is worried about the danger of discovery.

Guppy tries, by expounding the campaigns of Napoleon, to show there is no risk of being found out. Boris breaks in to ask how badly Collier is to be hurt, after which the following exchanges occur:

GUPPY: 'Not badly at all.'

BORIS: 'I really, I want to know . . .'

GUPPY: 'I guarantee you he will not be seriously hurt.'

BORIS: 'How badly will he be . . .'

GUPPY: 'He will not have a broken limb or broken arm. He will not be put into intensive care or anything like that. He will probably get a couple of black eyes and a . . . a cracked rib or something like that.'

BORIS: 'Cracked rib?'

GUPPY: 'Nothing which you didn't suffer at rugby, OK?'

The conversation continued with Boris saying, in the manner of one trying to wind up the proceedings, 'OK, Darry, I said I'll do it and I'll do it.'

The two friends then turn to discussing the relative merits of Second World War generals, with Boris reckoning Guderian was the best, while his friend's top three are Rommel, Patton and

Alexander, after which Guppy makes some concluding observations about Napoleon.

In 1993 Guppy was convicted of fraud and sentenced to five years' imprisonment. Immediately after he was convicted, Boris wrote a short piece about him in the *Daily Telegraph*: 'He lives by an Homeric code of honour, loyalty and revenge.' Boris did not entirely spare his old friend. He told the horrible story of how Guppy pursued a vendetta against his landlord in Oxford: 'On one occasion, after the landlord had hung up weeping from a midnight call, he picked up the phone the following morning to discover Darius still on the line.' But he also said that 'the joy of knowing Darius is the humorous self-deprecation beneath the idiotic flamboyance', and he praised his friend's 'ascetic, contemplative intelligence'.

Only when Guppy was already in jail did the tape get sent to Boris's editor at the *Telegraph*, Max Hastings, with a letter from a media enquirer asking him what he was going to do about it.

The tape could have done Boris very serious harm. Hastings consulted Jeremy Deedes, the paper's Editorial Director, and relates in his memoir, *Editor*, what happened next: 'Jeremy and I thought that it was impossible for the *Telegraph* simply to ignore an issue touching on the personal integrity of one of the staff. We flew our correspondent to London for a serious discussion. Boris easily persuaded us that he had never taken any action in pursuit of Guppy's proposal, nor had he intended to. We sent him back to Brussels bearing only a strongly worded note from me, suggesting that he would be rash to make such an error of judgement again, or even to indulge such a man as Guppy down the telephone. As a virtue, loyalty to friends has its limits.'

Boris drew those limits more widely, and less prudently, than Hastings would have done. So did Charles Spencer, who when Guppy came out of prison provided a house for him on the Althorp estate.

Ever since extracts from the tape were published in the *Daily*

*Mail*, on 16 July 1995, Boris has faced questions about his friendship with Guppy. Again and again, he has pointed out that he never supplied the address and that Collier was never beaten up. Sometimes he adds that his unfortunate friend was being 'hounded', while at others he says that Guppy 'was always a bit of a fruitcake'.

Some will say Boris should not have been Guppy's friend in the first place, but I cannot go along with this. I could see why Boris and Guppy were friends. Guppy had great charm. It is true that some people, including some of Boris's friends at Oxford, hated him, but when I met him for the first time in 1987 I liked him at once. He described himself as a poet and showed me some of his verses, and I liked those too. He had a quality of impertinence which was very attractive.

When I spoke to Guppy on the telephone – he now lives abroad – his tone of voice was exactly as I remembered it: high-spirited, affectionate, witty, and crazy in a way which before his downfall there seemed no need to take seriously. He was no longer in touch with Boris, but spoke with great fondness of him: 'I loved Boris. I was very attracted to him. I felt an affinity – I appreciated not simply his humour, but the warmth within his humour.'

Guppy said if he were Boris and being questioned about the tape, 'I would play it slightly differently. I would say the journalist concerned needed a knee-capping. I'm only sorry I couldn't provide him with the address. The guy was a prick, he needed a knee-capping, and the people I know would think I was a pussy for not chopping his head off and putting it on the Internet.' (Let me interject, lest anyone misunderstand this, that I am not in favour of knee-capping, or of chopping the heads off annoying journalists.)

Guppy went on: 'To be fair to Boris, a) he did not provide me with the address; b) he should have. The world would be a better place if he had, and you can quote me on this. Because I don't like journalists.' He added that he liked me, but he didn't like journalists: 'In fifteen years I have not spoken to one journalist.'

According to Guppy, 'people are so concerned about appearances' that they worry about justice being seen to be done, but are less concerned that justice actually *is* done. He prefers the customs of earlier ages: 'The Duke of Wellington fought twenty-five duels. Now if that had been under today's conditions he would have faced twenty-five counts of attempted murder.'

It has since occurred to me that the Duke would not have condescended to fight a duel with a journalist, and would more likely have said: 'Publish and be damned.' He did fight a duel when he was Prime Minister, but against a peer, the Earl of Winchilsea, and was severely criticised in the press for doing so.

Guppy refused to acknowledge that Collier's inquiries were entirely justified. He insisted that even today, many people, including 'Spaniards, Turks, Mexicans and South Americans', would have done the same as himself and gone after Collier. But in Britain, he thinks, 'a dreadful moral sanctimoniousness' has replaced any sense of natural justice: 'The English have this *Daily Mail* mentality and it is absolutely sickening.'

Guppy published a wooden account of his insurance fraud, *Roll the Dice*, in which he tried and failed to justify what he had done. As one who had once admired his literary gifts, I asked whether there was any chance of his writing something now, but he said: 'What I have to say is too controversial, I can assure you. I just can't be bothered with it – publishing stuff – the inevitable snide comment from the *Daily Mail*. I would not be allowed by law to seek redress. If someone says something bad about me my instinct is to go and beat them up. I never had a problem in prison because the prisoners could see this in me. If I came back to England I know I would do time for grievous bodily harm.'

He made the point that in a conversation between friends, one does not interrupt and say, 'Oh Darius, for the sake of any

tape recording . . .' and then place on record one's complete con-
demnation of what one's friend is saying.

'Now talking of addresses, Andrew,' he said in a joking tone,
'there's something you can do for me . . .'

Boris could see Guppy's defects. In June 1997, when commenting on the downfall of the Tory MP Jonathan Aitken, Boris
wrote: 'There is a touch of Darius Guppy about him, to take an
example from my own generation, a Walter Mittyish refusal to
face up to reality, and an inability to sort out right from wrong.'

Boris went on: 'Like all tragic figures, Aitken was the author
of his own downfall, and like most tragic figures, there was at
least an initial dash of greatness, if not quite of heroism.'

Should we just pass by on the other side when our friends get
into trouble? Part of Boris's trouble was his generosity. A nastier
man would have cut Guppy without a backward glance.

One of the journalists who wrote most about this affair was
Marcus Scriven, at the *Evening Standard*, the paper Max Hastings
went from the *Telegraph* to edit in 1995. In 1997 Hastings invited
both Scriven, who went with a girl friend, and Boris, who went
with Marina, to a lunch party in the *Evening Standard*'s box at
Newbury race course.

On the way to Newbury, Scriven played the tape to the girl,
wishing to have a witness in case the subject of Guppy came up.
After a pleasant lunch, for which Boris and Marina arrived late,
Scriven wandered round the course and placed a couple of bets,
before returning with his friend to the *Evening Standard* box.

Boris and Marina also returned to the box, and by Scriven's
account, the following conversation took place.

BORIS: 'Why do you keep writing about me and Guppy?'
SCRIVEN: 'Well, I don't really. I've only written about
        Guppy a couple of times. If you would go into print
        and write an apologia for him [a reference to the

article, quoted earlier in this chapter, which Boris wrote after Guppy's conviction in 1993]. You know him better than I do and you shouldn't indulge him by asking if this bloke is going to get badly hurt.'

BORIS: 'I don't think I said that.'

MARINA: 'I'm sure Boris wouldn't say that.'

SCRIVEN [withdrawing the tape from his pocket]: 'Yes, you did. Would you like to listen?'

Boris, according to Scriven, 'did a Bateman. The hairs stood up on the end of his neck, the white mop took off. And he left, he walked out. He came back later and said, "Let's just call it pax, shall we?"'

A time would come when Boris proved able to devise, at a decisive moment, a way of turning the Guppy episode to his advantage. But at Newbury races it was still a rather dreadful embarrassment.

# 14

## *A Telly Star Is Born*

BORIS RETURNED FROM BRUSSELS TO THE OFFICES AT Canary Wharf of the *Daily Telegraph*, where he was given the grand titles of Assistant Editor and Chief Political Columnist. A dialogue along the following lines took place between Boris and Richard Ehrman, one of the leader-writers.

> EHRMAN: 'Welcome back. It's terrific you're going to do a political column.'
>
> BORIS: 'I'm a bit worried I haven't got any political opinions.'
>
> EHRMAN: 'You must have some.'
>
> BORIS: 'Well, I'm against Europe and against capital punishment.'
>
> EHRMAN: 'I'm sure you'll make something out of that.'

He did make something out of that. Boris was being self-deprecating when he said he had no political opinions, but he certainly had no carefully worked-out system, or none that he was going to preach in a tedious way in his column. He could be eclectic and light-hearted and shove in whatever floated into his head, or whatever he thought *Telegraph* readers would enjoy. In

1997, he was made Commentator of the Year at the 'What the Papers Say' awards.

Some journalists would have rested on their laurels, composed a column a week and enjoyed feeling self-important. Boris was also the father of a rapidly growing family. Lara Lettice, born in June 1993, was followed by three more children all born in London at University College Hospital: Milo Arthur on 3 February 1995, Cassia Peaches on 8 September 1997 and Theodore Apollo on 4 July 1999. Theo only narrowly escaped being given an extra name, Washington, in honour of American Independence Day, after a certain amount of pink champagne had been drunk.

But while Boris revelled in being a father, that did not stop him being the most driven and ambitious man at the *Telegraph*. He was an astonishingly prolific writer, who more than made up in energy and rate of fire for those pieces which did not come off as well as they might have done. For a short period after he came back he wrote the political column in the *Spectator*, and one could often see that he had not devoted nearly as much time to it as he should have done, though Dominic Lawson, the then editor, said, 'I thought it was always very good.'

Boris also pursued his political ambitions. For the eighteen months up to the General Election of 1 May 1997, when the Conservative Party went down to its worst defeat, in terms of parliamentary seats, since 1906, Boris was the Tory candidate in the hopeless seat of Clwyd South, just over the border from Shropshire. He learned how to sing the Welsh national anthem and to order fish and chips in Welsh. But as he himself has written: 'I fought Clwyd South – and Clwyd South fought back.'

Losing Clwyd South was an excellent way of showing keenness to the party hierarchy, and Boris had done it in order to get a safe seat next time. Meanwhile he devoted himself mainly to journalism. One of the best things Boris did was a back-page interview in Monday's *Daily Telegraph*. As Charles Moore, who had succeeded Max Hastings as editor, says: 'He did it very well. He didn't just suck up [to his interviewees], but nor did he tear them apart.'

In September 2004, when Andrew Duncan came to interview him for the *Radio Times*, Boris told him: 'Bad luck you having to interview me. I used to interview people. Terribly difficult. You have a wonderful time with this chap, or girl, end up with a dumper truck of gravel from which you pick shiny pebbles to make your mosaic. It's seduction and betrayal.'

It is typical of Boris to voice the reservations others may feel about his work. He is a master of pre-emptive self-criticism. Before it has even occurred to us to accuse him of seducing and betraying his victims, he has accused himself. He enlists our sympathy by leaping to a harsher verdict on his conduct than we would have reached ourselves.

Not that this stops him from conducting a robust defence of his behaviour, in which he further implicates the rest of us. For as he explains in the volume of his collected journalism *Lend Me Your Ears*, while reverential interviews may still be acceptable in France or America, 'British readers, with their jaded palates, want something stronger. They want the revelations, the confessions. They want the sudden grabbing for the hankie. That is why the British hack approaches his interviewee with what is sometimes a frankly treacherous smile.'

This treacherousness, he says, has led PR men to become 'ever more ruthless' in their treatment of journalists, which in turn is why journalists 'have become ever more ratlike in their cunning'. Boris declares that he is 'in principle' on the side of the hacks, before saying a few more words in his own defence: 'For my own part, I have always tried to be faithful to the drift and mood of the conversation, even if there is a lot one must necessarily cut. I also tend to like my subjects, though Chris Evans and I were probably quite relieved when our game of golf was over.'

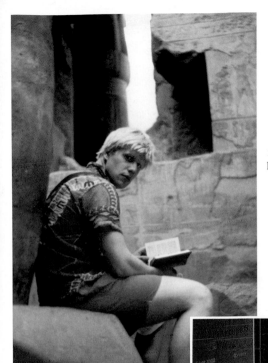

17. A thoughtful Boris on honeymoon in Egypt.

18. Conrad Black, former proprietor of the *Spectator*, with his wife Barbara Amiel. Black would not only give Boris editorship of the magazine, but also fail to sack him when Boris sought election to Parliament.

19. Boris at the *Spectator*: his secretary, Ann Sindall, tells him to concentrate on something that bores him.

20. *Spectator* supremo. Boris with colleagues at Doughty Street: Mary Wakefield at his feet; Ann Sindall sitting with her terrier Harry on her lap; Stuart Reid with clasped hands; Michael Heath in black; Clare Asquith over Heath's shoulder, Mark Amory on the right; and production editor Clarke Hayes leaning on a bust of Pericles.

21. Boris and his second wife Marina, after winning selection as the new Conservative candidate for Henley.

22. Boris, Kimberly Fortier and David Blunkett at a *Spectator* party.

23. Operation Scouse-grovel: Boris narrowly avoids deep water by apologising to the people of Liverpool at Albert Dock in October 2004, having been ordered there by Michael Howard after a *Spectator* editorial described the city as being 'hooked on grief'.

24. Petronella Wyatt, whose affair with Boris he famously and disastrously denied as an 'inverted pyramid of piffle'.

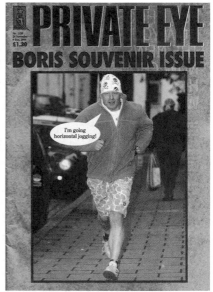

25. Boris makes the cover of *Private Eye* – one of the most famous shots of him during the Petronella affair.

26. A slightly dishevelled Boris, taking refuge at the home of his old Oxford friend Justin Rushbrooke, notices the long lenses of the *News of the World* while Rushbrooke points out that his car is about to be clamped.

27. Johnson *père et fils*, competing as ever while on the campaign trail during the 2005 General Election. Contrary to appearances Boris won the match easily.

28. Expect the unexpected: Boris was a handy rugby player in his day, and applied his skills against Maurizio Gaudino in a charity match before the 2006 World Cup. Unfortunately he was supposed to be playing football.

29. In 2005, Boris found himself overtaken by his fellow Etonian David Cameron in the party leadership stakes. Time will tell if Boris's unique style will one day find wider favour among his fellow MPs.

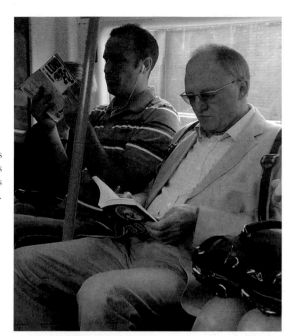

30. Ken Livingstone studies an earlier edition of this book, which he described as 'completely devastating'.

31. Merry England: in June 2009 Boris cheered everyone up by falling in the river. A woman jumped in beside him to try to rescue him.

32. Boris as Viking warrior while defeating David Cameron at tennis (see page 312).

THE RAKE'S PROGRESS 2011

RGJ

"IN THE MODERN VERSION HE BECOMES EDITOR OF THE SPECTATOR, MAYOR OF LONDON AND EVENTUALLY PRIME MINISTER"

33. In the 50th Anniversary Issue of *Private Eye* in October 2011, a cartoon by Richard Jolley suggests that an irregular private life will not stop Boris getting to 10 Downing Street.

His piece about Evans, a disc jockey who had also become the proprietor of Virgin Radio, describes how Evans agrees, not just to do an interview, but to 'give the *Daily Telegraph* a game of golf! . . . Just when he is needed most, Bill Deedes, the paper's answer to Arnold Palmer, is in Sudan. Someone, anyone, is needed to play golf with Evans. Have you ever swung a club in anger? the features impresarios ask, and, like a fool, I say yes.'

Boris turns his incompetence into a running joke: 'The last time I played golf was at school when one Major Morkill expelled me from the course for using only one club.' But he only has to play a few holes with Evans, whose own golf turns out to be mediocre – 'unless – ghastly thought – he was only being polite'.

For a while, Boris was comment editor, a role Charles Moore remembers him performing with 'maximum idleness'.

It was at this time that Boris started to acquire a vast new public through his appearances on television. He became the nearest thing most of us have seen to a real-life Bertie Wooster, and people loved him for it. While everyone else was trying to sound more classless, Boris went in the opposite direction, which was a much more enjoyable thing to do. Like his hero P. G. Wodehouse, but in another medium, he took us into a world of upper-class lunacy from which all nastiness had been removed. He acted like a public-school twit from the 1930s, yet by going on programmes on which most politicians would have been unable to cope, and on which most Cabinet ministers would consider it beneath their dignity to appear, he bolstered his democratic credentials.

The programme with which Boris has become most closely associated, and which did most to make him a television star, is *Have I Got News For You*. His first appearance on the show, in April 1998, proved painful, as he had not realised that it was the custom to spring a nasty surprise on one of the guests. Ian Hislop, the editor of *Private Eye* and one of the regular panellists, said: 'He was absolutely livid because I brought up the Darius Guppy tape, which I found immensely funny. He was in a terrific strop and blustered about an elephant trap.'

Boris was so angry he took his revenge by writing an article for the *Spectator* under the headline 'I Was Stitched Up' in which he said the programme was 'a fraud on the viewing public' because 'all that lightning repartee' was actually the result of careful preparation, scripting of even the bits where people are supposed to be ad-libbing, and an entire day of tedious editing before the programme went out.

Paul Merton, the other regular panellist, was infuriated by this article, for as Hislop said, 'Paul Merton gets very cross with suggestions that he's done anything to prepare in any way.'

Boris's career as a contributor to *HIGNFY* might have ended there. But it is not Boris's way to allow a feud to fester, and he cannot have wished to be on terms of permanent enmity with the *Private Eye* set. Quite soon peace broke out and Boris was invited back. After all, his disaster had been a thousand times more entertaining than a safe performance by someone else, and when Hislop said to him of the offending article, 'What a load of bollocks, Boris – you must have knocked that out in about twenty minutes,' Boris replied, 'No, it was shorter than that,' after which Hislop said, 'I expect you were pissed as well,' to which Boris responded, 'I might have been.'

Hislop felt disarmed by Boris's willingness to admit to virtually any charge made against him, and said: 'He apologised on air the next time he came on. It was quite endearing.'

On one edition of *HIGNFY* Boris faced a quiz about his party leader, Iain Duncan Smith, in which he was unable to answer any of the questions. Audiences loved such towering ineptitude. With many contestants, such behaviour might have become embarrassing, but Boris knew how to carry it off. He was tough enough to take the knocks, and the worse things went for him, the more he could make people laugh. The boy who had made Etonians roar with laughter by forgetting his lines was now playing to a nationwide audience. And although he was sending himself up, he was also sending up the very genre, the television quiz, on which he was appearing, by refusing to allow his every word to be controlled by the programme-makers, or to give the kind of glib performance which professional television people cannot help trying to create.

Once, while waiting in the wings, Boris said to Hislop: 'Do you know what the Tory policy is on immigration?' Hislop said 'No,' to which Boris replied, 'Nor do I.'

Boris was soon being asked to present the show, a role in which he maintained his unprofessionalism at a level nobody else could match. According to Hislop, most presenters 'spend two days rehearsing it, but Boris turned up at six p.m. on the day and had never read the script, which he proceeded to read in that dazed way of his. His insouciance was extremely funny.'

Charles Kennedy, the then leader of the Liberal Democrats, was the only politician before Boris who had done well on the show, but 'Chat-show Charlie' was attacked by his own party for being so good.

Boris has appeared only a handful of times on *HIGNFY*, which makes the reputation he has won there all the more remarkable. On a recent occasion when he presented the show, Merton paid him the compliment of saying he had actually got worse.

Some people thought it beneath the dignity of a Member of Parliament to go on such a programme. Boris replied that he would be a coward not to, and it was a way of reaching a much wider public, and he got paid £1,000 a time, which was enough to take two children skiing. He also said the real shocker was 'not that people are so foolish as to appear on TV, but that people are so idle as to watch it'.

Part of Boris's childhood on Exmoor was spent without television at all. His first love was books and one reason why his performances come off so brilliantly on telly is their throwaway character. Boris had become one of the very few politicians who could succeed on the television programmes people actually wanted to watch, and he hoped this would prove a decisive advantage. As he put it in an interview with *GQ* in May 2003: 'If you don't go out and mix it up a bit on the stuff that everybody watches, if you don't get involved in things that everybody thinks are amusing and if you're not prepared to get involved in vernacular, real TV and you just stick on Andrew Neil's late-night yawn-a-thon, then you're never going to get anywhere.'

Television fell in love with Boris. He has been on *Parkinson*, *Question Time*, *Breakfast With Frost* and *Top Gear*, among other programmes. If he had wanted, he could have given up politics and become one of the dominant television personalities of our age. But to Boris's credit, he did not want to sell his soul to television. His fiercest ambition was still political, and he was also heading for the top as a print journalist. His well-hidden seriousness of purpose has preserved him from becoming a television star with an income and an audience of millions. The nearer he got to power, the less inclined he was to prostitute himself in this way.

# – 15 –

## *Ape Gets Ming Vase*

BORIS WAS MADE EDITOR OF THE *SPECTATOR* IN JULY 1999, when he was thirty-five years old. This was a great chance for a youngish man, for although the magazine's circulation was only 57,000, everyone who was anyone in London read it. The *Spectator* was the oldest weekly in Britain and stood for a kind of irreverent conservatism, though much of it was not very political at all. It was part of Conrad Black's newspaper empire, which also included the *Daily* and *Sunday Telegraph*s. The post could be a springboard either to grander editorships within the group or to high political office. Having edited the *Spectator*, though in some cases after a considerable interval, Ian Gilmour became Defence Secretary; Iain Macleod Chancellor of the Exchequer; Nigel Lawson Chancellor of the Exchequer; Charles Moore editor of the *Daily Telegraph*; and Nigel Lawson's son Dominic editor of the *Sunday Telegraph*. There was no reason why Boris should not equal or exceed these predecessors.

Yet his appointment was not greeted with universal enthusiasm. When Sandra Barwick rang me up for a quote for the piece she was writing about Boris for the *Daily Telegraph*, I told her: 'It's like entrusting a Ming vase to an ape.'

How could I have said this? Partly because I thought Boris

would be slapdash, but mainly because I placed such a high value on the *Spectator*. I started reading it when I was a student, in about 1978, during the editorship of Alexander Chancellor. He not only persuaded interesting people to write for him, he also got them to do their best work, by giving them the intelligent appreciation that writers most desire. As a reader, you could relax in their company, and felt that they knew what was going on, but were not obsessed by politics or by success, and would laugh at people who deserved to be laughed at.

Richard Ingrams did a television column in which he treated telly people as the self-regarding idiots they so often are. One week he watched no television at all, but heard some through the wall of a hotel room in Hay-on-Wye. Jeff Bernard began 'Low Life', Taki reported on 'High Life', Ferdinand Mount was the political columnist, Auberon Waugh wrote 'Another Voice', Xan Smiley went to Africa, Murray Sayle was in Japan, Christopher Hitchens in Washington, Sam White in Paris and Andrew Brown in Sweden, Roy Kerridge was at a gypsy encampment somewhere outside London, Patrick Marnham, Geoffrey Wheatcroft, Richard West, Peter Paterson and Peter Ackroyd were all in full flow, and the great Shiva Naipaul spent several years having lunch with Chancellor before going on a journey and writing something which could not have appeared in any other magazine.

Boris could not edit in this style. He was far too busy, and also too restless. *Spectator* lunches, held in the small dining-room at the top of the house, used to be enjoyable because they were so leisurely, as well as because of the mixture of guests, who often included a famous politician or writer, but also took in some of the most amusing, though not necessarily most productive, people from Fleet Street. Boris could not pay host to that kind of long-drawn-out affair. Charles Moore said: 'There was a long-meditated lunch he gave for Debo [Duchess of] Devonshire at the *Spectator* – a weird mixture of people – random – someone from marketing, a friend of Ann Sindall's [Boris's secretary]. Almost as soon as lunch began, he left for the House of Commons – very typical. He enchanted Debo for twenty minutes, then departed.'

Like most editors, Boris was more excited by stories than by writers. 'Scoops are us,' he would say. When one considers that he shot from the hip, his aim was surprisingly good. He was in many ways a very fine editor, who did not expect other people to be as go-getting as he was. I was at this time returning to London from a stint in Berlin. He kindly invited me to be his unpaid Foreign Editor, and found it amusing that I did no editing and almost never went abroad. On one occasion he suggested I go to Papua New Guinea to write about penis gourds. Boris would have been there and back in a week, and would have written an account of the gourds which was just within the fairly elastic bounds of modern taste, but although I spoke to a man at the Pitt-Rivers Museum in Oxford, who knew all about Papua New Guinea and warned me it was quite a dangerous place, I never got round to going there. The articles I did contribute to the Boris *Spectator*, about places as far afield as Hackney, Surbiton and even Burnley, were paid at the generous rate of £500 a time, and usually appeared with the note: 'Andrew Gimson is Foreign Editor of the *Spectator*.'

Some editors treat their staff like galley slaves and expect them to produce a constant flow of 'ideas' for pieces (which is one reason why so much journalism is such nonsense, for many ideas which will pass muster as a phrase at an editorial conference are exposed as vacuous when some poor journalist is sent off to write about them). Boris was a humane editor who did not seem to mind if nobody but himself had any ideas, though Peter Oborne, who wrote the politics column, was usually rather good at coming up with something.

Never have I been to editorial conferences where such freedom of speech reigned. Leaning back on one of the sofas in

Boris's office, you could tell any joke that came into your head. There was a slightly brutish desire to 'get' Blair, but brutishness is one of the traditions of our free press, and Blair would have been an amazing scalp.

Oborne reported one week that Blair had been pheasant-shooting in the West Country, and recalled: 'Boris was electrified. He wouldn't stop ringing me up about it. He became quite obsessive about it. The resources of the *Spectator* were never engaged quite so fully and with such personal attention from the editor himself as on the Blair pheasant-shooting story. Jeremy Clarke [author of the 'Low Life' column] was sent down to Devon and found someone in a pub who claimed to have been out beating when Blair was shooting. Then the trail went cold, until a Tory MP said he'd sat next at dinner to a backwoods peer from Devon who could authenticate the story. Boris was in a state of frenzy. Then the peer started to withdraw a bit. Finally Boris rang up Fursdon, the friend Blair stayed with in Devon, who said: "No. Never. No. Absolutely not."'

Boris's right-hand man at the *Spectator* was Stuart Reid, a man a generation older than him. Dan Colson – Conrad Black's man of business – wanted an older and wiser person at Boris's side. The idea was that Reid would supply the sober judgement and attention to detail which Boris was unable to provide.

Reid is unquestionably a brilliant sub-editor, who can improve almost any piece of copy by making tactful changes to it. He is also devoid of the slightest trace of self-importance. But Reid said that people like Dan Colson misunderstood him: 'They got me completely wrong. I'm just as irresponsible as Boris but I lack his courage. I have actually urged caution and been utterly delighted when he went ahead anyhow. I've always voted Conservative but I'm not a capitalistic, Wall Street right-winger – I'm more of the Perry Worsthorne/Michael Wharton school. I agree with much of what George Galloway says about the war in Iraq.'

As a young man, Reid went to Australia, where he worked

for various publications, including the *Australian*, in which he had a column called 'On the Contrary', signed 'Matilda', and *Poultry News*. He drank enthusiastically, but at the age of thirty-eight thought it prudent to become a total abstainer. In 1975 he served for three months as editor of the *Catholic Herald*, where the headline on the leader in the week after he left was 'Return to Sanity'. He said of this period: 'My heart was in the right place. I was right to support Catholicism at the *Catholic Herald*.'

Reid barely knew Boris: 'I first got to know him when I was comment editor of the *Sunday Telegraph*. I always found him tremendously charming but a bloody nightmare. There'd never be any question of his copy arriving on Friday, nor first thing on Saturday. I'd ring him and he'd say: "Any second."

'At the *Daily Telegraph* I got to know him a bit. The first time I can remember speaking to him was on 3 September 1997 when he did that great piece about Lady Di – "A Latin American carnival of grief" – I sought him out in his office and praised him at length. He looked confused, bewildered and modest, as he does when you praise him.

'Not long after, I found him wandering round and round in circles. He had to write a column and he was saying, "Christ, what can I write?" He was in the shopping mall area of Canary Wharf. His shirt was hanging out and he was running his hand through his hair. My mind went blank. I couldn't help him at all.

'But from 1999, at the *Spectator*, we worked together as if we'd been colleagues – fairly close colleagues – for a long time, a fiction that helped us both.' Reid, whom I interviewed in June 2004, looked back on his life with Boris: 'We've been together now five years, and in that time I've only lost my temper once, and I don't know that he's ever lost his temper. He really is the nicest person I've worked for other than Kim Fletcher, and he's easy-peasy at a personal level.

'He's basically unreliable in terms of delivering copy or being around, and he doesn't seem to bear grudges – it's impossible not to forgive him. You see, he has to be a really nice guy, because if he weren't a nice guy he'd be dead. The anger doesn't have to do with personal nastiness. It's to do with him not being there, decisions not being made – and yet they always are made in the end.

'He's got this wonderful streak of creative irresponsibility. He's the sort of chap who can't see a red button marked "do not press" without pressing it. He's seen as anarchic. This is his appeal. And he is anarchic. He's a liberal libertarian. Legalise drugs. Let's not be pious about sex. Life is for living. Keep government off your back.

'I don't know whether he has any passionately held views. There must be more to him than a pastiche of an Englishman. I remember when the Americans went into Afghanistan and Boris said, "Wouldn't it be funny if – yeah – the Americans took a hiding." He's not anti-American, but he's mercurial. It would have been a better story.

'He is naturally a nice man. The mother of a kid he'd been at prep school with wrote to him and said her son had died, and did Boris remember him? Boris sent her a hand-written letter of about three pages, in which he not just remembered him, but remembered him with affection and told affectionate stories about him.'

Boris brought Ann Sindall with him from the *Telegraph* as his secretary. She was a very important person in his life and it was vastly to his (and her) credit that he wanted her to help run things. Sindall is a blunt, warm-hearted socialist from Batley, in Yorkshire, who dresses as if she is about to set off on a nineteen-mile hike across the moors and is capable of ferocious rudeness, both to her employer and to anyone else who has offended against her sense of right and wrong. She brought her dog, a terrier called Harry, to the office, but is the antithesis of the demure and elegant home counties girl whom ignorant people might have expected to find at the *Spectator*.

Sindall started at the *Telegraph* as a temporary secretary on the leader-writers' desk, when the payments system for the comment writers had collapsed. She sorted things out and they asked her to stay on.

Sindall was sceptical: 'Don't you want posh here?'

Richard Ehrman, one of the leader-writers, replied, 'We've had posh here and nothing works.'

Even when she started, in 1996, 'most of the calls I took were from people asking "Where's Boris?" Even then he was a rising star.'

The more famous Boris became, the greater the number of people who rang up wanting some of his time. Sindall defended him from these supplicants. Susan Clarke, a freelance journalist, rang offering a piece on the royal family and mentioned that next Thursday she was coming to lunch at the *Spectator*.

Sindall replied: 'Just because you're coming to lunch doesn't mean I know who you are.'

Television people had an insatiable craving to get Boris on their programmes. One day I went into Sindall's office and she was telling a TV company: 'He hasn't got time to spend two days going off pretending to be a boy scout.' As Sindall said after this call, 'However you deflect it, they just come back in a different way. It drives you mad.'

She described with affectionate scorn how Boris at a party would spinelessly agree to do things for people who came up and pestered him: 'Nodding dog stands there and agrees to everything they say.'

Boris was more than capable of annoying Sindall, and everyone else with whom he worked closely at the *Spectator*, but he knew how to mend fences. Sindall said: 'We can all hate his guts, we want to kill him, but then he can get us laughing again.'

Sindall's manner of taking important people down a peg or two gave enormous enjoyment to anyone sitting within earshot of her. When she was still at the *Telegraph*, 'Peter Mandelson rang up wanting to speak to Boris. He said, "He'll know who I am." I said, "That's fine, but I'm taking the message." He said: "Peter Mandelson." I said: "Can you spell that please?"'

Sindall's spelling was not actually very good. As she herself says, she got to the age of eighteen 'not even knowing I couldn't read and write properly'. After Paul Goodman, a *Telegraph* leader-writer who is now a Tory MP, criticised Sindall's written work, Boris reassured her: 'There's nothing wrong with your spelling. It's just different to everyone else's.'

Boris and Sindall were once at a function attended by Margaret Thatcher: 'He was like this schoolboy. He went running over to Margaret Thatcher saying "come on Ann, come on Ann". I had to go over and meet Margaret Thatcher. I couldn't think what to say to her. She was like a monster when I was growing up. Where I grew up there was absolutely no work. I said to her: "You changed the course of my life." I meant it sarcastically. She really did. I moved from the north because of her and ended up down south. She actually looked quite small and defenceless. Boris says I just treated her like a queen.'

There were strict limits to what Sindall would do for Boris: 'One day he came in wearing these trousers with a big rip in them. He was going on telly or something. He brought them in, he said, "Ann, you don't think you could . . .?" I said, "No way I could." The next thing, I walked in to reception and Alex Whitaker was sewing his trousers. He was sitting at his desk in his boxer shorts. Some girls will and some girls won't, but I won't do dry cleaning or sewing up trousers.'

Yet Sindall did help Boris in many other ways. When she started with him, his financial affairs were in total confusion. Unpaid parking tickets would increase in cost to £800 and the bailiffs would be about to break in.

She organised his speaking engagements and negotiated the fees. I caught a glimpse of this lucrative trade when Boris was asked by a German bank to speak at the tenth anniversary of the opening of its Guernsey branch. Boris did not have time and the bank needed another speaker at short notice. Sindall suggested me, billed as the Foreign Editor of the *Spectator*. I asked her how much I should charge and she said that as soon as the word 'bank' appeared in the name of an organisation, she charged a lot. How much was a lot? She urged me to ask for £3,000.

My freelance career was going through one of its worst patches, so I plucked up my courage and followed Ann's advice. The sophisticated gentleman who ran the bank paused for a moment during our telephone conversation when I mentioned this outrageous sum, and then agreed.

Sindall had the onerous task of making Boris's travel arrangements. He has an extraordinary, one might almost say a self-defeating, capacity to go to the wrong station, or to the right station but get on the wrong train. When Boris goes to an airport, there is a good chance his passport has not gone with him. Sindall said: 'I think that's just because his mind's so full of everything else.'

Boris craves action, including the action that flows from things going wrong. As Sindall said, 'If he hasn't got a crisis, he'll sit and say he's bored. He edited the *Spectator* on a knife-edge. He couldn't do it otherwise.'

Trevor Kavanagh, the Political Editor of the *Sun*, recalled a characteristic Sindall intervention: 'I rang Boris up about the identity of some people who might be involved in a story. He was going to give me some information he just couldn't resist giving to me when I heard Ann shout: "You're talking to Trevor Kavanagh. You can't do that!" And Boris said, "I'm sorry." He'd been caught red-handed.'

On one occasion I asked Sindall for the telephone numbers of some people to whom I wanted to speak about Boris, and added: 'Please don't feed his paranoia.'

Ann replied: 'It doesn't need feeding.' Boris is in many ways so robust, and so good at taking jokes at his own expense, that we perhaps forget he is also capable of paranoia.

But it is worth mentioning that Boris is in many respects brilliant at transacting business. Peter Oborne, who succeeded Bruce Anderson as Political Editor, said: 'The thing which struck me most of all is how efficient he was to deal with. We would speak once a week for about a minute, and in that minute you covered the whole ground. Boris had the gift that you never had to explain anything to him at all.'

# 16

## *Member for Henley*

BORIS HAD REACHED, WITH THE EDITORSHIP OF THE *Spectator*, a very exposed place in journalism, but he also pursued with ardour his hunt for a parliamentary seat.

Going into politics was no mere afterthought, but the deepest goal of his existence. He had set himself the goal of being in the Cabinet by the age of thirty-five, yet he had reached that age without even getting into the House of Commons.

He was determined to put that right. Michael Heseltine, the former Deputy Prime Minister, was standing down as MP for Henley after more than thirty years in the Commons. In the summer of 2000, Boris competed against 201 other applicants for this safe Tory seat. In the final round, which included a question-and-answer session for which Boris's television experience gave him an advantage, he defeated two lawyers, both of whom were closer to Heseltine on the question of Europe. In Henley as elsewhere, Tory activists were obsessed by Europe. They asked many more questions about it than about anything else, and were inclined to choose someone less pro-Brussels than Heseltine, whom many Conservatives had not yet forgiven for his decisive role in Margaret Thatcher's downfall. Boris could cope convincingly with Europe: here his

journalistic experience remained extremely helpful to his
political aspirations.

But there was one other matter which threatened to derail
him. A Henley Conservative stood up at the selection meeting
and accused Boris of having a skeleton in his cupboard. It was
the Guppy question, posed with such venom, according to
Boris, that it offended the audience's sense of fair play.

The candidate was able to reply: 'In so far as you accuse me of
keeping this Guppy business a secret, well, that seems a bit thin,
since I have actually been questioned about it on a TV game
show watched by I don't know how many millions.'

There was no need for Boris to add that he had not chosen to
be stitched up by the resident wags on *Have I Got News For You*.
The point was (as he says in his book about Henley, *Friends,
Voters, Countrymen*) that he had shown the ability to recover
under fire. This, he argued, 'was a bit of bad luck on the other
two [candidates], since they lacked the advantage of an embarrassing past to brush aside'.

It is a wonderful argument for taking foolish risks. How
better can a man show his resilience than by getting into trouble? Boris was not one of those percentage players, who never
does anything daring, and whose life furnishes no materials for
history.

Henley may sound small, but the constituency which takes its
name from the pretty town on the Thames covers a vast tract of
country between Reading and Oxford, and the *Oxford Journal*
ran a whole page about Boris on the day after his victory, ending
with the prediction: 'After the virtual disappearance of Michael
Heseltine following the last election, politics in South Oxfordshire are about to get very interesting once more.'

Even in 1997, a disastrous year for the Tories, Heseltine had a
majority of 11,167 over the Liberal Democrats, but the Lib
Dems boasted that they could take Boris on: 'We believe the
anti-Boris vote will be bigger than the pro-Boris vote.'

Boris himself used cautious language in victory. When something matters to him, he is perfectly capable of keeping quiet, and he had no desire to ruin everything in Henley by shooting off his mouth. There was a lot of stuff about being 'greatly honoured', and he insisted that his election to Parliament 'is absolutely not a foregone conclusion'.

But Boris also made clear that he hoped to pursue the risky course of remaining editor of the *Spectator*: 'I don't see a conflict of interest and it is not an unprecedented career path. I could mention Winston Churchill and Disraeli. It will probably be hard, but my plan is not to leave my job, not least because I would be broke.'

Disraeli and Churchill certainly showed that periods of intense literary activity were compatible with being an MP, though neither of them edited a weekly magazine. But from another point of view, these grand comparisons, offered with such skilful modesty ('I could mention'), were and are highly encouraging for Boris. Both men were written off as marginal figures, yet came to dominate politics.

Disraeli was an outsider who was at first regarded as ridiculous, and whose private life was scandalous, but who at the age of sixty-three 'climbed to the top of the greasy pole' and became one of the greatest of all Tory Prime Ministers. Churchill in the 1930s was likewise an outsider, who in 1940, at the age of sixty-six, reached the top. Boris still had another thirty years to achieve his ambition of becoming Prime Minister.

But it was nevertheless rather wilful of him to say that he saw no 'conflict of interest' between editing a magazine and being a Tory MP. The world of journalism looked askance at his move into politics, and predicted that he would fail. Richard Ingrams wrote in the *Observer*, 'What is rather sad about Johnson is that he has this desire to go into politics. For it is hard to think of a single successful journalist who has made any kind of mark as a politician. Most, including such illustrious names as William

Cobbett and Hilaire Belloc, failed utterly to shine when they were elected to Parliament.'

The assumption in Fleet Street was that Boris would be forced to give up the editorship once he actually became an MP, and Boris amused himself by inviting four of the candidates to succeed him – Michael Gove, Stephen Glover, Alice Thomson and Matthew d'Ancona – to lunch at the *Spectator*. In Gove's words, this was Boris's way of saying: 'I know what you buggers are up to – I can have a laugh at your expense.'

Less than a year later, when the election was called, journalists descended on Henley to write about Boris, confident that whatever else he did he would provide good copy. A. A. Gill wrote a notorious piece in the *Sunday Times*. He began by insulting the 'faux rural' area: 'Henley is a supermodel constituency – and like all supermodels it looks lovely on postcards but when you get up close and personal it's smug, selfish, demanding and vain.'

Gill moved on to Boris, whom he described as 'Quisling Boris' for abandoning journalism. The piece included a lengthy description of Boris struggling to find anyone to canvass on a summer morning in a commuter village, and ended: 'Boris Johnson is without doubt the very worst putative politician I've ever seen in action. He is utterly, chronically useless – and I can't think of a higher compliment.'

This verdict said more about Gill, and his desire to regard journalism as a higher calling than politics, than about Boris. The Liberal Democrats distributed Gill's verdict to the voters, but it made no difference.

At the General Election on 7 June 2001, Boris held Henley with a majority of 8,458 over the Liberal Democrats. A picture of him giving an enormous yawn was taken not long before dawn, when he was sitting waiting with his wife, Marina, for the result to be declared. He had worked very hard to ensure victory: when he commits himself to the great cause of getting himself elected, he spares no pains. In his victory speech, Boris urged people to 'go back home and prepare for breakfast'.

Henley was starting to take Boris to its heart, as a piece about him in July 2001 in the *Oxford Mail* made clear: 'It was the biggest ever attendance at the Macmillan Cancer Relief Lunch . . . The 37-year-old is juggling enough plates to dazzle a magician.'

Boris as usual arrived late, but nobody minded. 'I can't talk about politics because everyone thinks it's boring so I'm going to give a speech on the crisis of masculinity,' he confided to Katherine MacAlister from the *Oxford Mail*, while 'shovelling mouthfuls of duck noodle salad into his mouth'.

And the speech itself was a triumph: 'He had the Ladies Who Lunch eating out of the palm of his rather large hand . . . When his mobile phone went off in the middle he was terribly embarrassed and managed to utter, "Could you phone back, I'm in the middle of a speech," which had everyone splitting their Gucci sundresses with laughter . . . But don't be deceived. Beneath his famously dishevelled fair mop and innocent schoolboy face, lies a fantastic intellect and burning ambition that is making him more successful by the day.'

Boris told Katherine MacAlister: 'I don't go to parties. I'd much rather be at home with my kids and spend as much time as possible with them in the evenings and at weekends. My wife is being marvellous about everything.'

The last sentence of this reads a bit awkwardly. What exactly was the 'everything' to which Boris referred?

Boris's book about the campaign, *Friends, Voters, Countrymen*, came out in October. Simon Walters, who had written a book called *Tory Wars*, did a joint book signing with Boris at the 2001 Conservative conference: 'I'd written a serious book, while Boris had polished up a few sketches. One person came up to my desk. This person said, "You've libelled me – I'm going to sue." Boris was meanwhile being mobbed by hundreds of women. It was like Mick Jagger. They were going crazy over him. I thought, "This guy's got some special appeal, because the book's nothing."'

It is unkind to describe the book as nothing. As a light-hearted description of the trials and tribulations of life on the stump, it is good fun. It was serialised in *The Times* because Charles Moore, the editor of the *Telegraph*, would offer only a small sum for it, and it was quite favourably reviewed by Roy Hattersley, Jeremy Paxman and Christopher Silvester among others.

Not everyone warmed to Boris, however. Early in 2002, he was hit in the face with a bread roll as he addressed the Mayor of Henley's annual dinner. The roll was thrown by Eleanor Hards, a Labour councillor and the chairman of South Oxfordshire District Council, who was sitting three places away from Boris on the top table.

Councillor Hards said: 'He deserved it. He was making an overtly party political speech, worthy of the Tory conference. He mentioned at least three times that people threw bread rolls at him when they got bored. So I took him at his word.'

According to Tom Boyle, who reported the attack in the *Henley Standard*, 'The mayor's annual dinner is the social high point of the civic year. Over 100 guests packed the upper hall at Henley Town Hall on Friday evening, including dignitaries from Thame, Marlow and Maidenhead.'

In his speech, Boris said: 'Many people ask me "what policies the Conservatives have to offer?" At the risk of being hit by a bread roll I shall tell you some of my ideas.'

Boyle reported that Boris had lamented the state of public services, road conditions in Henley and rising crime, 'and was explaining his theory on nurses' pay when he was struck by the mini French baguette. Good-humoured heckling from the floor turned to gasps of horror when the roll found its target.'

The Mayor of Henley, Councillor Tony Lane, said: 'In all my

thirty-seven years in local government I have never seen anything as disgraceful. It was not the time or the place and it's left a rather unpleasant taste in my mouth.'

At Westminster, Boris faced a harder opponent than Councillor Hards in the form of Alastair Campbell, Tony Blair's director of communications.

Matthew Pencharz, who worked for Boris at the Commons, said that only once did he see his boss 'shell-shocked', and that was after Campbell had made 'terrible threats' against him at a meeting outside the Commons in New Palace Yard. This confrontation took place because Peter Oborne had revealed in the *Spectator* that Downing Street had pushed for the Prime Minister to be given a more prominent role in the Queen Mother's lying-in-state in Westminster Hall in April 2002.

Campbell was infuriated by this report, and the *Spectator* lacked the hard evidence needed to prove it. Oborne described the weakness of the magazine's position: 'I told Boris, "I can't stand this up. I can't provide documentary evidence that this is the case." So when Campbell first came on to Boris, Boris was a bit windy. He gave Campbell the impression we were on very weak ground. It was a bit like Hannibal at Cannae: we lured Downing Street on. I had a sleepless night because I couldn't stand the story up. I thought Downing Street had got us by the balls.'

Campbell, confident of victory, overplayed his hand, and was forced to back down when Black Rod, the parliamentary official in charge of the lying-in-state, declined to back No. 10's version of events. Boris's luck had held and he found himself on the winning side. It is easy to say that at many points in his career Boris should have been more cautious, but in journalism as in politics, victory sometimes goes to those who take risks.

While other new boys at the Commons kept their heads down and learned their trade in an obscurity from which some of them will never emerge, Boris operated in the full glare of publicity. It was not just in Henley that he was becoming popular. Up and down the land, he was the darling of the Tory rank and file.

Anne Jenkin, who knows the Tory party as well as anyone, and is married to Bernard Jenkin, the MP for Harwich and North Essex, said of Boris: 'When he came to speak at our constituency dinner, it was the only dinner that was not only sold out but had a waiting list. The kids all wanted their photo taken with him. He's absolutely my tip for the top. He's the only person who reaches beyond the political arena. Everyone else is so dull and political. Political life squeezes the character out of you.'

But Boris made a poor impression on many of his colleagues on the Tory benches. One senior backbencher described him as 'a blithering idiot. You never see him. I don't think I've ever seen him in the tea room.'

Another backbencher said: 'I was staggered at his economic ignorance. When he got in [in 2001], he was put by the Whips, to test his ability to do big, gritty subjects, on a committee giving detailed scrutiny to a Bill. He didn't make the reputation there he could have done for being able to do the nitty-gritty. There was a laziness.'

The 23-year-old Matthew Pencharz applied to become Boris's first researcher at the Commons, and went for an interview at which his future employer disconcerted him by scarcely giving him a chance to get a word in edgeways: 'Great for you to come in. Fantastic. Brilliant. So, err, well, um, not really given interviews before. How do you do it? Nightmare. Ah, you went to Haberdashers' School I see. Went there for a talk recently. Bright young thrusters. Fantastic. And you're a Cambridge man. Great!'

Pencharz began to grow desperate to say something. He blurted out that he was a 'genuine liberal', which caused Boris to bellow back: 'Not a Liberal Democrat!'

To Pencharz's astonishment, he got the job ahead of thirty or forty other applicants, apparently for the simple reason that he had the best degree. He loved working for Boris: 'He bounds into the office radiating bonhomie and energy, congratulating the team, asking for cups of tea and diet Cokes and barking orders.'

But according to Pencharz, his employer sometimes got 'very, very tired – the man overworked himself'. Boris was taking on too many commitments to be able to fulfil the demands of the Tories at Westminster. Pencharz witnessed how he could infuriate the whips, whose job is to get MPs to turn out and vote: 'After the fall of Baghdad in April 2003 Boris went to visit the city. Unfortunately he hadn't bothered to tell any of the whips. On Monday morning I received a very poor-quality call on a satellite phone from the "beleaguered Palestine Hotel" in Baghdad. "Hello old bean, Boris here!" the line crackled. "Yeah, I made it. Very interesting. Fascinating. What's going on? Any votes?" Yes, I answered, there's a three-line whip tomorrow. "Oh dear. Call up the whips and tell them I'm in Baghdad will you. Back Wednesday. Got a thing in Thame [a town in his constituency] to go to."'

The line went dead. Pencharz informed the whips that Boris could not make Tuesday night's vote, and went to lunch. On his return, there was a message waiting from Boris's whip: 'Boris, I do not appreciate being told, quite nonchalantly, by one of your staff on Monday morning that you're in Baghdad. Frankly that's not acceptable. I expect you to be in the House on Tuesday night for the three-line whip.'

Boris was not there. Nor, sometimes, did he get to other events. Pencharz sometimes had to stand in for him, to the disappointment of the packed audiences who had come to see and hear Boris. Pencharz also had to pick up Boris's people-carrier from a pound somewhere in an industrial estate beyond Woolwich, and cope when it broke down on the way back to Islington.

One of Boris's trickiest relationships was with the Tory party leader, Iain Duncan Smith. William Hague resigned as Tory leader after losing the 2001 election. Boris backed Ken Clarke to succeed him, and Michael Portillo also stood, but Duncan Smith came through and won. Interviewers made a point of asking Boris how he could remain loyal to such a dimwit, but Boris, with barely veiled satire, would say things like 'Superb man. Fantastic.'

When an interviewer for *Varsity*, an undergraduate newspaper at Cambridge, asked him in June 2002 'if he seriously believes that IDS is the man to lead the glorious Blue revolution', Boris accused the interviewer, Luke Layfield, of 'defeatism', then pretended to be 'paralysed by incredulity' by 'this most unexpected and unusual of questions', and ended by saying: 'Jeepers creepers. I just can't stand this negativity. He's going to do fine, absolutely fine.'

Negativity was breaking out all over the place. In September 2002, Boris published a piece by Peter Oborne which said the Tories were in chaos under IDS and predicted that within months he would be replaced by the sacked party chairman, David Davis.

The *Daily Mirror* quoted 'a Central Office insider' who said: 'This is a clear declaration of war and even amounts to mutiny. Iain will not take this lying down and those behind it will be dealt with. For a sitting Tory MP to publish an article in a magazine that he edits portraying the leader as a failure is unforgivable.'

But another Tory source said: 'Iain will have to play this one very carefully. Boris is one of the party's only stars and as a future leadership contender himself is unlikely to be intimidated.'

One can see why IDS's people might have regarded Boris as a traitor. IDS needed all the help he could get as a public speaker, and tried to make use of Boris's gifts as a debater by getting him, along with David Cameron and George Osborne, to come and brief him at the crack of dawn on Wednesday mornings, in preparation for Prime Minister's Questions. *Newsnight* filmed Boris arriving one morning on his bike, dripping wet and wearing a baseball cap and promising that they were going to kick Blair's butt.

The Tory leader felt he was not receiving quite the support he might have expected from Boris. At a party held by the historian Andrew Roberts for Henry Kissinger, IDS said to Conrad Black: 'I'd like to have a talk with you about Boris. I suspect neither of us is getting full value.'

But in Black's view, 'By laying most of the work [at the *Spectator*] on Stuart Reid we got the best out of Boris – IDS was losing out more than we were.'

By November 2002, in an interview with the *Scotsman*, Boris was lamenting 'the breakdown of authority' in every area of life: 'Adults are treated disrespectfully by children. In the Conservative Party we have total failure to respect the hierarchy.'

But Boris immediately corrected this verdict: 'No, it's total bollocks, isn't it? It's balls. No, forget it. It's a paragraph in a crap column. I tell you what the real problem is: there's no *esprit de corps* or will to win.'

Nobody could accuse Boris of lacking the will to win. In May 2003 he told readers of the laddish magazine GQ why they should vote Tory: 'Your car will go faster, your girlfriend will have a bigger bra size. It's an attested fact that under Conservative governments the quality of living of the British people has immeasurably improved, leading to better denticians, higher calcium consumption, leading inexorably to superior mammary development.'

We do not know of another politician who has promised the men of this country that if they vote for his party, their women will have bigger breasts. People reacted with incredulous joy to a Tory who would say such things. Boris was becoming the exponent of a new and vulgar Merry England conservatism, which appealed to rednecks but also to uptight liberals. He offered relief from the moral tyranny of the Blairites. People started to say what fun it would be to have Boris as Prime Minister.

# 17

## Conrad Black's Indulgence

HOW DID BORIS GET AWAY WITH IT? HOW DID HE manage at one and the same time to be an editor and an MP? There are precedents for this dual role, not least at the *Spectator*, but none which quite fitted Boris, who had in any case promised his proprietor, Conrad Black, that he would stick to journalism.

This Canadian magnate, who was ennobled as Lord Black of Crossharbour in 2001, rose and fell as a British press baron within two decades. Black bought the *Telegraph* cheap off the Berrys in 1985–86, acquired the *Spectator* in 1988, but suddenly started to lose control of his newspaper empire in the autumn of 2003, when his accounting practices came under intense scrutiny in the United States from disgruntled shareholders and from the Securities and Exchange Commission. In June 2004 the Barclay brothers bought the *Daily* and *Sunday Telegraph*s and the *Spectator*.

In the summer of 2005, Black and his second wife, the journalist Barbara Amiel, visited London, where they attracted a certain amount of adverse publicity. It was said that the American authorities were about to decide whether Black would face criminal fraud charges. Unkind souls also said that before arriving in town they had rung old friends encouraging those friends to have them to lunch or dinner. Boris had Black to lunch at the *Spectator*.

Black agreed to meet me for a drink one evening at the Berkeley Hotel, the luxurious establishment close to Hyde Park where he and his wife were staying. I have never had more than a passing acquaintance with him, but have always enjoyed his expansive manner, his love of the grand sweep of history and his fondness for orotund jokes, while also feeling slightly frightened of the power-mad bully who might at any time emerge. He is a very large man, who generally looks as if he is fighting a losing battle against his own greed.

His pugnacity seemed if anything to be intensified by his difficult circumstances. 'Envy is never far from the surface in this city,' he announced in an angry tone. He later added that journalists have 'a sort of grunting herd instinct when they use their position to destroy people with no sense of fair play'.

Black, who has himself written a considerable biography of Franklin Delano Roosevelt, asked whether Boris approved of having his life written. I said that at first he did, to which Conrad replied: 'He's so ineffably duplicitous you never know. FDR is one of the few people I know more devious than Boris. If FDR hadn't been devious God knows what would have happened to the world.'

It will be seen that Black admires duplicity – in this case the 'self-confident and Machiavellian' duplicity shown by FDR in the period before the United States entered the Second World War, when he was declaring his determination to preserve the peace while at the same time extending American territorial waters from 3 miles to 1,000 miles and letting Britain have 50 destroyers.

I asked Black how he first got to know Boris. 'I read his articles, I guess when he was in Brussels. He was a name much bandied about by Max [Hastings] in his last couple of years as editor [of the *Daily Telegraph*]. I may first have met Boris at the leader conference. I occasionally attended the leader conference when I thought Max's soggy tendencies were getting out of control.'

Black was intrigued by Boris: 'He's sort of like Hugh Grant in that he has rather predictable gestures. Boris tousles and retousles his hair and produces a number of imaginative adjectives – stonking – and he speaks in that syncopated upper-class way. He produces what purports to be a metaphor that's preposterous. I rang Boris up once and he said: "I'm hard at it transforming the *Spectator* into a McVitie biscuit. What I mean is an opening of solid meal followed suddenly and dramatically by a chocolate taste explosion." It's all rubbish, but it's imaginative.'

Black gave the impression that he was slightly over-awed by Boris, or at least felt powerless to control him. The powerlessness of the proprietor is one of the paradoxes of newspapers. In theory the proprietor is all-powerful, but in practice the only moment when he can exercise absolute power is when he hires or fires an editor.

The problem with sacking is that it cannot be done all that often without shaking confidence in the very publication you own. A disobedient editor therefore has much more freedom than may appear, at least as long as the publication in question is thought to be doing well.

Boris understood this. Black grew heated as he recalled how Boris had behaved: 'Jesus Christ, it all comes back to me, what a duplicitous scoundrel he is. When Max retired [as editor of the *Daily Telegraph*] we were in discussions with Dacre [Paul Dacre, editor of the *Daily Mail*]. Once Dacre just took our prospective pay packet back to David English [in charge at Associated Newspapers, owners of the *Daily Mail*], we re-interviewed Charles Moore and it became clear he was the man [to edit the *Telegraph*].

'Frank Johnson had a number of people call me to champion his cause – none of them was a grand elector – I didn't consider a call from a somewhat bibulous Woodrow Wyatt at midnight a clincher – but I told Frank he could have a try as editor of the *Spectator*. And then Frank didn't do anything.'

I said Frank was a good editor, who deserved to be backed rather than sacked, but Conrad swept on with his explanation: 'I again and again urged Frank to do the job. I said to him, look, you hired Anne McElvoy, if you want to change deputies it's up to you. Finally Dan Colson couldn't take it. The *Spectator* was rather lacklustre. There was no doubt the star in waiting, the man to make the *Spectator* a household name, was Boris.

'I saw Boris: he gave us his solemn word of honour that he would not seek selection for any party including the Conservatives. About two weeks later we found he'd thrown his hat in the ring in two constituencies. I was overseas so Colson interrogated him on the thing. Boris went through this tousling, oh God, I shouldn't have done this, you should fire me.'

Boris quite often told his employers he deserved to be sacked, but Black let him get away with it: 'We kind of endured it because the paper was doing well. Our view is that Boris's performance was outrageous, but the chief criterion is what's good for the *Spectator*, and Boris was a good thing for the *Spectator*. Still is.' This was how Black justified being so indulgent to Boris, under whose editorship the circulation of the *Spectator* rose from 57,500 to nearly 70,000.

When Boris became candidate for Henley, he rang up Charles Moore to ask his advice about how to handle Black, given that he, Boris, had faithfully promised that he would not become an MP. Moore at length wearied of Boris's apparent indecision and said: 'Look, Boris, what do you want?'

Boris replied: 'I want to have my cake and eat it.'

In only nine syllables, Boris had defined his programme, and on this occasion he actually managed, for several years, to carry it through. It is a popular programme, in the sense that it is what most people dream of doing, but by our mid-thirties most of us tend, in our unimaginative way, to have settled for something less.

Boris worked very hard to realise his dream. He lobbied everyone who might help him fulfil his ambition to be both an editor and an MP. At the *Spectator*, he spoke to his deputy, Stuart Reid, who recalled: 'When Boris decided to become an MP – to go for Henley – and I think he'd told the *Telegraph* there was no question of remaining editor if he got Henley – and vice versa – he asked me about it. Would I keep on working for him if he became an MP? I said yes. He was shoring up his position. But I did say to him I thought it was wrong in principle for someone to be both an MP and editor of a political magazine. And I still think it's wrong. But having said that, I think he's incredibly independent. He's run pieces about the Tory leader that I, as someone not committed to the Tory party, would have been terrified to run.'

When Boris appeared on *Desert Island Discs*, he was pressed by Sue Lawley to explain his conduct, and was unable to do so.

LAWLEY: 'You did as I understand it undertake to your proprietor Conrad Black that you wouldn't go into politics, you would just do the journalism, but you know, within a year you were running for Henley. I mean that was . . . dishonest?'

BORIS: 'Well, aaargh, it's probably fair to say I didn't tell them I was going to do it, that'd be a, you know.'

In April 2002 the *New York Times* did a profile of Boris, and it too asked him about his promise to Black. Boris claimed: 'The blessed sponge of amnesia has wiped the chalkboard of history.' Since Boris has an excellent memory, he must be referring to other people's amnesia.

The *New York Times* wanted a picture of Boris. I happened to be with him in his office at the *Spectator* when their photographer arrived downstairs, and Boris suddenly said: 'You pretend to be me!'

There was, we thought, a good chance that nobody in New York would realise, in the short time between getting the pictures and printing one of them, that they had got the wrong man. Boris went out and I posed for the photographer, who was completely taken in. Even when members of the *Spectator* staff put their head round the door and said, 'Where's Boris?' the poor man just said, 'Oh, are there two Borises who work here?'

But Kimberly Fortier, the American-born publisher of the *Spectator*, got wind of this childish joke, was not amused by it and put a stop to it.

One reason why Boris managed to remain editor was his ability to charm and amuse the many people apart from the Blacks and Dan Colson who thought they deserved to be amused. His predecessor, Frank Johnson, had found this an intolerable chore: 'There was this idiotic set-up where you had to suck up not just to Conrad and Dan Colson, but to the *Spectator* board.' This contained people like Norman Tebbit, the Tory politician who was most memorably described as a semi-house-trained polecat, and Algy Cluff, the former *Spectator* proprietor. Frank Johnson could not stand them, and would behave in a very surly fashion at board meetings. The consequence was that they could not stand him. Worst of all, he incurred the enmity of Kimberly Fortier. It is impossible to imagine that Boris would ever have made enemies in this way.

It was indicative of Black's continuing indulgence that, six months after Boris was elected MP for Henley, Conrad and Barbara threw a party in honour of 'the Boris Phenomenon'. Stuart Reid recalled the cardboard cut-outs of Boris which greeted guests as they arrived: 'I remember when Conrad and Barbara gave that party for him. Daniel Bernard, the French ambassador, was going up the steps. There were pictures of Boris everywhere and Bernard said: "It's a little bit like the cult of Pol Pot."'

Sarah Sands, then the deputy editor of the *Daily Telegraph*, and also the sister of the singer Kit Hesketh-Harvey, who performed at the party, said: 'The whole party was completely extraordinary – a celebration of Boris's treachery. My brother was asked to sing a song about Boris and his incredible unreliability. Everyone was laughing at things which were very, very close to the bone. At the end Kit went back to the piano to pick up the lyrics and they had gone – Boris had taken them, which was naughty.'

According to Kit, Black gave a speech in which he said that if Boris chose to run for No. 10, he, Black, was right behind him.

Charles Moore said: 'Kit and the Widow gave the cabaret and Conrad got quite angry because Kit was off-message. We left at midnight and my last sight was of Stanley Johnson in tartan trousers making a speech no one had invited him to make. The only words I can remember from it are, "One of my ex-wives . . ."'

But the Boris Phenomenon party was mainly famous for the indiscretions of the French ambassador. These would not have come to wider attention had Black's wife, Barbara Amiel, not publicised her guest's remarks in a piece for the *Daily Telegraph* in December 2001. Amiel said that during a reception at her house, the ambassador of 'a major EU country' had told guests the world's current troubles were all the fault of 'that shitty little country Israel', and had asked: 'Why should the world be in danger of World War Three because of those people?'

Other newspapers immediately identified Daniel Bernard, the French ambassador, as the author of these remarks. Bernard was outraged that a private conversation had been publicised. He at first said he could not remember saying what he was supposed to have said, and later insisted that his words had been distorted. But in July 2002 the French government transferred him from London to become ambassador to Algeria, and he died in April 2004 while still serving in that post.

I asked Black if he was intending to make Boris the editor of the *Daily Telegraph* when Charles Moore stepped down in the autumn of 2003, but he replied: 'More likely the *Sunday* [*Telegraph*] – and move Dominic [Lawson] to the *Daily*.'

Moore said Boris very much wanted the editorship of the *Daily Telegraph*: 'Boris tried pretty hard to get the job but they were determined not to give it to him. Colson was probably more adamant than Conrad.'

In Moore's account, this determination to deny Boris sprang from what Black and Colson saw as his deceitful behaviour as editor of the *Spectator*, when he had promised not to stand for Parliament only to go ahead and do so. Boris was no longer being allowed to have his cake and eat it. Some sort of high water mark had been reached.

According to Sarah Sands, Boris was offered the editorship, and said he would like to do it, but asked if the transition could be made to fit in with the next election, for he could not let down his constituents in Henley by causing a by-election.

Sands thinks Charles Moore, intent on arranging a smooth succession from himself to Boris, tipped off Boris about his departure several months in advance, while keeping her in the dark: 'I felt very hurt. I'd been Miss Goody-Goody, very loyal to Charles,' yet he did not tell her he was going until he actually did, which gave her no chance to campaign for the editorship herself. Charles had been in College at Eton, and she saw an 'Etonian understanding' between him and Boris. In the event, the relatively unknown Martin Newland was made editor, and lasted for about two years.

The embattled tycoon ended our conversation by declaring his innocence: 'It is more likely that I would get from here to John O'Groats by flapping my arms than I would ever violate the criminal statutes of the United States or any other serious country.'

One may note Black's assumption that it would be in order for him to break the law in those countries which he does not regard as serious. Conventions that might restrain lesser men were not for him. He had grand ambitions, and respected the grandeur of Boris's ambition to become Prime Minister.

On 17 November 2005 Black was charged by Patrick Fitzgerald, the attorney for the northern district of Illinois, with eight counts of fraud. Fitzgerald said: 'The indictment charges that the insiders at Hollinger [Black's company], all the way to the top of the corporate ladder, whose job it was to safeguard the shareholders, made it their job to steal and conceal.'

The day after Black was charged, I happened to see Boris at the *Spectator*. I asked him what he thought about Black. Boris was slow to answer: 'Let me think. He was terribly kind. He always treated me very, very well. No question of that.'

In 2007 Black was convicted on three counts of mail fraud and one count of obstruction of justice and was sentenced to serve six and a half years in jail. After protracted legal action in 2001–11, during which he was released on bail, his sentence was reduced. He was finally released from prison in May 2012 after serving a total of just over three years.

# – 18 –

## The Start of an Affair

A YEAR OR TWO AFTER BORIS BECAME EDITOR OF THE *Spectator*, he began a love affair which was to have very painful consequences.

Petronella Wyatt was already working at the magazine. She was the only daughter of Woodrow Wyatt, a raffish figure who as a young man had been a Labour MP, but was later raised to the House of Lords on the recommendation of his friend Margaret Thatcher. Woodrow moved in grand circles which encompassed the worlds of racing, politics and café society. He was in close touch with Rupert Murdoch, was chairman of the Horserace Totalisator Board and had innumerable famous people to dinner, about whom he wrote in his posthumously published diaries, which showed how rackety but also amusing he could be. Up to his death in 1997 he wrote a column in the *News of the World*, under the title 'The Voice of Reason'.

Petronella's mother, Verushka, was from Hungary and was the widow of Baron Dr Lazlo Banszky von Ambroz. Petronella had an exotic, hot-house air, and enjoyed behaving in a stylish and outlandish way. Michael Portillo, himself quite an exotic figure, has given an amusing description of her refusal to conform when as Defence Secretary he took a party of journalists to visit British forces in Bosnia:

It was winter and the troops' accommodation in the field was basic, so we issued a note to the press corps urging them to wear clothing that was warm and robust. We were billeted with the forces in a metal factory. At breakfast we joined the queue of soldiers in their fatigues and boots, rifles over their shoulders, with their mess tins ready to receive the man-sized dollops of scrambled egg, sausage and black pudding.

One figure stood out. She wore a tall Cossack hat, whose soft fur swayed like ripe wheat as she moved her lovely head. Her cashmere sweater plunged devastatingly at the neckline. Her legs were swathed in skin-tight moleskin jodhpurs and pirate boots. Petronella Wyatt looked wonderful, better for military morale than a whole concert performance by Gracie Fields. I asked one open-mouthed witness what he thought of her interpretation of the dress code. 'Very satisfactory,' he gasped.

Boris did not know Petronella before he went to the *Spectator*, but its offices are small and as assistant editor she would have seen him all the time. She was fascinated by political history, knew the Conservative Party well, including people like the former Chancellor of the Exchequer, Norman Lamont, and looked with favour on Boris's political ambitions. To be desperate to get to the top, but to make jokes about it, was for her a perfect mixture. His anarchic side chimed with something anarchic in her. Like her father, he delighted in causing consternation, or at least surprise, on social occasions where others were on their best behaviour.

A friend of the Wyatts said of Boris's attraction for Petronella: 'The key thing is that he's terribly like her father. He's identical to her father. They're both flamboyant, self-centred characters, very clever mountebanks, but what they've left behind is quite sparse.'

This is unfair to Boris, who is made to sound cruel and shallow. Petronella is also a very warm-hearted person. She may appear wilful and flighty, but she is capable of deep devotion, and she became deeply devoted to Boris. Friendship and the enjoyment of each other's company developed into love. They began a passionate affair.

From the first, there was one serious, and probably insuperable, obstacle to any kind of future together. Boris was married with four small children. A close woman friend of Petronella, whom for the sake of brevity we shall call Fop, defended her against the charge that she set out to break up Boris's marriage: 'She'd never before got involved with a married man. She didn't believe in it. I don't think women set out to take men away from other women unless they are complete bitches, and Petronella is not like that. She thinks divorce must be a terrible thing. She knows her father was terribly upset by his divorces, especially his third one.'

The affair was like any number of other office romances. It should not have happened, but once Boris and Petronella were attracted to each other, at least one of them would have to have shown a degree of self-restraint, if they were to avoid taking advantage of the opportunities open to them.

Boris and Petronella's warmest admirers would not say that either of them is notable for self-restraint. They incline towards boldness and impetuosity, rather than to the careful weighing-up of risks. They went out for long lunches and had assignations at the house Petronella shared with her mother in Cavendish Avenue, St John's Wood, which was within easy reach of the *Spectator* (by coincidence, the same road on which Boris's mother Charlotte had lived).

There was no reason why Boris's political or editorial colleagues should know he had broken his journey by bike from Westminster to Doughty Street at Petronella's house. Nor, if he went out to lunch, need anyone be certain where he had been.

If he wanted to see Petronella, he could postpone whatever lunch he had that day, tell the postponed character not to tell his secretary, Ann Sindall, what he had done, and pedal off to Cavendish Avenue.

Things were going very well for Boris. He saw no need to make the choices – politics or journalism, wife or mistress – which other men had to make. Boris got carried away and thought he could have it all. He said as much in an interview in the *Daily Mirror* in May 2002: 'I hate it when people say I'm a part-time MP. I work jolly hard. I am always at the 10 p.m. vote. I am a feminist icon. That's it! I am a juggler. I can have it all!'

Yet although the lovers were, as Fop puts it, 'basically very happy', Boris was also troubled: 'I know Boris felt guilty. He's family-minded. He adores his children – I think that was the big problem. And of course the children were very young. I mean, they still are quite young. But I don't blame him for not leaving Marina because I think it's impossible to leave four young children.'

Soon after the affair began, a woman of the world, a generation older than Petronella, asked her: 'How's your love life?'

Petronella: 'I'm having an affair.'

Woman: 'Oh good.'

Petronella: 'It's bad. He's married.'

Woman: 'Anyone I know?'

This sympathetic and intelligent woman takes up the story: 'I suddenly had a flash of intuition. I said, "Is it Boris?" I've always thought of Boris as a very faithful man. Petronella was very much in two minds about the whole thing – but obviously also rather smitten and very flattered. I think she was very thrilled by it all. And of course she hoped he'd leave his wife. And Boris quite rightly didn't. But I think she felt very betrayed by him. But this was a classic case of a man perhaps hinting he'd leave his wife. It's a classic story. It happens all the time. In this age of equality between the sexes, you would think it would work both ways. But single women are still very vulnerable to this. Some-one like Boris has got so much energy, and is so political – one can see how it would happen in an office. Boris behaved as well as one can under these very unfortunate circumstances, where one is bound to hurt people – he was as kind to Petronella as possible – he wasn't ruthless. Many men would have been much more ruthless.'

If Boris needed to be ruthless with anyone, it was surely with himself. He did not force himself to think through the conse-quences of having an affair. For him, and for his beloved wife and children, those consequences were likely to be even more severe than normal, because of the publicity which his adven-tures might attract.

Boris's gift for unclarity, and for avoiding inconvenient ques-tions, instead gave Petronella the idea that he was more committed to her than he really was. As a male friend in whom she confided said: 'Boris certainly gave the impression that espe-cially if she got pregnant there would be a future.'

Boris was wrong to start the affair, but it would be wrong to judge him too harshly for doing so. The pleasures of self-righteousness are repellent. Which of us, if we had had Boris's opportunities, and had found Petronella attractive, would have refrained from having a fling with her? He was only doing what any number of other men, including any number of other politi-cians and journalists, have done now and in the past. Once we start to demand a higher standard of sexual morality from politi-cians than from the rest of society, we imply that we want to be governed by politicians who are uninterested in sex. Yet politi-cians tend, with some exceptions, to have an above-average interest in sex.

One of Boris's lovers mentioned his predilection for canoodling in the back of taxis, which she thought was unwise as he doesn't tip much. Another woman, at whom Boris began to make a pass when left alone for five minutes with her, sought to explain, for the benefit of her husband, the way in which he is attractive: 'He's the male equivalent of a blonde with big tits. He's a powerful blond, he's quite funny and he's easy and he'd be in love with you for a bit. Then he'd piss off.'

Boris's writing is suffused with sexual imagery. He sees sex almost everywhere. After describing the 'pair of "acoustic couplers", a bit like a rubber fetish bra', which journalists were using in 1987 to transmit copy down a telephone line, he continued: 'No one who has done it can forget the semi-sexual sense of release when the electronic moaning and squeaking indicated that the article had arrived.' On riding to hounds for the first time in February 2005, as a guest of Charles Moore and the East Sussex and Romney Marsh hunt, he remarked on 'the weird semi-sexual relation with the horse'. He wrote of the women who tried a food writer's horrible recipes: 'They loved his "I eat anything" approach, with its flagrant sexual message.'

Life itself is often compared by Boris to a virility test. After mentioning the popularity of Ann Widdecombe as a speaker to Conservative audiences, and the difficulty of addressing people 'who have known the ecstasy of Widdecombe', he goes on: 'I imagine it is like being asked to make love to a woman who has just achieved bliss in the arms of Errol Flynn, or Robin Cook, or someone.'

Boris has also mentioned hearing his daughter play the James Blunt song which goes, 'You're beautiful', and describes how Blunt has no chance of getting the woman he has seen.

Boris had some blunt advice for Blunt: 'Come on, man: stop being so indescribably wet. If she's so beautiful, stop standing there in your T-shirt and floppy fringe, and hush your hopeless falsetto crooning. Go out and get her, is my advice.'

This captures something essential about Boris and women. If he sees an attractive woman, his instinct is to try to make a connection with her. A woman described being noticed by Boris in the deep-freeze section of the Holloway Road branch of Waitrose. Boris was with Marina, who was looking harassed, and their children, who were all in the trolley. The woman had her hand on a bag of frozen peas when she felt herself being watched. Whatever she leaned over, Boris leaned over. For the next few minutes, whichever aisle she was in, it seemed Boris was at the end.

Another woman, whom we shall call X, said: 'When Boris is taking no notice of you, you don't exist. He just seemed rather a juvenile kind of a guy. But when he turns it on, he becomes immensely charming and you feel very flattered to be noticed by him. It's digital – like a switch – I suppose that's what charm is like.'

The Englishman in love can be a sadly ineffectual figure, as the beautiful Canadian Leah McLaren complained in a cover piece published by Boris in the *Spectator* on 27 July 2002. But Boris was not like that. His pursuit of X could not have been more ardent, though his ardour, she thought, was in part an expression of the great strain under which he was operating: 'It's stress, it's pressure. If he's low and wants to cheer himself up I can get twenty text messages. And proposals of marriage. Phone calls in the middle of the night if he's feeling low. I've probably had 100 proposals in total over the year. He does believe it in the moment he says it, because it's the way to win the game. There's nothing he wouldn't do, nothing he wouldn't say, to get me.'

It follows that if Boris makes you a proposal of marriage, you ought not to take it seriously. He may mean it in that instant, rather as a journalist may believe some nonsense he is writing. But Boris is not the sort of literal-minded character who can be pinned down by a literal-minded analysis. He is more fluid, more passionate and more imaginative than a pedant could begin to conceive. Accuracy does not matter in the slightest to him.

Boris also takes a cavalier attitude to mere morality. The knowledge that he is being sincere is good enough for him. He wants everyone to have a good time, is seldom if ever censorious about other people's behaviour, and considers it distinctly uncalled for when they blame him. As X put it: 'He doesn't think he's a bad person. If you tell him, "You're sleeping with Petronella – you're betraying Marina," he doesn't have it in him to blame himself. I think the deal is basically that he's ruled by his feelings. The moment he feels not totally fired up and in love with someone, he needs that fix again. He has what Aristotle calls an incontinent personality.'

The Puritan element in British life is alien to Boris, and also to Petronella. They share an instinct not to do what they are told. The older woman already quoted above said: 'Boris shouldn't have started it – and he did start it – I think he absolutely went for her . . . He's very undisciplined, emotionally. He needs to be reassured, rather surprisingly . . . The reason he's so appealing is he's got this extraordinary energy, which brings with it a certain extra sexual energy. Like Lloyd George. It's wrong, bad and terribly hurtful. Nor do I think he can be excused by saying he's got more energy than other people. But he has. He's so ebullient it's bound to spill over in other directions. I think it's true to say he never intended to leave his wife. A slightly mitigating thing. Not much.'

Petronella's older friend contemplated her verdict on Boris: 'He's just larger than life – he's just got an incredible, cunning charm – there's enough genuine apologetic stuff – enough genuine remorse. He's a much more cunning man than perhaps people think. A Houdini of moral dilemmas.'

Other people in the office could see that Boris and Petronella's relationship was more ardent than is usually the case. Screaming matches occurred between them, and Petronella would weep, and Boris would make it up with her by sending her flowers. But staff at the *Spectator* did not realise their colleagues were having an affair until a taxi driver brought in a tape one day which Boris had left behind in a cab.

The tape was of Petronella singing songs from *La Bohème*, and Boris and Petronella had asked the driver to play it while they canoodled in the back. Not the least striking aspect of this story was the fact that they had left the tape behind. They were already displaying a very high degree of carelessness. This was something which came naturally to them. Like Boris, Petronella is the sort of person who forgets to take her passport to the airport.

The affair began to be talked about. Some have said that Conrad Black and Barbara Amiel promoted Boris's affair with Petronella, which they regarded with proprietorial pride as 'their adultery'. But Black told me: 'I did take it upon myself to say to Boris that he should bear in mind that his wife as I understood it was a divorce specialist.' Black also remembered saying to Boris: 'I don't care if you're charged with bigamy, but Boris, for the sake of that great cause which unites people up and down the land of "let's make Boris a greater figure", you'd better be a little careful.'

According to Black, Boris reacted with 'a complete motion scenario, like a cartoon, moving every joint and limb at the same time. I said, "Look, I will not raise it again. It's not a question of morals – that's not my business."'

While talking to me about Petronella, Black wished to check if his use of idiomatic English was correct. 'Tell me if I'm mis-using this phrase,' he demanded, before saying: 'I can understand the temptation when working at close quarters with Petronella to give her a seeing-to.'

Sarah Sands, who was at that time deputy editor of the *Daily Telegraph*, sent Boris a veiled warning, with James Fenton's harrowing poem, 'The Mistake', which she thought described all too accurately where Boris was going wrong. Nicholas Garland, the *Telegraph*'s political cartoonist, had shown her the poem. As Sands said with a smile: 'I've always tried to save Boris from himself. My message to him was that he was risking what was important by not choosing.'

Sands is a friend of Marina, whom she knew as a child, when their fathers moved in the same circles at the BBC. She remarked laughingly that while she had a friend in journalism, Melanie McDonagh, who believed in the stoning of adulterers, 'mine is more a nice, bourgeois matron's view of life, that men must behave'.

Once the affair was being talked about, it began, still worse, to be written about. Peter McKay started alluding to it in his Ephraim Hardcastle column in the *Daily Mail*. Columns of this sort thrive on some regular characters whose latest extraordinary exploits can be chronicled, and Boris became one of Ephraim's. A sort of teasing persecution began, which was all the more damaging for being based on fact.

As early as 8 February 2002, Ephraim wrote: 'Father of four Boris may be influenced unduly in his libertarian attitudes to sex by freethinking Petronella Wyatt, daughter of the late Tote boss Lord (Woodrow) Wyatt, with whom he works closely at the *Spectator*.'

On 30 May 2002 Ephraim did a piece about Petronella's thirty-fourth birthday party: 'Those invited included Miss Wyatt's editor/mentor at the *Spectator*, Tory MP Boris Johnson. The conspiratorial pair consult so often on work matters that there was a management inquiry into their sky-high mobile phone bills.'

Ephraim acknowledged that Boris was in the ascendant, reporting on 20 June: 'Custard-haired Tory MP Boris Johnson was 38 yesterday and is considered by friends to be well on track to achieve his ambition of being editor of the *Daily Telegraph* and Tory prime minister.'

On 27 September, Ephraim told the world that Petronella had said she was 'smartly but not revealingly dressed' when her 'clip-on silver and diamanté earrings' were seized by muggers in Kensington as she waited for a taxi: 'Be that as it may — saucy Miss Wyatt sometimes resembles a knife-thrower's glamorous assistant in a Continental circus – where was her mentor Boris Johnson, the Tory MP who edits the *Spectator*, when the attack took place?'

Petronella, according to a friend, 'was very annoyed and terrified' by Ephraim's coverage, because she didn't want news of the affair to get into the papers, 'which would make life very difficult for everyone'.

Members of Boris's staff were more and more often asked by *Daily Mail* readers what exactly was going on. Matthew Pencharz, who was working in Boris's office at the Commons, said: 'It tended to be the parents of friends. They loved Boris and they would all ask about it. I would say, "I know nothing. I don't know anything." But we all knew.'

McKay is unrepentant about the references he made to Boris's 'mentoring' of Petronella: 'I thought it would be a friendly warning to Boris that people were talking about it. Boris just seemed to be encouraged by it. I think Boris, like a lot of men, believed it was right to lie about sex. To give him his due, he never stopped my invitation to the *Spectator* summer party.'

Petronella had by this time started working for McKay at the *Daily Mail*. He pointed out that she is half-Hungarian, and suggested that a meeting of 'the wild east' had taken place between her and Boris. In McKay's opinion, if Boris had not been married, Petronella would have made a marvellous wife for him: 'She loves entertaining and she sings beautifully. She's very, very loyal. She's never said a single disloyal thing about Boris.'

Several times Petronella broke off the affair. On one occasion she even went to America for three months, and got engaged to an American, but the engagement did not last. To her mother's despair, she refused to marry anyone with whom she was not very much in love. Her mother had arrived in England at the age of eighteen as a refugee from Hungary, having lost everything, and took the pragmatic view that it was unnecessary to be in love with someone in order to marry them.

Petronella was a bit vague and forgetful about contraception, and early in 2003 she found herself pregnant by Boris. According to Fop, she told Boris immediately: 'He was never nasty about it. He said to her, "It's your decision. Whatever you do you have my full support." Many men in that situation would have gone and ordered her to have an abortion. He was very considerate.'

A woman friend of Boris said of Petronella: 'She told him that she was on the pill.'

Boris had much trouble with Petronella's mother, Verushka, who rang him all the time to tell him: 'You said you'd marry my daughter.' Verushka would not stop interfering and Boris felt unable to point out that Petronella was now a grown-up woman and should be allowed to lead her own life.

An agonising position now existed. Petronella's friends thought he was keeping her hanging on. She was under the impression he had said he was going to leave his wife, and Boris was under the impression he had not said this. He was protective of her, and was bad at breaking off the affair, or at keeping it broken off, because when he felt lonely he would ring her up. Petronella wanted a child with him, but at the same time was terrified of the consequences of having one. This impasse could not last for ever, yet went on a long time, threatening sorrow and even disaster for Boris and those closest to him.

# – 19 –

## *Sellotaping Everything Together*

LIKE MOST EDITORS, BORIS SOMETIMES FUNKED DEALING WITH problems to which there was no obvious solution, and he had more than half a mind to the political opinions of his proprietor, Conrad Black. But he was also out in front of the rest of his staff, scouting out new possibilities, seeing if he could pull off that surprise interview with Robert Mugabe, exploring anti-Americanism as well as paying lip-service to the neo-con line.

There were hawkish pro-Israeli pieces in the *Spectator*, of a kind that would have pleased Black, but Boris also published the pro-Palestinian pieces of Emma Williams, wife of his old friend Andrew Gilmour, who was by now working for the United Nations in Jerusalem. Boris's own report on the battle between George Bush and John Kerry to become President of the United States included a masterly put-down to both candidates: 'We don't have much of a choice in this election: between a man who inspires not much confidence and a man who inspires fractionally less.'

One of the most disagreeable tasks for an editor is to sack contributors who he thinks are not doing well enough. It was said that Boris took Susanna Gross, the *Spectator*'s bridge columnist, out to lunch in order to sack her, but slept with her instead.

'Who told you that?' Susanna said, looking fierce, when I had lunch with her.

'Well, I don't remember,' I said. 'I mean, as far as I know, it's what everyone in London thinks. Not that I go out much.'

'I'm outraged by the idea that he was going to sack me,' Susanna said. 'He certainly was not going to sack me. He was meant to be having lunch with me to tell me off because my *Spectator* column was always late, but he didn't even mention it, because he hates confrontation. We had such fun that we had a series of little lunches.'

I remarked in a mild tone that her bridge column was said, in the early days, to contain a lot of typographical errors, especially when Mark Amory, the books editor, who is also an expert bridge player, was not around to cast an eye over it, but she replied with indignation: 'Every bridge column has a lot of typos and it was teething problems in the first two months. I haven't had a typo for years.'

Susanna is a handsome woman of forceful views. She is literary editor of the *Mail on Sunday* and the daughter of Miriam and John Gross, eminent figures in literary London. She was so enraged by the thought that her bridge column could have been thought dispensable that I began to fear our lunch would be a failure. But I was eventually able to bring the conversation back to the altogether less controversial question of whether she and Boris had had an affair.

'No,' Susanna said. 'We had a flirtation but we didn't have an affair. Our non-affair was a few lunches. He was often dashing across town on his bike, so someone like Mary Wakefield [a member of the *Spectator*'s staff] thought he was having an affair. I like Mary Wakefield, but she's very mischievous.'

'Why was there no affair?' I asked, for I had been counting on Susanna to bulk out my as-yet rather meagre researches in this field.

'First of all because I was then with [the actor] Neil Pearson,'

Susanna said, 'and secondly because Boris was married with a mistress and with a crush on Mary Wakefield. Boris's wife had a crush on Neil, which completed the circle.'

'But could there have been an affair, had you and Boris both been free?' I asked, since she did not seem to resent this line of questioning. 'No,' she replied. 'I don't fancy him. He's too self-deprecating. I like a man to be a bit of a bastard. Also going about on his bike all day. Too sweaty. And also I was madly in love with my boyfriend – a very handsome actor.'

Susanna had something else she wanted to impart: 'I do think it's important to say in the middle of this that Boris and his wife are terribly happy. He loves her and she obviously loves him and thinks he's a wonderful father. They obviously still have in every way a very full marriage. He obviously loves having children. I think he'd be happy for his wife to have more children. The thing about Boris is that ideally he'd like more than one wife.'

Boris has an immensely strong but also rather extendable idea of family. He is in many ways a homely man, who after a meeting in some distant town prefers to drive back through the night to his wife and children than stay alone in a hotel. But like many enterprising men, he is attracted by the idea of maintaining more than one establishment. When he wrote about Jimmy Goldsmith, he referred in an admiring tone to the tycoon's 'three concurrent families' and eight children.

Susanna mentioned several times how cross she was with Boris for generally being late for lunch: 'When he was late for me the other day I was so angry – it's like training a pet – I saw him on his bike coming up to Soho House and I called him on his mobile and said: "There's no point coming in." He's the most good-natured man I've ever met. You can get as angry as you like with him.'

In the autumn of 2003, Boris brought out his second book, *Lend Me Your Ears*, billed as 'The Essential Boris Johnson'. It was a

500-page collection of his journalism, but did not include some of his most interesting work, including his defence of Darius Guppy and his attack on *Have I Got News For You*.

Lynn Barber, who used the book as the peg for an interview in the *Observer*, admitted that she had surrendered to his charm after only five minutes in his company. But she wondered, as so many others have, what Boris's sticking points are, what principles he would go to the barricades for, what he would consider a resigning matter. Boris tugged his hair, snorted and groaned: 'Uh. Ah. Ha. Mwa. I'm a bit of an optimist so it doesn't tend to occur to me to resign. I mean there are honourable people around who would seize opportunities to resign, but I tend to think of a way of sellotaping everything together and quietly finding a way through, if I can.'

Sellotape is useful stuff, but not all that robust. Boris was ludicrously busy, and it is tempting to suggest that he came unstuck because he had taken on more commitments than he could possibly satisfy.

Boris's column in the *Telegraph* continued after he became editor of the *Spectator*. The lateness of his copy drove some of his colleagues into paroxysms of rage. In the opinion of Charles Moore, the then editor of the *Telegraph*, 'Extreme unpunctuality is always a sign of selfishness.' He added that Boris was 'not horrible, but selfish'.

When a television programme was made about Boris, Charles said you could use of him the words used by David Niven of Errol Flynn: 'You knew where you were with Errol Flynn. He always let you down.'

Moore realised as soon as he had said this that it would be taken out of context. He had been asked what Conrad Black thought of Boris, and had replied that sometimes when Conrad thought of Boris, he was reminded of David Niven on Errol Flynn.

Boris also wrote about cars for *GQ*. Ann Sindall, his secretary, said: 'The car articles – so much work goes in to doing them. These guys at GQ deliver these cars. They leave them at his house and think he'll drive them to Henley. They get towed away and taken to the pound. I tell them they've got to get them from the pound. He came in once and said, "I can't find the car." I said, "What colour was it?" He said, "It's red or purple or green."'

Sindall once rang Paul Henderson at GQ and told him: 'If you're daft enough to give the guy an expensive car, go and find it yourself!'

Boris tended to miss the session at which he would have been shown by the delivery driver how to use the car. Sindall said: 'The thing is he's so busy sometimes I'll have Mary Wakefield outside the *Spectator* offices learning how to use the car. He'll ring me and ask, "How do I open the door?"'

Wakefield confirmed this account: 'He called me all through Saturday to get me to talk him through it, because he hadn't concentrated and couldn't work out how to open the door from the inside. He must have been stuck inside it. You had to turn a little dial to open the door.'

Boris loves driving fast cars – he mentions in a 2005 *Spectator* article that he has driven at 160mph on the M40 – and quite often describes them in sexual terms. He discussed a new Bentley in terms of penis size. He would sometimes be summoned to attend a 'bonding session' with other Tory MPs, and on these occasions it would amuse Ann Sindall to ensure that he arrived in a particularly expensive car.

But despite all the confusion behind the scenes, Boris was still the coming man. In October 2003, 'G2', the second section of the *Guardian*, appeared with a large, unnamed picture of Boris on his bike, and the headline, 'Only one man can save the Tories'. A month later Michael Howard made Boris a vice-chairman of the Conservative Party with special responsibility for campaigning. Boris's gift for cheering up the rank and file had been recognised. His talents were apparently so big that he could not be ignored.

Further promotion was not long in coming. In May 2004, Howard made Boris shadow arts minister. It was a minor post, which did not carry membership of the shadow Cabinet, but Boris made the most of it. Within minutes, as the following day's *Guardian* reported, he had issued a six-point programme:

Day one and I have a six-point programme. I haven't cleared this with anybody, but here's what I think.

On coming to power I am going to institute a Windows spell-check in English so that schoolchildren in this country no longer feel they have got it wrong when they spell words correctly.

The Greeks are going to be given an indistinguishable replica of all the Parthenon marbles, done in the most beautiful marble dust to end this acrimonious dispute between our great nations.

I am going to open up the bandwidth, so there is much more freedom on the radio stations. I am going to reduce some of the stuff allocated to the Pentagon, so you can get the Rolling Stones in Oxfordshire. I am fed up with just listening to treacly old Magic.

Fourth? I can't remember what point four is. Ah, yes. We are going to convene a summit with Damien Hirst and the rest of the gang at which they are going to explain to the nation what it all means. Let us have a national 'mission to explain' by the Saatchi mob, which will be massively popular.

We're going to have a national poetry Olympiad to restore rhyme and scansion. There will be some sort of stoop of wine for the winning prize.

Point six is to move away from Labour's grim, utilitarian approach to culture. I took particular exception to Charles

Clarke's attack on the Classics. If we can't study ancient languages, culture and art, we are deracinating ourselves.

Boris sportingly agreed to take part in an arts quiz devised by the *Daily Telegraph*, in which he scored only seven and a half out of twenty. Afterwards he said: 'I did terribly. My feelings of inadequacy and humility have been totally reinforced. But ask me again after I have done a year in the job, and I'd like to think I'd get them all right.'

No Labour minister dared take part in this quiz.

Eighteen days after his appointment, Boris made his first appearance at the Dispatch Box as a shadow minister. I was privileged to watch this event for the *Daily Telegraph*, and reported:

He wore a baggy light-grey suit in which he looked as if he had often fallen asleep as he worked on his question, and his pallor was such that one could guess he had not been out of doors for the past eighteen days . . . From the press gallery it was possible to note that Johnson had covered an entire A4 sheet of paper in messy handwriting, and as culture questions proceeded, he could be seen adding what looked like whole new paragraphs to his already lengthy question.

Some of his fans began to fear he might have over-prepared himself.

At last, when the tension had become almost unbearable, the Speaker called Johnson to speak.

He sprang to the Dispatch Box and started to flay the Government for allowing so many playing fields to be built over.

Last year, he pointed out, the Government had condemned no fewer than 404 playing fields to 'total extinction', and 'given the decline of contact sport in part due to litigation . . . will the minister, apart from encouraging people to run round concrete roads', arrange an annual meeting 'to arrest the decline of school playing fields?'

It was a magnificent question. In a desperate attempt to derail Johnson, Labour MPs started shouting 'too long', but he was unstoppable.

The belief that Boris would go higher was widely shared. Toby Young bet Dominic Lawson £1,000 that Boris would be Prime Minister within ten years. Young has since said that he was 'slightly in his cups' when he made this wager, but at the time Boris had such an extraordinary gift for making news that anything seemed possible. On Thursday 3 June 2004, the *Spectator* appeared on the streets of London with a political column in which Peter Oborne discussed the enmity between Tony Blair and Gordon Brown:

The underlying tension came to the surface last week in a most unexpected way. Boris Johnson, editor of this magazine, was sitting stationary astride his bicycle in Pall Mall, waiting for the traffic lights to turn green. Suddenly he found that he was not alone. Jonathan Powell, Downing Street Chief of Staff and Tony Blair's most senior adviser, had drawn up alongside. Johnson raised the subject of relations between No. 10 and the Treasury. Powell cast his eyes heavenward. 'It's a Shakespearean tragedy,' declared Powell. 'Gordon Brown is like the guy who thinks he's going to be king but never gets it. He's never going to be Prime Minister.'

Friday's papers reported Downing Street's reaction to this story. In George Jones's account in the *Daily Telegraph*, Blair's official spokesman admitted that Powell and Boris had met, but insisted Powell had not said that Brown would not become

Prime Minister: 'There was some light-hearted banter on Pall Mall but the last person Jonathan would confide his innermost thoughts to is Boris.'

Jones quoted Boris, who said Powell's memory 'must be playing him false'. Boris insisted the account which appeared in the *Spectator* was 100 per cent accurate: 'I'm absolutely certain – I went away and wrote it down afterwards. I have absolutely no doubt whatsoever.'

But Powell's partner, Sarah Helm, told me that 100 per cent accuracy was the last thing Boris could claim: 'There was an element of truth in it. There was a mention of Macbeth, but most of it was Boris telling a good story. Boris's question – "So you don't think Brown will ever become Labour leader?" – was put into Jonathan's mouth. It was a fantastic, Boris-esque example of a story being half-way there but not standing up.'

As with so many of Boris's stories, one could say that while the details were dubious, the general drift was right. Jones quoted an 'authoritative source' who described the atmosphere between the Blair and Brown camps as 'poisonous'. Boris had managed, with his mention of 'a Shakespearean tragedy', to dramatise something that unquestionably existed.

Ginny Dougary, who interviewed Boris not long after the Powell story, asked him whether he felt it was dishonourable to repeat what Powell had told him. Boris said: 'I did have a few qualms actually, to be honest. But I thought it was a jolly interesting story.'

What were his qualms? 'Well, that we were there in the fraternity of cyclists and [very big sigh] there you go, anyway, it's done.' Dougary, by the way, joined Boris's huge fan club: 'I would defy anyone to spend an hour in his presence and not be charmed . . . Boris for Prime Minister.'

Boris only took up cycling in London in 1999, but he was by now perhaps the most famous cyclist in Britain. He declared in a column that he was proud to be a member of 'that hated minority that rides a bicycle' and would defend his right to 'use my bike as my office'. He made these defiant remarks after he was upbraided by a woman in Islington for talking on his mobile while cycling. Boris had emerged as an outspoken champion of the right to use a mobile phone while on his bike: 'Just as I will never vote to ban hunting, so I will never vote to abolish the freeborn Englishman's time-hallowed and immemorial custom, dating back as far as 1990 or so, of cycling while talking on a mobile.'

In March 2006, Boris came off his bike for the third time in seven years, and was treated at Guy's & St Thomas' Hospital for an injured arm. In a short piece for the next day's *Guardian*, he said that he had been going at 'a responsible speed' towards 'a traffic light which was irrefutably green' when a group of French tourists started to cross the road. Boris shouted 'Ho!' and tried to weave around a large Frenchman who leapt directly into his path.

Boris identified 'the catatonically oblivious pedestrian, in particular the foreign tourist who thinks the traffic is coming the other way,' as the greatest threat to cyclists. This produced a letter from a *Guardian* reader, Andrew Stilwell, who said: 'If Boris Johnson casts his mind back to autumn 2005, he may just recall bicycling at top speed through a red light at the intersection of Bloomsbury Way and Bury Place as I was attempting to cross the road. I managed to avoid an afternoon at Guy's & St Thomas', but it was a close thing.'

When an interviewer remarked to him that 'cyclists drive other commuters ballistic', Boris replied: 'They're jealous. It's sheer jealousy at the way we pass them with ease and grace while they are stuck in queues.'

Cycling had several attractions for Boris. It was energetic, dangerous and anarchic: for most of the time, nobody controls the London cyclist and he or she decides from one moment to the next which rules to break. Biking was also the quickest way for Boris to speed from one job to the next in his recklessly busy life.

Mary Wakefield, his *Spectator* colleague, said: 'He tests his invincibility. If you go bike-riding with him, he will ride straight out into the traffic without looking left or right.'

This love of riding straight out into the traffic is quintessential Boris, capturing his bravery and brio but also his selfishness. He was by now taking such risks that he was riding for a fall.

# 20

# The Calm before the Storm

A FRENCHMAN, LA ROCHEFOUCAULD, SAID THERE IS something not displeasing to us in the misfortune of our best friends, but this elegant formula does not do justice to the British press. Our newspapers cannot bear it when someone is too successful. As soon as they have created a hero, they try to drag him back down into the mud.

In July 2004, Tom Baldwin, a political reporter on *The Times*, wrote: 'I don't know when I really started hating Boris Johnson, but I will try to tell you why.' Baldwin considered various reasons for hating Boris before saying it was none of those: 'No, *the* reason has something to do with him being perfectly pleasant to just about everybody and just about everybody apparently thinking he's great . . . I hate him because he's been built up and not yet knocked down. He has defied the usual laws of gravity.'

Boris was ripe for shaking, but was not the first person at the *Spectator* to get done over. The hounds of Grub Street first fastened their jaws around some of his colleagues. Within the space of a few months, the magazine acquired a reputation as a hotbed of illicit liaisons and became known to a wider audience as the *Sextator*.

It was possible, with the benefit of hindsight, to see the signs of strain building up months before. An editorial conference I attended on the morning of Thursday 27 November 2003, just after Conrad Black's troubles had burst upon an astonished world, indicated a degree of tension, even of hysteria.

Boris began by saying something about 'the magazine's future' – i.e., whether it would be bought by someone else because of Black's difficulties. In answer to this disturbing question, Boris said: 'I don't know.'

Christopher Fildes, the *Spectator*'s long-serving City columnist and a member of its board, said: 'I'd like to add my don't know to your don't know.'

Boris asked Fildes if Black would go to prison. Fildes said he thought not, as the problem was not fraud, but confusion between Black's private and public companies, leading to money getting into the wrong pocket. He said how sorry he was about Black, as he was a very fine proprietor.

Immediately after this conference, when Boris had left the room for a moment and Kimberly Fortier, the magazine's American publisher, had come in, a spectacular row broke out. Rod Liddle, the magazine's associate editor, who had been brought on to the magazine by Boris in 2002 after being sacked as editor of BBC Radio's *Today* programme, generally looked as if he had spent the night clubbing before crashing out for an hour or two on a park bench, but this morning seemed in an even rougher state than normal. He had almost lost his voice and was trying to get out of speaking at a debate organised that evening by Kimberly. After he lit a cigarette, the following dialogue took place:

KIMBERLY: 'You shouldn't smoke!'
LIDDLE: 'Don't you fucking well tell me how to live my life!'
KIMBERLY: 'If you've got bronchitis, you shouldn't smoke. I'm telling you that as a friend.'

LIDDLE: 'I'm not fucking speaking! I can't fucking speak!'

BORIS [re-entering the room] 'Pax vobiscum! Hey, hey, it's Thanksgiving! Peace!'

KIMBERLY: 'I'd rather be at home cooking the turkey.'

MARY WAKEFIELD [leaving the room]: 'I don't mind the row, it's the reconciliation scene I can't stomach.'

Next Thursday there was another row. The magazine had appeared that morning on the newsstands with a small but significant error. It carried the price for the Christmas double issue, which is twice the normal price, and Kimberly was frantic, convinced that we would lose 20 per cent of our newsstand sales. In what struck the editorial staff as a waste of our time, she brought in one of her staff to give us a lecture about late deadlines.

Boris, to his credit, threw Kimberly and her sidekick out of the room, after which for good measure he threw out a Channel 4 film crew who were filming the proceedings. He then readmitted the film crew, on condition that they did not show his row with Kimberly.

I rather liked Kimberly, and respected her ability to sell advertising, but she could get extremely cross with people. For most of the time, she was friendly to me, while also indicating that I was the kind of bumbling no-hoper who could never be of any interest to her. There were only two occasions when I incurred her wrath, both of which cast some light on Boris.

The first was after I had written a self-pitying piece for the *Daily Telegraph* in which I complained that my wife, Sally, wanted me to help look after our three small children. This article included an exchange in which Sally threatened to go back to work, to which I replied: 'Oh darling, you'd just be one of those horrid driven women.'

While writing this article I consulted Boris, who agreed that it was jolly inconvenient having a wife who went out to work. Boris has an acute sense of what can and can't be said, but it is clear that he very much regrets the rise of the career woman, at least in so far as it affects the home comforts of the career man. He offered me the following quote for my article, on condition that I did not mention him by name: 'Nobody takes any interest in whether you have any socks or indeed pants. My wife buys herself pyjamas, but she never buys any for me. I've totally run out.'

I put in this lament by a neglected man without saying who had uttered it, but Marina immediately spotted that it came from Boris, and teased both me and him about it the next time I bumped into them at a party. Her laughing reaction made me think how lucky Boris was to be married to her. Boris doesn't fall in love with horrible women, and in Marina he had found someone who could see the funny side even of male whingeing.

Kimberly, however, was not amused. She assumed, wrongly, that the article was about herself, and flew into a rage. The following Thursday she caught me on the stairs and told me that if I wanted a wife who stayed at home, I had no business wasting my time hanging about at the *Spectator* and should go off to the City and earn some real money.

The second time I irritated Kimberly was when I wrote an editorial for the *Spectator* attacking David Blunkett, the Home Secretary, for destroying our ancient liberties. Kimberly intercepted me on the stairs and said 'I didn't realise you were so nasty', while I wondered why she had taken the trouble to read such an unglamorous part of the magazine by ten o'clock on a Thursday morning. If anyone had put it to me that Kimberly was having an affair with Blunkett, I would have given an incredulous laugh.

In July 2004, Rod Liddle, the magazine's associate editor, was revealed to be having an affair with Alicia Munckton, the amiable young woman who answered the telephone at the reception desk on the ground floor.

Boris was highly amused by the exposure of the affair.

According to Liddle, 'Boris broke off discussing my next article to howl with laughter.' But Liddle's wife, Rachel Royce, cut up rough, and wrote at least a dozen articles denouncing him. She called his behaviour a 'classic philandering-husband-meets-muppet story' and said that having won ten tons of horse manure in a raffle, she would arrange for it to be delivered to the *Spectator*.

One could see why Royce felt furious. She and Liddle had lived together for eleven years but had only got married in January 2004, by which time, unknown to her, he was already seeing Munckton, a blonde who was twenty-one years younger than him. Worse than these admittedly provoking details, Liddle and Royce had two young sons.

So as usual in these cases, two stories ran in parallel: public soap opera and private agony. Liddle admitted in an interview with Cassandra Jardine in the *Daily Telegraph* that he was worried about his boys: 'I wish I saw more of them . . . It's scary to see how it affects them. I can't excuse my behaviour. It is tempting to say these things happen, but they don't unless you allow them to.'

The Liddle story was soon overtaken by the astonishing news that the Home Secretary was having an affair with the publisher of the *Spectator*. The story of Blunkett and Kimberly's affair broke in August 2004.

Boris himself still seemed in pretty good nick. On 14 September 2004 the launch party for his thriller, *Seventy-Two Virgins*, was held at the Travellers' Club in Pall Mall. The book, about a group of Islamic terrorists who seize the President of the United States while he is giving a speech at Westminster, is not a masterpiece, but it was still an amazing effort by such a busy man. It included a flirtation with anti-Americanism, and showed some sympathy and insight into a great diversity of characters, including William Eric Kinloch Onyeama, a traffic warden of kingly

West African lineage whose first three names are the same as the first three names of Sir Eric Anderson, Boris's old headmaster at Eton.

Quentin Letts, in a review for the *Evening Standard*, wrote: 'The Tory MP in the book is terrified that a sex-related indiscretion of his is about to be exposed in the *Daily Mirror*. It is interesting that Johnson should write so convincingly about a politician's fear of scandal.'

In the book itself, Boris's MP character, Roger Barlow, says after finding no revelations about himself in a tabloid newspaper: 'He felt like laughing at his own egocentricity. There was something prurient about the way he wanted to read about his own destruction.'

When Sue Lawley interviewed Boris on *Desert Island Discs*, she asked him about the book: 'Well as if you hadn't got enough on your plate you published a novel last autumn, didn't you, *Seventy-Two Virgins*, about a home-grown terrorist attack on London. It was chillingly prescient.'

> BORIS: 'Eerily prescient. Uncannily. Four suicide bombers, travelling from the north [as was to happen in London in July 2005], and the heroine was called Cameron.'
> LAWLEY: 'Yes, that's true, I hadn't thought about that.'
> BORIS: 'Right name, wrong sex.'
> LAWLEY: 'But it was weird.'
> BORIS: 'It was weird.'
> LAWLEY: 'But even weirder, actually, we have to say, it's a comic novel.'
> BORIS: 'It is, it is meant to be a comic novel, yes, parts of it.'
> LAWLEY: 'Well, it is quite comic and there's this chap called Roger Barlow who's sort of a bumbling Tory MP who rides a bicycle.'
> BORIS: 'Yes, I know, but that's been grossly exaggerated. He sort of fades from the scene a bit.'

LAWLEY: 'He doesn't. He crops up, I've read it.'

BORIS: 'Gosh, have you? You're incredibly kind.'

LAWLEY: 'And he's – you know what I'm going to say next, don't you – excessively exercised as to whether the tabloids are going to find out whether he's having an extra-marital affair.'

BORIS: 'I don't think you've read the novel with quite the attention it deserves, Sue.'

LAWLEY: 'Possibly not.'

BORIS: 'I think you need to go back, because otherwise people are going to come away with the wrong idea. I'm going to insist on this point. That's not what he's worried about. What he's done, if you remember, is he's invested unwisely in a – is it called lingerie? Lingerie – he's invested in . . .'

Barlow has lost £20,000 by investing in a lingerie shop called Eulalie. This revelation occurs at the very end of the book, for the rest of which we have been led to believe that the MP has been having an affair.

When P. G. Wodehouse ridiculed, in the figure of Roderick Spode, a fascist leader, he gave the would-be dictator a dark secret, which was to be the proprietor of a lingerie shop called Eulalie. Boris was following one of his literary idols. In the sunlit world of Wodehouse, Bertie Wooster can get into any number of scrapes, but is always rescued in the end, whether by Jeeves or by the self-defeating machinations of his foes or even, occasionally, by his own unexpected resourcefulness.

As the action in *Seventy-Two Virgins* reaches its climax, Boris allows Roger Barlow to get hold of a weapon and administer the *coup de grâce* to the chief terrorist: 'Then Roger drew back his arm with a wristy motion he had first learned as a child when thwacking the tops of the thistles in the meadow, and hit him very hard, on the base of the skull.'

There are thistles at Nethercote, the Johnson farm on Exmoor, which Boris had thwacked as a boy. He was drawing himself as the have-a-go hero who saves the free world. The book was a fantasy where an absurd and minor figure suddenly comes good.

At the start of September 2004, *Vanity Fair* magazine billed Boris as 'the Tory MP who could one day be Britain's Prime Minister'. It published an admiring profile of him by Michael Wolff, who ended by comparing him to two actors who went into politics: 'He is, it occurs to me, as he woos and charms and radiates good humor, Ronald Reagan. And Arnold Schwarzenegger . . . He is, I find, inspirational.'

No other British MP could have been compared to Reagan or Schwarzenegger. Only Boris was in a position to make the leap from celebrity, or ham actor, to serious politician. The public was willing him on, for it loves such implausible transformations, but the leader of Boris's party was about to cut this maverick exhibitionist down to size.

# 21

## Operation Scouse-grovel

WITHIN A MONTH OF *VANITY FAIR*'S PAEAN OF PRAISE, the storm started to break over Boris. The Liddle and Kimberly scandals can be seen in retrospect as the first flashes of thunder and lightning, heralding mortal danger for the man billed as the next Prime Minister but three.

The first bolt of lightning struck him in a most confusing and unexpected way. Many people will recall that Boris had to go on a mission to apologise to the people of Liverpool, without being able to remember exactly what he said about them that was so offensive. But even at the time it was hard to tell what exactly had gone wrong, especially from the brief phrases in the offending article which were quoted over and over again in other accounts of the row.

On Thursday 14 October 2004 the *Spectator* appeared with an editorial about the reaction to the murder of Ken Bigley, a British hostage who had been working in Iraq but came from Liverpool. The article criticised 'the mawkish sentimentality of a society that has become hooked on grief and likes to wallow in a sense of vicarious victimhood', and went on:

The extreme reaction to Mr Bigley's murder is fed by the fact that he was a Liverpudlian. Liverpool is a handsome city with a tribal sense of community. A combination of economic misfortune – its docks were, fundamentally, on the wrong side of England when Britain entered what is now the European Union – and an excessive predilection for welfarism have created a peculiar, and deeply unattractive, psyche among many Liverpudlians. They see themselves whenever possible as victims, and resent their victim status; yet at the same time they wallow in it. Part of this flawed psychological state is that they cannot accept that they might have made any contribution to their misfortunes, but seek rather to blame someone else for it, thereby deepening their sense of shared tribal grievance against the rest of society. The deaths of more than 50 Liverpool football supporters at Hillsborough in 1989 was undoubtedly a greater tragedy than the single death, however horrible, of Mr Bigley; but that is no excuse for Liverpool's failure to acknowledge, even to this day, the part played in the disaster by drunken fans at the back of the crowd who mindlessly tried to fight their way into the ground that Saturday afternoon. The police became a convenient scapegoat, and the *Sun* newspaper a whipping-boy for daring, albeit in a tasteless fashion, to hint at the wider causes of the incident.

It is not Boris's style to be wilfully abusive: on the rare occasions when he attacks people, he does it in a good-humoured tone. The author of the piece was Simon Heffer, whose original draft was nastier about Bigley himself. Stuart Reid, the *Spectator's* deputy editor, removed these taunts, by comparison with which the remaining insults thrown at Liverpudlians seemed so mild as to be harmless.

But the leader provoked what Boris himself described, in an article a few days later for the *Liverpool Daily Post*, as 'one of those sudden media firestorms: the cameras on the doorstep, the phone ringing off the hook, the endless requests for interviews, the shouted abuse'.

Some of this protest was genuine, but some was concocted by those who saw an opportunity to embarrass the Conservative leader Michael Howard or the party in general. It was, to say the least, extremely unfortunate that the article had grossly under-stated the death toll at the Hillsborough disaster, in which 96 people died, and had blamed drunken fans at the back of the crowd, when this cause was specifically ruled out by the inquiry report.

When Howard, a passionate supporter of Liverpool Football Club, was first asked to disown the piece, he thought a clarification issued by Boris might suffice. But it proved impossible for Howard's staff to agree a form of words with Boris, who was worried he would be disowning something in his own magazine. Heffer told Boris 'to tell Howard that I wrote it – I offered to own up – but Boris to his credit said no'.

As the story ran out of control, Howard was lobbied by people from Liverpool Football Club and by Tory candidates in the north-west. He was warned that when he attended a forth-coming Liverpool game, he would be booed, and on Saturday – two days after the offending piece had appeared on the streets of London – he ordered Boris to go to the city to apologise.

Boris was in two minds about whether to go. In retrospect, it seems clear that he should have refused Howard's order. The most handsome way for Boris to demonstrate his own inde-pendence, and the independence of the *Spectator*, would have been to resign his front-bench post, apologise for the errors of fact in the editorial, and make his own arrangements for any visit he might or might not make to Liverpool.

But he reluctantly agreed to Howard's request, having failed to realise (as Boris put it in the following week's *Spectator*) that 'Michael's brilliant spin-doctors would present this as some sort of disciplinary procedure, in which the ideal headline was intended to be: "Shamed Tory buffoon Johnson in Liverpool grovel – Iron Mike gets tough".'

Howard is in many ways a delightful man, but he also has a ferocious temper, and he cannot bear indiscipline among his subordinates. He got his way over the visit to Liverpool, but he and his staff grossly underestimated Boris's star appeal. As one of Howard's people put it, 'Boris was the story and we weren't prepared for that.'

The mission was conceived in such a way as to invite ridicule. Conservative Campaign Headquarters, which we shall call by its traditional name of Central Office as that was how most Tories still referred to it, was put in charge of the arrangements. It was decided that Boris should talk only to the Liverpool media, and not the national media. This was an untenable idea, for anyone who had given the matter a moment's dispassionate thought would have realised that the scores of journalists and photographers who were dispatched from London to cover Boris's trip were hardly going to accept that they could not see this national figure for themselves. Many of these correspondents already knew Boris quite well, and all of them realised they would be treated by their offices as total incompetents if they failed to find him.

Boris himself warned at a meeting two days before the trip that Central Office was getting over-involved, and suggested that it would be better to go up and do a press conference with everyone who wanted to see him. But Howard's people wanted to control everything, and insisted on treating the trip as an expedition into cannibal country. As one of them put it, 'We couldn't send him on his own. He would have been eaten alive.'

Another member of the team said: 'We booked him in under a false name at some hotel, which was probably in retrospect a mistake. Everybody felt it was a complete nightmare from start to finish. I've blotted most of it from my memory, I'm happy to say. They felt it needed large men to head up there because of expected trouble. They were going round the office the previous week saying, "You're large, you're large." Richard Shackleton, Nick Carter and Matt Cumani are all a good six-foot-plus, and the fourth member of the party, Ramesh Chhabra, is quite beefy. They were selected for their ability to take part in a rugby scrum.'

It must be said that not everyone took quite such a dim view of Boris's behaviour as Central Office did. It was quite common to hear people say that they agreed with him about Liverpool, and even in the city itself there did not seem to be many people who were thirsting to tear him limb from limb. In the press, too, he had eloquent supporters, including Michael Gove, whose defence of Boris appeared in *The Times* on Tuesday 19 October 2004:

> If we Britons love our shambolic bumblers, then we must expect them, sometimes, to bumble into something of a shambles . . . Alongside the disciplined ranks of parliamentary infantry, we need a few Cossacks, whose dazzling swordplay may not always hit the target, and may even cause the odd self-inflicted wound, but whose dash, verve and sheer élan help to lend the cause colour . . . For many contemporary Britons, part of the problem with Parliament is its crushing of individuality. A culture that seems to value the robotic on-messageness of a Hoon or Milburn over the freshness of a Boris must have something wrong with it. More than that, Boris himself seems to recognise, whether intuitively or through observation, that celebrity now plays the role in politics that possession of an aristocratic name or a distinguished war record used to perform. It gives you a right to be heard. Celebrity allows you into people's lives and homes, where they give you permission to share your views, in a way that others are denied . . . So I for one am happy to say: let us

acknowledge that his weaknesses as much as his strengths are all too visible, but let us cherish this free spirit while we still have him – the MP for Henley, the People's Boris.

Boris's four minders set to work to carry out the insane strategy of keeping him away from most of the press, and from just about the entire population of Liverpool. Shackleton and Chhabra formed the advance party, which went up a day early and carried out a reconnaissance of the places Boris would visit, including the Liverpool Institute for the Performing Arts.

Carter and Cumani had the job of escorting Boris to Liverpool on the evening of 19 October 2004. It was reported in the *Evening Standard* in London that journalists were staking out the stations, Euston and Lime Street, which Boris would use if he travelled from London to Liverpool by train. The airports from which one might fly to Liverpool were also being watched. The Conservatives therefore hired what one of Boris's minders called 'this enormous fuck-off top-of-the-range Range Rover, black with tinted glass, a monstrous brute. It couldn't have been more indiscreet. We took this brute up to Boris's house off the Holloway Road and drove round the block a couple of times just to make sure it wasn't staked out. One of us walked up and down his road, and knocked on his door. Boris went upstairs to pack his things, and at about 8 p.m. we set off. We had various plans in case we were followed. We were going to go to the House of Commons, drop Boris off with one of us at St Stephen's Entrance, walk him through the underpass and to Portcullis House and pick him up in the Range Rover there.'

But the Range Rover was not followed and they started the long drive to Liverpool. Boris sat in the back, either editing the *Spectator* or sleeping. According to one of his minders, Boris's mood varied between 'this is all an incredible pain in the arse and I'm hating every minute of it' and 'the schoolboyish sense that it was all a jolly wheeze'.

At two in the morning they arrived at a hotel in the Sefton district of Liverpool which belonged to a chain with which the Conservative Party had a corporate account. In the minder's opinion it was 'a pretty sleazy dive and freezing cold'. The rooms were booked in the name of Birkenshaw, but according to the minder, this was not an assumed name for Boris, but the real name of the man at Central Office who dealt with such matters.

The big story at breakfast time on local television was 'where is Boris Johnson – please phone in'. The hunt was on. Quentin Letts of the *Daily Mail* managed to contact Boris on his mobile phone: 'He was finishing off a newspaper column. Where the heck was he? "I don't know where I am," he blustered. "Can't talk, man. Gotta go!" Click, brrrrrrrr, went the receiver.'

Boris went for an early-morning breath of air in Sefton Park, where he met a jogger, who according to Boris said: 'Welcome to Liverpool. Never mind the bollocks.' Boris also did a quick exclusive interview with the evening *Echo*, which was sworn to secrecy.

His minders left him for a couple of hours at the hotel and did a final recce. It had been agreed that a 'pool' of twelve journalists would be allowed to follow Boris. One of the minders takes up the tale:

At this point we go into the dream sequence. What happened was so surreal, the picture goes a bit shimmery about the edges. I had to pick up the pooled hacks in a pub car park in Sefton and take them to the Liverpool Institute for the Performing Arts. It was a bit like taking a school outing. I called the register, someone distracted me and an extra person was smuggled in. I had twelve journalists with mobiles. It was just impossible. The first event was a photo call with Boris at the Institute. I got them there and we waited for him. Then the awful news came down my mobile that Boris was basically throwing a strop and they were going to be ten to fifteen minutes late. Boris told them: 'This is all a farce. This is going wrong. I know how to look after myself.' This was where the plan just fell apart. I don't know if you've seen the film *Zulu*, but it was a bit like that, when the British at Rorke's Drift suddenly see the Zulu *impi* coming over the brow of the hill. This army, this *impi* of hacks, with tripods and notebooks instead of assegais and shields, poured down the hill in a torrent. I was the only advance man there. I was swept aside. There was nothing I could do. Sixty seconds later Boris sweeps up in Matt Cumani's car, preceded by four police officers in a police Range Rover. Boris met the director of the Institute. There were shouts of 'Boris, have you come up here to apologise?' It was just bedlam after that. How were we going to separate the people in the pool from the rest of this Zulu army? I hadn't a bloody clue who was who. The antipathy towards us from the non-pool people was immense. At the bronze gates into the Institute we were vetting people and people were saying: 'Do you know who I am? How dare you keep *The Times* out?' All the time various broadcasters were ringing and asking how to get hold of Boris. The press office at Conservative HQ was also ringing and saying, 'This looks awful,' so I said to them, 'How do you think I feel?'

A press officer who had been left behind in London says: 'Those of us who were mercifully not sent on the mission but were watching the television in the office – our hands were wringing in total despair as it went from one catastrophe to another.'

According to Simon Hoggart, whose sketch of the occasion appeared beneath a large picture of the back of Boris's head on the front page of the next day's *Guardian*, the man at the eye of the storm 'performed rather well'.

Boris apologised for the hurt he had caused, and for the error made about the Hillsborough disaster. But he stood by the 'thrust' of the piece: 'It would be mad to say that I had undergone a pre-frontal lobotomy and everything I said last week was no longer operative.'

One of the minders takes up the tale: 'We were there for a good hour, with Boris watching various sorts of dancing shows, and then we slipped out the back, Matt brought his car round and we went to our next assignment, which was BBC Merseyside. Boris was being fairly game about it. He was going to do a phone-in and was going to abjectly apologise for his comments, or at least for Simon Heffer's comments. As we got there Kevin Bouquet was doing his piece to camera for the one o'clock news and Boris walked across behind him and said, "I never said that." The whole place descended into total confusion and laughter. The BBC thought it was so good they wanted it done again. Boris went and did his phone-in and a huge row erupted because George Eustice had promised Channel 4 they could go in and film the phone-in, and the BBC said they wanted to do that. We managed to resolve that.'

But Boris was still defying his leader by saying things like: 'Michael Howard was completely wrong to say that the article was "nonsense from beginning to end". I don't think he can have read it properly.'

Someone from Conservative HQ rang up one of Boris's minders to observe: 'It's all going horribly wrong, you prat. Get a grip on it.' Another apparatchik from Tory HQ actually rang a minder to say that Boris had got his lines wrong, and must be told to say the right lines.

Worse was to follow. Paul Bigley, the brother of the murdered hostage, phoned the radio programme to tell Boris: 'You're a self-centred, pompous twit; even your body language on TV is wrong. You don't look right, never mind act right. Get out of public life!'

Boris tried to apologise, but Bigley went on: 'Get out of private [sic] life, and leave us alone!'

Shortly before Boris left the phone-in, one of his minders found a woman dressed in pink lying in wait for him in the BBC car park.

Minder: 'Who are you?'

Woman: 'I want to talk to Boris Johnson. I'm a professional griever.'

Minder: 'What do you want to talk to him about?'

Woman: 'Alder Hey hospital. I want him to apologise for Alder Hey hospital.' The distressing case of Alder Hey hospital involved the retention of parts of dead children without their parents' consent.

The minder described what happened next: 'I wondered if BBC security could remove this woman, but they could not. We had to bring Boris past her. She pushed in. The television cameras pounced. Boris said: "Oh well, that's very interesting. I will report back to Michael Howard and he will write to you." The woman said: "I want a reply this afternoon." Then Boris went after her with a kind of strangling motion.'

The minder took more phone calls from Conservative HQ: 'This looks terrible.'

Minder to HQ: 'Well, what do you want me to do about it? Start assaulting the woman?'

According to the minder, 'Boris is beginning to get a bit pissed-off at this point.'

The *Spectator* sent over a copy of Boris's piece for that week's issue to the minder's BlackBerry. He found that Boris had written:

What makes Operation Scouse-grovel even more depressing is that I am attacked by my own troops for embarking upon it. In the journalistic equivalent of the fragging that GIs used to perform upon their officer, Stephen Glover, our own media correspondent, has said that in coming to Liverpool I am letting down the *Spectator*. He claims in Tuesday's *Daily Mail* that in going to apologise, at the behest of Michael Howard, the Tory leader, I am acting like a whipped cur . . . He ends his piece with words of dark foreboding about the freedom of the press.

The first thing to say is that Glover's piece shows, of course, the fearless independence of all *Spectator* columnists. Not only does he beat up Michael Howard and the Tory party, he also administers a resounding kicking to his own editor — with whom he had lunch less than a week ago, at which companionable and bibulous ceremony he requested and was granted a sizeable rise! That's the spirit, Glover! If that isn't freedom of the press, I don't know what is.

Boris rejected the idea that Johnson the politician was betraying Johnson the journalist: 'Johnson the politician apologises for and refuses to apologise for exactly the same things as Johnson the journalist.'

As the minder read this unrepentant piece, he thought 'Oh my God', but he also found that 'by that stage I was past caring'. On they went to the Granada studios, a huge round of local ITN interviews, and a photo call by the Albert Dock. They were supposed to go on to yet another radio station, but decided they had had enough, so Boris did that interview by telephone. They later learned that the station had been going to present Boris with an enormous humble pie.

The minders drove Boris to Speke airport and he flew back to London alone. One of the minders said: 'By that stage he looked like a wrung-out flannel. He really had been through the mill. We went back to the hotel, and those who weren't driving had stiff double whiskies. Then we drove back down in the huge Range Rover. We were laughing like lunatics at that stage. We were laughing so hard that we missed the turning from the M62 on to the M6. It was like the aftermath of the Charge of the Light Brigade – the survivors coming out of the valley of death. The usual debriefing meeting never happened. The idea was so flawed that the execution was a total irrelevance. The story played very big on the rolling news channels, but on the BBC *News at Ten* that night it had boiled down to only twenty or thirty seconds. But there was a certain *Schadenfreude* among elements of the parliamentary party, that Boris had been made to look a complete and utter chump.'

Susanna Gross said: 'He came and joined me and some friends for dinner on the night he came back from Liverpool. He was very annoyed with Howard, but as usual unbelievably good-natured. Boris just wanted to meet someone for a drink to unwind.'

Boris's attack on Liverpool gave him cult hero status among football supporters whose teams were playing Liverpool. Patrick Hennessy heard Chelsea fans chanting 'There's only one Boris Johnson' at the final of the Carling Cup in February 2005 at the Millennium Stadium in Cardiff.

Howard's people were not the only ones to have adopted an impossible plan. Boris had also adopted a career plan which could not long survive contact with reality. The Liverpool débâcle exposed the impossible contradiction between editing the *Spectator* and being a front-bench spokesman. When Sue Lawley interviewed Boris on *Desert Island Discs*, the following exchange took place:

LAWLEY: 'Well, let's move on to the Ken Bigley affair.'
BORIS: 'Why do we have to move on to that?'
LAWLEY: 'Because it does absolutely exemplify the dilemma, doesn't it.'
BORIS: 'Oh yes, good point.'
LAWLEY: 'Between the journalism and the politics. There

you are. You have to decide in that moment whether you're going to toe the party line because you're a front-bencher, or whether you're going to say what you really think, and you chose in favour of saying what you really think. In other words the paper won over the party. Is that fair?'

BORIS: 'Yes, what happened was that we had a very, very vigorous editorial which made some points about the culture of sentimentality, I'm racking my memory now . . . and that was what the editorial was meant to be all about.'

LAWLEY: 'Did you write it?'

BORIS: 'I take full responsibility for that editorial.'

LAWLEY: 'Did you write it?'

BORIS: 'I commissioned it, I edited it and I carried the can for it.'

LAWLEY: 'Ah, but you didn't write it.'

BORIS: 'And whether I wrote it or not is completely immaterial, Sue, because I'm the editor.'

LAWLEY: 'Of course, no, no, no, that's quite right.'

BORIS: 'And editors are responsible for whatever appears in the editorial columns.'

LAWLEY: 'But it would be quite interesting to know if you actually wrote it.'

BORIS: 'It would be. It would be. Er, but, I take full responsibility and I did, I went on this pilgrimage of penitence to Liverpool . . . to clarify and to apologise for the factual error which was related to the number of casualties at Hillsborough . . .'

LAWLEY: 'There were a lot of people who thought you just shouldn't have gone. You should just have resigned from the front bench. Do you think you should?'

BORIS: 'I think probably, yes, probably. Well, no, what I should have done, what I should have done is I should have resigned from the front bench and apologised for those things that we got wrong.'

Alan Watkins, one of the great political columnists of modern times, condemned both Howard and Boris. Watkins was at one time the *Spectator*'s political columnist, but was by now writing for the *Independent on Sunday*, where he observed that since the mid-1950s, when Ian Gilmour acquired it, the *Spectator* has been the most stimulating of all the weeklies:

Its editors have included, if Mr Howard will forgive me, three Conservative politicians of greater ability, intelligence and distinction than he possesses himself: Gilmour, Iain Macleod and Nigel Lawson. Who, not to put too fine a point on it, does this pipsqueak think he is, issuing orders to the editor of a great journal?

Watkins thought Howard had made 'an outrageous demand':

But once he had, it was Mr Johnson's clear duty to reject it, if necessary in the most forceful language.

If Mr Howard had then dismissed him from his front bench, Mr Johnson should have taken it on the chin. As it was, he chose to place his own political career or the interests of the Conservative Party or both above his duty as an editor. I do not want to make heavy weather about this, but he has let down his leader-writer, his staff, his contributors, his readers and, not least, himself . . . He has tried to ride two horses and has, I am afraid, succeeded in falling off both of them.

Many people agreed with Watkins. Boris's star was no longer in the ascendant. Gwen Halley, in the *Sunday Independent* in Ireland, attacked Boris's claim that there are two Boris Johnsons,

Johnson the politician and Johnson the editor: 'There are two Boris Johnsons all right: the Public Boris and the Real Boris. Charmingly sloppy and self-deprecating on the outside, arrogant and deeply driven on the inside. Boris Johnson has his nose in the bountiful trough of public life. The image of bonhomie he projects is a high art that will survive long after his comparably paltry achievements in journalism and politics are forgotten . . . like all babies – real or fake – Boris is indulged by those around him. Spoilt babies become spoilt adults, manipulative and morally degenerate.'

Yet it can also be argued that like many of the setbacks in Boris's career, the Liverpool débâcle did him no permanent damage. It amused a great number of people and made him even more famous. To subvert Howard's control freakery from the inside was perhaps more fun, and was certainly more trouble for the Tory leader, than a gentlemanly decision to resign from the shadow team would have been.

The story has a happy coda. Little more than a year later, on 2 December 2005, a party was held at Westminster to launch the all-party parliamentary group to support Liverpool in its role as the 2008 European Capital of Culture.

George Howarth, the Labour MP for Knowsley North and Sefton East, who set up the group, invited Boris to become one of its founder members, and Boris accepted this public gesture of forgiveness.

As Mr Howarth said, 'The people of Merseyside are nothing if not generous,' to which Boris replied: 'The quality of Mersey is not strained.'

There was a general air of contentment as Boris mingled with the dignitaries who had travelled from Liverpool to the reception. The Bishop of Liverpool, James Jones, told me he could confirm 'out of personal experience' that Liverpool is 'a very forgiving city'.

Not that Boris was about to yield any more ground than he had yielded at the time. He avoided answering questions about the original row by saying: 'You'll have to ask Michael Howard what I was apologising for.'

A beaming Howard arrived at the reception. It was only four days before he handed over the leadership of the Conservative Party to his successor, David Cameron, and he looked demob-happy. Howard was in no mood to dwell on his difficulties with Boris, and instead said: 'The difference between London and Liverpool is this. If you get into a lift in London, you will get out and no one will have said a word to each other. If you get into a lift in Liverpool, you can almost guarantee to come out laughing.'

Boris came out laughing from his contact with Liverpool, and did so by declaring a boundless affection for the place rather than by grovelling.

On 26 January 2006, when Boris appeared on the *Richard and Judy* show on television to publicise his programmes about the Romans, Richard Madeley took the chance to raise the Liverpool visit, and asked what Boris thought of Howard's order to go there: 'Were you actually furious about that? Why didn't you tell him to sod off?'

Boris replied: 'Because I thought it would be rude . . . It was fine . . . I love Liverpool. You can't get too much of it.'

# 22

# The Pyramid of Piffle

AS THE LIVERPOOL STORM BROKE OVER BORIS, HIS private life also reached a crisis. On the day before he set out for the city, Petronella aborted the second child she had conceived by him. In normal circumstances, this miserable event would probably have remained private, but for Boris the circumstances were not normal. He was by now so celebrated that news about him was at a very high premium, and on Sunday 7 November 2004 the story of the abortion broke in the press.

It should be said that Petronella rather than Boris reached the decision to have an abortion, and her friends are adamant that she has never sought to blame him. Fop, the close friend of Petronella quoted earlier, said, 'Nobody forced her into it. She didn't want to be a single mother, and she thought it would cause immense complications.'

The older woman friend of Petronella, also quoted earlier, tried to defend Boris: 'I think Boris didn't want Petronella to have an abortion. This is a way in which Boris is not a horrible man. Petronella wanted Boris to marry her, obviously. I think he was very upset by the abortion. I think he would have stood by her financially, visited the child, et cetera, if she had gone ahead.

He would think it was his responsibility if she had had a child. I don't think he would have chucked her.'

But many people, including many of Boris's friends, were indignant on Marina's behalf and distressed by the abortion. As one man put it: 'All that abortion stuff – it just didn't look good – it was horrible.'

Some of Boris's friends thought he was secretly glad to have the whole situation resolved. One woman said: 'I think Boris doesn't like hurting people and he'd got himself in a position where someone had to be hurt, and he couldn't do it because he's a big softy. He was paralysed. In a way the awful scandal when it came out was his way out, and I think there was a bit of him that was relieved. It took it out of his hands.'

This woman added: 'I think the public humiliation has been terrible for him. But let's not blow this out of proportion. Lots of men have affairs.' She expressed the hope that he would be able to restore his reputation: 'If he's given a shadow post I hope he can prove himself reliable.'

The private pressure on Boris, and on those near to him, was enormous, but to this was added a tidal wave of publicity which threatened his political career. Rival newspapers acted as a pack of hounds, each leaping at their common quarry, each drawing blood, and each emboldened by the others to fresh frenzies of aggression. Boris now lost his head and committed a very foolish error.

The *Sunday Mirror* of 7 November broke the story of the abortion, carried out on 18 October at the Portland Hospital in London, but without naming either Petronella or Boris. Meanwhile the *Sunday Express* said Boris was about to resign his post as shadow arts spokesman, 'amid rumours of a crisis in his private life', and referred to his 'close relationship' with Petronella. But it was the *Mail on Sunday* which did the fatal damage to Boris, or gave him the chance to do the fatal damage to himself.

Simon Walters, the Political Editor of the *Mail on Sunday*, has a formidable record of breaking big stories, and unlike his rivals he managed to get through to Boris and extract a comment from him. Walters' story appeared under the headline 'Boris, Petsy and a "pyramid of piffle"', with large photographs of both Boris and Petronella. The piece opened with Boris's famous, and disastrous, denial: 'I have not had an affair with Petronella. It is complete balderdash. It is an inverted pyramid of piffle. It is all completely untrue and ludicrous conjecture. I am amazed people can write this drivel.'

Boris had denied something which was known to be true. One can see why he did this. He reckons it is nobody's damn business who he sleeps with, so he is entitled to lie about it. He is convinced that his private life has no bearing on his fitness for high office, and believes that the press and public are motivated by a disgusting jealousy of his sexual conquests.

We know this is what Boris thinks, for he stated his case in a passionate defence of the right of politicians to lie about their private lives, published in the *Daily Telegraph* in January 1998. The piece takes the form of a defence of President Bill Clinton, who was under fire for having denied having 'sexual relations' with Monica Lewinsky when it was pretty clear that some kind of sex had taken place.

Boris observes that Lewinsky herself is not blameless. He suggests she may be lying, and accuses her of trying to seduce the President:

> It seems at least conceivable that she is lying her head off, a star-struck booby trapped in a fantasy malevolently encouraged by others ... Some have implied that the President coerced Miss Lewinsky. What tosh. The more footage we see of the pair together, the more obvious it is that she transpires at every pore with lust to be noticed by the 'big he', as she calls him. The more we learn about how

she used her Blue Pass to hang around outside the Oval
Office in a low-cut dress, the more one is inclined to
sympathise with Clinton's predicament.

Boris took the unfashionable view that Clinton was
Lewinsky's victim. He saw how vulnerable a powerful man
could be to this sort of harassment, and he sympathised with the
powerful man. But much more significantly, Boris tackled head-
on the claim that 'it's not the sex' but 'the *lying*' which is so
objectionable in such cases. According to our hero: 'It was a lie
about sex, the kind of lie we try to avoid, but which we would
all admit is sometimes justifiable, even, God knows, desirable.'
Boris has no time for the notion that a man who lies about
sex is untrustworthy:

> Extra-marital sex is said to be of immediate political
> relevance, and not just a matter for the couple concerned,
> because it is said to expose a basic treacherousness, 'If-a-
> chap-can-lie-to-his-wife . . .' etc. Oh really? Is Gladstone to
> be condemned, because of what we now know about his
> weird work with prostitutes? Was Thomas Jefferson a failure
> as a President, because he had an affair with a slave-girl?
> Does it really *matter* what Palmerston got up to with
> women in Hyde Park?

Nor does Boris accept the idea that politicians should 'set an
example' and help to uphold the institution of marriage, so that
children do not grow up without fathers, which makes them
more likely to turn to lives of delinquency and crime:

> Does anyone think a bunch of uniformly virtuous politicians
> would make the slightest difference? Of course they
> wouldn't. The decay of marriage, the rise in illegitimacy,
> are far more directly traceable to female emancipation,

unemployment and the vast welfare state, which so often supplants the role of the husband. The press wilfully muddles the issue, feeding on public prurience and jealousy.

We come to the heart of Boris's counter-attack against people who expose the affairs of politicians, including the late Robin Cook, who was found while Foreign Secretary to be having an affair with his secretary. The repellent motives of prurience and jealousy are at work:

Yes, jealousy. We know why these politicians are so attractive to young interns. It is because they have power, and *we* gave them that power. We want to delimit the consequences of electing them, to stop them enjoying the attentions of the likes of Miss Lewinsky; and how snivelling and short-sighted that attitude is.

We believe it is our democratic right to insist that Clinton and Cook have no mistresses, when it is nothing whatever to do with us. So politics is trivialised and turned into hell for so many of its practitioners.

Politics had become hell for Boris, but he made matters worse by claiming that the allegations were 'an inverted pyramid of piffle'. This bizarre phrase had already been used by Boris in a completely different context in a piece in the *Daily Telegraph* on 19 July 2001, and he may well have used it before then, for like most performers he constantly recycles his material, and finds certain phrases almost irresistible.

Boris's straight denial of the affair, to which the inverted pyramid was added as a flourish, gave the tabloids a perfect excuse to intrude on his private life. They could embark on a self-righteous mission to prove Boris a liar.

What should Boris have said? There was no good reply to give when the press started asking him about Petronella and her abortion, but the least bad response would have been: 'I don't answer questions about my private life.' This would have had the additional merit of being true, for the real meaning of the piffle quote, as a member of Boris's family explained to me during the writing of this book, was: 'Go away, it's got nothing to do with you.'

A version of this defence was successfully employed by David Cameron during the Tory leadership campaign, when he refused in a calm and amiable tone to say whether he had ever taken drugs. Most people believed he had every right to say this, and after blustering about it for a week or so, and ordering him to come clean, even papers like the *Daily Mail* were obliged to fall silent. To this day, we do not know about Cameron and drugs, which helps his friends to believe whatever they like on this controversial topic, while his enemies cannot drag him down by showing that he has lied.

Part of Boris's difficulty was that the papers already knew an awful lot about him, and he did not even know how they had discovered some of the worst bits. When the story of the abortion broke, a friend of both Boris and Petronella says: 'He was suspicious. He didn't understand how this came out. How did they know about the abortion? He wanted to know how they knew. He was really scared that Petronella had something to do with it. He wanted to be reassured that she had nothing to do with it, but he couldn't speak to her. But poor Petronella. The whole thing was horrible – really horrible to be in love with someone who was married – really horrible.'

Boris was one of the great loves of Petronella's life, but she was now cut off from him in the house in St John's Wood, just north of Lord's cricket ground, where she was living with her mother. She was offered a variety of safe havens by her friends, but chose to stay there. It is a fine, detached house, standing in its own garden, which is itself separated from the road by a reasonably high wall. Trees help to screen it from view. But a friend of

Petronella – the same Fop quoted before – said: 'It was horrible having the press camped outside her home, and the inaccuracies and lies written about the affair were horrible too. Petronella was very upset by a horrible article by Amanda Platell which accused her of sleeping with Boris because he was going to be Prime Minister. So much rubbish was written. Petronella bears no grudge at all against Boris, but she hated the way the affair ended with the press and all that. She had people standing outside the house with cameras all the time. She couldn't go out, and she couldn't ring Boris because she knew he was being watched too. All that she wanted was to be left alone. And then journalists were ringing up pretending to be other people.'

Verushka Wyatt at first went along with Boris's denial. In Monday's *Daily Mail* she said her daughter had a 'close relationship' with Boris, 'but that is all'.

According to Lady Wyatt: 'She has not had an affair with him. She has not been pregnant by him nor had an abortion. She has not been pregnant at all. She is in a stable relationship with someone else but I am not going to talk about that.'

Boris hates rows and confrontations, and may have harboured hopes, as one of his closest friends put it, 'that everyone would be frightfully civilised and Marina would just accept the situation. I do think he thought he could have two wives and two establishments and get away with it. I think that is what he wanted to do.'

But he now had to make a choice between Marina and Petronella. He could no longer go on having both of them.

As Fop said of Marina: 'Obviously she gave Boris an ultimatum. At that point Petronella was just terrified. She didn't want to see Boris because she so hated the press intrusion. All that concerned her was to be left alone.'

The news itself was not news to Marina. She had known about Boris's affair with Petronella for some time and she now took the view that it had been grossly exaggerated by the press.

She does not talk to journalists, and knew it would be a hope-less task to try to correct the inaccuracies in their stories, but she could not help feeling annoyed by the implication that she was a push-over. She reckoned Boris did not have an easy time with her. She also felt he treated her fine and that while the Petronella thing was unfortunate, it was not as bad as people made out. It was something which had happened, as she found when friends commiserated with her, to a surprising number of people.

But she was also very angry with her husband for seeing Petronella again a couple of times quite recently, and she threw him out of the house. Many others were distressed on Marina's behalf. A friend of Boris's mother said: 'How could Boris do the same thing to his wife that his father did to his mother? I don't think he enjoyed that moment when he was a boy.'

Another woman who knew Boris when he was growing up said: 'We don't think Boris is as funny as he thinks he is. His thing is to gloss over all the real damage and pain he's caused to people. His thing is to be like a little boy – a forty-year-old man being more irresponsible than a well-brought-up teenager.' She blamed Stanley for setting a bad example: 'I'm saying that Boris got the idea you could walk all over females and didn't have to take their feelings into account.'

But once one starts passing the blame back down the gener-ations, where is one to stop? Stanley's own father was no model of rectitude, while Ali Kemal, Stanley's grandfather, somehow lost contact with his children in England; an interruption with which the First World War, in which Turkey joined the German side, must have had something to do.

On being thrown out of the family home, Boris took refuge with Justin Rushbrooke, a friend since Balliol, who was 'very happy to help – if he hadn't rung me to say "Can I come?", I'd have rung him.' Rushbrooke is married to Nell Butler, daughter of Lord Butler of Brockwell, the former Cabinet Secretary. The couple were living with their children in Albert Street, Camden Town, in north London, and the tabloid press soon discovered that Boris was living with them.

Rushbrooke may have been an idle undergraduate, but by this time he had qualified as a barrister and was working at 5 Raymond Buildings in Gray's Inn, a chambers which has abbreviated itself to the more groovy '5RB'. He specialises in media law with a particular emphasis on defamation, breach of confidence and privacy, and described the period Boris spent staying with them: 'I don't know if you've ever had representatives of the press besieging your house but it's actually quite an unpleasant experience. Boris did tell them to bog off outside our house, which was quite commendable. Considering it can't have been very pleasant, he took the whole thing in reasonably good part.'

Meanwhile Rushbrooke resisted the temptation to tell the press: 'Do you realise I'm a barrister specialising in privacy law?' The furthest he went was to say to one reporter, 'Do you know you're invading my privacy?'

The press printed pictures which showed that Boris had worn the same clothes for four days running. In one photograph (reproduced as Plate 29) he can be seen on the doorstep with the unidentified figure of Rushbrooke, wearing a red dressing-gown, who is pointing and appears quite cross. 'It looks,' Rushbrooke said, 'as if I'm engaged in a contretemps, but the truth is much more mundane. Boris has spotted the *News of the World* paparazzi mobile parked about fifty yards away, which is clearly likely to have long lenses there, but equally Boris didn't have a parking permit for his car, which on the dot of 8.30 was going to get clamped. I also had a terrible hangover. I thought I should offer a bit of moral support.'

What made the whole situation more complicated was that Rushbrooke and his wife knew Marina very well. Rushbrooke had met Marina before she even started going out with Boris. This enabled Rushbrooke to tell Marina to tell Boris that 'the next time he came to stay he mustn't leave beer and coffee cups lying around. He was no better at clearing up in our house than in his own. But he was pretty self-sufficient in most respects. He used to go off running in the morning. He remains a prolific reader and when venturing down to the basement we would find three different books, all of which he was reading.'

Another old friend wrote a letter to Boris at this time. Darius Guppy told him: 'You must remember from our classical education and our love of the Greeks that family is everything.' Guppy received no reply, and hoped that Boris had not found his advice impertinent.

But the fact that he had gone to stay with friends of Marina, and not with friends of Petronella, was indicative of where Boris's deepest loyalties lay. Many wives would have been so furious with a husband who behaved like Boris that they would have hurled him into outer darkness and given him no way back. Marina, in her fond and cool-headed way, had been wiser than that.

# 23

# Toff Fired

FOR SIX DAYS BORIS'S FATE HUNG IN THE BALANCE. IT was not known whether he would be taken back by Marina, or whether he would be sacked from his front-bench post by Michael Howard, or even whether he would survive as editor of the *Spectator*.

On Thursday 11 November 2004, as luck would have it, Howard was presenting the awards at the *Spectator* Parliamentarian of the Year lunch held in the ballroom at Claridge's. I went that morning to the *Spectator* and after the morning conference had a word alone with Boris.

He said with deep feeling: 'I'm getting a bit fed up with it. Obviously I've been very selfish and stupid, but it's not me . . . There were things in the papers yesterday . . .'

There certainly were some fairly appalling things in the papers. Rachel Royce, the ex-wife of Rod Liddle, had expressed her sympathy for Marina in an excruciating piece in the *Daily Mail* headlined 'Confessions of an (ex) *Spectator* wife'. Royce described how she and Marina had struggled after a full day's work to get to a party at the *Spectator* 'full of glamour girls half my age who'd had hours to pamper themselves and would now be batting their carefully curled eyelashes at the paunchy, egotistical males strutting round the room like peacocks'. According to Royce,

> Men like Boris, with their power and celebrity, are so puffed up on their own egos they end up living in a parallel universe, where they think they can do what they please.
>
> Once they shut their front doors behind them in the morning, it's as though their homes disappear into the ether. Ties of loyalty to the women who have borne their children simply evaporate . . . They honestly feel they are at the centre of some mini-universe and they think no one else is as funny or clever as themselves.

If Royce had been feeling more charitable, she might have realised how bad this was for Boris. Marina saw him surrounded by predatory women, and knew how distorting their flattery could be.

Boris was certainly suffering that Thursday morning from the knowledge of the pain which people near to him were experiencing. He was also trying to think what to say in his speech at the awards, while at the same time coping with Kimberly Fortier, the publisher of the *Spectator*, who was refusing to release the names of the winners to the *Evening Standard*.

The usual arrangement was to release the winners' names to 'Londoner's Diary' on the *Evening Standard*, for use in the edition of the paper which appeared on the streets at two in the afternoon. This was clearly in the interests of the *Spectator*, which gained extra publicity for the awards without breaking the suspense of the lunch.

But Kimberly was refusing to release the names to 'Londoner's Diary' because she was angry about the things it had written about her affair with David Blunkett. Boris assured his sister Rachel's former boyfriend Sebastian Shakespeare, editor of the Diary, that Ann Sindall would phone the names of the winners over, whereupon Kimberly, who was not actually in the building but had somehow got wind of this arrangement, began to harass Boris. This extra complication prompted the editor to say, in a voice of agony: 'It doesn't make life any easier.'

Cars had been booked to take people from the *Spectator* to Claridge's, but Boris biked there. Pictures of him wheeling his bike along the pavement outside the hotel appeared in the next day's papers.

Politicians and journalists filled the ballroom at Claridge's with a buzz of laughter and conversation. We sat at large, round tables and lunch was served quite fast so that those MPs who needed to get back to Westminster would not be detained for long. Those of us who were drinking could drink as much as we liked. Kimberly had entered the hotel by some sort of back entrance. A place was laid for Petronella, but she had not turned up.

Much of the talk was about Boris and his prospects of survival. I found myself sitting next to Paul Johnson – no relation of the editor, but a *Spectator* columnist since the days of Alexander Chancellor – who said of Boris: 'Fortunately for him, he's a very hard man not to like.'

Towards the end of lunch, Boris and Michael Howard mounted a small stage at one side of the room. Boris began by twitting his party leader: 'We at the *Spectator* know that some-times it can be a very, very difficult burden on members of the Tory front bench to agree with every word we write.'

Then it was Howard's turn, and the ingenious and playful manner in which he discharged his task caused general hilarity: 'These are the *Spectator*'s awards and the *Spectator* is an incompa-rable magazine. There is nothing like the *Spectator* for stirring up and stimulating political controversy. Indeed in all senses of the word it could best be described as political Viagra [laughter]. And I must [prolonged laughter], I must take this opportunity of congratulating Boris on the tremendous enthusiasm with which you have approached your various front-bench duties. I had no idea when I appointed you as shadow minister for culture, media and sport that you would take to the task with quite such aplomb. You were keen to make your mark with the city of culture [i.e. Liverpool]. You wanted them to get to know you better. And you succeeded beyond my wildest dreams . . . All I can say is Boris . . . keep it up!'

The audience loved this, but Boris did not, and could be heard saying: 'I don't know how he's allowed to get away with this. Absolutely outrageous.'

It appeared, however, that Howard had decided to treat his shadow minister's exploits as a joke, rather than a hanging offence. Boris's punishment was to be laughed at in public, which was not pleasant, but seemed to put him in the clear as far as keeping his shadow post was concerned.

But relations between Boris and Howard were much worse than they appeared. Boris had indicated to Howard, after the Liverpool débâcle but before the Petronella affair broke, that he wished to resign from the shadow team. Given that Howard had only promoted Boris in May, this must have seemed both ungrateful and unserious to the Tory leader and his circle. But to Marina, it now seemed that Howard was fanning the flames of the Petronella affair as a means of getting rid of her husband, and she instinctively sided with Boris, who was certainly not inclined to resign under pressure. Nor did Boris consider that he had lied either to Howard or to Howard's aides. He reckoned that Howard could quite easily have stood by him, and had failed to do so.

Two days later, Howard sacked Boris. The *News of the World* claimed the credit, if that is the word. It splashed on its front page with the headline, 'Bonking Boris Made Me Pregnant'. According to a friend of Petronella, she 'loathed' this headline, because it made it seem as if she had herself spoken to the paper, which the rest of the story demonstrated she most certainly had not.

A second headline in smaller type announced: 'Liar FIRED after Tory chief sees *News of the World* evidence'. The newspaper gave the following account of Boris's Saturday afternoon sacking:

At **16.20**, when we put our revelations to him, he snapped: 'What I will say to you is, "Publish and be damned!"'

But by **16.30**, when Tory leader Michael Howard was informed of our story, it was Boris who was damned.

At **18.30** Mr Howard ordered him to be officially removed from his posts as shadow arts minister and vice-chairman of the Conservative Party – one of the fastest political sackings in history.

The *News of the World*'s 'revelations' were far skimpier than its presentation of them suggested, but both here and in Simon Walters' front-page piece in the *Mail on Sunday*, Verushka Wyatt had ceased to back Boris's version of events. The *Mail on Sunday* said Lady Wyatt had confirmed to the paper that Petronella did become pregnant by Boris and did have an abortion.

A close friend of Petronella is at pains to defend Lady Wyatt: 'A lot of people think her mother spilled the beans on Boris deliberately, but what happened was that a good friend who happened to be a journalist told her it would go no further, and then she started talking, and it appeared in the paper. Lady Wyatt is quite naïve about journalists. Some articles said it was the mother's revenge on Boris, but she adores him. Still does.'

Other papers were obliged to follow the story. Patrick Hennessy, who overlapped with Boris at school and university and was now Political Editor of the *Sunday Telegraph*, remembered: 'We got word that he was being sacked. I rang him at about 8 p.m. and he was very, very upset – really genuinely upset. What he really wanted to know was how the *News of the World* was playing it. I said if I could find out I'd ring him back. When the story was read over to him there was some phrase in it about "the snooty toff" and Boris replied: "Bloody hell, that's outrageous, I'm not a snooty toff."'

The phrase used by the paper was 'the snooty mop-haired toff'. Its story ended:

> Speaking through the letter box at a pal's house last night, Boris said: 'I am sorry this decision has been taken in response to stories about my private life.
>
> 'I am looking forward to helping promote a new Conservative policy on the arts, if only from the back benches, and I will continue to do my utmost to serve the people of Henley and south Oxfordshire. I am now going to have a stiff drink.'

One of Boris's warmest admirers said: 'I think Michael Howard wanted to get rid of him anyway. That's what I later heard from other Conservatives. I don't think Howard ever liked Boris, and I think he annoyed the Whips by not turning up for various things, and of course there's a lot of jealousy.'

Howard ran a tight ship, and sacked two Conservative candidates during the 2005 General Election campaign. He believed in discipline, and was harsh to anyone who gave so much as the appearance of indiscipline. That was the way Howard was, and it left no room for someone like Boris. But one should add that such rigid party management made a poor impression on many voters, and was one reason why Howard proved unable to extend Tory support beyond its core vote. His treatment of Boris indicated his limitations. For all his gifts, Howard was too narrow for the nation to take him to their hearts.

But the whole affair looked much, much worse for Boris. Few people doubted that he had suffered a very severe and perhaps terminal setback. The general line in the press was that Boris had been sacked for lying to Howard. The *Observer* said Boris was 'facing the end of what promised to be a coruscating political career, not to mention his editorship of a national magazine'.

Yasmin Alibhai-Brown, in the next day's *Evening Standard*, had no sympathy for Boris and expressed outrage on Marina's behalf:

This scandalous behaviour of Boris's, you imagine, must leave her both deeply hurt and seething. Only those who have been through it can understand the unspeakable anguish, what it feels like to be deceived so totally, to be humiliated and lied to, to be treated with such indifference by your husband and his lover, and, in this case, in public . . .

How do women like Petronella forgive themselves for wrecking the lives of so many people? . . . We take infidelity too lightly and forgive lying cads too easily, especially if they are charmers like Boris Johnson, charmers who come to believe it is their right to betray the mothers of their children and their lovers.

But at least Boris was back at home, as he showed the world when he emerged for a jog at 7.30 on the morning of Monday 15 November in his son's ski hat (generally, but incorrectly, described in the press as a 'bandana'). He told the press: 'I advise you all very strongly, go for a run, get some exercise, and have a beautiful day.'

On returning home, Boris found the door of his own house locked, and was asked as he waited to be let in if he felt unfairly treated, to which he replied in the words of Voltaire's Dr Pangloss: 'All is for the best in the best of all possible worlds.'

Boris was also asked if he had misled Howard and replied: 'No, I certainly didn't. Will you kindly hop it?'

The graver problem for Boris was not Howard, who was not going to be around for long, but other Tory MPs who were by now both jealous of his fame, and sceptical about his reliability.

# 24

# Theatricals

BORIS HAD COME DOWN TO EARTH WITH A BUMP AND nothing about his position looked very secure. On 15 November 2004 it was announced that Andrew Neil had been brought in as chief executive of the *Spectator*, which had by now passed, like the *Telegraph*, into the ownership of the Barclay brothers. Neil was close to the new owners, but this former editor of the *Sunday Times* was not someone whom one would expect to be in sympathy either with Boris or with the *Spectator*.

Michael Portillo took the chance, in the *Sunday Times* of 21 November 2004, to launch a sublimely self-important attack on Boris, which in 2016 turned out to be excessively dismissive:

> When I first met Boris Johnson, I marked him down as unserious. He came to interview me as Defence Secretary and arrived forty-five minutes late. Apparently, experienced political journalist that he was, he had thought the ministry was in Victoria Street, not in Whitehall. He had the decency to look flushed and sweaty, but also gave the impression that I should find his shambolic performance endearing. I pretended to do so.

Portillo contemplated Boris's prospects, now that he was known to have had an affair with Petronella: 'If this were France, Johnson's prestige as a politician would have soared for attracting such a mistress and we might be talking of him as a future leader of his party. Being Britain, his celebrity has increased and his earning potential with it, but his political career is over.'

If only Boris had taken Portillo's advice:

Nearly four years ago, when he had entered Parliament, I knew he was clever and discovered he had the right ideas (to my mind) about reshaping the Tory party. He wanted to be a future leader and of course he was highly media savvy. I advised him to focus on Parliament, stop being funny and resign from editing the *Spectator*.

I can see why he rejected my suggestions. His journalism and television work have brought him money and fame. Devoting himself instead to mastering a shadow spokes-man's brief would have been tedious and impoverishing. But if he calculated that he could leap from celebrity to leading the party he was wrong. His success had created too many jealousies among MPs and the buffoonery had gone beyond the point of recall.

Portillo ended his piece by predicting future greatness for a man who had acted as one of Boris's stooges at Oxford, but was not yet even a Tory MP:

Like Johnson he is a journalist, but unlike him he would never be late for a meeting. His name is Michael Gove, who long ago wrote a kindly biography of me. He survived that lapse of judgment and climbed the ladder. He has given up the prospect of editing *The Times* to become a humble backbencher in a party whose fortunes are at a low ebb. That is what I call serious.

The pressure on Boris and Petronella was soon relieved by new revelations about Kimberly and Blunkett. On 28 November 2004, the *Sunday Telegraph* reported that 'open war' had broken out between them, with Blunkett accused of 'fast-tracking' a visa for her Filipina nanny. Thanks to the collapse of his relationship with Kimberly, Blunkett was now on the downward path which led on 15 December to his resignation as Home Secretary.

When Kimberly found out about Petronella's affair with Boris she took a high moral tone about it, so now that Kimberly's own affair had become public, Petronella 'laughed like a drain'. She also wrote a piece in which she described introducing Blunkett to Kimberly Fortier three years before at Wheeler's fish restaurant in St James's, and how Kimberly flirted like mad with him, saying she had always wondered what it was like to sleep with a blind man: 'Mr Blunkett and I ate dover sole. Miss Fortier ate Mr Blunkett.'

Boris remained capable of marvellous ebullience. One of his friends was surprised to hear him say, in a buoyant tone, that things could be patched up at home without undue difficulty: 'Put on a good Christmas and it'll all be all right.'

On 16 December 2004, I sat opposite him at the *Spectator*'s Christmas lunch, held in a cellar at Berry Bros & Rudd, the grand wine merchants in St James's. Boris started his speech: 'It has been a difficult and turbulent year, in the immortal phrase of Norman Lamont.'

The reference was to Black Wednesday, 16 September 1992, when Lamont as Chancellor tried and failed to defend the pound's place in the Exchange Rate Mechanism against a wave of speculation. Lamont at one point raised interest rates to 15 per cent, and later emerged from the Treasury to say, 'This has been a very difficult and turbulent day.' Boris quotes this in the introduction to his book of collected journalism. Unlike many men who want to be successful, he also enjoys the comedy of failure.

In his Christmas address to the troops, Boris refused to be

downhearted: 'In spite of all our efforts to shake off readers . . . they continue to subscribe to us in ever greater numbers.' After some classical references – to Odysseus' dog and Caligula's horse – Boris described a visit to the *Spectator* by a girl from the magazine *Dazed and Confused* who expected to find 'people shagging in the toilets' but instead discovered it to be 'a place of monastic seclusion'.

Boris as usual thanked every one of the staff by name, including the humblest people in the advertising and circulation departments – a list of fifty or more people drawn up by Ann Sindall.

'Penultimately,' Boris said, 'I want to thank Ann Sindall, the be-all and Sindall.'

But Boris ended with a generous reference to Kimberly, who was at that point heavily pregnant with her second child and had been taken to hospital. Boris proposed a toast to 'absent friends and those who have done so much, now languishing in their hospital beds. I miss her, this is not a popular view, I miss her dynamism.'

One could say Boris was having it both ways. He got a big laugh for 'this is not a popular view'. But he was also behaving towards Kimberly with far greater charity than most of her colleagues did.

At the General Election in the spring of 2005, another Johnson took the field. Boris's father Stanley had got himself selected as the Tory parliamentary candidate in Teignbridge, a constituency in south Devon which had fallen into Liberal Democrat hands. Boris said: 'Never in history, as far as I know, has a father followed his son into Parliament. Our party cares about the older generation.'

There was some confusion among members of the public between the two Johnsons. Stanley was sometimes asked: 'Is it true that Boris Johnson is your father?'

Boris took time off from his campaign in Henley to try to help Stanley. He went down to speak for him in Dawlish (Stanley: '"How many other languages can he speak?" a Polish friend of mine asked') and on 22 April 2005 I saw father and son campaigning together in the small coastal town of Teignmouth.

Boris arrived from the constituency of North Devon, where he had campaigned earlier that day on behalf of Orlando Fraser, grandson of his grandparents' great friends Lord and Lady Longford. Boris was wearing a suit with no tie and a modest blue rosette, while Stanley's rosette was a good six inches across.

Stanley persuaded him to do a short walkabout in the rain, for the benefit of the considerable number of journalists who had come to watch. Boris was not keen and said: 'Sod the press.' A few minutes later he denied point-blank to me that he had said this.

We piled in to the Dairymaid restaurant, where I had earlier lunched with Quentin Letts of the *Daily Mail* and Valerie Grove of *The Times*. Boris said: 'So sorry to barge in. We're surrounded by the media.'

Boris and Stanley sat down on either side of two waitresses who were having their own lunch – it was about 2.15 in the afternoon. There was much laughter. Boris said as he left: 'Look, I'm so sorry to have troubled you.'

His apologetic manner, and the way in which he dissociated himself from the mob of reporters and photographers, helped to defuse any possible irritation, but did not always lead to promises of support. In Luders Patisserie, the woman behind the counter told Boris that she used to be a Conservative, 'but I would never vote Conservative again. Because of the Conservatives we lost our house, our business, everything.'

At the Carlton Theatre, a disappointingly small audience of forty-seven mostly Tory voters had come to hear Boris and Stanley, who competed to cap each other's jokes. The Johnsons were asked if it could really be right to send 50 per cent of school leavers to university – the target set by the Labour

Government. Stanley used this an occasion to mention that five of his children went to Oxford, and one to Cambridge.

Boris denounced 'these loony degrees in windsurfing from Bangor University', whereupon Stanley broke in: 'They also surf who only stand and wait.'

In a sketch for the *Daily Telegraph*, I quoted Boris's attack on 'loony degrees', which produced the following response in the paper's letters column from Dr David Roberts, Registrar of the University of Wales, Bangor: 'There are no such degrees, of course, at Bangor. What the university does have is an internationally renowned School of Ocean Sciences.'

A woman in the theatre said: 'I think if Boris were Tory leader they would get in without any trouble whatever.'

We drove through the rain to Newton Abbot, where Boris and Stanley played squash. Stanley wanted this match in order to show that he was still fit enough to be an MP. The encounter was built up, for the benefit of the press, as the greatest sporting contest of the campaign. Boris, who looked thin and attractive, but a bit pissed-off, beat his father easily.

After the match, Stanley gave Lauren Booth – the half-sister of Cherie Blair – and myself a lift to the railway station. He was on friendly terms with Lauren, who was writing a piece for one of the Sunday papers, and as we pulled away from the squash courts he started broadcasting through the loudspeakers mounted on his Hyundai battle bus: 'This is Stanley Johnson, your Conservative candidate, with Lauren Booth.'

Lauren took the microphone from him and said: 'This is Lauren Booth. I will not be supporting Stanley Johnson but I like him.'

Stanley never tired of repeating another joke made during the campaign: 'I visited a retirement home in Newton Abbot and was pleased when one of the residents confided that she had been impressed by my running in the famous Newton Abbot pancake race on Shrove Tuesday.

"'You were very good," the old lady said. "Are you a practised tosser?"'

This is not the kind of joke one is used to hearing from a Tory candidate, and it may not have amused everyone who heard it in Devon.

At the General Election on 5 May 2005, Boris held Henley with an increased majority of 12,793 over the Liberal Democrats, while Stanley lost in Teignbridge to the Lib Dems by 6,215 votes.

The man sitting beside me as Boris and Stanley performed in the Carlton Theatre had said: 'A theatre's the right place for these two.'

The same thought, at least as far as Boris was concerned, struck a number of people, including two of Boris's old friends from Oxford, Toby Young and Lloyd Evans, both of whom he employed to write theatre reviews and other pieces for the *Spectator*.

Young and Evans composed a play, *Who's the Daddy?*, which was put on at the King's Head Theatre in Islington in July 2005. The play was set at the *Spectator* and revolved around three couples: Boris and Petronella, Blunkett and Kimberly, Liddle and a young woman at the magazine who turned out to be an undercover reporter. The set included a picture of Margaret Thatcher which pulled down into a bed.

When the authors informed Boris about the play, he wrote back to them: 'I always knew my life would be turned into a farce. I'm glad that the script has been entrusted to two such eminent men of letters.'

Young wrote in the programme that they had both known Boris since they were all at Oxford in the mid-1980s, and asked: 'Could we justify stitching up our old mate?' He went on:

After much deliberation, the only argument we found halfway convincing was that Boris's status as a public figure had, to a certain extent, eroded the protection he was entitled to as a friend . . . As aspiring satirical playwrights, what sort of precedent would we be setting if we decided it would be wrong to take the piss out of a public personality just because he happened to be an acquaintance of ours? . . . Ultimately, the reason Lloyd and I decided to go ahead with *Who's the Daddy?* is because we felt that if we're serious about wanting to be writers – whether of plays, books or theatre criticism – the writing must come first: it must trump all other considerations. That may sound harsh, but it's a feeling that any writer with a sense of vocation will recognise. In your soul, you know you'll never be any good unless you're willing to sacrifice more or less everything in order to produce the best work you can.

This 'sell your own grandmother' approach recalled the worst excesses of Oxford journalism. The play contained many good lines, but was somehow joyless in its lack of charity. We saw Boris lying to Marina (by telephone) and screwing Petronella, while a Chilean cook attempted to get his visa extended by giving Blunkett a blow-job while pretending to be Kimberly. Tim Hudson played Boris and was good at conveying some of his heart. There were cruel caricatures of Kimberly and Liddle.

Boris did not come to see the play, but felt deeply hurt by it. He took to telephoning Young, begging him to scrap the projected transfer to the West End (which in the end never came off) and telling him that his life had become 'purgatory'. Yet he gave no public expression to his distress, and did not sack either Evans or Young. A couple of months later, when there was some question of both Boris and Young appearing on the television show *I'm a Celebrity, Get Me Out of Here*, Boris did allow himself to say: 'I can't think of anything worse than being trapped in the jungle with Toby Young.'

There were several other plays about Kimberly, Blunkett, Boris and co., including *A Very Social Secretary* by Alistair Beaton, shown on television in October 2005. But no fictional version of Boris's adventures has yet been more than a pale echo of the reality.

# 25

# Overtaken by Cameron

THE RISE OF DAVID CAMERON WAS ASTONISHINGLY SWIFT. He is two years younger than Boris, and although he came into Parliament at the same time, was much less well known. After Michael Howard led the Tories to their third General Election defeat in a row in May 2005, and announced that he would be stepping down, several months elapsed before the rules for choosing his successor were settled, and during this period David Davis was the firm favourite to succeed him.

Cameron only emerged as a serious contender for the leadership on 29 September, when he launched his campaign. Boris attended this event, which had the feel of a small but fashionable wedding, thrown by grand people but in such a way as to make everyone welcome.

The journalists had come straight on from David Davis's launch, which was larger, but felt like a gathering of golf club bores. Cameron seemed full of promise, while Davis gave the impression of being a dull man who was unlikely to transcend his own limitations.

The following week, at the Conservative Party Conference in Blackpool, Cameron delivered the same kind of promising speech as at his launch, including many of the same lines, but to a far larger audience. Davis failed by comparison, and although Kenneth Clarke and Malcolm Rifkind spoke well, they could not match Cameron's momentum.

On the last day of the conference, Boris used his *Telegraph* column to announce to a wider public his support for Cameron. He began by saying: 'Over the past few months I have lost count of the number of people who have asked me – satirically – why I am not standing in the current Tory leadership contest.'

Boris was not in a position to stand because he would have enjoyed virtually no support among MPs, and most of the people around Michael Howard had switched to Cameron. Howard himself preserved an appearance of scrupulous neutrality, but was reckoned to favour Cameron, whom he had promoted to the shadow Cabinet. Cameron looked new, but he was also the Establishment candidate, while the disappointed men in their fifties who felt unjustly ignored by Howard tended to cluster around Davis. There was not enough room for a third candidate, as Kenneth Clarke and several other aspirants were soon to discover.

The new leader was elected by the whole party, an arrangement which might have favoured Boris. But although he was immensely popular in the wider party, and had been assiduous in visiting constituency associations, the events of the last autumn, culminating in his sacking, made too many people fear he might turn into a liability. Boris had been given his chance to show what he could do as an apparatchik, but it was not in his nature to display the self-effacing steadiness and common prudence which were required. He was also very inexperienced. But so too was Cameron. As a public speaker, and also as a television performer, Cameron was much less experienced than Boris, at least as far as high-profile events and programmes were concerned.

The parallels between the two men were very close. Cameron is from a grander family, with aristocratic connections stretching

back into the Middle Ages, but as far as most people were concerned, they were equally privileged, for they had both been to
Eton. This presented them with a problem which has perplexed
Etonians ever since three of their number – Eden, Macmillan
and Douglas-Home – succeeded each other as Prime Minister,
only for the last to be narrowly defeated in 1964 by Harold
Wilson, who mocked his aristocratic lineage.

How could an Old Etonian succeed in such an egalitarian, or
at least pseudo-egalitarian, age? The next six leaders of the Tory
party – Heath, Thatcher, Major, Hague, Duncan Smith and
Howard – were all from relatively humble backgrounds, and
when Douglas Hurd, like Boris a scholar of Eton, stood for the
leadership, he made a fool of himself by pretending to be hum-
bler than he was. When Hurd said he was not really a toff, he
sounded as if he was denying his own background, even though
in traditional terms what he said was true.

Boris seemed brilliantly placed to crack this Etonian problem.
Far from denying his toffishness, he played up to it in such an
amusing way that hardly anyone held it against him. He was at
once gloriously traditional, and gloriously capable, unlike
Douglas-Home and Hurd, of communicating with people via
television. In class terms, Boris also carried less baggage than
Cameron, who had married an upper-class wife and was a
member of White's club.

Yet Boris had been sidelined, and tactful, charming, self-
possessed Cameron had come through. Boris now had the wit to
back him wholeheartedly, and urged his colleagues in Parliament
to back him too, 'for the entirely cynical and self-serving reason
that he is not only the best candidate, but that he is going to
win'.

Part of the charm of politics is its unexpectedness, but it must
have been a bitter blow to Boris to see Cameron overtake him.
A trace of disappointment appeared in one line of Boris's 'I'm
backing Cameron' piece: 'I like his constant repetition of "we're

all in this together"; indeed, I am vain enough to have a feeling that he nicked it from me.' But a woman who knows Boris well said that he is too proud to feel any real sense of disappointment, and is so confident of his own abilities that if he fails to become Prime Minister, he will not consider it his fault but the fault of everyone else in the party for failing to choose him as their leader.

Only nine days before the result of the Tory leadership contest was declared, by which time it was clear that Cameron was going to win, Boris made his appearance on *Desert Island Discs*. Tom Stoppard has a character in *The Real Thing* who is about to go on this programme and is worried that 'I don't like the pop music which it's all right to like . . . *I* like Wayne Fontana and the Mindbenders doing "Um Um Um Um Um Um".' But choosing the music was the least of Boris's worries. As we have already seen, Sue Lawley subjected him, under the guise of a friendly chat, to a ruthless interrogation. When people interviewed Boris for newspaper pieces, there was every chance he could win over the interviewer and ensure that a reasonably favourable piece appeared, with some of his prevarications and evasions omitted. But in Lawley's cross-examination, his refusal to give straight answers was exposed with terrible clarity. Boris sounded at times like a cashiered major who is desperately trying to keep up appearances. The conversation is punctuated by laughter – Lawley is amused by him, and at times she sounds flirtatious – but she is far too sharp to let him change the subject. One of Boris's difficulties may have been that he was trying to sound more serious, and less buffoonish, than he had in the past, in order to show that he would be a fit member of Cameron's team.

Cameron's impending triumph, the speculation about what post he would give Boris, and the awkward fact that Boris was still editor of the *Spectator*, enabled Lawley to go for the jugular. She confronted him with the choice he had been avoiding ever since he was elected an MP:

LAWLEY: 'If you had to choose between journalism and politics, and you might, who knows, one day, have to do so, you'd choose politics, would you?'

BORIS: 'Yes, of course, but I don't think I'd abandon journalism.'

LAWLEY: 'You'd have to. I mean people have told you time and again you can't ride two horses. You've probably proved you can't ride two horses.'

BORIS: 'I think I have successfully ridden two horses for quite a long time, but I have to admit there have been moments when the distance between the two horses has grown terrifyingly wide.'

LAWLEY: 'Split you right down the middle.'

BORIS: 'And I did momentarily come off.'

LAWLEY: 'But if you had to choose, you would choose, would you, politics?'

BORIS: 'Yes, of course. I always wanted to do it. I always knew I was going to be an MP . . . I had a sense that this was the single most interesting job that one could do, it was the job that involved testing one to the greatest extent . . .'

LAWLEY: 'So political ambition there is. David Cameron, were he to get the leadership, do you think he'd get you back on to the front bench?'

BORIS: 'Well, I've no idea. I think it would be pretty bonkers of me now to outline a job request.'

LAWLEY: 'What do you think your area is?'

BORIS: 'What I would love to do, the thing that I, OK, I'll tell you, the thing I would love to do is something to do with agriculture, trade, world trade . . . But hey, it's not for me, I'll take anything.'

LAWLEY: 'Did you know him, because I mean he was at Eton and Oxford a couple of years behind you.'

BORIS: 'I do, I do, I did know him, I do, I remember him,

he was younger than me, I hope it wasn't one of the
traumas I have to bear in my life, so we didn't know
each other that well, but I certainly knew him. I
haven't got a prayer of getting it, but, you know . . .'

LAWLEY: 'Have you got a prayer of becoming Prime
Minister, because that's what you'd really like, isn't
it . . . Was it your ex-mother-in-law who said, "Boris
is very ambitious and always said he wanted to be
Prime Minister"?'

BORIS: 'My ex-mother-in-law is in many ways a wonderful
woman. Did I used to say that? Maybe I did. I suppose
all politicians in the end are like kind of crazed wasps
in a jam jar, each individually convinced that they're
going to make it.'

As his first record, Boris chose 'Here Comes the Sun' by the
Beatles. His second was the theme tune of *Test Match Special*,
which brought 'very fond memories of playing cricket in the
yard with my brothers, all of whom are better than me at
cricket'.

Sue then probed Boris's ambition: 'You like testing yourself . . . You set your sights on things and go for it, because that's
what gets you going.'

Boris replied: 'You've been more or less programmed to want
to have these things. My silicon chip, my ambition silicon chip,
has been programmed to try to scrabble my way up this *cursus
honorum*, this ladder of things, and so you do feel a kind of sense,
you've got to . . . I think British society is designed like that.
Because what we need as a society, we need all these grasping
hacks and politicos to compete with each other and to advertise
their wares to the public, because if they don't they won't be
doing their job of serving.'

We see Boris avoiding responsibility for his behaviour by
developing a doctrine of necessity – he has been programmed to

try to scrabble his way up – and also by saying that this is what the public needs. For his third record he chose a piece of Bach from *St Matthew's Passion* – the tune also for the hymn 'Hail to the Lord's Anointed' – which was followed by the Rolling Stones' 'Start Me Up', 'the most fantastic, vigorous introduction to a rock song you could possibly have – it may be corny but it's brilliant'. Record number five was Brahms, 'Variations on a Theme by Haydn', followed by the Van Morrison song mentioned in the passage about Boris's novel, after which the dialogue continued with Sue observing: 'I haven't read a profile written about you, Boris, in which the interviewer doesn't come out feeling that they've been, you know, very unfair to you, as they've sort of pointed out all these misdemeanours, and you've sort of batted it back.'

BORIS: 'Yes.'

LAWLEY: 'But they all say they've been charmed by you, and isn't that the fact really that the strongest weapon in your armoury is charm?'

BORIS: 'Well again, I mean, it's very, very sweet of you to say this, Sue, but what are these misdemeanours you keep talking about?'

LAWLEY: 'We don't want to go back over them, Boris. I mean, I've left quite a few out.'

BORIS: 'What do you, I mean, for the benefit of your listeners, I think there are far fewer misdemeanours than there are demeanours, or whatever.'

LAWLEY: 'All right. Mishaps, I think. Mishaps. But what I want to know is whether the charm, whether it's all a bit of a ruse, or maybe you've always used it as a bit of a ruse, you know, to sort of get you by.'

BORIS: 'I suppose that could be, could be something. I was very deaf as a child, and I attribute, I used to have grommets, you know what I mean by grommets, I had terrible glue ear and could basically hardly hear anything anyone was saying, and I think I must have developed then a certain sort of evasiveness, because often really I couldn't follow what was going on at all, and if you can sort of guess what's going on but you're not quite sure, it's often as well to be a little bit vague.'

LAWLEY: 'Yes, but you are at the same time a comic institution, and you cultivate that image, because you go on *Have I Got News For You,* or wherever you crop up, I mean, you are highly entertaining, and I suppose what I'm asking is a question you can't answer, which is whether you do that in a calculated way or whether that's just Boris.'

BORIS: 'Yuuuh. I think the profound truth of the matter is it would be very, very hard to do it any other way. I think if I made a huge effort always to have a snappy, inspiring soundbite on my lips, I think the sheer mental strain of that would be such that I would explode, and I think it's much easier therefore for me to try to play what shots I have as freely as I can. Does that make sense?'

LAWLEY: 'Yes it does, but of course what happens is maybe the really clever and thoughtful Boris gets lost and people forget he's there, and that's the danger, isn't it?'

BORIS: 'Yeah, well, we need, we need to go and find him, we need to go and chivvy him out, wherever he is lurking in there . . .'

LAWLEY: 'Does he crop up quite often?'

BORIS: 'He does.'

LAWLEY: 'He does, does he? He's in there?'

BORIS: 'Yeah. He's there all right.'

LAWLEY: 'Record number seven.'

BORIS: 'Right. Ah, this is fantastic. It is The Clash, "Pressure Drop", and the great thing about The

Clash, of course, was apart from anything else, Joe Strummer was towards the end an avid *Telegraph* reader and it was the highest moment in my journalistic career when Joe Strummer actually sent me a letter saying how much he'd admired a column I'd written, about hunting funnily enough, and he was a fantastic man, a great hero of mine, a good poet as well as a fantastic rock musician.'

The last record, after Boris had said how on his desert island he would have 'a very disciplined approach to rebuilding civilisation as fast and as quickly as I could', and he enjoys making things out of wood, and would 'try to get to the heart of things' in his writing, was the opening of the last movement of Beethoven's Fifth Symphony. Boris said if he could only take one of the records it would be the Brahms. He chose Homer as his book – 'I think I could use up a few decades quietly translating that' – and mustard – specifically Moutarde de Meaux – as his luxury: 'any kind of meat is more or less bearable with mustard'.

On Tuesday 6 December 2005, David Cameron became leader of the Conservative Party. The next day, Cameron shone on his first outing at Prime Minister's Questions.

Two days later Cameron announced the remainder of his shadow Cabinet, and Boris got nothing. This was a humiliation, for which his appointment the next day to the shadow higher education post was scant compensation. Cameron had given his colleague a highly appropriate portfolio, but had also cut him down to size, especially as Boris was on the same day obliged to resign the editorship of the *Spectator*. The Tory party was not going to risk another Liverpool.

Petronella was still in love with Boris, and kept in touch with him, but she also managed to joke about how she had backed the wrong horse in the Tory leadership stakes. In a *Spectator* Diary she recalled how she met the young David Cameron, who was working for the Wyatts' great friend Norman Lamont, at that time Chancellor of the Exchequer. It fell to Cameron to organise his boss's fiftieth birthday party, held at 11 Downing Street, at which Petronella had been asked to sing: Lamont was particularly keen on her 'Lilli Marlene'.

After her performance, Cameron asked her to dance, which he apparently did 'with the grace of Astaire and the manliness of Gene Kelly'. He asked her to a Tory winter ball, but one of them was forced to cancel, and soon after that he began going out with Samantha Sheffield, whom he was to marry. Petronella ended her account: 'As Professor Higgins says, "Damn, damn, damn!" Oh, why did I muff my chance to become the wife of the next Conservative Party leader and perhaps First Lady? I have always looked rather good in the pillbox hats worn by Jackie Kennedy.'

Boris delivered a farewell speech to the *Spectator*'s staff at the Christmas lunch, held on 15 December at Franco's restaurant in Jermyn Street. When he rose to his feet he said he would be as quick as possible: 'I have a terrible feeling that I'm going to dissolve into great floods of blubbing sentimentality, and that would not be true to the traditions of the *Spectator*.' Boris used an image about his colleagues at the magazine which he had already used in public: 'For most of my time here I have been propelled by your talents, as a fat German tourist may be transported by superior alpinists to the summit of Everest.'

Like much of what Boris says about himself, this is funny because it is so wildly wrong. It is true that he owed an enormous amount to his staff, and that he left the routine editorial work in their hands. But it would be absurd, and he knew it was absurd, to speak of himself as a passenger. If Boris was climbing Everest, he would probably be wearing the wrong gear, and would have forgotten to bring a number of essential items of kit. But he would not want for physical courage and his instinct would be to get to the top first. He would want to be the leader who reconnoitres a brilliant new route to the summit, not some gormless passenger.

As usual Boris thanked every member of staff by name for their efforts: 'You have made my life each day for the last six and a half years.' Kimberly was present, and he asked where the magazine would have been without her: 'We might have slunk along without anyone paying any attention at all without Kimberly Fortier.'

Boris recalled that when he took over as editor it was likened to putting 'a Ming vase in the hands of an ape'.

'I think I know who said it. I think the Ming vase is in pretty good shape.'

'Who said it?' people asked, turning to one another. Nobody seemed to know it was me, and I was too far away from Boris to see whether he looked in my direction. Ann Sindall, who was sitting beside me, was weeping.

Towards the end of his speech, Boris said that if anyone asked them to leave 56 Doughty Street he would urge them 'to chain yourselves to the railings'. He added that 'I know Kimberly will fight like the Hyrcan tiger she is.' Not long after, *Spectator* staff heard they would be moved from Doughty Street to new premises in Westminster.

Stuart Reid paid tribute to Boris: 'Boris is an impossible act to follow . . . Boris leaves the magazine in better shape than it has ever been. We must carry on as before.'

Boris: 'Hear, hear.'

Reid: 'Without Boris guiding us.'

Boris: 'Oh yes.'

Reid: 'The *Spectator* is given to us in trust. It is more than just a product and more than just a brand.'

On 28 February 2006, Boris acted as Cameron's warm-up man at Vinopolis, a wine emporium in south London where the Tory leader was launching a platitudinous document called 'Built to Last'. Cameron, whose third child, Arthur, had been born two weeks before, began by saying he'd been having a lot of strain and some sleepless nights, and that was just thinking about Boris's introduction.

The joke went down well, but also expressed the implicit rivalry between the two men. Boris quite plainly remained a star speaker, and one with the capacity to ridicule Cameron as a man devoted to a mindless doctrine of 'change'. Cameron in this period was rather obviously repeating himself, and people were beginning to question whether there was any substance to him, or whether he would turn out to be one of the great bores of today.

# 26

# Roman Civilisation

BORIS SET ABOUT HIS DUTIES AS TORY SPOKESMAN ON higher education in a completely different manner to his debut less than two years before as arts spokesman. There was no spoof top-of-the-head manifesto, but instead a clear effort to be taken seriously.

On bumping into him in December 2005, soon after his appointment, I invited Boris to condemn Oxford University's plan to strip the colleges of the right to decide which students they admit. This sounded like an outrageous attempt to crush the colleges by subjecting them to a central management scheme. Yet Boris refused to dismiss the idea, and spoke well of Sir Tim Lankester, the President of Corpus Christi College, Oxford, who had chaired the working party which produced the proposals.

In his first appearance in the House of Commons in his new capacity, he called on the higher education minister, Bill Rammell, to dissociate himself from the deprecatory comments about medieval history made by Charles Clarke while Education Secretary.

Clarke had volunteered in 2003 that 'education for its own sake' was 'a bit dodgy', and that the study of medieval history was 'ornamental' and did not deserve taxpayers' money. Boris was incensed by these remarks. He was determined to defend the idea that the study of Latin, Greek, medieval history and other subjects which philistines might claim were of no practical value is worth it as an end in itself.

Not that Boris entirely abandoned his love of the frivolous. Early in 2006, after the rectorship of Edinburgh University had fallen vacant, he put in for it. But even here, he was at pains to emphasise that he was not simply trying to make some kind of joke: 'I am deadly serious about becoming rector of the University of Edinburgh. I believe I have a lot to offer as an ambassador for the students, the staff and the university.'

The rectorship has been held by eminent figures, including Gladstone, Churchill and Gordon Brown. The press reckoned Boris was the front-runner, and assumed he would have no difficulty beating the two other journalists in the race, Magnus Linklater and John Pilger.

But Boris's support for top-up fees provoked great hostility and prompted the Edinburgh University Students' Association, which has traditionally stayed out of elections for the rectorship, to launch an 'Anyone But Boris' campaign. Posters were distributed urging students to 'Practice Safe X – Don't Wake Up With a Dumb Blond Tomorrow'.

To most people's surprise, the election, held in mid-February 2006, was won by Mark Ballard, a 34-year-old Green member of the Scottish Parliament who had studied at Edinburgh University and of whom the students' association warmly approved. Linklater came second and Boris was only third. His campaign had been an unsatisfactory compromise: he could not give free play to his comic genius, nor could he match Ballard's earnestness.

Boris issued a statement: 'I salute the student body of Edinburgh and congratulate the new rector on his success. I am sure he will do the job in tremendous style. It has been a very enjoyable campaign fought with tact, honesty and discretion. I am sorry the student body came out against me, but democracy has triumphed. Given I am English, a Tory and broadly in favour of top-up fees, this was a commendable performance.'

In his first interview as higher education spokesman, Boris impressed Donald MacLeod, of the *Guardian*, by 'quoting accurately, and off the cuff, from a landmark decision on academic freedom in the US supreme court'.

Boris delivered the following message: 'If I want to do anything, I want to help vindicate academic freedom as enunciated by Justice Felix Frankfurter: the freedom to decide on academic grounds who should teach, what they should teach, how it should be taught and whom to admit. I think that's a very good definition of what we should be trying to do.'

But as MacLeod said, 'the note of gravitas is dissipated when he declares with feeling: "*Ich bin ein Frankfurter*."'

Boris then clutched his head and said: 'It'll be the headline, won't it? Oh Christ.' It was the headline, but in the interview Boris rallied and declared: 'I don't mind if that's the headline. If it gets Frankfurter's definition of academic freedom into the public imagination, it's a small price to pay.'

The liberalism of Boris's outlook was confirmed by his comment on the less academic university courses which are nowadays on offer: 'My instincts are not to go around trying to exterminate Mickey Mouse courses. One man's Mickey Mouse course is another man's *literae humaniores*.' So there were no more jokes about wind-surfing, of the kind which had so infuriated the Registrar of Bangor University only nine months before, and there were no wild promises. When Boris was asked if a Conservative government would raise the £3,000 cap on fees, he replied: 'That's exactly the sort of question I prefer to shirk at this stage.'

MacLeod was impressed by Boris's capacity 'to do what most politicians find almost impossible these days: think aloud', and also that he seemed 'intent on bringing joy into the debate'. Boris told him: 'There are certain things I've discovered about higher education that have been fascinating. And the first and most important is that it's a huge success story . . . There are 91,000 EU students alone, heaven knows how many non-EU students. We've got campuses being inaugurated in China, we've got programmes in India.'

Later the same week, the *Times Higher Education Supplement* published an equally positive interview with Boris by Anna Fazackerley. She reported that 'Mr Johnson's willingness to make some noise about universities – at a time when they have all but disappeared from the political agenda – is already winning him important friends in the sector . . . An insider at Universities UK reports that the group's chief executive, Baroness Warwick, was seriously impressed with Mr Johnson at a recent meeting. No mean feat considering she is a Labour peer.' To the 'amazement' of Universities UK, Boris had 'obviously digested the large pile of paper' it had sent him, 'and is keen to devour more'.

Fazackerley concluded her piece with the words: 'It is clear that those expecting controversy will not have long to wait. Mr Johnson has arrived. Let the show begin.'

At the end of the *Guardian* interview, Boris suddenly remembered to plug his new book, *The Dream of Rome*, which was published at the start of February 2006, accompanied by a two-part television series on BBC2. During one of these programmes someone says to Boris, 'I can see you are fascinated by empire – you would like to be an emperor,' to which Boris replies, 'Well, I can think of worse fates.'

Charles Brand, who produced the series, said that as a presenter, Boris 'proved himself to be a complete natural', and also 'didn't show the ego that TV presenters usually show'. In these programmes, he was like the best kind of schoolmaster: entertaining, energetic and plainly inspired by a deep love of his subject. He had visited some of the greatest Roman sites, and made one want to visit them too. At the Pont du Gard, the stupendous aqueduct which carried water to Nîmes, Boris remarked: 'Now one thing you can say about the Romans. They certainly were not cowboy plumbers.'

The Pont du Gard may have been started by the Emperor Augustus' right-hand man, Marcus Vipsanius Agrippa, in 14 BC. This was the cue for another joke: 'If Augustus had any kind of logistical or military problem his first reaction, I imagine, was to shout "Get Agrippa!"'

Boris interviewed scholars in French, Italian and German, and gave us a few words of Latin without making us feel hopelessly ignorant. Brand said the only problem they had was with Boris's English, which was 'too erudite for the BBC2 audience'. At the screening held in a Soho hotel before the programmes were broadcast, Boris said: 'What you realise about TV is it's a piece of cake to say something about ancient Rome. The tricky thing is to walk in a straight line as you say it.'

But some viewers thought he mucked up the Roman history by shoving in a strained comparison with the European Union. My wife watched for about three minutes before saying: 'There's such an ideological bent behind it, you can't believe a word of it. I can't watch it. I think it's just bollocks.'

My own view is that educated people have for many centuries allowed the ancient and modern worlds to intermingle and inform each other, and Boris stands in this grand tradition. The comparison with Rome does help to suggest why the European Union has failed to command our loyalties. Rome had an emperor, and an emperor cult, the EU does not. There is no Caesar on the Euro, but instead what Boris called the 'evasive symbolism' of 'bridges, culverts, drainage ditches'. Rome persuaded the people it conquered to want to be Roman citizens in a way that Brussels has failed to persuade us to aspire to European citizenship.

At the launch party held at Daunt Books in Marylebone High Street, Boris said, 'I occasionally wonder what people like me are doing in public life,' and answered: 'It is because we hope to become shadow spokesman for higher education.'

He described his latest work as 'what is in a not particularly hotly contested field my best book yet'. He was right. It is true that like much of Boris's writing, *The Dream of Rome* would be better if he had taken more trouble over it. Boris is not a scientific historian, someone who attempts to examine evidence in the most meticulous and fair-minded way. But if Boris had proceeded with that kind of care, he would never have got the book written at all.

And Boris as a historian still has great merits, and insights which would usually escape more professional scholars. Boris is a man for whom the past, and especially the classical past, is still alive. Like P. G. Wodehouse's work, his writing is filled with similes which would occur to nobody else. Boris said a statue of the Emperor Augustus with his arm aloft looked 'like Shane Warne doing his flipper'.

Boris also pointed out that in the dining-rooms of sophisticated Roman families one would find a marble portrait bust of the emperor, and remarked: 'Imagine the frisson of horror if you went out to dinner in Islington and looked up to see a marble rendition of Blair, or Thatcher, or even John Major. You'd think it was either a joke or a demented piece of idolatry.'

To the Romans, it was neither frivolous nor idolatrous to regard their emperor as a god. The early Christians were offensive to Rome, not because they had their own God, but because they insisted he was the only God, which meant they denied the divinity of the emperor. It is clear where Boris's sympathies lie: 'In their sophistication, their understanding of human nature, pain and pleasure, the Romans had a civilisation as exalted as anything we have seen.' Boris loves the glory-chasing, the ostentation and the 'ceaseless competition between macho males' in the Roman Empire: 'It was a world that believed above all in winners and losers, in death and glory.' The Romans had an amazing literature, they had no hang-ups about sex and they 'used the written word to celebrate innocent pleasures that were to become the subjects of Christian guilt and hysteria'.

The Christians were also deplorably meek, which is not a Roman virtue. In the last pages of his book, Boris says it is 'not fashionable these days to cite Edward Gibbon', before confessing that 'I cannot help feeling there is a grain of truth in the following mordant analysis', after which he gives us this account by Gibbon of why the Roman Empire declined:

> The clergy successfully preached the doctrines of patience and pusillanimity; the active virtues of society were discouraged, and the last remains of the military spirit were buried in the cloister: a large portion of public and private wealth was consecrated to the specious demands of charity and devotion; and the soldiers' pay was lavished on the useless multitudes of both sexes, who could only plead the merits of abstinence and chastity.

Abstinence and chastity count for nothing with Boris. He does not pretend that Christianity was wholly to blame for the decline and fall of the Roman Empire, or even the chief cause. But it is clear that he is inspired by the Romans, and even more by the Greeks, and repelled by the early Christians: 'In their suicidal behaviour, in their belief in an afterlife, and in their rejection of the values of the culture in which they found themselves, the early Christians evoke obvious comparisons with Islamic suicide bombers of today.'

When *Third Way*, a Christian magazine, interviewed Boris about his faith, he said: 'My family background is Muslim, Jewish and Christian, so I don't find it very easy to believe exclusively in any one particular monotheism. In fact, my children are a quarter Indian, so their ancestors adhere to a polytheistic faith. I'm a sort of – yeah, I'm Church of England all right, no question about it. I was confirmed in a Church of England church, but I don't kind of . . . Religion is a very private thing . . . Actually I once won the Wilder Divinity Prize, and the prep school scripture prize.'

Boris the politician has demonstrated how well equipped he is for the multicultural world of Muslims, Jews, Christians and Indian polytheists. But Boris the man has revealed virtually nothing of his own religion: he does not even mention that he was actually baptized a Roman Catholic. Later in the same interview, Boris said that like the radio signal for a London channel in the Chiltern hills, out towards Oxford, his faith 'sort of comes and goes a bit'. This makes him sound like a Christian who is troubled by doubts.

But beneath a top-dressing of Anglicanism, Boris remains a whole-hearted pagan. He is a pre-Christian figure who lives in a classical world of gods and heroes. A close friend said: 'He believes in god-like forces all of which are watching him. Because he is Achilles, chosen by the gods, he's put through these trials. Everything is always about him, and nobody is better than him. He can betray other people. It's all part of his drama, his trial by fire. He's very superstitious. He's Achilles and the gods are watching him and he's destined for greatness. He has funny obsessive-compulsive things. He reads car number plates and thinks of the first thing they could stand for. So BWW stands for Boris Will Win.'

This mixture of the educated and the popular – of classical literature and car number plates – is part of the essence of Boris.

# 27

## Coming Up on the Outside

BORIS'S EFFORTS TO PRESENT A MORE SERIOUS FACE TO the world were dealt a severe blow on 2 April 2006, when his old friends at the *News of the World* put him on the front cover again. The headline was 'Boris Cheats With a Blonde' and the story described how 'we caught the shadow minister enjoying a series of secret trysts with blonde beauty Anna Fazackerley, 29, at her London flat'.

The paper printed photographs of Boris leaving Anna's flat in the King's Road, Chelsea, on three occasions within ten days at the end of March. In one of the pictures Anna gazed fondly after him from the doorstep, while in another he waved at her from his bike as she left by taxi.

Boris wore a black beanie hat pulled low down over his forehead, which covered his hair but did not for one moment disguise who he was. If anything the hat merely served to emphasise his identity. To people worried about Marina, this was one of the most hurtful aspects of his behaviour: the lack of trouble he had taken to hide his meetings with Anna. But when I tried to put this point to Boris, he seemed to think that he had nothing to conceal.

It is true that he could just have been discussing higher

education policy with Anna, who after all had recently interviewed him on this very subject. One should also note that the *News of the World* offered, as so often, less evidence than its headline suggested, and was quite capable of completely misinterpreting what scraps of information its agents had managed to obtain.

The following Sunday, the newspaper claimed that on the Thursday after the first story appeared, Boris had shared a hotel room with Anna in Paris, on his way back from a trip to China. Quite friendly observers started to ask if he had gone mad. But the *News of the World* was wrong about Paris. If its reporters had troubled to discover from the hotel staff what the woman who left Boris's room at seven in the morning looked like, they would have learned that, unlike Anna, she was rather small and dark. She was in fact Boris's wife, Marina.

This ridiculous error cried out for correction. But the trouble about correcting errors is that you may end up implying that everything you do not correct is true. Marina accepted Boris's assurance that there had been no affair, but very reasonably decided not to get into an argument with such opponents.

It emerged from the *News of the World*'s coverage that Boris was still visiting Petronella as well as Anna. This was certainly not something on which Boris was going to comment. When Anna was asked if she would like to comment on her alleged affair with Boris, she said: 'Absolutely not.' Boris said: 'You're very kind. But no thank you. Absolutely not. No comment whatsoever. Thanks a lot. Bye.'

This was a vast improvement on his denial of his affair with Petronella, but the whole situation was still pretty horrible for Marina. The press descended on their house off the Holloway Road. Boris was at this point in China, on a fact-finding mission about higher education, and she found herself questioned by reporters in front of her children. She lodged a complaint with the Press Complaints Commission about this.

Marina otherwise maintained a dignified silence. So did her parents, though her father told a reporter that the story was 'rubbish'. He was infuriated to find he had instead been quoted as saying, 'I think it's rubbish, but I don't know.' In private, the Wheelers took a very dim view both of Petronella, and of her mother, Verushka Wyatt, for trying to seduce Boris away from Marina.

Meanwhile a friend of the Wyatts said Petronella was very upset, and felt 'heartbroken and betrayed', when the news of Boris's alleged affair with Anna broke.

Some of the tabloids made half-hearted calls for David Cameron to sack Boris, which the Tory leader quite rightly rejected, for it would have been ridiculous to set a precedent for sacking someone simply because they were said to have committed adultery.

Ephraim Hardcastle, in the *Daily Mail*, wrote daily reports on Boris, whom he diagnosed as suffering from satyrism, or 'unusually strong sexual desires'. He went on: 'Boris must re-establish himself as a serious political player. Why not portray himself as a victim of sexual addiction and seek treatment? This route was chosen by Hollywood stars Michael Douglas, Rob Lowe and Billy Bob Thornton.'

Shortly before he was done over by the *News of the World*, Boris used his *Telegraph* column to mount a robust defence of Silvio Berlusconi, who was about to lose the Italian General Election. Boris hailed Berlusconi as 'a standing reproach to the parade of platitudinous Pooters that pass across the stage of international diplomacy'. He gave some examples of the Italian Prime Minister's wild and tasteless behaviour, and asked why so many Italians still liked him: 'The answer is that they like him not in spite of the gaffes, but because of the gaffes. It is Berlusconi's genius that he has become the only world leader in the great queue of grey-suited line-toers who can be consistently relied on to say something eye-popping.'

One can see the bare bones of a defence of Boris here. He is more fun than the grey and cautious hypocrites who surround him. His very errors make him loveable.

Sue Lawley suggested to Boris on *Desert Island Discs* that he liked taking risks:

> LAWLEY: 'Aren't you somebody who, I mean, what, you like to play with fire.'
>
> BORIS: 'Sue, you're brilliantly good, you're a brilliant interviewer, but in the immortal words of, of Sue Lawley, more music please.'
>
> LAWLEY: 'You do like playing with fire though, don't you. It's all part of being tested.'
>
> BORIS: 'Well. I see. This is your, this is your theory, is it? . . . Well, I suppose there might be an element of truth in that, but anyway. Not unnecessary risks, no.'

Lawley was right to detect a craving for danger in Boris. He would find a life without risk intolerably dull. But he also craves comfort and reassurance. Unlike many Englishmen of his class, he actually enjoys the company of women, and acknowledges his need of them. He has also shown time after time that embarrassments which would make many people go away and hide in a hole in the ground were not quite so mortifying to him.

Boris found himself trapped in the role of celebrity. Without ever holding a political office of any significance, he had become more famous than most Cabinet ministers, but was also considered more irresponsible. There was a danger that he would turn into a kind of national treasure, to be wheeled out and laughed at on significant occasions, or occasions which television producers regarded as significant.

One of his weaknesses is an excessive desire to be liked, and he will be hurt if he does not come across as likeable in this book. Another flaw is his inability, or obdurate unwillingness, to make choices which would entail a degree of self-sacrifice. Asked if he would like A or B, he generally gives no clear answer and tries to have both.

He distracts our attention from this evasiveness by telling very enjoyable jokes, which along with his Woosterish persona have made him one of the most popular performers of our times. But the jokes can also make him seem to serious-minded listeners as if he does not believe a word he is saying. If he used to appear more grown-up than his contemporaries, by 2006 he was perhaps striking some of them as a bit juvenile.

Prigs think he needs to learn to be 'serious', by which they mean as dull as they are, and he has recently responded by giving a nod or two in their direction. The problem is that when he adopts a serious tone, he can begin to sound a bit like Prince Charles. But he is not without a sense of prudence, and has for years refused many more invitations to take part in mad stunts than he has accepted. He made an effort, when he was appointed shadow higher education spokesman, to show what a sober fellow he can be, but slightly spoiled the effect by giving a jokey, off-the-cuff speech to an audience of higher education dignitaries at King's College, London, who were expecting a considered account of Conservative policy.

The vein of anarchy in his character, and his impulse to do the opposite of what he is told, make it very hard for him to obey rules which seem to him to be an infringement of his right to do as he pleases. As Martin Hammond said of him when he was still at school: 'Boris sometimes seems affronted when criticised for what amounts to a gross failure of responsibility . . . I think he honestly believes that it is churlish of us not to regard him as an exception, one who should be free of the network of obligation which binds everyone else.'

This determination to do things his own way, even if it means breaking the rules, is one of the most characteristic things about

Boris. He was very successful as a journalist, but did not just grind his way on to become editor of the *Telegraph* or *The Times*. He started a parliamentary career which could easily end in failure, and when *Conservative Heartland* – a magazine for Tory party members – asked him in 2001 why he had taken this risk, he said he wanted to be where the action is, not just watching it, and went on: 'We all have tram tracks. All our lives . . . marriage, children . . . there is a lot to do, a lot going on . . . There comes a point where you've got to put the dynamite under your own tram tracks . . . derail yourself. See what happens.'

It is an extraordinary image. The last thing most people want to do is to derail themselves. Boris is braver and more optimistic, and finds stability more suffocating, than most of us do.

Before the 2006 World Cup, when he turned out for England in a charity football match against Germany, he conducted a rugby tackle on one of the German players. The video clip of this bizarre spectacle become one of the most popular things on the Internet. Boris had entertained people by doing something which nobody else would have dared to do, or even thought of doing.

That formula does not do justice to Boris's sex life, where he has done what many men have thought of doing. According to Balzac, men of all kinds, the distinguished man and the fool, desire both an ideal love and pleasure, 'which most often turns out to be a work in two volumes'. Boris has committed adultery, but when millions of other people have done likewise, it would be intolerably prudish and self-righteous to hold that this debarred him from high office. The diaries of Duff Cooper, a distinguished Tory politician of the 1930s, show him committing adultery with a prodigious number of women, but this did not prevent him from taking the brave and correct decision to resign in 1938 in protest at Neville Chamberlain's appeasement policy.

For Boris, it is a drawback that Parliament has many rules and people get quite cross if you break them. As an MP, you are expected to show an extraordinary degree of patience. Unless you spend hour after hour sitting in the Commons Chamber, the Speaker will not call you in debates, and unless you do your bit in committee the Whips will not rate you either. Boris lacked the time and docility to put up with day after day of this drudgery.

So although he is a brilliant debater, he has not yet established himself as a parliamentary performer. He is not among the few dozen Tory MPs who regularly turn up and speak. Even when Boris comes to Prime Minister's Questions, a highlight of the week which he often skips, he tends to stand behind the seat occupied by the Serjeant at Arms, a long way from the Conservative Party leader, David Cameron. There is no disguising the fact that while in the summer of 2004 Boris was still the coming man, by the summer of 2006, when these words were written, he looked a bit out of it, and was not one of the talented young group which had formed around Cameron.

But Boris was never the kind of politician who could expect to get to the top by dint of slow, inside work. This does not mean he has no chance of fulfilling his ambition to become Prime Minister. Insiders can become boring, and dangerously cut off. They can fail to see which way the world is moving, and can lose what capacity they may once have had to communicate with the wider public.

Boris is the opposite. He is very quick to see which way the world is moving and brilliant at reaching the wider public. These gifts have made him a successful journalist and may yet be of service to him as a politician. If he can lend his voice to public discontents which the insiders have ignored, he will at first be dismissed by the party establishment as a mere maverick, trouble-maker and populist, but may end by becoming the indispensable figure which it needs to show that it has responded to the public anger. Boris is willing to go out in all weathers and is likely to thrive best when times are worst. In the summer of 2006, he gave a fiery speech in the Commons, denouncing Britain's unequal extradition arrangements with America. One of Boris's own constituents was on the point of being extradited to Texas, and his anger at the unfairness of this proceeding came through loud and strong. It did not matter that Boris used one or two bizarre turns of phrase: his moral seriousness was unmistakable.

Yet even without wars, tumults and other great themes, Boris is likely to be needed by the cautious insiders, to demonstrate that they have some connection with Merry England. This is the generous conservatism for which he stands. He wants people to be free to enjoy themselves, does not rush to condemn anyone whose pleasures are not his own and sympathises with the little man who finds himself caught in an impossible position. While many politicians have the urge to perfect society, Boris believes in the imperfectability of mankind, and especially of himself. He does not seek to attain impossibly high standards, nor does he impose them on others. He is unpompous, which is yet another reason why people like him so much.

Hayek said in 1944, 'British strength, British character and British achievements are to a great extent the result of a cultivation of the spontaneous.' That is what makes Boris so British: his capacity for being spontaneous. He has never prepared himself properly, and this means his whole life has been a preparation for being unprepared. His real problem, an old friend of the family suggested, is to take himself seriously.

When he was worrying over lunch about this book, Boris leaned across the table and recited in heartfelt self-defence Othello's great last speech:

> Soft you, a word or two before you go.
> I have done the state some service, and they know't:
> No more of that. I pray you, in your letters,

When you shall these unlucky deeds relate,
Speak of me as I am. Nothing extenuate,
Nor set down aught in malice. Then must you speak
Of one that loved not wisely, but too well;
Of one not easily jealous, but, being wrought,
Perplexed in the extreme; of one whose hand,
Like the base Indian, threw a pearl away
Richer than all his tribe; of one whose subdued eyes,
Albeit unused to the melting mood,
Drop tears as fast as the Arabian trees
Their medicinable gum. Set you down this,
And say besides that in Aleppo once,
Where a malignant and a turbaned Turk
Beat a Venetian and traduced the state,
I took by th'throat the circumcised dog
And smote him – thus!

With these words, Othello stabs himself, kisses the dead body of Desdemona and dies. Boris is not Othello, and stern judges will think it was preposterous of him to recite those lines. But part of the charm of Boris is that he is willing to be preposterous. He has already done the state some service by entertaining us, and by popular demand he can still attain the highest office. In a world where Reagan can become President, it is not preposterous to think of Boris as Prime Minister. His rivals envy the love and admiration he evinces, while lamenting how unpopular our political system has become. If they try to exclude Boris because he is too colourful, too talented and too good at reaching the people, they will not be forgiven.

# 28

# How This Book Was Received

THE SUGGESTION AT THE END OF THE LAST CHAPTER that Boris could yet become Prime Minister attracted a certain amount of ridicule when this book was published in the autumn of 2006. Alexander Chancellor, Stephen Glover and Paul Routledge were among those who greeted the idea with incredulity, with Glover telling readers of the *Daily Mail*: 'In the unlikely event of the British people so taking leave of their senses, I shall be buying a one-way ticket to New Zealand'.

Nor can it be said, as I write these extra pages for the paperback edition, that the passage of nine months has brought the prospect of Boris the Prime Minister appreciably closer. There seems no pressing need to embark on the second volume, provisionally entitled *The Statesmanship of Boris Johnson*, which I hope one day to offer the world.

On occasion Boris still seemed more determined to upset the dreary, pious consensus than to show any kind of steadiness. A fine example of his iconoclastic style can be found in the *Daily Telegraph* of 12 October 2006, where his column appeared under the headline, 'Give Iran the bomb: it might make the regime more pliable'.

And yet there are moments of encouragement. I was heartened

to hear my Westminster colleague Simon Carr, parliamentary sketch-writer for the *Independent*, say of Boris's performance at Foreign Office questions on 5 December 2006: 'It was the first time I'd heard him not sounding like a comedian'.

The questions posed by Boris in the 'new voice' which Carr had detected were as follows: 'What can the Foreign Secretary say to disprove the withering verdict of the US State Department official, Kendall Myers, that Washington has systematically ignored British advice over Iraq? Can she give a single concrete example of any piece of advice given by her or the Prime Minister that was accepted by Washington and without which the catastrophe in Iraq would have been even worse?' The Foreign Secretary, Margaret Beckett, responded with empty bluster.

The commonest mistake in politics, Lord Salisbury said, is clinging to the carcasses of dead policies, and this is not an error to which Boris is prone. In December 2006 he told some students at Portsmouth who accused him of having blood on his hands over the war in Iraq: 'If I have my time again I certainly would not vote for it. I regret it. It was a colossal mistake and misadventure.'

A few weeks later he said in reply to a question from a reader of the *Independent*: 'It is the sheer number of casualties, the chaos, that persuades me that we did the wrong thing. I voted for this bloody disaster not because I believed Blair, but because I thought it would be a good thing to get rid of Saddam. And it was a good thing. It is just that the price has been way too high.'

While the Tory leadership hesitates, for fear of looking cowardly and inconstant, to make such admissions, Boris has already cut and run. His approach is less reliable, but more realistic. He connects with people by using the language they too use about 'this bloody disaster'.

But it cannot yet be said that he connects with them very often by this means. When he blazes forth into national prominence, it is still by comic performances in which he spreads a kind of incredulous joy that such things can happen outside the pages of Evelyn Waugh.

One such eruption occurred at the start of September 2006, when Boris remarked in the *Daily Telegraph*: 'For 10 years we in the Tory Party have become used to Papua New Guinea-style orgies of cannibalism and chief-killing, and so it is with a happy amazement that we watch as the madness engulfs the Labour Party.'

Jean L Kekedo, Papua New Guinea's High Commissioner in London, was enraged by this attribution of cannibalism to her country: 'I wish to state that I am shocked and appalled by such comments from a seemingly well-educated person of very high standing, in fact the alternative minister for higher education in the House of Commons. How far removed and ill-informed can Mr Johnson be from the reality of the situation in modern-day Papua New Guinea?'

Boris responded with one of those vivid and amusing statements which come so easily to him at moments of crisis, and which so seldom amount to a full apology: 'I would like to thank the High Commissioner very much for her clarification. I meant no insult to the people of Papua New Guinea who I'm sure lead lives of blameless bourgeois domesticity in common with the rest of us. My remarks were inspired by a Time Life book I have which does indeed show relatively recent photos of Papua New Guinean tribes engaged in warfare, and I'm fairly certain that cannibalism was involved. I'd be happy to show the book to the High Commissioner but I'm of course also very happy to take up her kind invite and add Papua New Guinea to my global itinerary of apology.'

After issuing this statement, Boris rang me to ask if I still had the book, which had fascinated him as a child and which he had lent me while trying to persuade me to go to Papua New Guinea for the *Spectator* – a generous offer which, as related in chapter 15, I never got round to taking up. I ransacked my study in a vain search for the Time Life book, before coming to the view that I had either returned it to Boris or else passed it on to Mary Wakefield, who is more adventurous than I am and was thinking of offering to go to Papua New Guinea.

About ten days later, on 18 September 2006, the first edition of my life of Johnson was published, and I was extremely anxious to know what Boris thought of it. He asked to see the book a few days before it came out and Simon & Schuster sent one to his Commons office. On publication day I was at the Liberal Democrat conference in Brighton and spoke to Boris after I had dined with some Liberal Democrats. We had a long and genial talk, during which Boris asserted: 'You've done more than enough to avoid any charge of sycophancy.' He asked how sales were going and expressed the hope that the book was not doing well. He also wanted to know the identity of one or two people who had made disobliging comments about him, which I naturally refused to reveal. Boris began to make guesses, which I soon refused to answer for fear he would arrive at the answers by a process of elimination.

A fortnight later, at the Conservative conference in Bournemouth, Simon & Schuster had arranged for me to sign copies at the Westminster Bookshop stall in the Bournemouth International Centre. In an effort to drum up interest for this signing, flyers were distributed among Conservative party members assuring them that this was the funniest book on politics they would read all year.

This feeble hucksterism did no good. Very few people came to my table, which was piled high with copies of this book, while only a couple of yards away Ann Widdecombe was selling vast quantities of her novels. Widdecombe has a powerful personality and an adoring Tory public and virtually no one who came within ten yards of her was able to avoid buying at least one of her books. I bought one myself and got her to inscribe it to my mother. Widdecombe's fans were drinking the wine and eating the olives provided by my publishers, yet buying only her books, which she promoted in a loud voice as containing no indecent language.

I could not pretend my own work was as chaste as Widdecombe's. In desperation I rang Boris, who had told me he would 'do his best' to put in an appearance after speaking at a fringe meeting. I got through to his answering machine, on which I outlined the humiliation which was being visited on a book which was after all about himself.

Within a few minutes Boris had arrived on the scene and the battle was transformed. Copies flew off my table. People crowded round Boris, begging him to sign the book. It was a minor example of his ability to change the whole atmosphere. Some of the customers who had got Boris's signature came over and asked for mine too. He had found many different forms of words in which to rubbish the book, including this, found in a copy which he signed for one of my godchildren:

This book is all wrong!

Ignore everything within.

Best wishes,

Boris Johnson

P.S. It's balls

The writing of rude comments in each copy struck me as a better way to deal with the book than by retreating into a frosty and dispiriting boycott. At the same time Boris managed to sell quite a few of his own books.

This brief frenzy was as nothing compared to what happened the next day. Boris has never had any time for faddy feeders, or for intolerant attempts to boss us about, and he told a fringe meeting: 'If I was in charge I would get rid of Jamie Oliver and tell people to eat what they like.'

The Tory leader, David Cameron, had just praised Oliver to the skies, saying that the TV cook's campaign to improve school food had done more than the Department of Education to raise standards. Yet here we had Boris dismissing the Oliver line on school food: 'I say let people eat what they like. Why shouldn't they push pies through the railings?'

Later that afternoon, Boris arrived in the large, domed hall on the seaward side of the Bournemouth International Centre where the press was quartered. Journalists surrounded him, asking him about his anti-Oliver and pro-pie remarks, which had been reported by Peter Henley, political editor of BBC South.

Boris batted these inquiries away and retired into a screened-off part of the hall which the Tories were using as their press office. Here he asked if he could borrow a computer in order to write a piece for the Times Higher Education Supplement. A computer was provided for him and he began typing.

Two or three photographers outside the enclosure began shouting for Boris. Soon there were about ten photographers banging on the metallic walls and calling for him. One of them climbed up a ladder and put his camera over the top of the partition.

A Tory press officer approached Boris and asked in a friendly way: 'Can I just get this straight? Have you said, if anything should be got rid of, it shouldn't be pies, it should be Jamie Oliver?'

Boris: 'I've said nothing of the sort, Jamie Oliver is a saint.'

Press officer: 'This is what the journalists are all saying you said.'

Boris: 'I suppose it's conceivable I said something along those lines. But they've misinterpreted it.'

Press officer: 'So you did actually say it.'

Long silence.

Boris: 'Well I suppose I did actually use those words, but it was purely to make a point which they all misunderstood.'

The press officer was by now slightly perturbed: 'It was clear to me there was a problem. Whether or not he had been misunderstood, he clearly had said those words.'

Outside the stockade, more and more journalists were gathering. A camera team from Newsnight on BBC2 was filming a team from BBC1 which was filming the dozens of other photographers. Within 45 minutes, well over 100 members of the media had gathered, for this was next to the desks where we all filed our stories, and nothing much else was going on. I took my place in the throng, where Matthew Parris of *The Times* was trying to get a chant of 'Boris, Boris, Boris' going.

Within the stall, the sense of being under siege rapidly increased. The first journalist they saw looking over the top of the partition wall was Dave Wooding of the *Sun*, who gave a great big grin and passed on the news that Boris was still inside. The noise grew louder and louder. A kind of jokey hysteria was enveloping the journalists, many of whom had spent the last three weeks on the road at the party conferences, where one cannot feel one is entering into the spirit of things if one misses the drunken late-night receptions. Seven or eight Tory press officers conferred among themselves and established that there was no way out except through the door by which Boris had entered. The BBC found a ladder and sent a cameraman up it to film what was going on inside.

At six o'clock, the Tories were intending to brief journalists on David Cameron's keynote speech to the conference to be delivered the following day, but the Boris affair had completely taken over. Shadow cabinet ministers who wanted to get into the Tory press office had to battle their way through the scrum of media people outside. Boris, who as higher education spokesman was not in the Shadow Cabinet, just sat there, typing his

34. In 2012, during the London Olympics, Boris managed to get stuck on a zip wire – a mishap which somehow made him more popular (see chapter 33).

35. In 2015, while playing rugby in a madly competitive spirit for a few moments in Tokyo, Boris knocked a ten-year-old boy to the ground. The boy and the Mayor of London were both unhurt.

36. On the afternoon of Sunday 21 February 2016, Boris revealed to the media scrum outside his house in Islington that he had decided to join the Leave side in the EU referendum campaign.

37. On 11 May, Boris launched his Vote Leave battlebus campaign by brandishing a Cornish pasty in Truro.

38. The misleading claim on the bus, that by leaving the EU Britain could spend £350 million a week more on the NHS, exposed him to much criticism.

39. Boris and Michael Gove formed a powerful double act on the campaign trail. Here they inspect a bottle of hand wash in Stratford-upon-Avon.

40. On 23 June, Boris and his wife, Marina Wheeler, arrived to cast their votes in the EU referendum . . .

41. . . . as did Gove and his wife, Sarah Vine. She would later be described as 'Lady Macbeth' by observers who claimed she persuaded her husband to betray Boris.

42. Following the Leave campaign's victory, David Cameron wrong-footed his opponents by at once announcing, with his wife Samantha looking on, that he would be stepping down as Prime Minister.

43. Gove listens as Boris makes his first public statement after winning the referendum. They look exhausted rather than triumphant.

44. Boris supporters: Sir Lynton Crosby, the rugged Australian campaigner brought in to run his leadership campaign . . .

45. . . . and Ben Wallace MP, for several years Boris's main supporter in the House of Commons.

46. Gove supporters: Nick Boles MP, a close friend who was found to have sent foolish and disreputable texts on Gove's behalf . . .

47. . . . and Dominic Raab MP, in whose gaze is seen a touch of the ideological fervour which made Gove the chosen candidate of some Eurosceptic Tories.

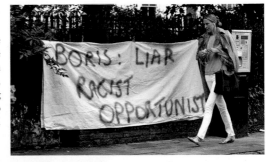

48. A banner draped on the railings opposite Boris's house shows how low he has sunk in the estimation of his opponents, who accused him of taking Britain out of the EU in order to seize power for himself.

49. Angry protesters proclaim their hatred of Boris, who has to be protected by a considerable number of police officers.

50. Boris cannot quite conceal the intense pain he feels as he waves to his supporters and tells them, to their astonishment, that he is abandoning his bid to become Prime Minister.

51. Andrea Leadsom, surrounded by her stern, unbending, Eurosceptic admirers, announces that after coming under ferocious pressure from the media, she too is withdrawing from the leadership race.

52. Only twenty days after the referendum, on Wednesday 13 July, Theresa May, pictured here with her husband Philip, celebrates becoming Prime Minister.

53. May's most dramatic early appointment was of Boris as Foreign Secretary, seen entering his new department with his most senior official, Sir Simon McDonald.

54. The new Foreign Secretary aroused far greater interest than any other member of May's Cabinet.

55. On his first visit to Brussels as Foreign Secretary, Boris amused his Spanish, Belgian and Maltese counterparts.

56. Boris was welcomed by John Kerry, the American Secretary of State, at their first joint press conference, but was accused by American journalists of having 'an unusually long history of wild exaggerations and frankly outright lies'.

57. At May's first Cabinet meeting, Boris sits immediately to her left, with Sir Jeremy Heywood, the Cabinet Secretary, on her right.

58. Only Amber Rudd, the new Home Secretary, and Philip Hammond, the new Chancellor, now separate Boris from the new Prime Minister as she takes questions in the Commons for the first time.

article and sometimes looking up, a smile playing about his lips. He had not arranged this spontaneous demonstration of his pulling power, but he was in some ways enjoying it.

Theresa May, one of the few women in the Shadow Cabinet, who is perhaps better known for her shoes than for her politics, turned up and asked in the press office: 'What on earth's going on – can I do anything?' It was suggested that she might as well flash her shoes, which she did, but that wasn't what the media had come to see.

As soon as Boris had finished his article, he wanted to leave and three press officers were deputed to accompany him. It was put to Boris that it would be best if he said no more about Jamie Oliver, the thinking being that there were already two versions of the story and it would only make matters worse to have a third.

Boris: 'That's fine. I won't say a word.'

The door opened and out he went. A scrum like a huge balloon formed round him as he turned to the right, which was the wrong way to go. Apprised of his mistake, he turned back and made his way to the doors giving onto the seafront. The balloon narrowed and squeezed through the doors with him, resuming its normal shape in the open air and accompanying him down the hill towards Bournemouth pier. Throughout this performance Boris talked freely with the reporters nearest to him, asking them if they didn't think they were getting things a bit out of proportion.

High on the cliff behind Boris, outside the Highcliff Hotel, an old lady and her companion watched this astonishing spectacle.

The companion said: 'What on earth is that?'

The old lady said: 'It must be Maggie. She's back.'

The moment Boris had departed, reporters began ringing the press office to ask if he was going to be sacked. The press office checked with Cameron's office, which said: 'You've got to be joking – Boris sacked?' By the end of the conference, Boris had managed to convey his revised opinion that Oliver is a 'national saint' and a 'messiah'.

Cameron's reaction to having the show stolen from him was different to what Michael Howard's would have been. The new Tory leader was more liberal in temperament than the old, and also wished to be seen as more liberal. There was nevertheless a hint of headmasterly asperity as Cameron alluded to the affair at the start of his speech the next day: 'Even Boris made it all the way to Tuesday afternoon before he put his foot in it.'

Cameron paid tribute to the 'amazing job' Boris had been doing going round our colleges and universities, before adding: 'We don't mind if people go off message. We like it actually. Just try not to do it all the time.'

Boris has since been trying not to do it all the time.

To my relief, few errors of fact have been detected in the book. Boris objected to the photograph of him as a young child where he is described as looking 'not very happy' and said: 'The whole point of the photograph is that I have a bean stuck up my nose.'

Me: 'Why?'

Boris: 'I was illustrating some point.'

He promised to correct other errors in the book, but then thought better of this, and said the mistake about the bean was the most serious.

In February 2007 Lord Ashcroft delivered a presentation at Conservative headquarters at which he summarised the results of private polling carried out for the party. This showed that outside the present leadership, there were two people the public associated with the Tories.

Up came pictures of Margaret Thatcher, looking imperious, and of Boris Johnson, eating a bun.

# 29

# Mayor Johnson

DAVID CAMERON HAD NO INTENTION OF GETTING BORIS TO run against Ken Livingstone in the election for Mayor of London to be held on 1 May 2008. If the idea of Mayor Johnson entered Cameron's mind, it was swiftly dismissed. Boris was a liability. At the last party conference he had stolen the show from Cameron, and although Boris had tried to behave himself since, the Tory leader knew his unruly colleague would be unable to resist stealing the show from him again if given half a chance. It would be madness to select such an unreliable figure as Boris as a champion of the new conservatism (in actual fact a very old conservatism) which Cameron and his team were putting together.

So various implausible people were approached to ask if they would consider becoming the Conservative candidate. The trouble was that Ken was generally regarded as invincible, and to take him on demanded a boldness and optimism not widely found in a party which had lost the last three general elections. It was also desirable to field a candidate who was well known, and virtually no one in the party who was below retirement age could claim that.

By April 2007 the Tories found themselves in a humiliating predicament. After a prolonged search, which included rejections from Lord Coe, the Olympics supremo, and Lord Stevens, the former head of the Metropolitan Police, the best potential candidate they could come up with was Greg Dyke, a former Director General of the BBC, who like Lord Stevens was not even a member of the Conservative Party.

Not all Tories were enthused by Dyke, who was perhaps best known for introducing Roland Rat, a glove puppet, to viewers of breakfast television. Charles Moore wrote in the *Spectator*: 'Mr Dyke is very exciting to some because he is quite famous, quite unTory in demeanour and a former Labour supporter. Unfortunately, as any student of the Hutton affair and reader of his lachrymose memoirs, *Inside Story*, will know, he is also, politically, a moron.'

The word 'moron' is a bit harsh, for Dyke was astute enough to reject the Tories' offer, or at least to say he would only accept it if he could run as an independent with Tory and Liberal Democrat backing. The Lib Dems turned down the proposal and that was the end of Dyke.

As a result of his Dyke piece, Moore received an e-mail from Mary Wakefield at the *Spectator* in which she said, in a flash of inspiration, 'Why not Boris for mayor?', to which Moore replied: 'No, Boris for Mayor of Henley.'

Boris was shown this e-mail, and it has been said that he was so stung by it that he decided to run. It is an amusing thought that his feelings of rivalry with Moore prompted him to become Mayor of London, and if Boris were a character from a P.G. Wodehouse story it would even be true.

But when the real Boris was urged again and again over the next few weeks, in the most friendly and persuasive way, to run against Ken, he was at first no more than cautiously keen. Of course his competitive spirit and addiction to popularity contests were engaged, but Boris did not wish to jeopardize his chances of promotion at Westminster. He had made a big effort as shadow higher education spokesman to prove that he was serious. A lot of people in the world of higher education were impressed by his mastery of detail which, contrary to popular belief Boris can hoover up at astonishing speed when he puts his mind to it, and he believed he was in line to be rewarded for his assiduity by Cameron. This did not seem the moment to throw away his safe seat at Henley and abandon the Westminster route to the top.

If Cameron had not harboured such a deep distrust of Boris, he could without much trouble have kept him beavering away as a loyal shadow spokesman. It is true that Boris regards himself as unquestionably the more brilliant figure. But in truth, Cameron would only have had to praise Boris for doing good work and offer him some modest promotion, and he could have had Boris eating out of his hand.

Boris instead was forced to start asking himself why Cameron was not giving him any encouragement. Boris could see too that as Mayor of London, he could be a leader rather than a follower, which would enable him to play to his strengths. The boy who had wanted to be world king could at least run a world city: London was an interesting proposition. Boris later recalled receiving a lot of advice from the Tory MPs whom he consulted, including 'don't stand', 'absolutely don't stand' and 'Ken is unbeatable'. What spurred him on to defy this advice was his growing doubt about whether he was going to get anywhere under Cameron.

That doubt was confirmed in the clearest way on 2 July 2007 when Cameron reshuffled his team of shadow ministers, a move necessitated by Gordon Brown's entry into 10 Downing Street. Brown decided to split the education portfolio and promote his right-hand man, Ed Balls, to the new and totalitarian-sounding post of Secretary of State for Children, Families and Schools.

Who would get the key job of shadowing Balls? The existing shadow education secretary, David Willetts, was out of the running, having by accident set off a row about grammar schools which had caused grave embarrassment to Cameron. Many Tories were appalled by their leader's opposition to the creation of new grammar schools, and said in a resentful tone that it was all very well to take that view if you had parents who could afford to send you to Eton.

Cameron chose Michael Gove to shadow Balls: Gove who at Oxford had been happy to act as Boris's stooge. Gove was recognized as a man of outstanding ability, but had only got into the Commons as recently as 2005, as had two other MPs, Jeremy Hunt and Nick Herbert, whom Cameron also promoted to the Shadow Cabinet.

Boris, who had been in the Commons since 2001, was left with the job of shadow spokesman on higher education, in which he would still be answering to David Willetts, who was himself demoted to the less significant role of shadow Secretary of State for Innovation, Universities and Skills. Having looked for love from Cameron, Boris found himself kept at a chilly distance.

In fairness to Cameron, one should say that many Tory MPs, alarmed by Boris's unpredictability and jealous of his fame, thought that was exactly where he should be kept. They too saw him as a maverick whom it was only prudent to exclude from power, and from any post where he could cause the party serious embarrassment. The last thing the parliamentary party wanted was for such a loose cannon to be given official encouragement. Nor, given the chippiness stirred up by the grammar school row, was this the moment to bring another alumnus of Eton and the Bullingdon Club to the fore.

There is something about Boris which is an affront to serious-minded people's idea of how politics should be conducted. By refusing to adopt their solemn tone, he implies that they are ridiculous, and the dreadful thing, from their point of view, is that a large part of the British public agrees with Boris. So it is not just lefties, but people from every part of the political class, who cannot bear his unwillingness to take them as seriously as they take themselves.

It was after all a Tory leader, Michael Howard, who had sacked Boris, and Howard's chosen successor, Cameron, has similar instincts about what does and does not constitute reliable behaviour.

Boris and Cameron are often described as friends, but this is highly misleading. It would be more accurate to say that they are on friendly terms, but have never spent or wished to spend much time with each other. Many people who have known Boris well since Oxford days have never once met Cameron with him. As a well-placed observer said: 'They have no history of friendship and Boris has never been part of Cameron's set. Boris would find the idea of going on holiday with the members of that set atrocious.'

For while Cameron is a favoured son of the establishment, and takes the establishment's view that there are certain things which are just not done, Boris is an outsider, a loner, a man who likes to be on genial terms with everyone but who has no circle of political intimates. Cameron is a man of astonishing gifts, including cool judgement under pressure, but his instinct is to work within the existing framework of rules. Boris frets under such restraint and is always ready to drive a coach and horses through it. Cameron believes in order: Boris believes in being free. Cameron is bound to regard Boris as bit disreputable, while Boris is bound to regard Cameron as a bit limited.

To be excluded from the Shadow Cabinet showed Boris he was going to get nowhere by playing the parliamentary game. Two days after Cameron left him out, news broke that Boris might run for Mayor of London. The Tories denied the story, but were forced to retract the denial after Boris issued the following statement:

Being Mayor of London would be a fantastic job and anyone who loves London would want to consider the possibility very carefully.

I want to stress that this idea did not come from David Cameron or from anyone in his office but I have, of course, been very struck by the number of people who have been urging me to run.

In my case, there are huge obstacles – above all my commitment and responsibility to my constituency. It is hard to see how those difficulties could be overcome – but I am ruling nothing out.

Boris was becoming more and more attracted by the idea of running for London because it offered him the chance to perform a grand out-flanking manoeuvre, where his ability to connect with the British people would more than compensate for the invincible suspicion he inspires in party managers. Just as the Mayor of Paris can ascend from the Hôtel de Ville to the Elysée Palace, so, if he won, he could pioneer a new route via City Hall to 10 Downing Street.

And among the Cameroons, the realization belatedly dawned that Boris would be a far stronger candidate than any of the able but unknown Tories who wanted to have a go. Nick Boles, the founding director of the Policy Exchange think tank and a man who attracts rave reviews from those who have worked with him, was the preferred candidate of the Notting Hill set round Cameron, despite being unknown to the public. But Boles received the alarming news that he was suffering from cancer, and had to withdraw.

George Osborne, the shadow Chancellor of the Exchequer, was the first prominent Cameroon to urge that Boris be adopted as candidate. To take on Ken, the party needed a big personality who was extremely well-known and would have the chutzpah and energy to make things happen. Boris as mayor would not have his finger on the nuclear button, nor would he have the pernickety task of steering complicated legislation through Parliament.

On the last possible day, 16 July 2007, Boris launched his

campaign to become the Tory candidate for Mayor of London. Not everyone was optimistic about his chances: Colin Brown of the *Independent* described him to me as 'a butterfly who will have his wings ripped off', a view shared by many members of the parliamentary press gallery.

At my suggestion, Simon & Schuster sent some copies of this book round to Ken, who was photographed reading it on the Tube and described it as 'the scariest thing I've read since *Silence of the Lambs*.'

But as so often, perhaps the most vehement attack on Boris was made by Polly Toynbee of the *Guardian*, who wrote: 'David Cameron has just made his worst mistake. He will bitterly regret the day he encouraged Boris Johnson to stand as London's mayor. What does it say about the desperate state of the Conservatives that they will put up a clown to run a great global city?'

Yet Toynbee was rattled: 'Jester, toff, self-absorbed sociopath and serial liar, the man could still win.' One cannot help feeling that the great columnist reveals here her low opinion of Londoners.

On 27 September 2007, the Tories announced that Boris had beaten by a distance the three other people who had entered the open primary held by the party to decide who its candidate would be. Boris said: 'As I visited all of London's 32 boroughs in the last few weeks, the message is loud and clear – King Newt's days are numbered.'

But this looked a rotten time to be the Tory candidate. When the Tories gathered a few days later in Blackpool for their party conference, it was widely expected that Gordon Brown would call an early general election and win it. Brown was riding high in the polls and his plan was to smash the Tories while they were down.

On the morning of Monday 1 October, as I went into break-fast at the De Vere golf hotel on the landward side of Blackpool, the fire alarm went off and I met Boris as we went outside. Clad in an ordinary white shirt, of the sort one might wear with a suit, and shorts, he set off for a jog round the golf course while the rest of us stood in the car park.

Half an hour later, as I was breakfasting in the hotel, he came and sat down at the next table and a genial chat ensued about whether there would be a general election. I predicted that Brown would funk it, but asked Boris whether, if there was an election, he would fight Henley.

Boris gave a good imitation of choking on his cereal – perhaps on a bit of bran, or else on a bit of fruit – before replying: 'I'll play it by ear.'

'This disinclination – no, much worse than a disinclination – this evasive refusal to give straight answers is damn annoying,' I scribbled in my diary. At a time when Boris should have been demonstrating his single-minded determination to become mayor, he was instead clinging to his old, self-destructive, cake-and-eat-it approach. It was ludicrous to think he could remain MP for Henley as well as winning London, but perhaps it was asking a bit much of him to get him to agree to give up the one before he had gained the other.

On the following day Boris performed with Lord Strathclyde, Oliver Letwin and David Willetts at a fringe meeting chaired by Sheila Lawlor of the Politeia think tank. Boris told the Tories, 'We need to bring back the idea of failure to the classroom.'

Boris has often proclaimed the educational value of failure, but I wondered if this was the kind of bracing message he would want to give in his mayoral campaign. When someone asked him about housing, he condemned 'rabbit-hutch dwellings' and also 'some of these very large phallocratic structures'. His audience was surprised by the word 'phallocratic'.

That autumn the Tory leadership became very worried about Boris. It had managed to frighten Brown out of holding a snap general election: during the Blackpool conference George Osborne promised to cut inheritance tax and David Cameron delivered a speech without notes which was far superior to Brown's address the previous week to Labour. The polls moved at astonishing speed in the Tories' favour and Brown had suddenly missed the chance to ask the voters for his own mandate.

But the last thing the Tory leadership wanted was a joke candidate in London. They needed someone who would give them momentum and show they were ready for power. More than enough people had already written their man off as a clown without Boris himself giving credence to this view.

Ken's campaign tried for good measure to get Boris written off as a racist, by going through every article he had ever written and quoting a few words such as 'piccaninny' out of context. As far as I could see, this campaign only worked with those people on the left who were already disposed to think the worst of Boris. Throughout the campaign, Ken's people found it difficult to get ordinary members of the public to hate Boris.

Boris's campaign was spluttering and fizzling. It felt improvised and unconvincing: when I agreed in an early television interview that he is a poor administrator, he rang me up himself and said: 'I'm the bloody Napoleon of organization' – a ludicrous and megalomaniac claim, though it is true that he is a very good employer of administrators. Boris's PR lady said of her client: 'I'm not going to stop Boris doing anything. I'm going to let Boris be Boris,' and her firm sent out a Christmas card bearing the jokey message: 'Let us deal with your nightmares in 2008.'

Something had to be done. This was the moment when Cameron and the people round him had to accept that Boris was their candidate and needed their unstinting support. As George Osborne realised, 'We have to get behind this and get on top of it.' Osborne agreed with Boris that Lynton Crosby, the tough Australian campaigner who had worked for Michael Howard during the 2005 general election, would return to London to run Boris's campaign.

In their determination to exploit Gordon Brown's increasingly cack-handed leadership – his dithering about whether or not to call a general election was soon matched by his dithering about whether or not to nationalize the Northern Rock bank – the Tories pulled together. Brown had by that winter emerged as a hopeless employer, who was unable either to take decisions himself or to allow his subordinates to take decisions, with the result that large parts of the government were in a state of paralysis, waiting on orders from Number Ten which never arrived.

Cameron, to his credit, is good at getting the best out of his team, and that team now expanded to include Boris. The press wrote this up as a desperate attempt to control Boris, but Boris is quite intelligent enough to know when something is not working, and to accept worthwhile offers of help. For the time being his and Cameron's interests coincided: they were bent on inflicting a further humiliating blow on Labour and creating the sense that the Tories were now the party of hope, dynamism, ideas and efficiency.

This meant that if Boris won, he had to be ready to govern well from day one. So Nick Boles, now recovered from the cancer which had scuppered his bid to become the Tory candidate, set about recruiting the capable people Boris would need to run things. Boles was trusted by Cameron and Osborne to take astute decisions in a way that neither of them would trust Boris.

Boris himself understood that to win, he had to grit his teeth and make concessions. He broke decisively with the self-destructive style of politics which he had learned from his father Stanley: the style according to which absolutely everything has to be treated as a joke and played for laughs, however seriously one may inwardly be taking it.

It is not that Boris became serious – in my view he has always been seriously gifted, energetic and ambitious – but that he began to evince an unexpected steadiness. Gone were the gaffes on which the press feasted with such delight. In their place was a grasp of policy which sounded the equal, in most respects, of Ken's, allied to a far greater determination to do something about questions – knife crime, children terrorizing elderly people on buses – about which Ken seemed to have given up, or to have nothing new to say.

From February 2008 Boris opened up a lead in the YouGov polls conducted for the *Evening Standard*. Ken sought to dismiss these polls, but it was becoming clear that he faced a desperate struggle for survival. The *Standard* backed Boris to the hilt, and gave Andrew Gilligan any amount of space to chronicle the deficiencies of Ken's proteges at City Hall. Gilligan had received stalwart support from Boris after coming under heavy fire from Alastair Campbell for reporting that the Government had 'sexed up' its account of Iraq's military capabilities, part of the chain of events which led to the suicide of David Kelly. At City Hall, Gilligan and others found rich pickings.

One should not forget that the more formidable Boris looked, the more determined many Londoners became to vote for Ken. This was becoming a two-horse race, in which first the Greens and then the Lib Dems got squeezed. It is worth noting that if Boris himself had been useless, or repugnant, or just wooden and off-putting, all the help in the world from the *Standard* would have availed him nothing, and would merely have made that newspaper look idiotic.

Perhaps the most damaging single thing to appear about Ken's regime was a television documentary by Martin Bright, political editor of the *New Statesman*, which gave chapter and verse about Ken's cronyism and the way he had promoted so many of his closest allies from the far left to top jobs at City Hall. This was the left, or a significant part of it, turning on Ken and reminding itself why ever since the 1970s and 1980s it had detested and distrusted him for doing down decent, moderate Labour politicians. Ken had benefited in the past from his status as the anti-establishment candidate, but that was not a pose he could adopt during his horribly forced joint campaign appearances with the increasingly unpopular Gordon Brown, with whom the mayor himself had until recently been at daggers drawn.

Tory canvassers found 'very, very wide' recognition of their candidate. You only had to say on the doorstep, 'I'm campaigning for Boris', and people would know what you were talking about. Boris got people talking about politics, a subject which self-respecting Londoners often prefer to ignore. He and Ken were demonstrating that to get people to come out and vote, you needed interesting candidates on the ballot paper, not tedious party clones.

In February 2008 I sat next to Boris when he was the guest speaker at a lunch in the Commons press gallery. Rosa Prince, my colleague from the *Telegraph* who was covering the campaign, and I asked Boris for jobs. After all, we said, if Ken had given jobs to his friends, why shouldn't Boris?

There was a time when Boris would have entered wholeheartedly into a joke of this kind, and would have been unable to resist inventing ludicrous job descriptions for us, involving executive functions for which I at least would be totally unsuited, with inflated salaries to match. But now he did not respond at all.

So I asked how he was going to avoid the temptation of cronyism. Boris said he would reign like the Emperor Augustus, living in a simple room. This struck me as an amusingly grand comparison, but not exactly a trivial one. I suggested that Augustus preserved the outward forms of the Roman Republic, but was a tyrant.

The atrocious crime of being an Etonian was often flung at Boris during the campaign, and is one which he attempted neither to palliate nor to deny. But in March 2008, when I went to Harlow in Essex to sample public opinion for the *Telegraph*, I found nobody who objected to David Cameron's Etonian background: Gordon Brown's Scottishness was a much greater drawback.

The British public are more fair-minded than one would think from reading the British press. The idea of Eton irritates commentators, many of whom went to less grand fee-paying schools, more than it annoys the man or woman on the Clapham omnibus. In Harlow, Cameron was spoken of as a normal family man, while Brown was seen as abnormal and incapable of getting on with people.

Some observers seem to imagine that to be an Etonian is to be effete. But as a Macmillan Tory – an old lady buried deep in the English country – observed to me of Etonians as a type when Cameron was under greatest pressure: 'If they're really pushed, they can fight very, very dirty. They're very, very tough.'

Boris campaigned with indefatigable energy, devoting much time to the outer suburbs, many of which had never seen Ken, whose own campaign was late and patchy. In the final days, Ken's people put out a postcard which said: 'Imagine Boris in charge of running London. Suddenly he's not so funny.'

It was true that Boris was not so funny, but that was because by this point he was trying very hard not to undermine himself by telling jokes. In the final stages of the campaign, journalists complained that it was almost impossible to get him to talk to them at all.

Both camps said the election was 'on a knife-edge', a line they had to take, because they were desperate to get their own voters to come out, but it really was hard to know who was going to win. The race attracted greater and greater interest, with correspondents arriving from the United States and the continent of Europe to write long pieces about Boris, the 'Drôle de tory' as *Le Monde* called him. YouGov, in the *Evening Standard*, said in its last poll that he would win by 53 to 47 per cent, but other opinion polls suggested Ken could still scrape home. I had met many more people who had once voted for Ken, and were now going to back Boris, than the other way round, but I still felt unsure of the result. It was difficult to write off such a skilful campaigner as Ken, and the thought of a Boris victory still prompted feelings of incredulity.

\*

On the day of the election, Thursday 1 May 2008, the *Guardian*
used its second section to run a section in which 'Zoe Williams
and other Londoners imagine what it would be like if this
bigoted, lying, Old Etonian buffoon got his hands on our
diverse and liberal capital'. A degree of bogus hysteria – of
people saying what they thought they ought to think about
Boris – was apparent in many of the contributions to this fea-
ture. Arabella Weir, an actor and writer, parodied the genre by
telling the *Guardian*: 'I will go on hunger strike and throw
myself in front of the next horse at Ascot if he wins. Failing that
I was going to say I'll sleep with him, but he'd probably say yes.
So instead I'll chain myself to the railings of his house. And then
I'll move out of London.'

Soon after the polls closed it became clear that Labour had done
atrociously in the local elections held on the same day in many
other parts of England and Wales, but the counting in London
took much longer than it should have done and the result was not
announced until five minutes to midnight on Friday evening in the
Chamber at City Hall. Boris's wife Marina and their four children
had arrived a few minutes before, looking delightfully happy, for it
was generally accepted by then that he must have won. In the final
stages of the campaign, Marina appeared several times with Boris,
and photographed well with him. Once the two of them went out
with David and Samantha Cameron, and an amusing picture was
printed of David Cameron looking a bit wary as Boris held forth.

When Boris trooped onto the stage at City Hall with the other
candidates, he looked more serious than I have ever seen him. Here
was no trace of vainglory, but a kind of full-hearted emotion. Boris
knew he was entering upon a great responsibility which could be
the making of him. At one point as he stood in the row of candidates he seemed to look fixedly at me. I wondered what to do: it
did not seem quite the thing to raise a thumb, or even an eyebrow.

In the first round, Boris led by 1,043,761 votes to 893,877 for
Ken. Once the second-preference votes of the other candidates

had been distributed between them, Boris won by 1,168,738 votes to 1,028,966 for Ken, or by 53 to 47 per cent. The turnout was eight per cent higher than in the mayoral election of 2004 and Ken had received over 200,000 more first-preference votes than he did then, performing far better than Labour did in the rest of England and Wales.

This was not an easy victory: Boris had triumphed over one of the greatest survivors of modern British politics, achieving perhaps the most famous Tory victory since the general election of 1992, and certainly the largest personal mandate. In May 2005, Boris had polled a mere 24,894 votes in Henley, which happened also to be 53 per cent of the vote. In a hoarse but trenchant tone, Boris congratulated Ken on 'your courage and the sheer exuberant nerve with which you stuck it to your enemies especially in New Labour'. Boris likes his predecessor, and was perhaps pleased that Ken was going to come and watch his performances at City Hall. For Boris craves attention and Ken, the gifted loner who never got anywhere in the Commons, is closer to him than all those conformist Tory MPs who have never taken a risk.

In his acceptance speech, we heard Boris the public servant, dedicating himself to all the people of London and promising to 'work flat out' to gain the trust of those who voted against him, and also of those 'whose pencil hovered for an instant' above the ballot paper before deciding to back him.

Boris ended with the words, 'Let's get cracking tomorrow – let's have a drink tonight,' and off he went to have a drink with David Cameron and other Tories on Millbank. But Boris himself did not give way to triumphalism, and looked almost embarrassed as Cameron took hold of him and raised their arms aloft.

Rachel Johnson, his sister, nearly spoiled things by making remarks which sounded insufferably arrogant, about how they had celebrated with oysters, caviar and champagne, but Boris's demeanour during his first days as mayor confirmed the impression that he knew what he was doing. He himself denied that he had changed, and said in an early interview: 'I am just totally fed up with this artificial distinction . . . this sort of Arian controversy about the old Boris and the new. There is no distinction.'

But there were signs of a continued determination to deny the media the pleasure of seeing him fall flat on his face: 'You are like some ravening Hyrcanian tiger which has been deprived of his mortal prey – a Johnson blooper.' The last person I had heard him call a Hyrcan tiger was Kimberley Fortier, as noted at the end of Chapter 25. Incidentally, one hopes Boris does not get into the habit of referring to himself by his surname. It is not generally a good sign. A much better sign was his decision to stand down as MP for Henley.

The *Guardian* had the grace to publish a letter from a reader, Steven Emmott, who wrote: 'Boris Johnson's victory will go a long way to helping solve the housing problem in London, what with all those *Guardian* readers having promised to leave if he was elected.'

As soon as he had won, Boris asked Ann Sindall, who was still working at the *Spectator*, to go to City Hall to work as his personal assistant. Once again the Yorkshire socialist would be protecting him from creeps and time-wasters.

A member of his inner circle asked of Boris: 'Has he acquired the ruthlessness required to be an effective leader – if leadership requires you to tell some of your friends to fuck off?' There has at least never been any doubt of Sindall's ability to say this on his behalf.

In his first week, the new mayor banned the consumption of alcohol on the Tube and buses: a popular decision and one which indicated his determination to restore discipline to the public realm where it has broken down.

Boris's great hero is Pericles: for a bust of the Athenian leader in that city's golden age see the picture in this book of Boris and the staff of the *Spectator*. Thucydides tells us that Pericles said: 'Taking everything together then, I declare that our city is an education to Greece.'

And this was the astonishing chance which now opened

before Boris: to make London, if not an education to the rest of the United Kingdom, at least a demonstration of what the Conservatives could do. He could show that the Tories are good and competent people, or else that they are clowns and liars.

# 30

## *Generous Errors*

THE PUBLIC WATCHED WITH AMAZEMENT AS BORIS continued his ascent of the lofty and treacherous precipice which separates mere celebrity from statesmanship. People studying his climb from the comfort of their hotels in the valley were excited, as they sipped their Glühwein, to see whether he would lose his footing and tumble back into the abyss of mere notoriety, where his punishment, equal to any of the horrors found in classical mythology, would be to end his days listening to Jeffrey Archer.

Expert commentators warned that Boris was moving at reckless speed. They pointed out in a dismissive tone that he was too lightly equipped, and had no team of sherpas to carry essential supplies of food and oxygen. They observed that he lacked the technical ability for a climb classified as extremely severe.

From time to time an avalanche of bad publicity threatened to sweep Boris off the mountain. Yet there was method in his madness. He knew this ascent was one that could only be accomplished at speed: to pause for breath would be to lose momentum and fall back relative to his competitors. How intolerable if some younger, fitter man or woman were to power on upwards and overtake him as he rested, exhausted, upon a boulder.

And Boris needed to do things his own way. Simply to wait around for events to move in his favour would bore him to death. As the air got thinner, he hoped to refresh himself with the oxygen of publicity, of which he was confident of being able to generate an unlimited supply.

The role of mayor was Boris's audition for the top job. His aim was to establish himself as Prime Minister in waiting: the only senior, elected Conservative willing and able to stand up to Cameron, and the man to whom the Tories could not avoid turning when Cameron faltered.

At a party thrown by the *Spectator* soon after his victory, Boris attracted more attention than Cameron. The press began to talk of 'Borismania'. Cameron is a fine actor, but even he needed a few rehearsals before he could answer questions about Boris's future prospects without flinching. The Tory leader still had to endure two years of auditions before becoming, as he hoped but could not take for granted, Prime Minister.

Cameron avoided reminding people that he had never wanted Boris to stand, but pulled off the delicate balancing act of acclaiming his rival's victory, while keeping his distance in case it should all go horribly wrong. Fraser Nelson of the *Spectator* put it to Cameron that Boris might want to become Prime Minister after being Mayor, and the Tory leader responded: 'I am a big Boris fan. I have known him for a long time. I have always said to people, do not underestimate the brains and ambition of this guy. So when I've had a go, I'm sure there will be a queue of people looking to take over.' One notes the subtle deprecation by which Cameron's rival is lost, at the end of this, in a queue.

Boris had managed to jump the queue, only to find himself faced by a task on an altogether different scale to anything he had done before. As he said in an interview with Geordie Greig of the *Evening Standard* to mark his first year in power: 'Becoming Mayor was like having a baby in that you have this shattering sense that the world will never be the same again.'

It soon became clear that Boris was under-prepared for this form of fatherhood. The Cameroons, by contrast, had spent their careers getting ready to move into government: from their earliest days in the Conservative Research Department, the key figures – Cameron, Osborne, Letwin, Steve Hilton, Ed Llewellyn – were schooled in the processes of government, and knew that good staff work was essential if ministers were to avoid disaster.

One of Boris's most successful early appointments was of a journalist, Guto Harri, whom Hilton had also tried to recruit. Harri had just gone to New York for the BBC when Hilton approached him and invited him to become Cameron's press man. Harri went to a lunchtime barbecue with Cameron and got on 'very, very well with him'. But while Harri was thinking it over, Osborne persuaded Cameron that Andy Coulson, a former editor of the *News of the World* and therefore a link with Rupert Murdoch, was the right man for the job. This decision later came to cause Cameron grave embarrassment when it emerged that Coulson was more deeply implicated in the phone-hacking scandal than the Cameroons were willing to believe.

By hiring Harri, an affable and astute Welshman, Boris had done the prudent and professional thing, while Cameron, the son of a stockbroker, had taken a calculated (or ill-calculated) bet on Coulson which failed to pay off. Perhaps Boris was starting to grow up.

But soon after he was elected Mayor he dismayed Harri and Boles by telling them he'd got this other job, as a columnist for the *Daily Telegraph*, for which he was going to be paid £250,000 a year. As Boles exclaimed, 'Talk about getting off on the wrong foot!' For Boris had only just become mayor, which by most people's lights was a full-time job, and carried a salary of £137,579, which for most of us would be more than enough. Boles feared this would be 'a defining disaster' which would confirm that Boris was a selfish dilettante.

Harri says Coulson was obsessed by the subject. 'Andy kept saying, "This is a car crash. This is going to sink the whole mayoralty within a few weeks. You are going to piss off every newspaper he is not working for."'

So Harri came up with the idea that Boris should give a substantial amount away, and Boles established that the London College of Communication could set up scholarships funded by Boris for students of journalism.

According to Harri, 'Nick [Boles] was the driving force but it was me that had to ask Boris. We went to ITV Daybreak at dawn. I said, "Boris, I'm going to have to ask you a very expensive question."'

Harri proceeded to ask whether Boris was prepared to give away a proportion of his income.

BORIS: 'How much?'
HARRI: 'Fifty K.'
BORIS: 'OK.'

But neither Boris nor Marina was happy about this. As Boles recounts, Marina accused Boles of raising the tax rate on her husband to 75 per cent: 'Marina rightly behaved like a tigress protecting her cubs. Who were these bloody apparatchiks, giving away what amounted to two children's school fees, skiing holidays, and a new car?'

The impression was given that Boris would donate £25,000 a year to students of journalism, and £25,000 to Friends of the Classics, to promote the teaching of Latin in London. It seems unlikely that as much as this will have been given, but Boris has funded three bursaries a year for four years, which means he will have paid for 12 journalism students out of taxed income, and he has also sent some fees directly to Friends of the Classics. Harri bridles at any suggestion that his boss has fallen short: 'Show me anyone else in public life who's remotely as generous. But I can't say it's been the most popular recommendation I've made.'

The curious thing about this affair is that the fears of Boles and Harri turned out to be misplaced. In Boles's words, 'We were completely wrong about the column. It stops him just disappearing into London.'

Boris's acceptance of the suggestion that he give away a large sum of money indicates that he felt insecure. It took him time to grow into his new job: a problem that often afflicts newly elected politicians, though Cameron showed no sign of it. Part of the difficulty was that apart from Harri and Sindall, and Boles who stayed on for the first couple of months, Boris had no team to support him. As one outsider put it after being hired in a hurry: 'He didn't have any people.'

Boles therefore set about finding some people. He brought in Kit Malthouse to be Deputy Mayor with responsibility for policing. According to Boles, 'I persuaded him to take Boris seriously, and vice versa.' Malthouse proved to have what it takes. So did Munira Mirza, recruited by Boles from his think tank, Policy Exchange, to be Boris's cultural supremo.

But in part because of the haste with which people were recruited, there was an embarrassingly high attrition rate. Within a few months, Boris lost the services of James McGrath, his chief political adviser, for making a remark that could be construed as racist ('Well, let them go if they don't like it here,' said of older Black Caribbean people); Ray Lewis, the Deputy Mayor for young people, for making exaggerated claims in his curriculum vitae; and Tim Parker, yet another Deputy Mayor, who was brought in as chief executive and left when it became apparent (a somewhat elementary point) that City Hall could not be run in the same way as a business like Kwik-Fit, where Parker had stripped out costs with ruthless efficiency. In June 2009, Boris also lost Ian Clement, Deputy Mayor with responsibility for government and external relations, for making fraudulent expenses claims.

To lose one deputy mayor may be regarded as a misfortune, but to lose three looked like incompetence. Yet there was a stronger case for the defence than the bare facts suggested. Boris was more willing to look to outsiders – in some cases to untried outsiders – than is usually the case. He did not make the prudent but dreary assumption that it was only safe to hire people who had already proved themselves as politicians. He wanted to get away from the inward-looking, self-important, self-perpetuating clique who give the public the dismal impression that politicians are all the same.

Ray Lewis, who was born in 1963 in Georgetown, Guyana, and came to London at the age of one, was an outsider with whom Boris formed a very close bond. Lewis had set up the East Side Young Leaders Academy in Forest Gate in east London, which aimed, by the application of tough discipline, to reform black youths who were in danger of being thrown out of school and going to the bad.

The Tories were enthusiastic about Lewis, who received what he calls 'a steady stream of middle-class white men looking for some urban credibility'. Nick Boles, David Cameron and Iain Duncan Smith were among those who made the pilgrimage to Forest Gate, but as Lewis says, it was Boris who made the deepest impression.

'We just hit it off straight away. There was an amazing chemistry. I relate to Boris not through his intelligence: there's something intuitive about him, almost metaphysical. Boris made a speech to the boys. He was Boris Johnson and they were black boys. It was like King Herod running a crèche. There seemed to be no obvious connection. The boys were saying, "Who the fuck is this guy?"'

Yet according to Lewis, Boris connected with the boys because they thought he was being genuine. After he had gone, one of the lads said, 'I'd like to go to Eton.' Soon Lewis was supporting Boris's election campaign, helping him to arrange inner-city visits.

Lewis gave a flavour of the rushed and unprofessional arrangements made after Boris's victory. On the Saturday, so less than 24 hours after the result had been declared, he was bidden to Boris's office at the Commons. Boles was there, and Boris, who was 'exhausted', invited Lewis to be Deputy Mayor for young people.

Lewis says: 'I didn't realise it was a senior, serious job in politics. I work with black boys in a boot camp context. It all went very, very fast, and the speed of it was probably our enemy.'

Boles told Lewis he would have to be interviewed to establish that he was a fit and proper person, and needed to bring his curriculum vitae with him. Lewis said he had no curriculum vitae.

Boles told him to compose one, in which he was to put down all his interests. Lewis duly stated that he had been appointed a magistrate. He knew his appointment had not yet been approved by the Lord Chancellor, but thought this was a mere formality.

Off Lewis went to City Hall: 'I was thrust into this whole new world and quite frankly I didn't have a clue.' Yet Lewis could be a formidable performer. Soon after he started, I happened to see him at a public hearing about youth crime, where he told Cherie Blair that schools should stop 'blaming their customers for their own failings'.

Mrs Blair bridled at this, and asked, 'How are schools failing?'

LEWIS: 'I don't think I need to articulate it, Ma'am. They are failing . . . to provide an education service that is fit for males, let alone black males.'

BLAIR: 'What's so special about teaching males?'

LEWIS: 'I'm surprised you ask me a question like that. I think it's obvious. Males have a different psychology to girls. The presence of female teachers who don't look like the boys in their care . . . is unhelpful.'

Blair went pale with anger, and the corners of her mouth turned down. As I watched Lewis's defiant encounter with her, I had a sense that one era was giving way to another; that here was a black man of conservative disposition who could rely on the whole-hearted support of the new mayor, however shocking his opinions might be to old-style feminists. Boris agrees with Lewis that semi-criminal boys cannot be saved by extra geography lessons given by well-meaning women. Such youths need to be given the chance to take physical risks and test their courage in a hard school run by men they respect.

But journalists began to follow Lewis around, and to find elements of wishful thinking in his CV. It was correct that he had been ordained as an Anglican priest, but the Church of England had barred him from practising. The Church authorities took a dim view of him. He had also been investigated by the police on allegations of blackmail, theft and deception, though no charges had been brought.

Various accusations were flung at Lewis, but although he had answers which most fair-minded people would have accepted, there seemed to be no way of getting these answers across in the midst of a media storm: 'I'm not sure the team we had in place was all that skilled at managing that kind of flak.'

Boris tried to regain the initiative by holding an emergency press conference with Lewis at City Hall. The Mayor hoped to forestall further revelations by getting his version of events out first, but his version turned out to be inaccurate, based as it was on Lewis's inaccurate curriculum vitae. The press was in full cry, demanding to know why Lewis had not been vetted – a precaution for which there had seemed to Boris and Boles to be neither need nor time.

I watched the press conference on television in the *Daily Telegraph*'s office at the House of Commons. The general view among political journalists was that Boris had blundered, and should just have gone to ground. Boris's most recent biographer,

Sonia Purnell, says the event was 'universally derided as a "shambles" and "farce"', while Ken Livingstone describes it in his memoirs as 'disastrous'.

Boris has held few press conferences since. But it struck me, as I watched, that the Mayor was demonstrating a remarkable degree of loyalty to the man he had appointed and whom he still trusted. Instead of issuing mealy-mouthed bulletins from the bunker – 'thank you for all your hard work . . . may I wish you well for the future' – he was out there fighting to save his friend. The black press noticed this.

Boris was at his most anguished during this affair. Lewis himself says of Boris, 'He has at times an incredible emotional intensity.' Harri recounts how 'when we had all the cameras assembled up on the ninth floor' of City Hall, and Lewis was about to go out and tell the press that he had resigned, Boris seized hold of him by the arm and said, 'No, you can't do this.'

According to Harri, Lewis replied: 'This patient is dead. On a life support machine. You have got to show some testicular fortitude and allow the patient to die.' Lewis remembers his own words slightly differently: 'I said, "Boris, I've always said to you, and I've said to my boys [at the East Side Academy], there are times in a man's life when he has to find his testicular fortitude, and this is such a time."'

Lewis recalls that he then 'wrenched' his arm out of Boris's grasp and went out to resign in front of the television cameras. Boris often said after this, 'I hate myself for letting Ray go.' He always wanted to bring Lewis back, and after a couple of years got him back in the unpaid role of mentoring champion.

This episode prompted Boles to say of Boris: 'He is basically a decent guy. He wanted to do the right thing. Appointing Ray, sticking with Ray, that was entirely admirable. Boris has real qualities of loyalty, and admiration for virtue in others.'

Boris had made a mistake, but it was a generous mistake. He had shown he could be loyal to a fault. In the case of Ian Clement, whose misuse of a City Hall credit card was indefensible, Boris even wondered whether they should invite him back for the Christmas party.

One begins to discern the outlines of a generous, Merry England conservatism which was not quite like anything that had gone before.

Enoch Powell believed the nation's very existence was threatened by excessive levels of immigration. His pessimistic assumption that while immigrants might be needed to staff the National Health Service, they could not be absorbed in very large numbers into the British tradition, deprived the Tory party of a rich source of recruits. Boris proposed an amnesty for illegal immigrants. He, and others like him, have recognised that immigrants provide an infusion of conservative values (religion, family, hard work, freedom, the monarchy, love of adopted country). And with Boris, this did not remain just a heartwarming theory. When his instinct tells him to trust an outsider, he does so.

The man who did more than anyone else to bring order out of chaos at City Hall was himself of immigrant descent. Simon Milton's father, Clive, had arrived in London from Hanover in 1939, on the *Kindertransport* by which German Jews sent their children to safety, and in the early 1950s set up Sharatons, a successful chain of patisseries. Simon was born in 1961 and was educated at St Paul's School and Gonville and Caius College, Cambridge, where he became chairman of the University Conservative Association and president of the Union: politics rather than pastries had claimed him. He was elected a Westminster City councillor in 1988 and led the council from 2000 to 2008. In 2006 he became one of only two Tories in local government to be awarded a knighthood during Tony Blair's prime ministership.

On the Monday after the mayoral election, the call came from Boris and Milton rushed off to City Hall. The introduction had been made, as usual, by Boles, who was himself a former Westminster City councillor. Ken Livingstone observes that Boris relied heavily 'on the old Westminster Council mafia that succeeded Lady Porter'. Boris persuaded Milton to become Deputy Mayor for policy and planning.

Robert Davis, who spent 23 years as Milton's partner and is yet another Westminster City councillor, described what happened next. Milton realised at his first meeting with Parker, the chief executive, that 'this couldn't last', because Parker 'just didn't get' that local government was different to business. Very soon Parker had been forced out and Milton had moved his desk so that to get to Boris you had to pass him and Ann Sindall. Roisha Hughes, a survivor from the Livingstone era for whom Boris professes an intense admiration, was also in this ante-room. 'She's lovely,' Davis said of Roisha. 'There's a lot of laughing and humour in that room.'

Humour eased the sometimes almost intolerable pressure of working for Boris. Boles said that working for the new Mayor 'was utterly maddening', yet also 'a total delight', for one of the 'enchanting' things about Boris 'is that he can't resist a joke'. Melissa Crawshay-Williams, who was his secretary at the Commons from 2001 to 2006, found she had far more work than most of the other secretaries, but she also found Boris 'very buzzy, motivating,' and loved the thank-you notes and letters he would leave for her.

She has kept a selection of these. A simple note of thanks for dealing with his vast correspondence might just say:

Dear Melissa,
Great letters!
Many thanks.
Boris.

A more elaborate letter, dated 22 December 2005, incorporates an apology for being late and disorganised:

Dearest Melissa,

I wanted to thank you for the lovely ["lovely" underlined twice] ties [her Christmas present to him] and for arranging such an extremely jolly Xmas lunch.

I am sorry I cut it a bit fine and PROMISE we will have a real blitz on the organisation in the New Year.

Happy Xmas to you and all yours.

Love, Boris.

Melissa has also preserved a letter from Boris's children:

Dear Melissa,
We loved the humbugs
you gave us.
They were delicious.
We've already finished
them. We look forward
to meeting you.
Yours
The Johnson Kids

In some respects, Boris has very bad manners. He tends to be late, does not care about being late, and dresses without much care, though he has been observed to rumple his hair when it is too neat.

But these failings should not obscure the ways in which he is well brought up and a pleasure to deal with. He writes thank you letters, tries at once to mend fences with those he has offended, and makes people laugh. He does not pull rank: he will listen to a teenager or pensioner met at random. On the whole, he is a good employer.

The team Boris needed at City Hall was coming into existence. Robert Davis explained why in his opinion the
partnership between Simon Milton and the Mayor worked so
well: 'Both had brilliant minds. Simon very much enjoyed
working with someone who had a mind equal to his.'

Davis and others portray this as a partnership of equals: 'Boris
would never make a decision without Simon being consulted
first. Simon was at most of the meetings, and would sum up and
say what we're going to do.'

At weekends and in the evenings, Boris and Milton were 'on
the phone all the time'. In Boris's first summer, when big negotiations were taking place about transport funding, 'Simon was
crucial at being the broker between Philip Hammond [the
Transport Secretary], the Treasury and Boris.' Milton would
spend a sleepless night thinking through a problem and rise at
dawn to send an email giving the solution.

People used to ask Milton, 'What's Boris really like?' Milton
would reply, 'Just like he is on the telly.'

But Milton was ill, which was why he had decided he could
not run for mayor. In 1990 he had been diagnosed with
leukaemia. In 1998 he had a bone marrow transplant from his
sister, Lisa, but while his immunity was down, his lungs sustained
serious damage. From then on he had the lungs of an ailing
75-year-old. The slightest exertion put him out of breath, and
every winter he had to spend time in hospital.

But he always recovered, which was why his last illness, which
struck him when he was 49 years old, took everyone by surprise.

On Thursday, 7 April 2011, he had a minor heart attack. He
was taken to the London Clinic and put on a breathing machine,
but on Saturday his condition worsened and he was moved into
intensive care. Boris came to see him and chatted with him. On
Sunday, Milton was put on a dialysis machine and his doctors
had to sedate him. Davis says, 'Boris came in to see him and
started telling jokes. Simon started nodding. He responded.'

At three a.m. on Monday, Milton had another heart attack. Ruth, his mother, and Davis rushed to the hospital. Milton was in a deep coma, his lungs clogged with pneumonia. His doctors were trying 12 different drugs to clear it.

Davis continues the story: 'Boris came in and spent a lot of that day with us, in the morning and the afternoon. Boris came back at six p.m. Eventually at eight in the evening Simon died. We were all there. Boris stayed with us for a good hour afterwards.'

During the illness, Davis said, 'Boris was just what anyone would expect of a friend. He was trying to make a few jokes to keep Simon cheerful. He couldn't have behaved more perfectly. He was supportive to us. He went out of the room when medical procedures had to be performed. Afterwards, for the first two weeks he'd phone me regularly to see I was OK.'

A Labour apparatchik who worked at City Hall said: 'When Simon Milton died the whole building was sad.'

Many of us have no idea how to deal with death, and persuade ourselves we must not intrude on the bereaved. Boris can be infuriatingly evasive, but he did not evade his right-hand man's death.

'A Service of Thanksgiving to Celebrate the Life and Work of Sir Simon Milton' was held at Westminster Abbey on 31 October 2011.

Boris gave one of the addresses. He spoke of Milton's ability 'to sum up in about fifty words what I had been trying to say all morning'. He also said of Milton and Davis, 'Their partnership was a significant step forward in the modernisation and improvement of the Conservative Party.'

Wesley Kerr, chairman of the Heritage Lottery Fund's London Committee, said of this address: 'I've never heard Boris sound so statesmanlike.'

Boris had made his accommodation with the existing system of local government, which Milton knew better than anyone how to work.

There was no radical de-Baathification programme, of the kind that went so disastrously wrong in Iraq. But not all the old guard were as safe as they thought they were. Sir Ian Blair, Commissioner of the Metropolitan Police, appears to have had no inkling that Boris was going to get rid of him. The Mayor, after all, had no power to do that. In theory, at least, the Home Secretary, Jacqui Smith, was in charge.

But Smith was clearly not going to do the right thing, so in October 2008 Boris did it for her. He showed her up. The Prime Minister, Gordon Brown, raged to his friends in the press that the Mayor's conduct was intolerable. But those friends could not denounce Boris with any conviction. Blair's response to the shooting by his officers of Jean Charles de Menezes, an innocent and unarmed Brazilian carpenter, on 22 July 2005 had been grotesquely inadequate. Having seized the moment to bundle Blair out of Scotland Yard, the Mayor proceeded to mend fences with Smith and agree with her on the appointment of Paul Stephenson as the next commissioner. No lasting political wrangle was allowed to undermine the policing of London.

This was the episode which established Boris as a serious player. The muzziness of the rules, and his acute sense of timing, had enabled him to dominate a transaction in which he ought to have been no more than a junior partner. Some of his friends had imagined he was too soft ever to sack someone. My own belief is that any sense of mercy was outweighed by his burning indignation at the treatment of de Menezes. But Boris will also have known that many Tories considered the Commissioner much too close to New Labour.

Part of the charm of politics is its close resemblance to a game of Snakes and Ladders. You can rise or fall at amazing speed. The morning of Monday 2 February, 2009 was very bad for Boris. Snow had fallen and Transport for London decided to shut down its entire fleet of buses 'on the grounds of safety'. It claimed that on Sunday evening there had been 30 bus-related accidents, and that because of inadequate gritting many of its vehicles could not even leave their garages. All but one tube line was shut down too. By the time Boris was informed of these pusillanimous decisions, some time after six on Monday morning, it was too late for him to do anything about it.

Boris was left struggling to defend a policy which he himself would never have adopted. He was in danger of being written off as the mayor who couldn't cope with a light fall of snow. People said London's buses had kept going during the Blitz, so there was no reason why they should not keep going now.

Hence the extreme agitation with which Boris reacted the following day, Tuesday 3 February, when Keith Vaz, the chairman of the Home Affairs committee of MPs, said the Mayor would not be able to appear as a witness before the committee because of 'more pressing matters', namely the snow. Boris leapt on his bike, pedalled in eleven and a half minutes from City Hall to Westminster, declared to anyone who would listen that Mr Vaz was talking 'epic bollocks', and insisted on his right to appear before MPs, who were taking evidence on a quite different matter.

Mr Vaz and his colleagues wished to know what Boris could tell them about the strange affair of Damian Green, a Tory MP who was arrested on 27 November 2008 by the Metropolitan Police in connection with their inquiry into Home Office leaks.

Boris recalled, in his evidence, the astonishment with which he heard from the police of the impending arrest: 'It seemed to me at first blush that if the facts were as they stated them, then obviously there would be a hoo-hah, or a kerfuffle, or a commotion, or a controversy. . . I think the phrase I used was that this one would go off like a rocket. You would have to have pretty good reason to ensure that the arrest of a member of this House was not a disproportionate response to a leak inquiry.'

The committee wished to know when precisely Boris was told about the arrest, to which he replied that it was 'at about lunchtime', after which he narrowed this down by saying 'a conventional lunchtime, not a Spanish lunchtime'.

Boris has never seen why he should submit himself to questioning of an unduly exact or pedantic nature. Just as an aircraft can evade incoming missiles by emitting strips of metal foil known as chaff, so Boris baffles inquiry by emitting a stream of badinage known as chaff. The committee was trying to catch him out by suggesting that he had held improper conversations about the arrest with Green and other politicians. Gwyn Prosser, the Labour MP for Dover, asked whether the Mayor had discussed the arrest with Green in his capacity as mayor, as chairman of the Metropolitan Police Authority, or as a friend.

Boris replied, 'I would invoke the doctrine of the Trinity and say I was three in one and one in three.' The doctrine of the Trinity is hard to grasp, but the message that Boris was not going to allow himself to be pinned down was clear.

The committee also wished to know whether the Mayor had taken the chance, during a service at Southwark Cathedral on the afternoon of the arrest, to discuss the arrest with David Cameron. Boris said any conversation he had on that occasion with Cameron was 'perfunctory' because Brown, who was also at the service, was 'appalled' to see the Mayor sitting next to Cameron and got Boris moved.

The idea of the Prime Minister intervening to change the seating plan somehow threw most people off the question of what Boris had or had not said to Cameron. But Boris also vouchsafed that 'not only did I not have any valuable information, but I didn't furnish him with it'.

I have quoted these in themselves rather minor exchanges as an example of how hard it can be to pin Boris down about anything so inconvenient as a fact. But perhaps this is true of all politicians, and his evasions are just more idiosyncratic than most.

On 4 February 2009, the day after he had insisted on appearing before the Home Affairs committee, Boris employed another technique. He swore down the phone at Mr Vaz: 'I'm unbelievably disappointed at the way my evidence is being treated ... So fucking angry ... This is fucking ridiculous ... This is fucking bollocks ... I fucking warned you beforehand that I would not be very good on details ... Fucking smear tactics from the Labour Party.'

In April 2009 Boris almost got up and left when another group of MPs, the Transport committee, tried to question him about the snow debacle. Boris accused this committee of 'talking tripe' and said it was 'not within my competence to stop the biggest downfall of snow we have had over the skies of this city for 20 years'.

But it was within Boris's competence to stop Transport for London behaving in such a feeble way the next time it snowed, and this he did when snow fell in December 2010. The streets of London were now so well gritted that the buses ran pretty much as normal.

Buses matter to Boris. During the 2008 campaign he had made a very good thing out of defending the Routemaster bus and promising to get rid of bendy buses. Once elected, he proceeded to hold a competition to design a new Routemaster, with an open platform at the back, and to phase out the bendy buses. There can be no doubt that this was a highly popular thing to do.

Bikes matter to Boris too. Ken had been pro-bike without actually knowing how to ride one, but Boris saw through the introduction of a bike hire scheme which was universally agreed to have been a success, especially compared to the scheme in Paris, where many of the bikes were stolen.

But the most imaginative, if least immediately practicable, transport scheme pursued by the Mayor was for a new airport to be built in the Thames estuary. This was a classic example of Borisian optimism in action. Practical objections which would have daunted any other leading politician did nothing to deter Boris, who was entranced by the idea of creating a really big, new airport. During his first term he put this case so forcefully that more and more people started agreeing with him, though not, as yet, the Government.

One of the problems about transport projects is that most of them take a long time to come to fruition. Boris benefited from improvements initiated by Livingstone, such as the transformation of the North London Line. Boris's successors will benefit from some of the plans for which he obtained money.

Meanwhile the standard of service on the tube remained distinctly unsatisfactory. Boris and Harri were travelling late one night on the Jubilee Line. The Mayor received many complaints from passengers about the service, with one man even asking him to intercede with his employers, who were about to sack him for arriving late at work. Boris duly recorded a message which went something like, 'Please do not sack Mr Smith for being late, if you find that the Jubilee Line was genuinely down that day. You can check whether it was on the Transport for London website.'

Boris continued to amuse the nation by doing things it was hard to imagine other politicians doing. He fell in a river while standing next to an attractive young woman. While bicycling home one evening, he rescued another woman from some yobs. He built a hut on the balcony of his smart new house in Islington which had to be demolished because it contravened planning regulations.

And in Beijing on 24 August 2008 Boris gave what is probably the funniest speech delivered at the closing ceremony for an Olympic Games. His intonation can only be appreciated by watching it on YouTube, but here is the peroration:

Virtually every single one of our international sports were either invented or codified by the British, and I say this respectfully to our Chinese hosts who have excelled so magnificently at ping pong.

Ping pong was invented on the dining-tables of England in the 19th century and it was called wiff waff.

There I think you have the essential difference between us and the rest of the world.

Other nations, the French, looked at a dining-table and saw an opportunity to have dinner, we looked at a dining-table and saw an opportunity to play wiff waff. That is why London is the sporting capital of the world.

And I say to the Chinese, and I say to the world, ping pong is coming home.

Even Gordon Brown could be seen laughing uproariously at this. Critics said Boris had let the side down by not dressing as respectably as the Chinese would have liked. But none of the critics had ever given a speech that gave so much pleasure.

# 31

# Wrestling with the Prime Minister

DAVID CAMERON HAD FALLEN SHORT. IN THE GENERAL election on Thursday 6 May 2010, the Conservatives gained 97 seats, but were still 20 seats away from an overall majority. Their share of the vote was 36.1 per cent, a mere 3.7 per cent higher than in 2005.

But Cameron's performance in the days after this disappointment was masterly. His cards were weaker than he had hoped, but he played them so well that he compelled the Liberal Democrats to make him Prime Minister. Boris was no longer the top elected Tory. Cameron and Osborne were dealing with a far more important task than he was: they were rescuing the country from bankruptcy.

In December 2010 I seized the opportunity, during a drinks party at 10 Downing Street, to ask the Prime Minister if he could contribute any material to my updated Life of Johnson. Cameron launched with gusto into an account of a one-to-one negotiation about money between himself and Boris.

The Treasury had prepared a brief for the Prime Minister which stated how much money he could offer at the start of the negotiation, how much more he could offer if Boris pushed him, and the absolute maximum he could go to if the Mayor got really difficult.

Boris attempted to snatch this piece of paper off Cameron. This is something Boris does from time to time: a few years before he had made 'a desperate lunge' for Piers Morgan's notepad.

The Prime Minister resisted, and a wrestling match ensued. My mind was filled with a picture of Cameron and Boris rolling over and over on the carpet as they grappled for possession of the Treasury brief. It appeared to me that Cameron, being taller, would have the longer reach, which might enable him to hold the paper just outside his opponent's grasp; but that Boris, as a former prop forward, might be able to deploy greater muscle power, as well as the 'sudden spasms of uncontrolled aggression' which he used at school in the Wall Game.

Although the Prime Minister declined to volunteer a blow-by-blow account of the fight, there was one point he was determined to stress: he said he was 'so desperate' to keep control of the briefing paper that he managed to do so. In other words, he won.

Not until November 2011, during the party to launch his book about London, did I get round to asking Boris for his account of the fight for the Treasury brief. Like Cameron, Boris launched with gusto into the story, but there all similarity ended. According to Boris, 'I won. I had him basically pulverised. He was calling for Osborne. I snatched it off him. He'd hunkered down. I pushed him far into the sofa when he started whingeing for Osborne. Soon there was a knock on the door from Special Branch. After I'd extracted provision of Crossrail and the Tube upgrades, I desisted.'

In this account, Boris emerges as a clean-cut hero from the pages of John Buchan, single-handedly defending Londoners against the evil Cameron-Osborne regime; after which he shows a kind of scornful mercy to his defeated opponent, to whom we may imagine first aid being administered by the Special Branch officers.

We cannot judge for certain who was telling the truth, or more of the truth. But leaving that question on one side, we see how intense the rivalry between the two men was, how anxious each of them was to declare victory, and also how ready each was to treat the whole thing as a game, or indeed as a joke. One hoped that the next time they had a wrestling match they would hold it in public. A cage fight at Wembley between Boris and Cameron could have been just the thing to re-engage the public's interest in politics.

The two men were sporting enough to hold a tennis match in Trafalgar Square as part of the International Paralympics Day celebrations. Each man had a partner in a wheelchair, and they played only one game. Boris and his partner won, thanks in part to a ferocious smash by Boris. A picture was widely reproduced of Boris baring his lower teeth, his mouth stretched to a thin line as he clenched his left fist and held his racquet in his right hand like a club. It was all too easy to imagine he might be descended from Goths, as posited at the start of Chapter Two. The Mayor looked the epitome of ferocity, while Cameron kept his gentlemanly cool. Viewers naturally preferred Boris's more uninhibited performance.

An hour after his victory, Boris got a text message from Cameron which went something like this: 'As you're up for re-election before I am I thought I'd better let you win on this occasion. But if you're on for a proper match, come to Chequers any time.' Cameron is a much better tennis player than Boris, so would probably win such a match.

In 1947 Stephen Potter published *Gamesmanship*, defined as 'the art of winning games without actually cheating'. This was soon followed by *Lifemanship* and *One-Upmanship*. Potter captured the unending battle for supremacy which is waged even in the seemingly most innocent and inconsequential areas of

English life. This is the comic yet also tragic tradition in which Johnson and Cameron took their place. Boris should have been irretrievably one down: he was, after all, only Mayor, while Cameron was Prime Minister. But how often Boris managed, by brilliant one-upmanship, to turn the tables on his rival, and to emerge as the coming man for whom Cameron was just the warm-up act.

I was fortunate enough to see a prolonged exhibition of the two men in action against each other at the beginning of the general election campaign in April 2010. On an idyllic spring morning they carried out a joint visit to the Royal Hospital in Chelsea.

David Imrie, a Chelsea pensioner who had served in the Black Watch, said of Boris before he arrived, 'I hope he brushes his hair when he comes here.'

Boris had not, of course, brushed his hair. One of his favourite gambits is to make Cameron look too carefully turned out. Boris came by bike, with scruffy hair and an anorak, and held an impromptu press conference just inside the gate with a gaggle of journalists. Already he was undermining the careful stage management of the event by Cameron's staff. Boris suggested to Cathy Newman of Channel Four News that she 'give me a grand to stay married'. This was plainly a satire on Cameron's plan, about to be unveiled, for tax breaks for married couples. But one wondered whether it was also a hint that all was not well with Boris's own marriage.

More members of the press had somehow slipped through the gates of the hospital than had been intended. An up-tight young woman working for Cameron said to one of her colleagues, 'David's about to arrive. We need to get all of them out.'

But it was too late to reduce the press pack to those of us who had got proper accreditation. Cameron arrived, and Boris hastened up to him. Otherwise, it seemed, the journalists would have stayed clustered round Boris, awaiting further indiscretions.

The moment the two men were within speaking distance, battle was joined for control of the conversation:

'Dave.'

'Boris.'

'Brilliant.'

'You were on the radio this morning,' Cameron said, as if encouraging a junior aide who had done awfully well to get such coverage.

They made for the passage to the infirmary, ushered by their host, the lieutenant-governor. A pensioner in an invalid carriage got trapped behind a black tape which had been erected to keep the press back, and became distressed. Cameron turned in the twinkling of an eye and said, 'Sir, do you need a hand?'

Cameron has about the best manners of anyone I have met. He is the sort of man who at breakfast passes you the marmalade before you even realise you want it. It was to his credit that even while trading blows with Boris he alerted everyone to the pensioner in distress.

And yet these good manners keep people at a distance. Cameron is so quick, so agile, so considerate, so well-brought-up and well-prepared that he becomes impermeable. He is an English gentleman who cannot help doing the right thing. As his cousin Ferdinand Mount has observed of Cameron's mother's family, the Mounts: 'A high moral tone came naturally to them.' Cameron himself is an example of Christian self-control modulated into the manners of an English gentleman. No wonder so few of the political commentators understand the first thing about him, for they would not know a Christian gentleman if they saw one, and would consider the term at least a hundred years out of date. Cameron himself gives them no help. He says nothing about his own gentlemanliness and even conceals it, both because it would be ungentlemanly – immodest – to say 'Look at me, I know how to behave', and because toffs (or anyone liable to be mistaken, by our indiscriminate press, for a toff) nowadays find it expedient to conceal their toffishness. In Cameron's case, it may also be the case that in fields such as music and television he has a number of genuinely popular tastes.

Yet try as he might during the 2010 election campaign, Cameron could not make an emotional connection with the British people.

Boris is no gentleman. He takes his place in the long line of English debunkers who cannot resist mocking the pretensions of those who assert, no matter how tactfully, their claims to higher status. Boris loves Chaucer 'with his bawdy, his mockery, his self-mockery, his pricking of hypocrisy and his terrible puns' (the quotation is from Boris's book about London).

On their visit to Chelsea, Boris behaved like a very strong, shaggy, affectionate, over-grown young dog, who is never happier than when bounding into your lap, getting hair all over your clothes and sweeping the tea cups off the table with his tail.

Nobody manages to get Boris to walk at heel for very long, and part of the joy of watching him with Cameron was waiting for the moment Boris would commit some gross act of indiscipline. The day before they met, Cameron had launched the voluntary 'national citizen service' for 16-year-olds. Boris proceeded to declare, in a ludicrous display of loyalty, 'I think it should be compulsory.'

'Come on, Mayor,' Cameron said, trying to close down the conversation. Guto Harri afterwards offered an ingenious justification for Boris's call for compulsion: 'That's a very enthusiastic way of saying it's a great idea.'

Soon the two politicians, with nine pensioners resplendent in their red coats, were taking tea and making sprightly conversation at a table in the sun. Boris, waving at the press, who were once again confined behind a tape, told a pensioner, 'This is just a selection of . . .' What would he say? Riff raff? But it is not Boris's custom to insult his old trade, so he began again: 'This is just some of my entourage.'

Cameron made immaculate establishment conversation. At one point he called out to Boris, 'This gentleman served with Ian Gow. Troop leader. In Berlin.' Gow was a Tory MP who was murdered by the IRA. But Cameron also tried to establish that he is as much of a bad boy as Boris: 'When I was in the Cadet Force I was always the one who was caught smoking and was made to do all the washing up.' Cameron also rather cleverly asked if the pensioners had 'any questions for the mayor'.

Boris even more cleverly turned the conversation back on Cameron with the words, 'Now what we need to do is extort a promise from the future government.'

The Mayor proceeded to extort a promise from Cameron that if the Tories won the election they would pay for Crossrail, an astonishingly expensive railway to be built under London. I lost count of the number of times Boris called on Cameron to back Crossrail. A less self-controlled man than the Tory leader might have started to look cross about Crossrail.

But the pensioners came to Cameron's aid with a prolonged bombardment of Boris on the question of the 211 bus. The Mayor was told that one pensioner had been kept waiting 55 minutes for a 211.

Boris kept saying sorry, to which the pensioner retorted, 'You may be sorry, but what are you going to do about it?' With his back to the wall, Boris resorted to the diversionary tactics of which he is one of the finest living exponents. He asked how many men were killed in the Charge of the Light Brigade.

After tea there was a group photograph of the pensioners with Boris and Cameron. This roused Boris's martial instincts and led him to cry, 'Steady the Buffs. No surrender. Fight to the last man. Lock and load.'

The visit ended with Boris and Cameron giving some joint interviews for London television channels during which Boris proceeded, with magnificent unhelpfulness, to turn to Cameron and say, 'You do agree with Crossrail, don't you?' Cameron had no choice but to say that he agreed with Crossrail.

Afterwards, Boris claimed that there was 'glutinous harmony' between them: a favoured expression which he has used on other occasions too, for example on *Newsnight* on 5 October 2009, when he spoke of the 'almost glutinous harmony' between himself and Cameron at Oxford.

The Cameroons recognise, as one of them put it to me in April 2011, that 'every month Boris has to do at least one thing, if not two, that distances him from the Government'. They know Boris cannot afford to be painted by Labour as a mere Downing Street stooge, and that there is no point in getting angry with him when he demonstrates his independence. 'I hope we all understand that's part of the deal,' the Cameroon told me. 'It's in all our interests. Boris winning in 2012 would be a momentous achievement, an enormous reverse for Ed Miliband.'

But the ardour with which Boris attacked the Government was nonetheless still rather breathtaking. He could not see an unguarded flank without attacking it. He spent very little time denouncing Ed Miliband, and not much more on Ken Livingstone. For most of the time, his fire was concentrated on his own leader. It is something he did very well – better, some would say, than Miliband, who never brought much brio to the role.

There were moments when Boris, not Miliband, sounded like the true leader of the opposition to Cameron. To give an exhaustive account of his attacks would burst the bounds of this volume. But here are a few of the highlights.

In August 2008 Boris ridiculed Cameron's claim that we live in a broken society: 'If you believe the politicians, we have a broken society, in which the courage and morals of young people have been sapped by welfarism and political correctness. And if you look at what is happening at the Beijing Olympics, you can see what piffle that is.'

In April 2009 he blasted the timidity of the Cameroons' approach to education: 'The answer, as everybody knows but dare not admit, is to allow state schools the freedom once again to select on the basis of academic merit. Everything else is just blah. Look at what is happening to social mobility. Look at the way the fee-paying schools are lengthening their lead. The whole thing is outrageous, and to cap it all we are now letting Martin McGuinness – who spent decades trying to blow us up – get away with abolishing the grammar schools in Northern Ireland. What a disaster, and what putrid hypocrisy on the part of the entire British ruling class, who either use private tutors to give their kids the edge, or else send them to private school.'

Not all of Boris's attacks have proved prescient. On 7 March 2011 he wrote an outspoken piece about Libya:

It is some days since Lord Owen captured our imagination with his call for a 'no-fly zone'.

As time trickles by and the casualties mount, it is frankly more likely that Col. Gaddafi's planes will be immobilised by snow or volcanic ash than by Western firepower . . . The war has provoked such deep distrust of our motives as to make any action in Libya virtually impossible . . . The world knows it and Gaddafi knows it. How he must sneer at our confusion and laugh at our weakness.

To which one may add that Cameron was more confident than Boris about what might be possible in Libya, and that Gaddafi, having met his end on 20 October 2011, is no longer able to laugh or sneer. But Libya in 2016 is in a sorry state.

Although Boris is not a great man for going round picking fights with people, in May 2011 he accused the Government of being feeble about bringing in tough anti-strike laws which would help to stop walkouts by London Underground staff: 'I want to see more action. The Government at the moment seems to be caught in limbo, you could even say they are being lily-livered.'

As the Government's spending cuts began to bite, Boris became a great worrier. On *Any Questions* on 25 March 2011 he said: 'There are aspects of the cuts that worry me ... housing benefit ... I worry about the Education Maintenance Allowance.'

There had already been a fierce row about housing benefit in October 2010, when Boris said he would not accept 'any kind of Kosovo-style social cleansing of London'. This produced a public rebuke from Cameron's spokesman, who declared that 'The Prime Minister doesn't agree with what Boris Johnson has said or indeed with the way he said it.'

But the attack on the Government which I found most outrageous was carried out by Boris in the spring of 2011 when he said, 'I was absolutely scandalised the other day to hear a Government minister tell me he did not want to see more families in Sheffield able to afford cheap holidays. Absolutely disgraceful, a bourgeois repression of people's ability to take a holiday. It is a matter of social justice.'

'Impeccable sources' revealed that the minister in question was Oliver Letwin, Cameron's head of policy. Letwin was door-stepped, during which he told reporters, 'I do not ever comment on things that are alleged to have been said in private conversations, but I would never knowingly say anything offensive to anybody.' Letwin became the fall guy, and a rash of third-rate articles appeared in which he was dismissed as a snooty, gaffe-prone, former investment banker.

I happen to have known Letwin since 1977. We were at university together, he in the year above me at Trinity College, Cambridge. I cannot think of anyone who uses his intellect in a more generous and honest way. His ability to hold productive conversations with people who are less intelligent than he is, and who hold opposing political views, is exceptional. His high-pitched laughter at his own misjudgements is infectious. Yet our gaffe-obsessed press just mocks him for his lack of worldly wisdom. When he was found to be dropping constituency correspondence in the litter bins of St James's Park, nobody said how fortunate the people of Dorset West are to have an MP who begins each day by dictating answers to the 20,000 or so letters they send him each year, some on matters of quite minor importance. Everyone just mocked Letwin as an idiot.

So I felt indignant on Letwin's behalf when Boris exposed him to public ridicule and contempt. In one of my notebooks about Boris I found myself writing: 'I suppose Boris is cross he is getting nowhere with his estuary airport project. But the episode crystallises for me the sense that he is a cad: no gentleman: a selfish bastard: an unscrupulous, unreliable, self-serving adventurer.'

I offer this autobiographical excursion as an example of how angry with Boris even a mild-mannered fellow can become. This uncharitable outburst is not my considered verdict, though I suppose I shall see it quoted as if it were, but it is the sort of thing that even Boris's friends sometimes find themselves thinking. A source at Number Ten said of Boris's conduct during the Sheffield affair: 'Very, very poor behaviour. Not what one would expect, particularly from a fellow Etonian.' According to this source, Letwin had not said what was attributed to him, about not wanting people in Sheffield to go on holiday, but from an excess of honourable feeling did not wish to issue a correction, for fear of making things difficult for Boris.

An intelligent Cameroon told me not to get so hot under the collar, and said of Letwin, 'Oliver's not going to lose his job over this.' This Cameroon also said that 'Boris would rally round if the Government was in real trouble.' That is doubtless true, though one can imagine that Boris's recovery plan would include making him leader.

But it was Letwin himself who calmed me down. When I told him the Sheffield incident had shocked me, Letwin replied, 'But he apologised so charmingly afterwards,' adding with a rueful smile,

'I shall never stand up for regional airports again.' But it was clear that Boris had yet again managed to leave no residue of rancour.

There are two subjects on which Boris harried the Government more often than on any other. The first is Europe. Cameron decided that once the Lisbon Treaty had been ratified, it was no longer practicable to allow the British people to give their verdict on it in a referendum. Boris repeatedly challenged this line, for example at the Conservative Party Conference in October 2009. After that particular act of defiance, Boris received a text in Italian from Nick Boles, '*La vendetta è un piatto che va mangiato freddo,*' which means 'Revenge is a dish best eaten cold.' Boles insisted, on being asked about this, that he was 'old friends' with Boris and 'one of his biggest fans', and continued the joke by saying, 'I know Boris will be disappointed, but you wouldn't believe how hard it is to get hold of a horse's head these days'. This was a reference to one of Boris's favourite films, *The Godfather*, in which a horse's head is left in a man's bed as a warning.

Perhaps this is the moment to point out how good the Cameroons sometimes were at turning Boris's weapons on himself. Cameron himself did this to brilliant effect at the *Spectator* Parliamentarian of the Year Awards in November 2010. The previous year, Boris had twitted Cameron about claiming money on expenses for wisteria.

This time Cameron gave a speech in which he paid tribute to his favourite *Spectator* editor: 'We went to the same school, the same university and of course I've got a soft spot for him. A man of huge intelligence and huge ambition. An irresistible charmer with an enviable head of hair. Always bursting with brilliant turns of phrase and bright ideas. Yes, my kind of political maverick.'

The audience of parliamentarians and press imagined that Cameron must, for some curious reason, be paying an unexpected tribute to Boris. But instead the Prime Minister paused a moment for effect and said, 'Ian Gilmour.'

It was a beautifully unexpected name. Readers who wish to be reminded of the Tory Cabinet ministers who have edited the *Spectator* will find a list at the start of Chapter 15. Gilmour was a leading Tory wet who was sacked by Margaret Thatcher in 1981. Cameron followed up his advantage: 'I'm not quite sure what went wrong for Ian. I suppose he rubbed the Prime Minister up the wrong way and never really recovered. Shit happens. Anyway, there's always the chance of becoming our ambassador in Pristina, I suppose.' Pristina is the capital of Kosovo, and the row about Boris's reference to 'Kosovo-style social cleansing' had occurred only a few days before.

Andy Porter, the political editor of the *Daily Telegraph*, saw at once the significance of this speech (composed as I later discovered by Gove), and under the headline 'Cameron warns Boris: Don't rub me wrong way', began his report with the words, 'David Cameron has delivered a four-letter swipe at Boris Johnson for hinting at prime ministerial ambitions.'

This was a clear invasion by Cameron of Boris's territory, or perhaps it would be more accurate to describe it as a retaliatory raid. For Boris kept on making extraordinarily provocative attacks on the Government. Apart from Europe, the most frequent stick with which Boris beat his friends in Downing Street was tax. This had the advantage of being another subject for which Boris had no responsibility, so could afford to be irresponsible, or what Cameron and Osborne regarded as irresponsible.

There is scarcely a tax which Boris has not at some point wanted to lower. He has at various times called for reductions in VAT, National Insurance and fuel duties. Most often, he demanded a cut in the top rate of income tax. In a particularly cheeky intervention, which appeared in the *Telegraph* on 28 January 2011 under the headline 'Tell us how you'll cut tax, Chancellor,' Boris informed Andy Porter that the coalition needs to develop its 'Norman Tebbit side'.

As Porter recognised, the calls for tax cuts were attacks on the Chancellor of the Exchequer rather than the Prime Minister. At that time, Osborne was Boris's main rival for the succession to Cameron. Except for a small group of trusties, Tory backbenchers tended to feel spurned by both Osborne and Cameron. They complained that Osborne had behaved with insufferable arrogance towards them, and taken them for granted, ever since becoming shadow Chancellor in 2005. They accused Osborne of being interested only in politics, and of subordinating economic questions to narrow calculations of party political advantage.

The Commons is full of disillusioned men (they are still mostly men), a substantial proportion of whom now sit on the Tory benches. They knew they had virtually no hope of attaining ministerial office in that Parliament, because a disproportionate number of the available jobs went either to Liberal Democrats or to Tory women, regardless of whether these were the best candidates for promotion. Many of the 2010 intake of Tories had their interest in politics first aroused by Margaret Thatcher: they believe in low taxes and national sovereignty, and did not get elected in order to sell out those ideals.

Boris had set about showing these malcontents that he is a better bet than Osborne. As he said at Oxford, 'The terrible art of the candidate is to coddle the self-deception of the stooge,' and his task now was to coddle as many backbench stooges as he could find into believing that he is a better bet than Osborne.

It was nevertheless with some surprise that in September 2011 I heard a Tory backbencher express 'growing respect for Boris Johnson's judgement' on both Europe and tax. Another prominent Tory said of Boris, 'He's maturing. He's calming down.' This Tory thought that Boris showed the ability 'to distil the European issue' in a way no Tory since Thatcher had managed to do.

At a much more serious, intellectual, level, Robin Harris, a

Thatcherite who in the autumn of 2011 published an impressive history of the Conservative Party, says of Boris, 'Although we would I am sure disagree about many things – he is obviously more liberal than I am, which is not difficult – I do consider him at a deep level to be conservative, and I certainly would not say that about Cameron.'

Are these Tories right to take Boris seriously? Not in the sense that he is a serious economist. Nor, by the standards of Enoch Powell's heirs on the Tory benches, is he a serious eurosceptic. Boris loves Europe. He may have made his reputation by mocking the pretensions of Brussels, but that does not mean he disagreed with everything that Brussels was doing. He mocked Cameron, but again, might well do many of the same things once he himself was in power.

Yet these caveats are not quite the end of the matter. Boris would, I think, be more inclined to go for tax cuts than either Osborne or Cameron, because he has a greater sense of daring: a greater desire to see what will happen. Boris is attracted by the idea of doing outrageous things, or things which more cautious politicians would shrink from doing, for fear of what supposedly enlightened metropolitan opinion-formers might say.

This relish for saying the outrageous has led Boris into frequent declarations of support for bankers. As he put it in his Tory conference speech in October 2009, 'I know how unpopular these bankers are and I know how far out on a limb I now seem to be in sticking up for these pariahs. But never forget, all you banker-bashers, that the leper colony of the City of London produces nine per cent of Britain's GDP and 13 per cent of value-added taxes that pay for roads and schools and hospitals across this country.'

On Europe, Boris's taste for being outspoken prompted him to suggest as early as June 2011 'that Greece would be better off in a state of Byronic liberation, forging a new economic identity with a New Drachma' instead of struggling to stay in the euro.

In October 2011 Boris followed this up with a piece in which he complained that to say that 'any country will either default or leave the euro' is regarded as 'the height of bad taste and irre-sponsibility', but that the whole thing was bound to end in 'some sort of rupture and reorganisation'.

Boris commended himself as a politician who possessed the necessary bad taste to say that the euro could no longer survive.

Perhaps we have hit here on a way of describing the decisive difference between him and the Cameroons: that he enjoys saying surprising or unfashionable or tasteless things, while they are always wondering whether what they really think or feel is the kind of thing they dare say in front of the public.

In 2011 Cameron gave a tenth anniversary dinner at 10 Downing Street for all those Tory MPs first elected in 2001 – an intake which included himself, Boris and Osborne. Boris as usual was late and entered to a huge cheer, though it was impos-sible to tell how far this was genuine and how far ironic.

Later in the evening, Boris turned to George Osborne and said, 'When's the recovery going to begin?'

Osborne at once replied, 'Oh, I think it'll start next June,' the month after Boris would be standing for re-election.

Boris asked when there would be tax cuts, to which Osborne responded, 'Oh, we're saving those up for when we need to be re-elected.'

The person who told me this story said, 'The atmosphere really was very sharp.'

It was said that even if Cameron won an overall majority at the next general election, expected in 2015, he would with any luck have the sense to stand down after about eight years as Prime Minister, or in about 2018, the calculation being that both Thatcher and Blair grew hopelessly out of touch after they had served that long. So Boris could hope to win re-election to the Commons in 2015 and be in a position to challenge for the leadership in the middle of that Parliament. There would be any number of Tory associations who would be delighted to have him as their MP.

But meanwhile, he had to be patient, for Cameron and Osborne were in command of the party machine, and controlled the wells of patronage. Only when they stumbled would Boris get his chance. At that point, however, his route to the summit looked as if it could be clearer than it had ever been before.

# 32

# The Merry England Candidate

BORIS IS AT ONCE THE MOST OPEN AND MOST SECRETIVE of men. On many subjects where conventional politicians would hesitate to express an opinion, he delights his listeners by plunging in. But on anything to do with his private life, the most formidable interviewers have failed to penetrate his defences. Lynn Barber, known as 'the demon Barber' for the ferocity of her work, asked Boris whether it is true, as suggested by an anonymous woman in Chapter 18 of this book, that 'As well as being a philanderer, he's a great family man.' Barber described Boris's response: 'This brought on one of his yelping, snorting, hair-rummaging routines to give him time to devise his answer and eventually it came: "I took a sort of vow ages ago that when bowled any kind of ball like that, the great thing to do is to watch it very carefully for as long as possible as it flies through the air, and then you stick your bat straight out, put your foot forward, block it and retire into your crease. That's the only way to deal with that one."'

There is no attempt to hit Barber's delivery back over her head for six. The Mayor tells us he is going to behave like an orthodox batsman. But Boris knows this is a dull way to play, or indeed talk, so peps things up by flattering his interviewer and introducing a new and more painful image: 'I'm not going to say anything except that I hugely admire the elegance with which you framed the question and the elaborate way that you dug the hole and placed the stakes at the bottom – but I'm not going to fall in.'

Much the most likely person to make him fall in is Boris himself, at some moment when he is not being interviewed, and forgets he is in danger of being impaled. This is not the kind of moment which I am much good at precipitating. I cannot pretend, in what follows, to have lived up to the high standards of modern biography, in which the sex lives of the famous are reported with pitiless candour. The women with whom Boris has slept would regard with an admirable disgust the idea of selling their story to a tabloid newspaper, or even telling it for free to an insinuating biographer.

One of these women explained why they do not kiss and tell: 'Because they would look worse than Boris if they did. And he picks women who are middle-class and don't go in for that kind of thing. It's something they'd consider to be in bad taste, not some magic spell he puts on them. It's difficult to hate him. He amuses me.' She described the only expensive present she got Boris to buy for her. He is not a man to whom this kind of gesture comes naturally, and 'was white with shock.' Boris does not buy his women: he tells them jokes and makes friends with them.

But this woman warned against the romantic illusion that Boris only sleeps with women with whom he is in love: 'He does it so often he can't be in love with all of them. I know more women he's had sex with than you know about – things that lasted for a week or less – he is completely sex mad.'

On the morality of his behaviour, Boris has remained clear. He sees no reason why he shouldn't practise what he doesn't preach about, but this is a subject he finds easier to broach when discussing past ages. When it emerges, in *Who Do You Think You Are?*, the excellent BBC programme about his ancestors, that

Boris is descended from the illegitimate child of an actress, Friederike Margrethe Porth, who lived from 1776–1860, he remarks that 'an actress could be a euphemism . . . we may be about to turn up a prostitute here . . . not that I mind. I want you to know they can get up to anything, my ancestors, they have carte blanche to commit whatever acts of fornication they want as far as I'm concerned, but I want to know.'

On the other hand, Boris wants us not to know what he is up to now. He prefers to revel in the exploits of the dead. The longest essay in his book about great Londoners draws the life of John Wilkes, the 18th-century libertine and campaigner for liberty. Wilkes became an MP and launched a subversive paper, the North Briton, which George III's ministers made botched efforts to suppress, in the course of which the freedom of the press was entrenched. Wilkes was too popular with the London mob for the authorities to be able to suppress him, and towards the end of his life served as Mayor of London as well as an MP.

Boris describes Wilkes's early studies at Leiden in Holland, then a more prestigious institution than either Oxford or Cambridge:

At university he learned the habits of debauchery that were to last him a lifetime. It is not that he wasted his time at Leiden. He sharpened his mastery of Latin and French; he loved the classics. He first met some of the intellectuals who were to welcome him during his exile into the circle of the *philosophes*. But he was a firm believer in what you might call a rounded education. As he later said, 'I was always among women at Leiden. My father gave me as much money as I pleased, so I had three or four whores and got drunk every night. I woke up with a sore head in the morning, and then I read.' For the first time since the fall of the Roman Empire, it was now acceptable to discuss fornication in this way, as the supreme recreation of a civilised society. Wilkes associated sex with intellectual creativity. As he once told Boswell, 'Dissipation and profligacy ... renew the mind. I wrote my best North Briton in bed with Betsy Green.'

One can imagine the excitement if David Cameron were to write a book commending sex as the supreme recreation of a civilised society, and a spur to intellectual creativity. But when Boris did so, it caused barely a ripple.

The woman quoted above agreed that Boris's views on Wilkes are an accurate guide to his views now: 'He just feels monogamy is very stupid and uncivilised. He's very unrealistic about it, but it's what he wants to believe.'

The unreality of Boris's position lies in the fact that he is also, as Barber reminded him, a great family man. Nobody who knows Boris and Marina doubts their devotion to each other. Yet even if his affairs present no serious emotional threat to her, they are bound to be hurtful, especially on becoming public.

Experience had demonstrated that this is bound sometimes to happen. It happened in July 2010, when the tabloids published a story about Helen Macintyre, a 36-year-old art dealer with whom Boris had an affair in early 2009. In November 2009 she gave birth to a fair-haired daughter. Her then partner, Pierre Rolin, a dark-haired Canadian whose property business was getting into difficulties, discovered he was not the father and cut up rough. Macintyre was by now living with William Cash, a twice-married journalist. It is not clear how the story, which speculated that Boris was the father, got into the papers, but the speculation turned out to be correct.

Rolin gave an interview in which he accused Boris of lacking 'a moral compass', a term once used by Gordon Brown. I invited Macintyre to tell me the whole story. She said almost everything in the tabloids was wrong, but declined this valuable chance to correct it.

It appeared that, in normal circumstances, Macintyre was good company: an affable and warm-hearted woman who could enjoy a joke as much as the next man, and was capable of surprising directness. I had been told that in May 2010 she went to a birthday party at which someone said to her, 'I gather you have a baby,' and she replied: 'Yes, it's Boris Johnson's.' But the experience of being chased by the tabloids had evidently impelled her to become less outspoken.

A colleague at City Hall described Boris's reaction when the Macintyre story broke: 'He was so consumed with self-loathing off the back of that, because of what he'd done to Marina. He was very, very deeply traumatised.' But this is not a side of Boris that is on general view. When I asked the woman quoted at the start of this chapter how bad Boris felt about the way he treated Marina, she replied: 'Not as bad as he ought to feel, frankly. Occasionally he would roll his eyes and say poor Marina, but he didn't seem wracked by remorse.'

The whole episode was wretched for Boris's family. According to one account of an early evening in July 2010 at the Johnson home, 'It was quite dramatic. Marina was saying, "Right, that's enough, I'm off to the country." Ten minutes later Boris got back and was saying, "Is she here? Where is she?" and had to persuade her not to go.'

It was instead Boris who went, moving out to a small flat in the same road. As on the previous occasion when Marina turfed him out, he had not been hurled beyond reach. She was tough-minded enough not to take the obvious course, which many wronged women would have taken, and decide in a self-righteous way that she would have nothing more to do with him. No marriage could last a day in which each spouse was not prepared to tolerate the other's failings, and though Boris's failings were horribly conspicuous, he was also more fond of his wife and more prepared to make a go of family life than many men who have never put a foot wrong. He was permitted to pay visits to the family home, and the press noticed his laundry being taken round to him. He was able at this time to do a good deal of work on his London book.

Among the uses to which Boris puts his *Telegraph* column is as a noticeboard. On 4 April 2011 he used it to tell the world that he and Marina were back together. Not for Boris the portentous column which opens with a swift dive into a cold bath of abstract argument, where he and his readers would swiftly die of boredom. His pieces almost always start with a prolonged passage of autobiography, which turns out, by means of some more or less Woodhousian twist, to be related to some wider issue of the day, on which Boris ventures in his penultimate paragraph to express the modest thoughts of a plain man drawing on his own humble experience of life's ups and downs. Here is Borisian rhetoric in its classical form: most of it is about himself, and although there are moments of trenchancy, there is never anything as tactless or preachy as an attempt to ram his opinions down anyone else's throat.

In this particular piece, Boris started with the weather:

I don't know about where you are, but it was spectacularly lovely here in London yesterday morning ... Everywhere you could hear the noises of a perfect spring day in a much-loved municipal park: the laughter of children, the barking of well-disciplined dogs, the mating calls of the birds and the gasping sobs of middle-aged men as they tried to retrieve the high-speed cross-court passing shots of their younger, fitter wives.

I was the one playing tennis, and after losing another rally I looked up to see a familiar figure ... As he drew closer I saw that it was none other than my old chum Tom Baldwin, who is now the Labour Party's official spokesman and the apostolic successor to Alastair Campbell.

He was talking on his mobile phone ... But then my

wife hit another of her cross-court zingers and I went puffing to retrieve the ball from the corner of the court.

The chance meeting with a key insider is a favourite Borisian device, though what he overhears Baldwin saying into the mobile phone turns out to be some way short of a scoop: 'From our point of view, the key message today has got to be that it's all a complete mess.'

To ensure that the message of marital reconciliation had got across, Boris and Marina were photographed together on 5 May 2011 at the Hanover School polling station in Islington, where they voted in the referendum on the alternative vote. And when Boris was asked in an interview published on 17 May 2011 who he admires the most, he replied, 'Aristotle, Marilyn Monroe and Scarlett Johansson – in fact, I think she might have overtaken Marilyn Monroe – and my wife, of course. My wife is way ahead of Aristotle. She's beaten him in the final furlong.'

When rioting erupted in Tottenham, in north London, on the night of Saturday 6 August, 2011, the ruling classes were away on their summer holidays. David Cameron and his family were staying with two other families in a Tuscan villa with 15 bed-rooms and a billiard room.

Boris, Marina, and their children were touring the Rocky Mountains in Canada in a camper van. The Winnebago, billed as 'the most trusted name in motor homes', had the disadvantage of being so big that Marina's feet could not reach the pedals.

This was a problem for Boris when word reached him of the riots. He felt he could not just bail out and abandon Marina and the children with the Winnebago. A second problem was that his mobile phone ran out. His daughter Lara had a phone with ten minutes left on it, but that ran out too.

Guto Harri was in Spain, in some mountains near Seville. He

rang Lara's phone in order to arrange for Boris to give an interview to the BBC on the Sunday. The hope at this point was that
the riot in Tottenham was a one-off event and Boris would not
need to abandon his wife and children and fly home. For so
much of the time his job comes first, and here was a chunk of
time he had set aside to spend with them, thousands of miles
from the distractions of City Hall.

But on Sunday evening there was rioting in Brixton, Enfield,
Islington, Wood Green and Oxford Circus. The television
footage was shocking. The eyes of the world were on London.
People wanted to know why this was happening, and whether it
was going to go on getting worse. The fear was that the police
had lost control of the streets.

Still Boris resisted. According to a source at City Hall,
'He didn't want to come back. He was being begged to
come back. He put family first. He said he couldn't come
back as he was five hours from Calgary. He only came back
when Theresa May came back.' The Home Secretary forced
Boris's hand by deciding she really must break her holiday.
On the evening of Monday 8 August it was announced that
the Mayor was interrupting his family holiday in order to
return to London to deal with the riots. That night there
was looting, arson and rioting in parts of Battersea, Brixton,
Bromley, Camden, Chingford Mount, Croydon, Ealing, East
Ham, Hackney, Lewisham, Peckham, Stratford, Waltham Forest and
Woolwich.

By Tuesday lunchtime Boris was back. He and the Home
Secretary paid a joint visit to Clapham. This first contact with
people who had suffered in the riots was a disaster. Boris, as one
of his staff put it, 'was caught between a rock and a hard place.
He had angry shopkeepers on one side and cameras on the
other. One woman said, "Why are you talking to the cameras?"
He immediately used humour and it was completely inappro-
priate. His trademark humour for the cameras didn't work with

the crowd. It was just a complete disaster. It could have made him completely irrelevant. The riots were his lowest point. They showed him to be completely out of touch.'

Another mayoral adviser said of the Clapham debacle, 'That was Boris in ill-prepared transmit mode. Ed Miliband was very much better received, in palpably listening mode. Boris was on the wrong side of the police tape, and he thought because he had good people in front of him it would all be OK. He was not aware of the anger of people whose houses had been trashed. The first thing he should have done was get on the right side of the tape. That was a very low point, and Boris knew it. He said it was awful, it was a catastrophe.'

Fortunately for Boris, everyone else was ill-prepared too. Theresa May slipped away while he was talking, hardly the action of a loyal colleague. Ken Livingstone did attack cuts in police budgets, but also relied on Lee Jasper to respond to the disturbances. Jasper interpreted the trouble as a replay of the 1980s riots, which it was not.

Tuesday night was peaceful in London, though not in several provincial cities where copy-cat rioting broke out. The police had regained control of the capital by deploying far larger numbers of officers. They could also depend on the support of the very large number of law-abiding Londoners who were appalled by the three nights of looting, thieving and arson. But pictures of Boris with the broom brigades who turned out to start clearing up the streets were by no means sufficient to re-establish his authority.

On Tuesday night David Cameron entertained Boris to an informal dinner in the Downing Street flat. The only other person present was Ed Llewellyn, Cameron's chief of staff. The Prime Minister served melon and parma ham, followed by pan-fried steak and potatoes.

Boris revealed nothing of his plan for the following morning, when he went on the *Today* programme with a clear idea of the question he wanted to answer. He suggested on air that John Humphrys, who was conducting the interview, 'might want to ask me ... whether I think there is a case for cutting police budgets'. The following dialogue took place:

HUMPHRYS: 'I was about to come to that.'

BORIS: 'Well, let me anticipate your question. In the light of these events then my answer to that would be no. I think that case was always pretty frail and it's been substantially weakened. I think that this is not a time to think about making substantial cuts in police numbers.'

HUMPHRYS: 'The exact opposite of what the Home Secretary told me this time yesterday morning ... So you're totally opposed to the policy that the Home Secretary and Prime Minister are still supporting ... that there should be severe cuts to the police budget?'

BORIS: 'Well, as I say, I think if you look at what's happening today I think most people, commonsensical people, looking at our country, we're going forward to the Olympic Games next year, we're welcoming the world, and I do think it's, it's very sad what's happened.'

HUMPHRYS: 'Yeah, yeah, but what's the answer to my question.'

BORIS: 'I think the answer is yes. I can't remember what the question was exactly ... You're always quite rightly trying to find a way in which I'm opposed to the Government.'

HUMPHRYS: 'You offered it, with great respect. It was your suggestion.'

BORIS: 'All right. Good point. I think it would be a good thing if the Government had another look, how about that?'

Shortly after Boris had betrayed the official line there was a meeting of Cobra, the Government's disaster emergency committee. Boris arrived late.

The first thing Cameron said to Theresa May was, 'Has Boris discussed this with you?' The Home Secretary replied, 'No.'

When Boris turned up, Cameron was so angry he could barely look at him. But on Wednesday evening the two men had a long phone call which, according to Boris's people, ended up with the pair getting on well again.

Harri says of Boris's decision to go public on the need for a debate about police budgets without warning Number Ten: 'Well obviously they weren't thrilled about that.' According to Harri, Boris had long been saying in private that you need about 32,000 people on the payroll to police London properly, and now was the right time for the Mayor to go public. 'I encouraged him to do that. That was where the people of London were at that time. It had the advantage of shifting the coverage onto serious matters – we need a serious debate about police numbers. It worked a treat for us. It didn't for central government.'

A Tory MP expressed admiration for the way Boris had 'turned on a sixpence' and 'torn up the policy he had followed for the last three years'. One can certainly argue that he was right to do this. Democratic politicians must be allowed to change their minds when the facts, or circumstances, have changed. On Thursday 11 August, when Parliament held an emergency session to debate the riots, Ed Miliband, the Leader of the Opposition, failed to challenge Cameron anything like as strongly as he could have done about police budgets.

It was Boris rather than Miliband or Livingstone who had seized the moment to articulate the public's fears.

But Boris had retrieved his own position at the expense of his colleagues. Another Tory MP, who sits for a London seat and has had many dealings with Boris, described him as 'a selfish bastard', and said that if Sir Simon Milton had still been alive, he would have stopped the Mayor's U-turn on police budgets.

One of Boris's own staff said of his behaviour, 'If he had cleared his lines with George and Dave it would all have been rather different.' Osborne and Cameron were understandably cross that Boris had not told them what he was about to do. Boris also tried by means of premature publicity to bounce Downing Street into matching a 50 million-pound fund scraped together by Peter Rogers, the Mayor's adviser on regeneration, to repair the damage caused by the riots.

Cameron declined to be bounced in this way, and during a magisterial parliamentary performance he also refused to be panicked into abandoning the spending limits set for the police, which he said would still allow enough officers to be put on the streets at times of crisis.

No one knew quite what the Mayor's analysis of the riots was, but order had been restored. On 6 September 2011 Boris gave evidence on the riots to the Home Affairs committee of MPs, chaired by his old enemy Keith Vaz. For the first time ever, I went to sleep during one of Boris's performances. He was being deliberately ponderous. At least twice he deployed the cliché, 'The proof of the pudding is in the eating', a phrase he would find easy to embroider, but which went unembroidered here. Few statesmen have refrained, on occasion, from boring their adversaries into submission, and here was the Mayor showing he too could do so. It looked as though Boris had matured.

Ken Livingstone agreed with this judgement. As he said of Boris in an interview in October 2011: 'You'd assume he was my father or grandfather. He sounds about twice my age.' Ken was at this point 66, while Boris was 47.

Lynton Crosby, the rugged Australian who was again running Boris's campaign, declined when I interviewed him in early December 2011 to predict what the result of the mayoral election would be. But Crosby reckoned that if it came down to a choice of who Londoners wanted to be Mayor, Boris would win. This view was supported by polling carried out in early autumn 2011 by Peter Kellner, who established that one in five people who would vote Labour in a general election campaign intended to vote for Boris in the mayoral contest on Thursday 3 May, 2012. Kellner said this was 'by far Ken's biggest problem' and explained why these Labour voters were going over to the other side: 'They tend to think that Ken has lost touch with ordinary Londoners, and that Boris is decisive and sticks to what he believes in.'

Ken faced the alarming possibility that just as people used to enjoy voting for him in order to annoy Tony Blair, so they would now vote for Boris in order to annoy Cameron. The task that faced Ken was to redefine the election as a Tory-Labour contest, whereupon he rather than Boris would become the anti-Cameron candidate. For as Ken pointed out when I interviewed him in November 2011, 'If Boris was re-elected on May 3, that evening you'd have Cameron and Osborne saying this is a vote of confidence in the way we're running Britain.'

So Ken needed to convince people that Boris was at heart an evil, ideological Tory, one of the enemy as far as Labour voters were concerned. But Ken could not resist also dismissing Boris as 'Britain's Berlusconi' who 'just gets away with things nobody else could' and 'doesn't really do the day job either'.

The difficulty of defining Boris, his continuing political indistinctness, was making it difficult for Ken to land blows. The two lines of attack on Boris – as a frivolous maverick, or a serious Tory – cancelled each other out. Nor did Boris do Ken the favour of attacking him, or even of showing much interest in him: he instead missed no opportunity to ignore him.

And in much of what Ken said about Boris, I thought I detected an undertone of admiration. Ken predicted future greatness for his opponent: 'He will be the next leader of the Tory party even if I beat him.' This was in part an attempt to accuse

Boris of using City Hall as a mere stepping stone to Downing Street, but it also painted Boris as the coming man, while Ken had been around for longer than most Londoners could remember.

At the Conservative Party Conference of October 2011, Boris cheered the faithful without rocking the boat as violently as he had in previous years. Jill Kirby, a former director of the Centre for Policy Studies, wrote of his conference speech, 'His exuberant self-assurance makes us feel confident too: confident about being Conservative and confident that Conservatives in power can get things done.' Kirby's piece, published next morning in *Conservative Home Daily* for distribution among Conservatives at the conference, appeared under the headline 'Boris reaches the parts that Cameron doesn't', and ended with what sounded like a plea for Boris to take over: 'I bet that there were more than a few Conservatives in Manchester this week thinking they'd like to see him go head to head with the Lib Dems – and indeed with the European Union.'

Ray Lewis, whose forced resignation Boris had failed to avert in the summer of 2008 (an episode described in Chapter 30), opined in November 2011 that the Mayor has come on a lot since then:

> Boris has grown in stature. I say this with a pinch of salt but he's becoming very mayoral now. I've noticed he's picking up the mantle of who he is. I'm not saying he's sold out. There's still the lightness, the lovingness, the playfulness. But his political prowess is growing.
>
> I think in a year or two he'll be absolutely formidable and ready for more seniority. He's awakening. This is a man with a growing sense of destiny. London will be too small for Boris soon.

Not everyone is impressed by Boris. He unsettles some of his colleagues by continuing to take what they regard as an unprofessional approach to his duties. One critic said that 'Boris has learned some things', including how to chair a meeting, 'but I don't actually think he has an aptitude for government.'

In place of a mastery of the technique of government, Boris offers, according to that observer, '*Triomph des Willens* with Guto Harri as Leni Riefenstahl'. The suggestion is not, of course, that Boris is a Nazi, but that he achieves things through the triumph of his will and brilliant propaganda rather than by learning how to do them properly.

This strikes me as unfair. There is of course room for more than one reading of Boris, and indeed for more than one reading of this book. I was pleased that Ken Livingstone read it twice. He described it as 'completely devastating', and devoted several pages of his own memoirs to quoting some of what he considered to be the most damaging material.

But it is evident that Boris has not fallen flat on his face in the way that the *Guardian* predicted before he became Mayor. He has not been exposed to public ridicule as a clown and a liar. In *Just Boris: The Irresistible Rise of a Political Celebrity*, published in October 2011, Sonia Purnell reveals a wealth of previously unknown detail, but her 433 pages contain no revelation that forces us to revise our opinion of him. She pays Boris the unintended compliment of making immense efforts to trip him up, and not quite managing to do so.

Yet suspicions remain, in part because people sense that Boris is a risk-taker. They feel they never know quite what he is going to do next. Some of his warmest admirers describe him acting on intuition or instinct. This does not necessarily make him wrong: it could make him quicker to detect the right course of action. And at times of political crisis, it is often more important to act swiftly, than to wait for complete information, by which time the options have narrowed.

To those who fear he is reckless, Boris's caution as Mayor provides some reassurance. He has surrounded himself with

competent people, and has not tried to reinvent vast organisa-
tions such as Transport for London. 'Steady as she goes' has more
often been his policy than one might think.

But there is still something imponderable about him. Boris does
not suffer from the fear which makes so many of our politicians so
dull and reduces them to an indistinguishable mass of apparatchiks,
namely the fear of saying or doing something new, which could
turn out to be wrong, or be derided as wrong, which would be
just as bad. He has permissive instincts. In both economic and
social matters, he is a genuine liberal, who considers it wrong and
counter-productive to try to suppress people's animal spirits.

The Tory element in this is twofold: a love of existing institutions, and a recognition of the inevitability of hierarchy. As
usual, Boris finds this easier to say when writing about the past,
notably in his essay on Samuel Johnson in his book about
London. The modern Johnson hides behind the coat-tails of the
mighty 18th-century Tory, from which place of safety Boris ventures to observe that even today we might 'reluctantly' agree
there is a 'grain of truth' in Dr Johnson's dictum, 'No two
people can be half an hour together, but one shall acquire an evident superiority over the other.' Boris gives us Dr Johnson's
arguments for inequality, including the reply to a Mrs Macaulay,
'the Polly Toynbee of her day', who claimed we would all be
better off if we had the same sized plots of land and nobody
could domineer over anyone else.

Nonsense, Dr Johnson replied, mankind is happier in 'a state
of inequality and subordination'. If everyone was equal, there
would be no leisure, so no intellectual improvement. Nothing
would get done, added to which, 'Men will submit to any rule
by which they may be exempted from the tyranny of caprice and
chance. They are glad to supply by external authority their own
want of constancy and resolution, and court the government of
others, when long experience has convinced them of their own
inability to govern themselves.'

I cannot remember Boris saying anything half so trenchant as this on his own account. He lacks Dr Johnson's urge to derive general doctrines from particular cases. But he did say, in an interview with Gina Thomas published in the *Frankfurter Allgemeine Zeitung* on 2 April 2009, during which he dismissed with unusual vehemence the anti-banker demonstrations taking place at the G20 summit in London: '*Wir sind abhängig von der Ungleicheit. Leider haben alle Gesellschaften kommerziell mit einer Art von Elite funktioniert, es hat immer Reiche und Arme gegeben.*'

Thomas has not kept Boris's original English, but the German version might be translated as, 'We are dependent on inequality. Unfortunately, all commercial societies have functioned with a kind of elite, there have always been rich and poor.' The insincere word here is 'unfortunately'. Boris does not consider the existence of elites to be in the slightest bit unfortunate. He sees things as they are, not as the idealists think they ought to be. He is a Tory realist, added to which he loves competing. But one should add that his realism is infected with the distinctly un-Tory quality of optimism.

For Boris, one of the merits of having no explicit doctrine is that he can avoid digging massive fortifications at what will most likely turn out to be the wrong place, and can instead fight a war of movement, reacting at lightning speed to unexpected events and expressing the public mood before the public even knows what its mood is. To Boris's detractors, this looks like opportunism, and recalls Lord Beaverbrook's remark about Lloyd George: 'He did not seem to care which way he travelled provided he was in the driver's seat.' But it can more generously be described as an adventurous pragmatism. The more one examines his claim that Heathrow airport is in the wrong place, the more justified it seems. While others say it is all too difficult, Boris wants to go for it.

As he said on 21 November 2011, when relaunching his airport plan at the Institute of Directors in Pall Mall, 'I don't think that financing is the number one issue. The number one issue is political will. Britain is a trading nation. We are a great country and we are currently suffering a poverty of ambition. It is time for our government to look at these proposals, to take them up and act. I don't think we can afford to wait.'

While writing this study, I happened to be reading, for light relief, Roy Jenkins's volume on Chancellors of the Exchequer. It contains this complaint, in a letter written on 12 August 1928 by Neville Chamberlain, then Minister of Health, about his colleague Winston Churchill, who was Chancellor of the Exchequer:

> Winston is a very interesting but d——d uncomfortable bedfellow ... In the consideration of affairs, his decisions are never founded on exact knowledge, nor on careful prolonged consideration of the pros and cons. He seeks instinctively for the large and preferably the novel idea such as is capable of representation by the broadest brush.
>
> Whether the idea is practicable or impracticable, good or bad, provided he can see himself recommending it plausibly and successfully to an enthusiastic audience, it commends itself to him.

That is Boris: a man who loves to sketch daring enterprises, and will fill in the details later. Boldness, which the world often finds indistinguishable from shamelessness, is a characteristic of almost all great politicians. In his book about Bill Clinton, *All Too Human*, George Stephanopoulos asks of his boss's behaviour during the Monica Lewinsky affair, 'How could a president so intelligent, so compassionate, so public-spirited, and so conscious of his place in history act in such a stupid, selfish, and self-destructive manner?'

Stephanopoulos begins to work out the answer: 'I came to see how Clinton's shamelessness is a key to his political success, how his capacity for denial is tied to the optimism that is his greatest political strength.'

The Clinton comparison occurred to Stephen Robinson, a former Washington correspondent, who wrote of Boris in a piece for the *Sunday Times* magazine on 28 December 2008: 'As with Bill Clinton, there is a carnal quality to his meet-and-greet technique.' We have already seen, in Chapter 22, how in 1998 Boris stood up for Clinton during the Lewinsky scandal. This admiration persisted long after Clinton, who was President from 1992–2000, had stepped down. As late as July 2007, Boris wished, in an interview in *GQ*, that we could get Clinton back:

> The world was better run under him as President, there was a greater sense of optimism, the potential for harmony between different countries and religious groups. And we didn't have this terrible thing that Bush has brought in of this 'you're with us or against us' mentality... I'd love to see Bill Clinton back to restore things. He represented America better, and that is so important. I love America.

The Bushes, father and son, were born into the Republican establishment and became its candidates. Cameron too was born into the establishment and became its candidate. Boris is drawn instead to the poor boy from Arkansas who gave the world a less belligerent idea of America. He wants people to walk away from the table feeling good about themselves.

This overwhelming desire to make people feel good is one reason why, in the writing of this book, I have found myself reaching for the words 'Merry England conservatism' to describe what Boris stands for. The time has come to try to define a term which is not yet in general use.

Merry England has nothing to do with thatched cottages: Kingsley Amis's hero in *Lucky Jim* may well be right that 'Merrie

England . . . was about the most un-Merrie period in our history.'
In politics, the Merry England style is not a hankering after an
ideal past, but a subversive and disrespectful reaction to the pieties
of the present. The Merry Englander laughs at the earnest politician striving to implement a scheme of general improvement
which ignores the character of those who are to be improved.
Political commentators seldom require such a term, for their stock
in trade is to explain what the politicians are trying to do, and to
criticise it for not being earnest enough. They value their status as
insiders, while Merry Englanders are relaxed about being outsiders.

A Merry Englander should not be confused with a Little
Englander. Boris is a case in point. He loves going abroad, and
is well-disposed towards foreigners who settle here. As he said
during the BBC programme about his ancestors, his own family
shows that immigrants can become as British as anyone else: 'It
is interesting to look at how British I can feel, and yet actually
what a completely mongrel composition I really am.' He added,
as a precaution, the hope that 'the people of Henley will bear in
mind that at least half my antecedents are English'. But Boris
does not feel threatened by newcomers to these islands, in the
way that Little Englanders tend to do.

Nor is Boris's attitude to the European Union dictated by fear.
When he sees the EU trying to assume some unwarranted
power, or launch some impractical project, his instinct is to laugh
such vanity to scorn. This was his line when he made his name
as a correspondent in Brussels – he mocked the eurocrats. Boris
the Merry Englander took his stand as a man of common sense
who could see the absurdity of the EU's pretensions. He did not
take his stand on the doctrine of national sovereignty, as Enoch
Powell and others have done. Boris feels relaxed enough in his
own skin to tolerate or even approve of considerable schemes of
European co-operation. But he knows that when the peoples of
Europe find themselves being ordered about by a remote and
undemocratic apparat, trouble will follow. It is not just England

that will no longer be so merry: nor will the rest of Europe.

The Merry England style of politics entails often being rude to people. The ancient and enjoyable right of an Englishman to tell another Englishman when he is being a fool is upheld by Boris. But Boris gets this message across in a curiously elliptical manner which recalls the lines of Alexander Pope in his *Epistle to Dr Arbuthnot*:

Willing to wound, and yet afraid to strike,
Just hint a fault, and hesitate dislike.

Yet Boris's rhetoric is less spiteful than this. His tone is never nasty. In Boris, we find a unique combination of the clear and the evasive, the learned and the popular.

One of the paradoxes of democracy is that although this form of government is generally assumed to be favourable to freedom of speech, it is impossible to say what one really thinks about various subjects, when one's views are so unfashionable that one will be written off as mad. Boris tries to get round this problem by an artful imprecision: he says something which is on the borders of acceptability and then retreats from it, or cracks a joke. In Merry England, many a true word is spoken in jest.

Merry England craves entertainment, and Boris provides it. In June 2011, when he accompanied the Metropolitan Police on a drugs raid, a suspect called Rambo exclaimed on seeing the Mayor of London, 'What the fuck are you doing here?' This is politics as soap opera, with Boris as one of the main characters. His implausibility is one of his attractions.

The politics of envy are not found in Merry England. It is relaxed about people being rich; is even, in Lord Mandelson's words, intensely relaxed about people getting filthy rich. Boris wants everyone − and especially himself − to have a good time, and no puritanical moralising to spoil our pleasures by making us feel guilty.

But Merry England is not relaxed about people being poor. Poverty is not a merry condition. The state can help by keeping the burden of taxation as light as possible, while paying its own employees above the bare minimum: Boris froze City Hall's share of council tax and adopted the London living wage. But it is an illusion to imagine that the state can end poverty by imposing punitive taxes.

Boris is more inclined to put his trust in free trade. He has also urged the bankers whom he has defended to make munificent donations to charity. Boris's demeanour is that of a compassionate Conservative.

On the morning of Friday, 9 September 2011, two men who had known each other since they were at Oxford in the mid-Eighties met in Hammersmith, west London. They were there for the opening of a most worthy institution: the West London Free School, founded by a group led by Toby Young, last heard of writing a hurtful satirical play about Boris. A third Oxford man, Michael Gove, who started his political career as 'a stooge in the Boris machine' at the Oxford Union, was by now the Secretary of State for Education, and had given his enthusiastic backing to the new school.

Boris paid tribute to Gove, claiming he had added a new inflection to the verb 'to give' – we give, they gave, he gove. As an example of the new usage, Boris proposed, 'He gove us these fantastic free schools.'

So Merry England had its joke. But Merry England was also engaged in more valuable work than had once seemed likely. A generation of Oxford hacks had come of age. Boris was still a long way from being a statesman, a status generally requiring a wider field of action than running a city can provide. But his performance at City Hall had persuaded many people that he deserved his chance at national level.

And the day may come when the Tories decide they need a Merry England candidate.

– 33 –

## *Stuck on a Zip Wire*

Boris won the 2012 mayoral election, which took place soon after the last edition of this book went to press. His opponent, Ken Livingstone, managed to make him lose his temper, by accusing him during a radio interview of avoiding paying tax. Boris raged at Livingstone during a journey to the roof of LBC for photographs. He proceeded to disprove Livingstone's accusation by publishing his tax return.

But much the most memorable event of 2012, as far as Boris was concerned, was the London Olympics. Many Londoners feared the Games would be an embarrassment, with the trains and buses unable to cope with so many visitors. Boris expressed his confidence that the whole thing would go off well, and he turned out to be right.

Before the Games began, Mitt Romney, the Republican candidate for US President, was unwise enough to question 'just how well it will all turn out'. Boris responded at a mass rally in Hyde Park: 'I hear there's a guy called Mitt Romney who wants to know whether we're ready. He wants to know whether we're ready. Are we ready? Yes we are.' Screams of approval for Boris greeted this sally.

He proceeded to dominate every joint appearance which he

made with the Prime Minister, David Cameron. It was not that Cameron was bad: just that Boris was better at connecting with the crowds. And during the Games, Boris managed to get stuck on a zip wire: a mishap which greatly amused people, and somehow made him more popular.

At the final rally in front of Buckingham Palace to celebrate the athletes who had taken part, Boris said, 'We've come now to the final tear-sodden juddering climax of the summer of London 2012,' and told the competitors that 'you produced such paroxysms of tears and joy on the sofas of Britain that you probably not only inspired a generation but probably helped to create one as well'.

This earthy language gave much pleasure to his audience, and is I hope a sufficient reminder of how successful Boris was in his ambassadorial function as Mayor of London.

## 'Do You Have a Golden Toilet?'

Boris had said he would not seek to return to the House of Commons until his mayoralty came to an end in May 2016, but he broke that assurance and in September 2014 was adopted as the Tory candidate for the seat of Uxbridge and South Ruislip, on the western fringes of London and a few miles north of Heathrow Airport, which he proceeded to fight at the general election of May 2015. During that campaign, I sketched him on the campaign trail for ConservativeHome, and perhaps because of the unusual nature of the event, detected for the first time one of the reasons why he forms a better connection with people than if he were the kind of politician who takes no interest in his audience, and just wants to preach some standard message at them. This is a slightly modified version of my original report:

Boris Johnson almost looked nervous. There was no trace of bumptiousness about him as he waited yesterday morning to take questions from an audience of over 500 people in Uxbridge and South Ruislip.

It did not seem to matter to him that none of these people had a vote. Nor did it matter that most of them were not even born in 2008, when he became Mayor of London. The children of Colham Manor Primary School had his undivided attention.

It is true that about fifty members of staff witnessed the event, and some of the children may have gone home and told their parents about Boris. But this was not one of those confected occasions which takes place mainly in order to provide attractive pictures for the television news. No cameras were present and I was the only journalist who saw this event, which included some enquiries at least as tough as Andrew Neil would have posed. But the Mayor began by asking the children a question: 'Does anybody know why I'm late?'

Hands shot up. This was not one of those school assemblies where no one dares address the visiting dignitary. It was very soon established that he had got stuck in the traffic, and had indeed became so frustrated that 'the steering wheel was almost bent into a pretzel'.

'Whose fault is the traffic?' Boris went on. Various possibilities were canvassed: the traffic lights could be a factor, as could the lollipop lady.

'Me,' Boris said, and the way he said it provoked laughter. 'The traffic is entirely my fault.'

Here was a strange politician: one prepared to admit blame. But let us not exaggerate that aspect of his character, for his next question implied there were deeper causes at work: 'Why do you think the traffic is so bad in London?'

The answer, it turned out, is that the population of London has grown by 600,000 since he became Mayor: 'Last year there were more babies than in any year since England won the World Cup.' So there is more traffic, meaning more pollution, meaning we need cleaner vehicles. And what might those be?

'A Porsche,' a small boy said. For a moment, I thought Boris would agree. But with statesmanlike restraint, he extolled the merits of bicycles, which he said are 'good for the soul'.

'Do you have a golden toilet?' No one had expected this. The six words suggested with admirable brevity the possibility that Johnson is a corrupt despot who leads a life of impudent luxury.

'The answer to that is certainly not,' Johnson said. 'It would be a total waste of money.' He added that under him there was not only no golden toilet, but the council tax had been cut.

'Who wants to be Mayor?' Johnson asked, and about 250 hands went up.

'It's a wonderful job,' he agreed, because 'London is the greatest city on earth'.

'Why are general elections held on Thursdays?' a pupil asked.

Boris said it was so you could get the results on Fridays, and then had the weekend to sort things out and 'send in the removals vans' if needed, not that they would be on this occasion.

We moved to a classroom, where each member of the class had a question: 'Have you ever thought about running for Prime Minister?'

'I've thought about David Cameron being Prime Minister again,' Boris said.

'How many friends do you have?' someone asked.

'That's a very good question,' Boris replied. 'Enough.' He wondered aloud how many serious friends it was possible to have in politics: 'Uneasy lies the head that wears the crown.' But he went on: 'I've got enough friends, and some very good friends too.'

'Did you want to be a politician when you were small?'

Boris responded by describing why he found his first career, as a journalist, unsatisfactory: 'Being in journalism, you're always being cruel to people, even by mistake. People got so upset.'

It occurs to me that one reason why Boris is so good on the stump is that he does not want people to be upset – a characteristic which is often described as one of his weaknesses. If someone comes up to him who is worried or distressed about something, then at least while he is talking to them, he too is worried or distressed. Instead of trying to keep their trouble at a distance, he enters into it and tries to alleviate it.

Good manners can be used, in England, to keep people at a distance. Boris has the kind of good manners which entail listening to what they have to say, and imagining what it must be like to be them.

He is in one respect the rudest men I have ever met: I have never known anyone so consistently late for appointments. At Colham Manor Primary School, he was an hour late, though his staff had phoned ahead to warn he was held up. The children were not brought, beautifully behaved and a credit to their teachers, into the hall where they were to meet him, until he was actually there.

As soon as Boris arrived, he made up for his rudeness not just by being amusing (in itself a highly welcome characteristic), but by being attentive. When at last he performed, he was determined to connect with his audience.

And so it was when he moved on from the school to talk to members of the public outside Uxbridge Station, served by the Metropolitan and Piccadilly lines. It was like being at a carnival. What an orgy of smiles, giggles and selfie-taking broke out. Without apparent distinction of age, sex, ethnicity or religion, people wanted to have their photograph taken with Boris, and about ten professional photographers pursued him too.

Members of the RMT union stopped the love-in becoming too sugary by shouting 'The man's a crook', and by waving placards which said 'Keep Uxbridge Ticket Office Open'. But to balance this, another man stood by Boris as he was being filmed by a camera crew and shouted 'Boris for Prime Minister. Yeah.'

When I asked this man, who gave his name as Eric from Ealing, why he wanted Boris to be PM, he replied: 'He's got charisma. He's the one we need. Full of blood, full of charm, says what he thinks.' It turned out that Eric 'won't be voting for anyone' this time, for he has yet to get over supporting the Liberal Democrats in 2010: 'They really disappointed me.'

A sweet old man invited Boris to condemn embryo research,

'because when we have an embryo we have a life'. Johnson replied that he doesn't 'take a maximalist position on this'. He is a moderate, who thinks that the sufferings of severely ill people should be taken into account, for their pain might be relieved by such research.

Several people at the back of the crowd began spontaneously to discuss whether Johnson would make a good Prime Minister. 'The Opposition seem to lack gravitas,' an elderly gentleman said. 'I think he'd be quite good on the international stage.'

A man upset by the closure of a local day centre for people with learning difficulties spoke at some length to Johnson, who passed on the complaint to Ian Edwards, a local Conservative councillor, who assured the man: 'We'll take that up for you.'

In 2010, Sir John Randall retained Uxbridge and South Ruislip for the Conservatives by 11,216 votes, and in 2015, Boris was returned with a majority of 10,695, so only 521 fewer. In May 2016, Boris stepped down as Mayor of London, and flung himself into the referendum campaign and its amazing aftermath, which are described at the start of this book.

# Picture Credits

The publishers have made every effort to contact the copyright-holders of material reproduced in this work. Where this has not been possible the publishers will be happy to hear from anyone who recognises their material.

1, 2, 4, 7–13, 15–17: Private collection; 3: Sophie Baker; 5, 6: Micky Böl; 14: *Tatler*; 22: Nigel Howard; 18: Dave Bennett/ Getty Images; 19, 20: *Spectator*; 21: John Taylor/Pressnet.co.uk; 23: Christopher Furlong/Getty Images; 24: Simon Brown; 25: *Private Eye*; 26: *News of the World*; 27: Richard Austin/Rex Features; 28: Mike Walker/Rex Features; 29: David Hartley/ Rex Features; 30: Big Pictures; 31: Photoshot; 32: Getty Images; 33: Richard G Jolly; 34: Getty Images; 35: Rex Features; 36–44: Getty Images; 45–6: Rex Features; 47: Getty Images; 48: PA Images; 49: Rex Features; 50–7: Getty Images; 58: PA Images.

# Index